The Resident Assistant

Working with College Students in Residence Halls

Third Edition

Gregory S. Blimling
Louisiana State University

Lawrence J. Miltenberger
Indiana State University

KENDALL/HUNT PUBLISHING COMPANY
2460 Kerper Boulevard P.O. Box 539 Dubuque, Iowa 52004-0539

Cover photo courtesy of North Carolina State University

Interior photos by Thomas M. Comeaux, Baton Rouge, LA

Copyright © 1981, 1984, 1990 by Kendall/Hunt Publishing Company

Library of Congress Catalog Card Number: 89–64327

ISBN 0–8403–4963–7

Printed in the United States of America
10   9   8   7   6   5   4   3   2

Contents

Preface

The foundation of nearly every residence hall program across the country is the resident assistant (RA) position. These student-staff members fulfill a most difficult assignment: supervising and assisting an entire floor of undergraduate students. The resident assistant is in the vanguard of the field of student development. The daily contact the RA has with students makes it possible for the RA to have a significant impact on the development of these students. The authors believe that whether the RA is prepared to accept this responsibility is directly related to the quantity and quality of education received for the role.

This book is designed to be used as a text in courses taught to resident assistants in colleges and universities. In institutions where courses for credit are not provided, the book may be used by residence hall staff for in-service education programs. The book may also be used as a personal manual to assist RAs in doing the best possible job with a difficult assignment.

The responsibilities of RAs are similar across the country. As a result, the authors have provided information that should be basic to the RA positions in almost all locales, but it is expected that residence hall staff on a particular campus will add to, alter, or otherwise enhance the information in such a way as to tailor usage to the individual campus environment.

The book is divided into six parts. The first part contains chapters on the history, philosophy, and influence of residence halls on the development of students. This section also includes a discussion of the RA position. The chapters in Part Two focus on aspects of college student behavior including: patterns of student development, adjustment problems, peer counseling, interpersonal communication, and human diversity. Behavior problems, conflict resolution and suicide are topics covered in Part Three. Part Four deals with common problems encountered by the RA, including substance abuse, human sexuality, cults, and violence on campus. Part five covers two very important aspects of the RA position: the development of community in the residence hall setting and residence hall programming. The final part is directed at the personal development of the RA. The chapters in this section focus on time management, stress management, and study skills.

The Resident Assistant

Part One

The History and Foundation of Residence Halls

Chapter 1
The Roles of the RA

You have probably heard the expression "overworked and underpaid" many times. If it ever applied to a job, that job is the Resident Assistant, or an RA, as this person is commonly known. If you are now at the stage where you are contemplating becoming an RA primarily because of the financial assistance it may offer, understand that the job simply does not pay enough. You can earn more money and spend much less time doing any number of part-time jobs in college. Most RAs receive minimal remuneration, usually a single room and a meal contract for the year. Some also receive a small stipend. This simply is not enough for all the work that you will be expected to do.

What is perhaps more important is that an RA's experience in college is uniquely different from that of other students. You need to consider this very carefully. As an RA, you cannot always be a part of the group activities in the living unit. Some students in the unit will ostracize you because of the authority that you represent. You will be intentionally left out of some group discussions and often not invited to share in the "inside information." Many tasks within the building will be required of you, and some will force you to reorder your personal priorities. You will be among the first students back to school in the fall of the year and among the last to leave in the spring. The same will be true of each vacation period.

Other students and the student affairs staff will place great demands on both your personal time and study time. Many activities with which you want to involve yourself must take second place to duty nights, working at the information desk, or advising students in the living unit. Even your friendship patterns will be somewhat defined by the residents that you are assigned to advise. You assume all of these demands, requirements, and expectations when you accept the responsibility of being a resident assistant. It is not an easy job. Think very carefully before you accept it.

Though the responsibilities are very great and the demands that will be placed on you throughout the academic year may be even greater, you will also benefit greatly from this experience. The RA fills a unique role as a teacher and a leader that few students are privileged to experience. No other group of students receives the training, assistance, and attention that you will as a resident assistant. This is an opportunity to grow, to learn, and to experience responsibility in a work situation.

Expectations of the RA

From campus to campus the responsibilities of RAs vary. Following are responsibilities common to most resident assistants throughout the country:

Administrative Details

1. Prepares necessary reports and records.
2. Assists with public relations by being able to explain residence hall programs and staff duties to faculty, guests, parents, and students.
3. Assists with room checks as required by hall operations.
4. Assists with communications among staff members, students, and residence program leaders.
5. Keeps residence hall director informed of major plans developed by students.
6. Maintains a good liaison relation with housekeeping personnel.
7. Regularly staffs the hall information desk.

Helping to Provide Control

1. Sets an example by adhering to rules and regulations of the college or university.
2. Knows the institution's and residence hall's regulations.
3. Knows the rationale for institution's rules and regulations.
4. Assists students in knowing what is expected of them in the college or university.
5. Explains the reasons for given rules and regulations.
6. Encourages students to confront other students with violations.
7. Assists in individual growth toward accountability.
8. Knows and interprets the institution's philosophy of discipline.
9. Reports behavioral infractions according to determined policies.
10. Supports or does not openly disagree with the institution's regulations.

Helping to Establish a Healthy Residence Hall Environment

1. Helps students develop a respect for each other's rights and freedoms.
2. Helps students develop a respect for private and institutional property.
3. Encourages residents to attend residence hall and institutional programs.
4. Encourages faculty to visit his or her floor to talk informally with students.
5. Knows and communicates well with the residents.
6. Is tolerant of different life-styles.
7. Encourages an atmosphere conducive to study.

Assisting Individual Student Needs

1. Becomes aware of individual student goals, abilities, and potential for achievement.
2. Becomes aware of social isolates and helps them make friends and become a part of the campus community.

Parts adapted from Greenleaf, Elizabeth A. (1967), *Undergraduate Students as Members of the Residence Hall Staff* (Washington, D.C.: NAWDAC).

3. Becomes aware of attitudes and behavior patterns of the residents in his or her floor.
4. Knows resources in the campus community to help students.
5. Refers students for help when they need it.
6. Becomes aware of adjustment problems new students experience.
7. Makes himself or herself available for casual contacts and develops a pattern of available times for students to visit.
8. Applies good listening and counseling skills.
9. Applies good interpersonal skills.
10. Becomes aware of his or her own strengths and weaknesses (is self-aware).
11. Shows concern for people and their problems.
12. Follows up with students who have had a problem to see the results and to learn whether other assistance should be given.
13. Assists students with class scheduling.
14. Assists students in developing effective study habits.

Hall Government Programs

1. Encourages students' responsibility for their own residence hall programs.
2. Helps students to get involved with university clubs and organizations.
3. Provides creative suggestions for hall programs.
4. Initiates activities and programs on his or her floor.
5. Supports hall programs by personal attendance.

The RA as a Role Model

No matter what responsibilities you are specifically assigned as an RA on your specific campus, there are four basic roles that you will assume. The first and perhaps the most influential role that you have as an RA is as a role model. Remember, when you are placed in a living unit within a residence hall as a staff person, the very fact that you hold this position says to every student that you possess certain characteristics that the university respects and considers important. New freshmen view you as a model to emulate. This is one of the reasons for providing undergraduate RAs in undergraduate residence halls.

At one time, graduate students were used as RAs for undergraduate halls because it was thought that these older students would be able to assert more control over undergraduates and provide better counseling. However, one of the elements in finding appropriate role models is to locate ones with which students can easily identify. If the role model is too far removed from what the individual believes he or she can become, the role model has less influence. The standards and behavior exhibited by the role model must be perceived as attainable by the undergraduate student. Much of the behavior and many of the accomplishments of the graduate students were not seen as attainable by entry level undergraduates.

The advantage that undergraduate RAs have is that their experience is not too far removed from the experiences of incoming freshmen. The incoming freshmen can usually identify more easily with younger RAs than with older ones.

As an RA, you model behavior that others will come to assume as appropriate behavior for students in college. If you have good study skills, there is an increased chance that new students in your living unit will emulate this pattern of study. Likewise, if you spend most of your time throwing a Frisbee up and down the hallway, drinking beer with people in your living unit, or continually find that your time is occupied by your boyfriend or girlfriend, you are setting an entirely different model of behavior.

As an RA you are expected to live by the rules and policies that your institution has set. Unless you can abide by them, do not expect your residents to do so. If you cannot abide by these policies, do not consider becoming a resident assistant. When you accept responsibility as an RA, you also make a commitment to the position as it is defined. If you disagree with the administration's policies or regulations, try to change them through the appropriate supervisory channels. If you cannot change them and still cannot live with them, resign. Do not do yourself, the institution, and your residents a disservice by not enforcing the rules or by pretending that the policies and regulations do not exist.

Understand from the onset that your RA position extends outside of your residence hall and onto the campus. This does not mean that you go about campus enforcing random rules and regulations, advising students on this and that, and asserting your staff position in places where it is not welcomed. It does mean that your role modeling responsibility carries beyond your living unit. If you believe that you shed the cloak of resident assistant when you leave your living unit, you are mistaken. While on campus—and at some universities off campus as well—you are expected to conduct yourself as a member of the staff. It is amazing how many RAs believe that as soon as they leave the residence hall they can become as wild and reckless as they please. Not only is this illogical, it is irresponsible.

Nor should you misuse your role as an RA. Perhaps the classic example of misusing one's position as an RA comes in writing editorials for the school newspaper. As a student you are entitled to submit whatever opinion you wish to your newspaper. The fact that you are an RA need not enter into it. Some RAs, however, feel they must initial every item they submit as though they were making official policy statements. They send in their editorials and sign their names and their position title. Unless you have been elected to make an official policy statement for your residence programs office, avoid attaching your personal opinions to your position. Remember that the views you hold as a resident assistant do not necessarily reflect the views of every other resident assistant in your hall or institution as a whole. Readers might assume that you speak from a position of authority and responsibility and that your opinion should carry more weight because your are an RA.

Your role as a model for other students is one of the most important duties that you will assume. Handle the responsibility carefully and with the respect it deserves.

The RA as a Counselor

The second role that the RA serves is as a counselor, consultant, or advisor. The word *counselor* may be a misnomer. The RA might more appropriately be considered to hold a helping role. This function is an important part of being an RA. Students undergo many adjustments, stresses, and crises throughout the academic year. They are separated from their families, the comfortable and familiar surroundings of their homes, and their established friends. They are asked to live among a group of peers whom they do not know and asked to study and produce more than they have ever had to before. At the same time, they are undergoing tremendous psychological adjustments in their transition to adulthood. In the day-to-day living environment of the residence hall, many of these growth experiences, emotional traumas, and crises come to light. In the residence hall the students' values will be challenged by other students. Their knowledge of themselves and their ability to work with other people will be tested. For students accustomed to a quiet, private environment, a group living situation can be threatening and difficult. You as an RA are expected to help students through this experience.

Think for a moment how many hundreds of challenges are placed before a student just within the first two weeks of college. Think back to your own experiences when you first entered college. You did not know how to register for classes, or how to get a meal pass, or what to do if you were ill, or who to see if you were experiencing some problem with a professor. Simple issues like these can become real problems for students who want to be accepted and are afraid to ask someone for help. New students fear that they will be labeled as less mature, less intelligent, or not part of the group. You are the person with this information and the one charged with responsibility to see that students get it. Providing information and helping are important functions of the RA position and among the primary reasons for its existence.

To provide such information in a counseling framework, you must begin to establish a positive, friendly relationship with every person in your living unit—not selectively with only those you like, but an open, understanding, and warm relationship with each person in the unit. You must be accessible to everyone. You must be viewed as fair, consistent, and knowledgeable about the institution. Only then will people come to you with their concerns. Only after they know you as a person will students come to you with their problems. People do not share personal information with people they do not know and trust.

The helping role can be taken one step further. The RA has the best opportunity to help students who are experiencing minor problems and to identify students who are experiencing major problems. Identification of students who are undergoing some form of personal crisis or severe depression can literally save a student's life.

The RA as a Teacher

The third role that the RA assumes is that of a teacher. This role includes teaching in a formal sense, not simply the informal teaching involved in role modeling. The RA teaches many things, specifically: (1) general information about the university, about events happening on campus, and about services offered; (2) inviting speakers to the living unit, in conjunction with residents, thereby creating a situation in which formal learning takes place; (3) group-process skills in floor meetings, in groups planning an activity, in floor elections, through student activities within the building, and through intramural activities; (4) values, both through his or her own personal behavior and through late-night discussions (bull sessions) in which such issues as sex, religion, politics, and career plans are discussed. The RA is an agent in this teaching process and at the same time becomes a learner; for not only does he or she challenge other students' values, but his or her own values are also challenged.

Of all these teaching roles, educational programming is probably the most visible sign of teaching. It is the time in which the RA has the opportunity to bring a host of different ideas to the collective experience of the members of his or her floor.

The RA as a Student

The fourth role the RA has is that of a student. Although most RAs rank as their first priority their goals as students, their responsibilities as students usually come to take second place to the RA position. This is unfortunate. The first responsibility of the RA should be to his or her studies. However, RAs often find their studies pushed to a second priority, and the RA position becomes all-consuming. People place unreasonable demands on RAs' time, and wishing to do a good job, many RAs find an increasing amount of their time spent working with other people's problems while their own studies are neglected.

Though some RAs find that the additional responsibilities make them better budget their time, many find that they enjoy being an RA much more than they enjoy being a student. They put all their time and energy into being an excellent RA, while their grades slip. Obviously, it does no one any good if the RA loses the position because of poor grades. So when you take time to study and pursue important academic interests, you will be fulfilling one of the expectations that the student affairs staff has for you as an RA.

Do not be afraid occasionally to post a note on your door asking people not to disturb you for an hour or two unless it is an emergency. You will find that students will contact you at the times you are available. Some of your residents will want to occupy all of your attention and will often spend their time in your room procrastinating. It is easy for these people to consume monumental amounts of your study time. This can create a difficult situation, because you do not want to alienate your residents by refusing to spend time with them. There is a balance between ordering your personal priorities—that is, studying and having your own social life—with attending to the needs of your residents. If you have an exam or need to do some important studying, many of the routine questions can wait until you take a break or have finished your studying. If you have established a positive relationship with your residents, you will find that they will interrupt you only for truly important discussions. If there is a crisis of some type, you will be interrupted. If there is a personal problem with which a resident needs to talk to you, he or she will need to consider it pressing enough to interrupt you during your study time.

Part of the limits to your availability can be explained in your first floor meeting. You should reinforce on every occasion during the floor meeting that you are available, that you are accessible, and that you want to be consulted about matters of concern to the residents. At the same time, you should make the point that you, too, are a student who needs to study. Close your door when you are studying and leave it open when you are not. An open door is an invitation to be interrupted. When you are not studying and are in your room, leave your door open so that the students will feel welcome to come and talk with you.

Conclusion

The RA serves one of the most comprehensive roles in the student affairs division. No student problem escapes the RA's involvement. This job is one of the most difficult student positions to hold and to perform well. To be called to do so many tasks, to hold so many responsibilities, and to be accountable for so many other people during the time when you are shaping your own education is one of the greatest challenges you will face during early adulthood.

Chapter 2
The History of Residence Halls

The Origin of Residence Halls

One of the most comprehensive examinations of the origins and early history of residence halls was written in 1934 by W. H. Cowley (who later became the President of Hamilton College). According to Cowley, residence halls owe their origin to the housing problem created during the middle ages by thousands of "wandering students" flocking to universities in Bologna, Paris, and Oxford. The number of these students was considerable. Thompson (1946) describes the situation in the middle ages as follows:

> In 1262 at Bologna, the faculties were lecturing to 10,000 students—twice as many students as there were people living in the local town. In 1257, there were 30,000 students enrolled at the University of Paris. There were more students than townspeople. And so it has been down through the ages. Any time that a group of learned men band together for the purpose of imparting knowledge, the youth of that age gather about them, sometimes in numbers which create very difficult problems in the field of housing (p. 95).

The sheer numbers of these otherwise homeless young men, most of whom were only 14 or 15 years old, created considerable problems in the customarily small medieval cities of the early to mid-1200s. James (1917) says that "the number of students was so much in excess of any possible provision for them that they lived in tents, they camped in the fields, in fact some places they burrowed into the sides of hills" (p. 101). In time, students moved from living with school masters and townspeople to rented houses that became known as *hostels* in Bologna, *paedagogies* in Paris, *halls* or *colleges* at Oxford, and *Bursens* at German universities. For the most part, these houses were self-governing democratic groups. However, by the mid-1400s these houses had come under the control of university authorities.

Roots in the British Collegiate System

Because many of the students attending universities during this period were poor, Oxford University established *domus pauperums* (endowed hostels) as charitable institutions. The endowed halls, which subsequently appeared at Cambridge, came to be known as *colleges*. This system of colleges flourished from the fourteenth to the eighteenth century throughout Europe, but began vanishing on continental Europe in the 1800s. The Reformation begun by Martin Luther showed concern over any institution that remotely resembled the monkish orders of the Catholic monasteries. The idea of young men living together in a Bursen resembled too closely the monkish trappings. The French Revolution and the Encyclopedist Movement—which advanced the position that the purpose of education was pure knowledge—further sealed the fate of college-operated housing for students on continental Europe. The collegiate system of colleges and halls, which had its origin at the University of Paris but grew to maturity in Britain, survived at Oxford and Cambridge (Cowley, 1934).

You might be wondering at this point how the often-used term *dormitory* came into being. Charles F. Thwing, president of Western Reserve University and Adelbert College, explains in 1909 that

> The word "dormitory," in its present meaning, is a new word in academic language; in its present meaning standing for a building used by a college for housing students. Mullinger, the historian of Cambridge, uses the word in contrast with *study* in speaking of a student of his university of about the year 1550. The present meaning was formerly taken by the "hostel" or "college" or "hall." The hostel of the English universities of three hundred years ago was a lodging house under the charge of a principal, where students resided at their own cost. The word was never transferred to America. . . . The word *college* as applied to a building, has been the favorite word in American academic usage. . . . The brick row at Yale of eight buildings was composed of colleges, though *hall* was the term applied in the earlier time to the first. *Hall* is still used and to it have been added *house* or *cottage* or *halls of residence,* especially as applied to women's colleges. *Dormitory* has within fifty years, come into good use. It can hardly be called a fitting word except for those who wish, in their earnestness or wit, to represent the college as torpid (p. 34).

Origins in the United States

When the English colonized North America, they brought with them the traditions and concepts of education learned in mother England. In 1636, the Congregationalists founded Harvard University using as their model what they had known as students at Oxford and Cambridge. With the exception of the Philadelphia Academy and the College of William and Mary, the original nine colonial colleges (Harvard College, New Jersey University, Yale University, College of William and Mary, King's College, Philadelphia Academy, College of Rhode Island, Queens College, and Dartmouth College) were founded by graduates of either Oxford or Cambridge. The College of William and Mary was founded by James Blair, a graduate of Edinburgh University, and the Philadelphia Academy was founded by Benjamin Franklin. Cowley (1934) says that "The British background of the prerevolutionary college organizers had more to do with the establishment of residential colleges in America than any other factor" (p. 708).

The collegiate system of Oxford and Cambridge focused on building a student's character and intellect to develop a member of the English gentry who was both a scholar and a gentleman. The residential colleges were the focus of this learning. The faculty worked closely with students serving as role models and mentors for students.

Unfortunately, the American system of residence halls did not provide students with this same intellectual atmosphere and social spirit. Part of this is due to the abandonment of the class system of England and part to the pioneering fashion in which the American colleges grew (Cowley, 1934). Students as young as 13 and 14 attended American institutions. Attending college frequently required traveling great distances during a period of time when travel was difficult and often dangerous, so living and boarding at the college was a necessity.

Unlike the English system of residential colleges, faculty at American colleges were expected to assume all manner of duties, from proctoring residence halls to classroom instruction. At Oxford and Cambridge, deans, proctors, and bedels had been employed to attend to these affairs, leaving the faculty free to engage students in scholarship and expose them to the social rules of being English gentlemen. Cowley (1934) says that responsibility for student discipline was one of the more practical reasons why the collegiate system of residence colleges had such difficulty in establishing itself in the American college. He cites the disciplinary conflict between faculty and students as one of the primary reasons residence halls in American colleges never came to serve as the core of the educational program as they did in England. Cowley writes:

> In America, . . . the faculty member living in the dormitory became the student's natural enemy. Circumstances made him a martinet, and conscientiously he lived up to his responsibilities. The results are well known. Student riots and rebellions against the faculty have bespattered the historical records of every college up until the inception of athletics and extracurricular activities in the last decade of the nineteenth century (p. 709).

Nineteenth Century Disregard for Student Housing

And, indeed these were difficult times for American colleges. Historian Frederick Rudolph (1962) describes some of the problems associated with dormitory living in the 1800s, writing:

> In the commons room of the dormitory at South Carolina College in 1833, two students at the same moment grabbed for a plate of trout. Only one of them survived the duel that ensued. Among the victims of the collegiate way were the boy that died in the duel at Dickinson, the students who were shot at Miami of Ohio, the professor who was killed at the University of Virginia, the president of Oakland College in Mississippi who was stabbed to death by a student, the student who was stabbed at Illinois College, the students who were stabbed and killed at the University of Missouri, the president and professor who were stoned at the University of Georgia, and the University of North Carolina. For this misfortune these victims of the college life could thank the dormitory, the time house of incarceration and infamy that sustained the collegiate way (p. 97).

It is little wonder that in 1852, President Henry Tappen of the University of Michigan converted one of the university's dormitories into classrooms. Shay (1964a) quotes Tappen as giving this rationale: "The dormitory system is objectionable in itself. By withdrawing young men from the influence of domestic circles and separating them from the community, they are often led to contact evil habits and are prone to fall into disorderly conduct" (p. 181).

Tappen was not alone in his condemnation of dormitory life. President Francis Wayland at Brown University and Frederick Barnard at Columbia University shared his sentiments on dormitories. Tappen and many other educators came to embrace the "Prussian system of education," which placed no value on what students did outside the classroom. Faculty educated at German universities fought to replace the "overbearing paternalism of their clerical predecessors, and . . . (substituted) impersonalism" (Cowley, 1949, pp. 19–20). Student housing and social life were viewed as beyond the concern of the university, which was to expand the fields of knowledge and train the minds of young scholars. Following the Civil War, many German scholars and Americans trained in German universities joined the faculties of American institutions, which further ingrained this educational philosophy into the character of American universities.

American colleges attempted to regulate student behavior by imposing prescriptive sets of rules. One small denominational and coeducational college in 1870 published its rules in a small book, which President Kolbe of Drexel University read to the Eighteenth Annual Conference of the National Association of Deans and Advisers of Men in 1936. President Kolbe (1936), quoting from this book of student regulations, described the following rules for students of the 1870s:

> Students are expected to be kind and respectful to others.
>
> Students, while connected with the college, are strictly forbidden the use of intoxicating liquors and tobacco, profanity, or indecent language on the college premises, or so far as the college has any jurisdiction.
>
> Students must refrain from all improprieties in the halls, boisterous talking, or scuffling.
>
> Young men and women are not allowed to take rides or walks without permission.
>
> No student will fire gunpowder in college buildings, or on the premises, or engage in card playing or any other form of gambling in college, or in the city, or commit injuries upon the person or property of any student.
>
> The faculty shall have the authority to visit and search any room in college, using force if necessary to enter, and assess all damages occasioned by the violation upon the offender (p. 11).

In 1862 Congress passed the Land Grant College Act, which established 69 state colleges. This act, and other pieces of legislation by the government encouraging state supported higher education, assured the preeminence of secular education in the United States (Cowley, 1949). A second factor contributing to secular education was the gradual demise of religious affiliation by such institutions as Harvard, Yale, Princeton, and Columbia at approximately this same time (Cowley, 1949). The result of this secularization was a loosening of the controls that the institutions wished to or chose to exercise over students. The rigid codes of obedience and hours of compulsory chapel exercises were replaced over time by conduct regulations that granted students greater freedoms. With the lessened concern for student welfare and a freeing of students from the control of clerics, much of the the violence associated with student behavior vanished.

However, in time this diminished concern for residence halls took its toll on the facilities available for student housing. Ill-kept, disheveled, rat-invested, and dilapidated are appropriate adjectives for college-owned student housing in the late 1800s. Students lived where they could. Townspeople, faculty, and the presidents of colleges all boarded students. Other places that served as housing in this period included the basement of the town meeting house for students attending Hiram College and the attic of the first building constructed at Oberlin College. At Amherst College the same rooms were used as bedrooms, classrooms, study halls, and chapel (Leonard, 1956). Most of the dormitories built earlier in the century were still in operation, but they were not well maintained by the colleges.

Some students who were dissatisfied with these living conditions took refuge in privately owned dormitories that had been established in a few communities, organized or joined a fraternity which had developed residential functions, or found other accommodations. At the turn of the twentieth century, Thwing (1909) explains that

> Most state universities have declined to accept special responsibility for the domestic interests of students. These men and women have been left in no small degree to shift for themselves. Funds given by the state or by the individual have been required for the erection of libraries, laboratories, and other halls. The ordinary home has opened its doors to students, glad to avail itself of the means of increasing income, and students have not been loath to accept (p. 34).

The attacks on dormitories and the collegiate way were most pronounced at the Eastern colleges; Midwestern and Western colleges appeared to be largely indifferent.

Early Twentieth Century American Residence Halls

The collegiate system of residential colleges was not easily vanquished. There were those who kept alive the idea that college should educate both the character and intellect, as in the system epitomized by the English colleges. Arthur T. Hadley, president of Yale; William Rainey Harper, president of the University of Chicago; A. Lawrence Lowell, president of Harvard University; and Woodrow Wilson, president of Princeton University, all spoke on behalf of the English residential system and the importance of the collegiate experience. The rebirth of interest in student housing started at Yale, where there had remained an adherence to "the English philosophy that the communal life of students has high educational value" (Cowley, 1949, p. 21).

Woodrow Wilson, while president of Princeton, suggested in 1907 that dormitories be joined to form quadrangles and that unmarried faculty be housed with students in what he termed the Quadrangle Plan. His plan was motivated by a desire to disband the powerful men's social clubs at Princeton by substituting residence halls that would be under the control of the university. Although Wilson's plan initially met with the approval of the Princeton University trustees, it ultimately fell under attack from the men's social clubs and the influential alumni of these organizations who opposed it. But as Shay (1964b) points out, "Wilson had lost the Battle at Princeton, but helped the War for the Residence Hall" (p. 29). The debate over the residential system of colleges sparked discussion at other universities which later served as inspiration for an expansion of college-owned residence halls at Harvard (Cowley, 1934).

Typical of this philosophy supporting residence halls and the value of the collegiate experience are the comments of Richard C. Hughes (1909), president of Ripon College, who wrote:

> The purpose of a college education is not only to educate the student in formal disciplines, but to aid him in discovering his own powers and to train him in the best use of these powers for effective work in life; in other words, to discover the profession or calling in life for which he is best fitted and to prepare him to be a good citizen. A large part of this most important work is done outside of the classroom and laboratory, during the hours when the student mingles freely with his fellows, expresses himself without restraint, and takes on the habit of thought and speech and life of the crowd with which he associates. The education of the classroom may be training in one direction while education of his chums in the dormitory is training him in the opposite direction. In other words, the first factor in solving the problem is to recognize that for good or evil, success or failure, life in the dormitory is a powerful influence in the life of a student. The strongest lines of social influence are always horizontal. We are more powerfully affected by the opinions of our peers than by those of our superiors. The student will listen with respect to the teaching of the faculty, but he will accurately imitate the language and life of his chums (p. 47).

At the turn of the century, in most universities, the vivid recollections of the old dormitories with their myriad problems and manifold abuses had mellowed into pleasant recollections and funny stories of days long since past (James, 1917)—thus lessoning the objections of faculty who had often worked as tutors or proctors within the halls. There was also a revival in student activities and increased attention paid to college life on campus. It was marked in the late eighteen hundreds by such activities as intercollegiate athletics, which Cowley (1934) dates as beginning with a boat race between Yale and Harvard in 1852 on Lake Winnipiseogee. Intercollegiate football games followed 17 years later. Other activities associated with college life included an increase in student participation in social clubs, student publications, drama clubs, and intercollegiate debates.

Edmund J. James (1917), president of the University of Illinois, upon laying the cornerstone of the first woman's residence hall at that institution, gave the following reasons for the revival of residence halls at American universities in the early 1900s:

1. In the first place, the people outside may not keep up an adequate supply of rooms, and the prices for rooms may be excessive. . . . The addition of university residence halls will tend to relieve this pressure, and even if they do not take all of the students, . . . they will do something to relieve the situation. . .

2. A second reason is that they will do something to help standardize the conditions of life. A student needs for his work as peculiar and distinct a room and equipment as the grocery man needs for his, as the iron man needs for his work . . . and it is very difficult to get people who rent rooms to students to understand that point of view and to provide the proper kinds of furniture and equipment.

3. A third reason which is often assigned for the university residence hall is to be found in the fact that it offers a certain kind of social organization which is not so easily supplied by the students if they live at random throughout the houses of the community.

4. While we are getting our university education, our knowledge of Latin and chemistry, and other subjects, we ought to be getting a lot of other things that help to make a civilized people. We ought to be acquiring polished manners. We ought to be acquiring a certain ability to live easily and efficiently, so to speak, with our fellow men. . . . And residence halls properly constructed, properly organized, properly administered, can do something toward crystallizing and helping to form and shape what may be called the social life of the student body.

5. Another reason sometimes assigned is that students who live scattered about through the towns do not get in touch with the university spirit. Some people come here . . . and insist that they would not send their boys or girls to institutions which could not provide what they called the opportunity for the development of college spirit. And so they insist upon a kind of institutional life which the college dormitory may develop. . . . A student who comes to the university and lives here four years and goes away without having increased his desire for profitable and wholesome human companionship will certainly have lost one of the greatest opportunities which college life can bring (pp. 105–106).

One cannot overlook the importance of women's colleges and the role they played in the revival of residence halls. It was one thing to let men fend for themselves in a community and quite another to permit the same liberty to women. Women's colleges such as Vassar, Smith, and Mount Holyoke all were founded in the late nineteenth century and all were strictly residential. Maria Mitchell was a professor at Vassar College in the late 1800s and wrote in her diary (Mitchell, n.d.) about the residence halls at Vassar.

We are a community of 500 people. The students are a family of about 350. The lady principal is the "Mother" of this family. She knows every girl by sight and in time, by character. She has eight corridor teachers, to assist her, each of whom has care of about 40 girls. These 40 students live in one half of one floor, the floors being divided by the broad staircase. These 40 students are a small community which is like a village. The corridor teacher has her office hours, at which time these 40 students can receive her advice or can repent to her their omissions of rules, etc. The corridors are divided into suites of rooms. . . .

These little families of a half dozen girls, submit to college laws—to the corridor laws—to their class laws—but they also make laws for themselves in their own parlors.

The moral tone of the college is exceedingly high but in that respect, I suppose it is not unlike that of other female communities (as quoted by Pillinger, 1984, pp. 7–8).

Marion Talbot (1909), a professor at the University of Chicago, believed that women's residence halls held great potential for the training of young women. For her, residence halls should be organized to "bring all into relation with all and to have all recognize the privilege and obligation" associated with living in a community (p. 43). Talbot (1909) thought that this sense of community responsibility could be realized through such activities as learning the social graces, exercises in hospitality, participation in some charity, interest in the affairs of the university, and cooperation in a common interest such as setting quiet hours for the house or determining how Sundays should be observed. These experiences, and others like them in the residence halls, as Talbot (1909) observed, lead to "the opportunity to acquire that power of expression, that facility in social intercourse, that ability to meet situations of an unusual and unexpected character, that dignity and poise, which ensure that the intellectual and scholarly results of the academic experience will be made available in full measure" (p. 5).

Most faculty and administrators at colleges and universities were men. Findlay (1937), in writing about the history of this period, notes that when women joined institutions that had been exclusively for men, "it turned out that women's problems were frequently of a different nature than those of men students. Convention required a stricter supervision of women than was expected of men. These facts, together with the earlier establishment of women's dormitories and the influence of the American Association of Collegiate Alumnae in its desire for a special adviser for women students—all served to bring into existence a new administrative officer—earlier called 'the lady principal' or preceptress" (p. 105). These female administrators soon came to be known as deans of women—preceding the deans of men on most campuses. In 1902, at Northwestern University, deans of women entered into a national association, which they called the National Association of Women Deans. Cowley (1934) observes that this organization was a "powerful influence, especially in the direction of bringing the attention of administrators to the housing of women students" (p. 761).

Deans of men on most campuses were appointed later, between about 1910 and 1930, but unlike the appointment of deans of women, deans of men were not appointed principly over concern for housing male students. According to a survey by Findlay (1937) of all the institutions affiliated with the National Association of Deans of Men in 1936–1937, the reasons for establishing the office of Dean of Men were as follows:

1. Increased enrollment	47
2. Need for adviser of men (counseling)	36
3. Extracurricular development (and centralization)	33
4. Administrative reorganization	30
5. Relief for the President or general administration	27
6. Influence of the dean of women's work	22
7. Housing problems	13
8. Request of students	11
9. Enlarged service for the institution	9
10. Discipline	5
11. Study of other college programs	5
12. Had been doing it unofficially	5
13. Campus morale demanded it	4
14. Aftermath of the war	3

Twelve other causes are given, for each of which only one or two votes are offered (p. 115).

It can be seen from the survey that problems with housing were among the reasons for appointing a dean of men at a college; however, it was not one of the principal reasons for establishing this office. Of the 262 schools surveyed, 22 or only about 8.4 percent of the schools established the dean of men's office because of housing problems. The administrative press presented by increased enrollments, although not entirely unrelated to the need for housing, was the most often cited reason for establishing this position.

Another influence supporting the revival of residence halls in this period was the increasing disparity in wealth between those students from rich families and those from poorer ones. This inequity was often the distinction between those who could afford to live in private dormitories or fraternities and those who were forced to live in the meager accommodations offered by the college. Charles W. Eliot, president of Harvard University, took exception to this situation because it developed a form of caste system and perpetuated cliques of students from the same backgrounds. In commenting on the differences between private dormitories (which were established in Cambridge in the late 1800s and early 1900s as investment properties by private individuals to cater to the wealthier students) and the college dormitories at Harvard, Elliot (1909) writes:

> I like better to have the youth go into the college dormitories. . . . The college dormitories are not occupied by any one class of students at all. They are occupied in the most promiscuous manner as regards the classes from which their occupants have come, and they are occupied in a completely democratic manner as regards the school from which the occupants have come and the parts of the country from which they come. In these private dormitories there is a great deal of grouping by sets of fellows who have known each other before, who, for instance have come from St. Paul's school, or from some other boarding school in some other part of the country. For my own part, I prefer the breaking up of those groups when they come to college, but is a very natural thing that in the private dormitories they seek precisely to create or prolong the life of these groups formed elsewhere. It is merely a case of birds of a feather flocking together (p. 58).

Fraternities became influential organizations on many campuses. They went from secret societies to social bodies with lodges and, eventually, to democratically run houses. Birdseye (1906) defended fraternities, writing that they were, "homebuilding agencies, wherein many rich and influential alumni and earnest and energetic undergraduates are laboring together to erect college homes and thereby solve to a limited extent the modern problems in the college family life arising out of increasing numbers and changed dormitory and social conditions" (p. 221). Fraternities were so successful as to cause some universities, like Amherst, to stop construction of dormitories for lack of student interest (Cowley, 1934). However, this same "success" of the fraternity system catering to the needs of a particular class of students was viewed by others as antithetical to the democratic principles of egalitarianism that were central to the educational mission of many state universities and religious colleges. Shay (1964b) notes that because access to fraternities was "based upon grounds which were repugnant to the

American concept of democratic life, wealth—and high social standing . . . (fraternities) . . . acted as a stimulus to the development of college residences not so much because it was a model institution, but because it came to be seen as an unhealthy influence which might wither away if the college provided residence halls" (p. 29).

Residences after the First World War

Following World War I, enrollments at colleges and universities increased. By the mid-1920s, many institutions were experiencing overcrowding due to increased enrollment. Some institutions began to build more residence halls. In 1926 the Virginia State Board of Education authorized $1 million dollars of state funds for "dormitory needs" of state institutions under the Noel Act ("Funds for Dormitories," 1926). Similarly, President Coffman of the University of Minnesota, after being denied state funds, embarked on a plan—which had been successful at other universities—of selling bonds to finance residence halls ("Dormitory System," 1926).

The most popular approach to organizing residence halls at this time was to establish residential colleges which were usually composed of a group of halls segregated by gender and by class standing. This plan was proposed by a committee of the faculty at the University of Michigan in 1927 ("Proposed Residential Colleges," 1927). The most popular and well published of these new plans was Harvard University's house plan. Harvard President A. Lawrence Lowell (1929), like his predecessor Charles Elliot, objected to the "cliques based upon similarity of origin and upon wealth" and believed that "Great masses of unorganized young men, not yet engaged in definite careers, are prone to superficial currents of thought and interest, to the detriment of the personal intellectual progress that ought to dominate mature men seeking higher education" (Lowell, 1929, pp. 262–263). A gift of $3 million from Edward S. Harkness, a graduate of Yale University (class of 1897), made it possible for Harvard to build two houses. Harkness earlier had made this same offer to Yale, but the faculty committee established to study the idea did not respond in time to meet Harkness's deadline; he then took to Harvard his offer to build residence colleges similar to those at Cambridge.

The aim of the Harvard house plan was to "bring into contact a body of students with diverse interests who will by attrition provoke one another to think on many subjects, and will have a corporate spirit" (Lowell, 1929, p. 263). Each house was a cross-section of students selected from the students who resided the previous year in one of the freshmen residence halls that Harvard established in 1911. Upperclassmen and house authorities (faculty) residing in the houses selected students upon their voluntary application. President Lowell intended for the plan to encourage scholarship, intellectual interests, and increased personal attention. Perhaps most of all, Lowell envisioned that the houses would become communities of scholarship dedicated to enhancing the learning process. He believed that through what he called the "spirit of emulation" and informal group discussions that would grow from the day-to-day contacts naturally occurring among students and faculty living together, the residence houses would enhance the formal classroom instruction "with all men not destitute of mental appetite" (p. 264)

Yale University established residential quadrangles in December of 1929, principally because the undergraduate schools were so overcrowded that life at Yale had lost some of the important benefits that students had when classes were smaller ("Residential Colleges," 1929). Although the problem of overcrowding was recognized earlier, it had become acute and relief was needed.

Residence Halls in the 1930s

However, inadequate housing facilities for students seemed to be the rule rather than the exception. In a survey of 44 of the 52 land grant institutions by the Office of Education in 1931, housing facilities existed for approximately 15 percent of the 136,000 students. Two institutions (the University of Nebraska and Colorado Agricultural College) had no residence halls, and eight were still waiting for state legislatures to make appropriations ("Student Housing," 1931). The other institutions surveyed had either constructed residence halls through issuing bonds, by establishing nonprofit corporations, or by some other creative financing arrangement ("Student Housing," 1931).

Life in the residence halls during this period emphasized making the college residence hall a "home." The college authorities believed it was their responsibility to mold a student's character. The courts had also recognized this as the responsibility of colleges, acknowledging as early as 1913 in *Gott* vs. *Berea College* that college authorities were to act in loco parentis. The court stated "College authorities stand in *loco parentis* concerning the physical and moral welfare and mental training of the pupils, and we are unable to see why, to that end, they may not make any rule or regulation for the government or betterment of their pupils that a parent could for the same purpose" (cited in Young and Gehring, 1977, pp. 1–13).

This concept came to be a guiding principle for much of the early work with students outside of the classroom. Some of the dormitory regulations for women at Louisiana State University in 1934 illustrate the scope of control which the colleges sought to exercise over the daily lives of students in serving in lieu of parents.

1. Smith hall residents are under regulations from the time they register in the university until they sign out to leave for their homes at the close of school.
2. Smith Hall residents who leave the campus for any reason are required to sign out on the register in the general office, stating destination, time of leaving, and expected time of return, and sign in immediately upon return to the campus. Each student must sign for herself.

3. Women students who have permission to attend a dance or a special function must return to Smith Hall within fifteen minutes after the time set for closing, or leaving, such functions.
4. Women students are not to visit a house where men reside exclusively, unless a chaperone approved by the dean of women is present.
5. Students are held responsible for the conditions of their rooms at all times, subject to daily inspection (L.S.U. Student Handbook, 1934–35, pp. 41–44).

Other regulations included a 10:30 P.M. curfew on weekdays and a midnight curfew on weekends, a dormitory roll call each night at 8:15 P.M., and a requirement that all lights be out and students in bed by 11:15 P.M. on school nights. Regulations for men were often more liberal, but they too had curfews, room inspections, and roll calls, and men were usually required to sign in and sign out when leaving the campus.

This concern with shaping the lives of students was also reflected in the landmark statement of "The Student Personnel Point of View" issued by the American Council on Education in 1937 to express the philosophical purposes and functions of student personnel administrators during this time. In this statement, 23 functions or services were enumerated as the responsibility of student personnel practitioners. Included among these was an acknowledgment that student personnel administrators had responsibility for "assisting the student to reach his maximum effectiveness through clarification of his purpose, improvement of study methods, speech habits, personal appearance, manners, etc., and through progression in religious, emotional, social development, and other nonacademic personal and group relationships" (p. 3).

Life in the residence halls cannot be viewed apart from life on campus and the influence of national social and economic upheaval. The 1930s were a time of social change and economic confusion. There was strong sentiment favoring socialism and communism as viable economic systems for the country. "Calls to use teachers and students as tools in a process of social reconstruction stood side by side with concern for teacher and student freedom" (Sorenson, 1985, p. 80). Extracurricular activities on campus became so important that it gave cause for Cowley and Waller (1935) to defend such activities, writing "Other factors, of course, contributed to the widespread opinion that the campus has seemed to swallow up the classroom. These include the values of activities in educating for a competitive world, the consonance of activities, education, and Babbitry, and so forth. Our fundamental point, however, is unchanged: The function of all student organizations must be canvassed and evaluated in terms of the fulfillment of human purpose" (p. 385).

Low-cost student housing was developed in the late 1930s as a means to assist those less able to afford higher education and as a way to meet the demands of the increased number of students enrolled. At the University of Wisconsin, for example, the enrollment increased from 8000 students in 1935 to 11,400 students in 1938. To meet the increased demand for housing and the needs of low-income students, the university constructed cooperative housing facilities that had varied rents depending on the amount of services supplied by the university and the amount of services students supplied themselves. Rates for these low-cost dormitories ranged from a low of $70 per year with optional food service in dormitories where the students performed all of the housekeeping responsibilities to a high of $96 per year for room and $245 per year for food with daily maid service ("Low Cost Housing," 1938, p. 623).

Iowa State University opened a "cooperative dormitory" for women students in 1922 and a second one in 1938 to accommodate women who required reduced living expenses in order to attend college. These accommodations were run on a cooperative basis in which the women planned, cooked and served their own meals and performed other household tasks. The room rent was approximately the same as the traditional residence halls at the university—approximately $32 per quarter—but the women in the cooperative dormitory paid about half the board rate—amounting to a savings of approximately $2.25 per week ("Cooperative Dormitories," 1938, p. 344).

Public higher education benefited from government-sponsored work forces such as the WPA. Stewart (1941) says that "During the past decade (1931–1941), it may surprise you to know that publicly supported universities and colleges in America have launched such a gigantic program of construction for student housing as to constitute one of the major developments in American educational history" (p. 110). He estimates that institutions of higher education invested in excess of $150 million, which was matched by the federal government for the construction of student housing facilities. Universities, supported by government subsidies, reduced or eliminated tuition and fees for many students unable to pay.

Findlay (1936) explains the plight of many students during the early thirties when describing the organization of The Independent Men's Association at the University of Oklahoma for the purpose of helping integrate nonfraternity men into the mainstream of campus life:

> The Depression gave the university an increasing number of nonfraternity men who were attempting a college education "on a shoe string." A large portion of these men were leaving school at the end of nine months—maladjusted, disappointed with their experience, still unacquainted with their fellow students, and poorer in health than when they first set foot on campus. Their slim pocketbooks did not permit attendance at the usual social events. Many did not attend a party or a social function all year.
>
> When scholastic troubles came on, there was no chapter preceptor or tutor available for them and they had no money with which to hire the services of a private tutor (p. 156).

Residences during the Second World War

World War II lead the United States from the Great Depression and moved it from its customary isolationist view of the world. The war years on college campuses saw most young men leave to join the service or in preparation to become officers through the Reserve Officer Training Corps activity on most campuses.

To participate fully in these programs, universities were expected to provide some form of housing facility, offering yet another incentive for constructing residence halls. War training units came on campus; many members of the faculty were given leaves from their academic posts to serve in various military positions or to work in research related to the defense industry. More women attended college and comprised the majority of the student body on many campuses.

Residence Halls after World War II

Sixty percent of those veterans who were eligible to enroll in institutions of higher education after World War II enrolled within approximately two years after the war; the GI Bill made it financially possible for 25 percent more veterans to attend college than would have been able to attend without government support (Brown, 1951). The students who returned to the campus after the war were much different from the ones who had left. They were older, more experienced, and more serious about their studies. Many campus restrictions designed to "parent" students were out of place when applied to veterans. Campus organizations that flourished before the war seemed frivolous to many students after having experienced the war and the loss of loved ones.

The surge of this new breed of student caused housing problems. For the first time on many campuses, colleges were asked to provide housing not only for the student but also for the family that accompanied the student. The federal government responded to the needs of the war veterans by making temporary housing available to servicemen. This was done in June 1945 by amending the Lanham Act, which had been established to provide temporary housing during the war years. The amendment to this act, known as Title V, allowed universities to seek financial support for the housing of students.

To meet the demands for housing, colleges developed temporary quarters for married students. Often these took the form of converted barracks or trailer parks. The University of Illinois housed about 300 veterans in the gymnasium and secured from the Public Housing Authority "275 temporary shelter-type houses" (Thompson, 1946, p. 100). The University of Michigan was able to place most of their single veterans in one of nine residence halls, but had problems in trying to integrate students with families (Ferris, 1946).

The problems associated with the increased need for student housing was impetus for S. Earl Thompson, Director of Housing at the University of Illinois, to call on the housing officers at other universities to attend the First National Housing Conference held at the University of Illinois on July 28–30, 1949. Within three years, the housing officers, attending what became an annual meeting, formed an association (1951) and subsequently adopted the name of the National Association of College and University Housing Officers (The Association of College and University Housing Officers—International, 1985).

Universities were reluctant to undertake the construction of permanent structures after the war under the belief that this new student was a temporary manifestation and in time the campus would return to the pastoral academic communities of the prewar years. As one indication of this, Abernethy and Arbernethy, faculty members at Rutgers University, in 1949 wrote a monograph outlining for faculty members how they might go about entertaining students in their homes. They write, "If . . . we think of ourselves as teachers of students, their problems, their questions, their vocabulary, their aims in life, their family backgrounds, the better teachers we will be. Very little of this information can be garnered in the classroom or formal conference periods. Most of it will come out quite naturally in the informal setting of a home, to the mutual benefit of the teacher and student" (p. 5).

Residence Halls in the 1950s

Although the direct influence of veteran enrollment rose and fell in a relatively short time—the decline beginning in about 1952 and lasting until about 1955, when veteran enrollment was considered negligible (Mayhew, 1977)—a return to the days when faculty members knew most of the students at the college and could invite them into their homes in small numbers was not to be regained on most campuses. Francis Brown, staff associate for the American Council on Education, forecast the problem facing higher education in his 1951 address to the National Association of Deans of Men. He said:

> If you look at the long range future, in terms purely of the matter of births, an appalling situation faces higher education. The present 18-year olds were born in 1932 and 1933—take 1932 as illustrative. During the year 1932 there were 2,059,000 babies born in the entire United States. In 1947 there were 3,656,000 babies born in the United States. In the last six months of 1950 there were more than 2,000,000 babies born, indicating more than a 100 percent increase in the birthrate at the present time, as contrasted with the declining birthrate of the 1930s. . . .
>
> But one wonders what this means. We are seeing it now in elementary schools. It will move into the high school, and by 1956 and 1957 it will begin to strike the colleges. This is not a bulge in the birthrate. It is apparently a permanent and continuing plateau that turns only upward (p. 108).

Mr. Brown's forecasts for enrollment increases came to pass. In 1946, institutions of higher education in the United States enrolled 2,078,095 students. By 1957 enrollments had increased by approximately one third to 3,036,938 students (National Center for Educational Statistics, 1981). To meet this increase in enrollment, universities built new residence halls. But, these were not the small quaint halls, steeped in tradition and built to join students in companionship with the community of scholarship. Instead, buildings were constructed to meet demands for the housing of large numbers of students. Decisions were often made on the basis of cost-per-square-foot assessments determined by a formula that would allow the residence halls to generate enough funds to pay for the bonds sold to build the facility and to cover the operating costs of the building. The idea was to make the residence halls self-financing—a financial auxiliary of the university. Shay (1969) describes this self-financing idea as an "unfortunate policy . . . [which forced] many an unhappy administrator to choose between providing a rigid institutional environment or charging exorbitant rents which impecunious students cannot afford. Most administrators have tried to split the difference, resulting in our brightly colored barracks with opulent lounges which can hardly be classified as educational facilities" (p. 77).

Unseem (1966) calls the period after 1950 in which there began a surge in the building of residence halls the "traditionless period." She describes the characteristics of student housing built in this period:

1. The number of students housed within any unit has increased. The units are sometimes grouped together in complexes, and occasionally the complexes are coeducational.
2. The halls are managed by professionals or what I have called members of professionalizing occupations: housemothers have become resident advisers, janitors and cleaning people have become maintenance personnel. . . .
3. Services to students have increased both in quantity and quality. The bare minimum provided in a dormitory room has increased to include lamp fixtures, bedspreads, built-ins, and venetian blinds.
4. Investments must be protected, accounted for, managed, and organized. And to do this students have to be managed, too. Rules and regulations have become more depersonalized and, from the point of view of students, seem to be imposed by the professional staff rather than learned from students and self-enforced.
5. With the increase in campus size, more services and activities that were once on central campus have had to be decentralized. . . .
6. Much the same standardization has happened and will continue to happen in residence halls as has occurred in other organized-administered activities of modern mass society. I sometimes call this the "Residence Hall Beautiful" or the Howard Johnson syndrome, for residence halls are repeatable from coast to coast.
7. In some of the freshmen halls, in the absence of traditions, adolescent behavior tends to take over; and this must be managed and controlled by the professional staff (pp. 118–119).

These new buildings lost much of the esthetic appeal of the smaller residence halls of the past. Shay (1969) described them as "gilded barracks with glamorous appurtenances . . . far less homelike than many of the halls built as WPA projects in the late 1930s" (p. 77).

The personnel who managed the residence halls had also changed. Cowley said in 1957 that there were "Three kinds of people engaged in student personnel services professionally: the humanitarians, the administrators, and the scientists, more especially psychologists" (p. 174). The first group of student personnel administrators, those who founded the field, he described as coming from the ranks of humanitarians—and some distorted sentimentalists. But the second wave of administrators, and the ones Cowley described as predominating the student personnel field in 1957, were administrators. He says that, "By and large, those who have come into the field during the past 25 years to administer the huge coordinated programs that have been developed have been appointed primarily because of their administrative ability rather than because of any compelling interest in students. They are primarily executives in charge of large and important operations" (p. 175). Those who came from backgrounds in psychology, Cowley notes, were in the student personnel field since about World War I, but were just now—1957—beginning to be a force within the field still dominated by the "administrative types." And, to some extent, the predominance of the "administrative types" may help explain why universities built the high rise, sterile environments of concrete and glass and expected students to enjoy the experience of residing in them.

This is not meant to imply that those who worked with students as resident counselors or hall directors were insensitive to the needs of students. Indeed, much of the literature (Orme, 1950; Lind, 1946; Strang, 1949) of the late 1940s and 1950s was concerned with the counseling and advising of students. However, these people were not the administrators usually making the decisions about construction of facilities. On most campuses these decisions were left to top administrators, architects, and those in the college business office.

Residence counselors were engaged in helping students learn social skills that would give them greater flexibility in social and professional situations. Typical of this approach was a book written by Irene Pierson, the Social Director of the Illini Union, first published in 1946 with a second edition in 1956 and a third edition in 1962, entitled Campus Cues. The book was written to help "those who are unknowing in the area of manners to gain information and in reassuring those who have good manners that they know and are doing what is socially acceptable" (p. 1). In it Pierson details for both men and women how they should act by answering some of the questions that have plagued college students for generations, such as

Q: Is it considered correct to kiss the girl on the first date?

A: If you try to kiss every girl you go out with, you could be labeled as promiscuous and thus admit that you are not at all particular. It is rare to get to know a girl really well enough on that date to consider a good-night kiss proper (Pierson, 1962, p. 88).

To the question confronted by many a coed

Q: What is the correct procedure when a girl has a Saturday night date and her boy friend from out of town pops in a half hour before time for the date?

A: "Tell the boy friend you have plans for the evening and cannot break them as you do not want the reputation of being a person who is not dependable. The boy friend was inconsiderate in not calling in advance. You could have been out to dinner and not have been located by him all evening" (p. 52).

The late 1950s were also a time in which many in the United States felt threatened by communism in Europe and the Far East. On October 4, 1957, Americans learned that the Russians had launched a space satellite called Sputnik into orbit around the earth. By early November, the Eisenhower administration had found a palatable explanation to offer the American public for the Russian's advanced technology, and the U.S. Office of Education released a report—which had been prepared eighteen months earlier—describing the emphasis on science, math, and engineering in the curriculum of the Russian educational system. *The New York Times* recounted this information to the American public on November 11, and on November 13, President Eisenhower in a television address told the nation the reason the Russians had a space satellite and the United States did not was that the Russians were able to produce 80,000 engineers to our 30,000 and that their educational system emphasized math, science, and engineering (Moynihan, 1975). Eisenhower called on Congress to expand the National Science Foundation, established in 1950, and requested the enactment of a number of special educational programs in math, science, and engineering as temporary emergency measures (Gladieux & Wolanin, 1976). Out of this was born the National Defense Education Act of 1958 (NDEA), which was an unprecedented expansion of the involvement of the federal government into higher education.

Residence Halls in the 1960s

In the ten years following the NDEA, enrollments on college campuses more than doubled, going from a national student enrollment of 3,226,038 in 1958 to an enrollment of 6,928,115 in 1968 (National Center for Educational Statistics, 1981, p.92). This increase in enrollment cannot be attributed solely to the NDEA. The enrollment increase was also the result of what has come to be known as the "baby boom generation" reflecting a higher birth rate following World War II.

The increase in enrollments helped create the community college movement, transformed many state colleges and normal schools into comprehensive universities, expanded the size and character of the already large state universities, and increased the size of professional school education (Carnegie Foundation for the Advancement of Teaching, 1976). With these changes came a continuing increase in the size and number of residence halls to meet the increased demand for housing.

Although institutions grew in size, Mayhew (1977) argues that between World War II and 1968 American higher education, in substance, changed very little. He explains that,

> Until 1968, although fluctuations can be noted, the higher education community largely believed that higher education was rational and intellectual. It was an "academic" activity provided to a growing, but still limited, segment of the population for the quite specific purpose of screening these young people into preferred positions; enculturating them into at least a portion of the high intellectual tradition of society. Egalitarian sentiments were expressed, to be sure, and egalitarian efforts made; but as new kinds of students enrolled in college, they were expected to conform to the orthodox and traditional practices of a residential—or simulated residential—campus (p. 2).

Higher education was changing throughout the 1960s in large part due to the increasing involvement of the federal government, which provided special funds to students and universities as part of President Johnson's "War Against Poverty" and as a result of the civil rights movement. Educational programs such as the 1963 Higher Education Facilities Act and the Higher Education Amendments Act changed the character of higher education.

This federal intervention in higher education brought a different kind of student to campus and significantly increased the enrollment in institutions of higher education. Of particular importance to the construction of residence halls was the Higher Education Facilities Act of 1963, which permitted universities to borrow money at low interest rates from the federal government to build residence halls. Many of the highrise residence halls standing on campuses today were built with loans authorized under this act. Among the items that could be funded under this act were building fixtures, defined as any items built-in or otherwise permanently attached to the building structure. The reason that many residence halls have built-in beds, desks, and dresser drawers can be traced to the provisions of this act, which permitted these "fixtures" to be financed through the loan authorization.

These structures were of the same sterile variety begun in the late 1950s. Bess (1973) says of the residence halls being built at this time that:

> With the recent rapid growth in higher education, huge complexes of dormitory residences have been built with little thought to the ways in which residence life might be integrated into academic life. Often beset by unwieldy state and federal restrictions on costs per square foot, institutions have cut financial corners by creating space-saving devices without thinking about the educational life of students, let alone their personal living space. The typical long corridors, bolted down furniture, monolithic exteriors, and cramped lounge spaces are cases in point (pp. 37–38).

It is little wonder that students rebelled against living in dormitories. Most students did not like life in the dormitory with its rules and policies; they sought to live off campus (Greenleaf, 1969). Van der Ryn and Silverstein (1967) suggested that "the need for independence, a diversity of activities and friends are characteristics of successful student living. And yet, it is the search for these conditions that drives many students out of the dormitory" (p. 28).

This was a time when students were dissenting against the established practices of university and the government. Sentiment against the Viet Nam War was strong, and students questioned the value of traditional education and, instead, sought approaches more "relevant" to the issues of the day.

Prior to this time, students under the age of 21, in most states, were considered minors. When the federal government changed the age of majority to 18, which was subsequently adopted by the states, institutions of higher education had to reexamine their relationships with students. Already, public universities were prohibited from exercising their disciplinary authority over students without affording students due process (*Dixon* vs. *Alabama State Board of Education,*

1961). In roughly a 10-year span (1962–1972), policies regulating student behavior in the residence halls moved from strictly enforced curfews for men and women, sign-in and sign-out logs, strictly enforced dress codes, strict rules governing the use of alcohol, limited visitation privileges for men and women, to no curfews, abandonment of dress codes, more tolerant attitudes about student drinking, open visitation, and coed residence halls. Residence hall counselors and undergraduate students serving as peer counselors or resident assistants (RAs), accepted as their principle roles that of counselor and adviser. They were educated in understanding the psychological problems of college students, in drug use intervention, suicide prevention, counseling skills, and similar psychosocial and developmental issues. Housing officers defined their relationship with students by a housing contract that students were required to sign upon requesting to live in a residence hall. Access to a student's room changed from an unchallenged right of the university to one defined by the housing contract and dictated by court cases related to warrantless searches.

Students challenged in the courts the priorital regulations of universities which required students to reside in residence halls (*Prostrollo* vs. *University of South Dakota,* 1974). In this decision the courts originally rejected the university's argument that the reason students must live in the residence halls for their freshmen and sophomore years was to ensure that enough money was generated to pay the bond obligations of the residence hall buildings. But, on appeal the university emphasized the special educational programs and benefits to be derived from living in a residence hall, and the court reversed its original decision upholding the right of universities to require on-campus residence for reasons related to the educational benefits that were to be gained by exposure to this environment.

In 1970 the Association of College and University Housing Officers (ACUHO) approved a proposal to its Research and Information Committee to publish a journal dedicated exclusively to student housing, and in July, 1971, ACUHO published the first edition of this journal which it titled *The Journal of College and University Student Housing.* The ACUHO organization, established in 1951, grew from fifty member institutions to 658 member institutions in 1984 (Association of College and University Housing Officers—International, 1985).

Residence Halls in the 1970s

Mayhew (1977) notes that "Residence halls during the 1970s appear to be considerably more popular with students than they were from approximately 1965 to 1970, although the significance of this shift is difficult to gauge" (p. 298). In the mid 1970s, many financially pressed students sought to live in residence halls for the economic advantages they offered over the rising costs of off-campus apartment rents and utility costs. Some universities experienced an increase in student housing, while others—predominantly comprehensive state universities located without easy access to urban areas—experienced marked housing declines.

Students of the seventies were described by Levine (1981) as more narcissistic, career oriented, less concerned with social issues, and disillusioned with the credibility of established social institutions such as higher education, church, and the family. He once (1981) characterized the students of this time as "Going First Class on the Titanic," noting that they believed that they would survive and be economically successful, but other students would be experiencing significant economic hardships.

The 1980s and Beyond—Future Demand for Residence Halls

In 1981, when the entering college freshmen were surveyed (Astin, King, and Richardson, 1981), engineering and business were the career fields most often chosen by students as their preferred academic disciplines, and the objectives students considered most important were becoming an authority in their chosen fields and being well-off financially. Over 60 percent of the students entering college in 1981 planned to live in a college-owned residence hall, although this was the preferred residence for only about 46 percent—the difference accounted for by those who preferred to live in an apartment off-campus but for some reason were unable to.

Little changed in the same national survey conducted with 1985 freshmen (Astin, 1985). Most students were still interested in business and engineering, wanted to be a expert in their chosen fields, and wanted to be financially well off. Similarly, almost 60 percent of the freshmen students planned to live in college-owned residence halls, with only 42 percent actually preferring this option—again with the difference accounted for by students who wished instead that they could reside in an off-campus apartment.

It is estimated that higher education will see a 23 percent decline in enrollment by 1997, with a period of enrollment stability between 1988 and 1991 and a sharp decline between 1991 and 1997 (Carnegie Council on Policy Studies in Higher Education, 1980). As the 1980s began, Blimling and Schuh (1981) estimated that the decline in enrollment and other factors would have the following effects on residence halls in the decade of the 1980s:

1. Enrollment declines due to fewer high school students and economic constraints will mean lower occupancy for residence halls on many campuses.
2. Inflation, enrollment declines, and related economic factors will force universities into retrenchment, open admissions, and concentration upon retention.
3. Since they will be able to choose more freely among universities, students as consumers will demand more services, better facilities, and more freedom in residence halls.
4. Universities will be asked to meet the needs of a more diversified student population.
5. The government will continue to regulate universities, and more university policies and actions will be challenged in the courts (p. 98).

As Blimling and Schuh noted in undertaking this assessment of residence halls, "Predicting the future is a little like hitting balloons on a carnival dart board. Some balloons are easier to hit than others, but the darts are weighted against you" (p. 95). It would appear, as of 1989, that their darts have fallen somewhat short of the mark. The predicted effects of enrollment declines were short lived. Judicial involvement and government intervention has continued, but it has not presented significant problems for residence hall administrators. Similarly, inflation and energy costs have generally continued to rise, but not at the rate anticipated and not with the effect predicted.

Conclusion

History reveals that residence halls have been both the herald of and the bane of higher education. At times residence halls were viewed as the focus of building a student's character through the companionship of faculty and fellow students seeking to be scholars and gentlemen. Later it became synonymous with all manner of hedonistic and insidious activities of wayward youths. There was a revival of residence hall construction for all the cherished educational reasons and a reorganization into highrise sterile structures for all the wrong reasons.

It is apparent that the history of residence halls is driven by factors other than a consistently held, conscientiously applied, and well-reasoned guiding philosophy. The pattern of this evolution has been essentially one of reacting to other influences in history. Although in the early development of residence halls they were acknowledged and promoted as an important educational tool, in recent years their growth has been predicated on enrollment trends and considered on many campuses as a service provided for students. The same enrollment-driven expansion that fostered the often-cursed highrise residence halls was also the genesis of a new commitment to the education of students living in residence halls.

Because of the complexities associated with fulfilling a commitment to have residence halls become a meaningful part of a student's education, practitioners in residence hall work have had to become more sophisticated in their approaches to structuring these peer environments and more analytical in assessing the value of the residence hall environment.

Chapter 3
The Educational Philosophy of Residence Halls

Before you examine a philosophy to guide residence halls, it is important to consider some realities of operating a residence hall system. At public universities most residence halls are considered to be "auxiliary" organizations. This means that they have self-generating funds and receive little or no state support. The money to construct residence halls at public universities is usually borrowed from the state through a bond issue offered by the state government or borrowed through a special funding program offered by the federal government. The fees students pay to live in residence halls pay for the operation of the halls and help retire the bonded indebtedness or federal loan.

Private institutions usually take a similar approach to the operation of residence halls—that is that they must be self-supporting. At private institutions funds for building residence halls are sometimes donated by wealthy alumni, but more often, the money is borrowed from a lending agency or from the institution's endowment, to be paid back to the institution with interest from monies generated by the fees students pay.

At both public and private institutions the cost of residence halls are usually subsidized by renting the rooms to conference groups in the summer.

What this all means is that the first responsibility of the director of residence life or housing is to be a good money manager. No matter how laudable the director's intentions may be, nor how educationally directed he or she wishes to be, a large part of what occurs in residence halls is dictated by the financial stability of the residence hall program as a whole. Resident assistants (RAs) and other staff members are an expense incurred in the operation of residence halls, just like the bond retirement expense or cost of utilities. When the cost of housing is determined, the cost of professional staff and RAs are factored into the overall cost residents are asked to bear. Students are purchasing your services and your skills.

Effective residence hall programs have developed a balance between the cost of operation and the financial reserves of the residence hall program. If a director were to operate a residence hall without a continuing process of maintenance, refurbishment, staff training, and renovation, the residence halls, like any other resource, would be depleted. The physical environment and social atmosphere of the building would soon drive students away, and the financial stability of the residence hall's operation would be disrupted.

By the same token, if the director were to establish exorbitant rental rates for rooms, students would seek accommodations elsewhere. Student housing is a cost that people consider along with tuition when they select an institution. Even if the institution has a requirement that students live in residence halls for one year, the cost of this may be a factor in the overall financial attractiveness of the institution when the institution recruits new students. Thus, a balance must be struck among what the financial market will bear for cost of a residence hall room, and the educational programs, residence services, and operating costs of the residence hall.

Four Philosophies for Working with Students in Residence Halls

Throughout its history residence halls have been guided by many philosophies. In the early years, residence halls were viewed as a necessity and as a method for controlling the behavior of students. They were considered an extension of the educational philosophy of the school and were used to help instill piety and obedience in students. As was noted in Chapter 2, the philosophy toward students in residence halls changed with the imposition of the "German model" of higher education. In this context, residence halls were viewed merely as places of residence having no influence on the institution's relationship with students.

Today four different philosophies exist in residence halls. In identifying these four philosophies, it is important to note that the lines of demarcation are not always clear, and that some approaches may share characteristics of several philosophical commitments.

The Student Services Approach

One of the early philosophies for guiding the experience of students in residence halls holds that residence halls are a *student service* provided by the university. In this view, residence halls fall into the same category as services provided by the health center, or the services provided by on-campus dining services. As a service, it is important that it is managed effectively and efficiently. One may also refer to this as a *business approach,* because it views residence halls first and foremost as a business, appropriately managed to the best interest of students. Educational programs, RAs, intramurals, and hall government are services provided to the student.

An extension of this student services approach is a greater emphasis on consumerism. The belief is that residence halls should be operated in a businesslike manner, marketed to students, and those services with the greatest student appeal should be retained, whereas those of less interest to students should be eliminated.

The Custodial Care and Moral Development Approach

Many private universities and Bible colleges use an approach that can best be described as a *custodial care and moral development approach* to running residence halls. The living environment of students is used as an extension of the philosophy or dogma of the institution. At institutions where the belief is that the institutions must control all aspects of the young person's life, residents may be restricted from having radios or televisions in their rooms. They may be forbidden to smoke cigarettes or to drink alcoholic beverages on campus and may be subjected to periodic room inspections, curfews, dress codes, and nonvisitation periods.

The idea behind this philosophy is that by controlling the behavior of the individual, the institutions instill in students values consistent with religious or educational values of the institution. The rules by which students live create a social environment that supports and fosters what the institution believes to be a healthy environment for the student. Removed from temptation and monitored closely, it is believed, students are helped to become more moral.

The Student Affairs Approach

The *student affairs approach* holds that residence halls serve to guide the educational experience of students outside the classroom. One might describe this as a nondirective approach in which students are provided with a variety of opportunities to get involved. When students experience problems, RAs and other staff people are available to advise the student. Residence halls are managed with the knowledge of the history and purpose of residence halls being part of the educational system. Hall government, RAs, and residence hall programming exist to promote an educational milieu in the residence halls. If the social environment of the residence halls can be maintained and enhanced, students who live there should have an enriched educational experience.

The focus is on maintaining the components that contribute to a positive educational environment in the residence halls. For example, RA training is done to help all RAs develop a variety of skills so that they may respond to the variety of demands placed upon them by the residents. If the RAs do their job well, the students are more likely to have a successful learning experience in the residence halls.

The Student Development Approach

In 1972, Robert Brown authored a monograph on student development. This was the culmination of an ongoing program sponsored by the American College Personnel Association to reconceptualize the fundamental concepts, rules, functions and methods of student personnel work. This *student development approach* is characterized by the following:

1. Acceptance of the belief that individuals develop in stages that are sequential, cumulative, increasingly complex, and qualitatively different
2. Acceptance of the student as the principal agent for change
3. A belief that the role of residence hall staff is to assist students in accomplishing goals that they have set for themselves
4. A recognition that one must consider the development of the whole individual, intellectually, physically, emotionally, and spiritually

Residence hall programs that have adopted this approach may begin by assessing each individual student's personal goals through either testing or through personal interviews. A plan may be designed for each student based on opportunities in the residence halls to help that student accomplish the goals he or she has set for himself or herself. A system of monitoring the student's progress through either testing or keeping a record of the student's participation in educational experiences in the residence hall may be used to give the student feedback about his or her progress. New goals are then set with individual students based upon the progress they have made in attainment of goals that they have already set.

Using this approach requires a strong theoretical knowledge of experiences that facilitate cognitive, psychosocial, and moral development. The assessment techniques and interpretation of instruments require professional training and experience. Because of this, this approach requires professional staff who work individually and in small groups with students. RAs are generally used to help implement educational programs, counsel students, and give feedback to professional staff on the progress individual students and groups are making.

What often occurs is a somewhat less intense approach to student development in the residence halls than the one just described. The recognition that students are confronting different developmental issues in different stages of their lives guides decision making in designing educational programs for residence halls and in designing intervention to enhance the social environment of a residence hall.

A Blend of Approaches

Although four separate philosophies were identified for working with students in residence halls, there is on most college campuses a mixture of approaches. The approaches are a reflection of the orientation or attitudes of the people who are operating the residence halls. The philosophy of the residence halls on a campus combines the experiences the students and professional staff bring to that environment. It is blended with the tradition and heritage of the residence hall system on the campus, and with the educational philosophy and mission of that institution.

Residence hall philosophies on individual college campuses change. They may take the best of the student development approach and try it, keeping elements that work while discarding elements that have not proven successful. They may use the student services approach to control facilities, yet focus the residence life and educational aspects in the tradition and heritage of the student affairs approach. The one concept that all of these approaches hold in common is the philosophy that residence halls provide an educational benefit to students. The experience of living and participating in a residence hall enriches the intellectual, emotional, physical, and spiritual life of students who live there.

If residence halls do not adopt a philosophy of education, there is no real justification for universities to support them. It is surely easier to operate residence halls as hotels than as an extension of the educational mission of the institution. Were residence halls not provided on college campuses, in most communities the private sector would be quick to respond with low-cost housing for students. It is only because the educational community believes that there is value in living and sharing the educational experience of college that residence halls on college campuses exist. They are a principle method by which the educational experience of the classroom is joined with the out-of-class experience of the student.

As you will see in the chapters which follow, the involvement of the student in the experience of education through the residence halls and in other ways enriches the quality of the educational experience. This involvement helps sustain the student's intellectual pursuits throughout college.

How does this discussion apply to you as an RA? It reveals the reason that the university employs you. You help facilitate the education of students outside the classroom. This is why your institution spends time training you in human relations skills, crisis management, counseling techniques, and all of the other skills necessary to aid students in their personal development. Your function is to serve as a catalyst, an identifier of services, a role model, and as an informal assessor of students' strengths and weaknesses.

Goals for Residence Hall Programs

If the philosophy of residence halls is educational, it must be directed to accomplish educational goals. In 1986, the Council for the Advancement of Standards for Student Services/Development Programs (CAS) issued a set of standards and guidelines for student personnel programs on college campuses. The mission established for housing and residential life programs is the following:

> The residential life program is an integral part of the educational program and academic support services of the institution. The mission must include provision for educational programs and services, residential facilities, management services, and where appropriate, food services (CAS, 1986, p. 51).

The standards identify four goals to accomplish this mission. These goals are:

1. a living learning environment that enhances individual growth and development;
2. facilities that ensure well-maintained, safe, and sanitary housing conditions for students, and otherwise accommodate residential life programs;
3. management services that ensure the orderly and effective administration of all aspects of the program for food, dining facilities, and related services that effectively meet institutional and residential life program goals in programs that include food service;
4. food, dining facilities, and related services that effectively meet institutional life program goals in programs that include food services (CAS, 1986, p. 51).

The first two of these goals are of particular importance to you as an RA because they define the standards for your living conditions and for your educational purpose in residence halls. Figure 3.1 elaborates on the opportunities, experiences, and activities that residence halls need to provide to individuals and groups to accomplish the educational and developmental goals of residence halls and to ensure that the residential facilities in which students live are comfortable and conducive to study.

To effectively fulfill its mission and goals, the program must provide the following:

1. Individual and group educational and developmental opportunities. Opportunities should include activities and/or experiences in:
   - living cooperatively with others
   - developing and clarifying values
   - developing independence and self-sufficiency
   - developing appreciation for new ideas, cultural differences, and life-style differences
   - enhancing respect for self, others, and property
   - exploring and improving interpersonal relationships
   - making educational and career decisions
   - acquiring and using knowledge
   - understanding and managing personal health requirements, personal finances, and time
   - developing and exercising leadership skills
   - exploring and managing the use of leisure time
   - promoting and demonstrating responsible social behavior such as nonexploitive and nondiscriminatory racial and sexual relationships
   - promoting and demonstrating a proper understanding of the results of drug and alchol use

Educational programming, advising, and supervisory activities of the residential life staff should address developmental objectives and will vary in accordance with locally assessed needs. Examples include

- introduction and orientation of students to services, facilities, staff members, and staff functions;
- education of safety, security, and emergency precautions and procedures;
- encouragement of student participation in institutional and residence hall programs;
- encouragement of an atmosphere conducive to academic pursuits;
- explanation of institutional and residential living policies, procedures, and expectations;
- provision of information about relevant civil and criminal laws;
- provision of written institutional disciplinary policies and procedures;
- encouragement of students to develop a sense of responsibility for their community through
  - participation in policy decisions
  - confrontation of and education about inappropriate and disruptive behavior
  - participation in mediating conflict within the community
  - assessing fair charges to individual(s) responsible for damages, and participation in evaluating the housing program
- provision of academic information
- provision of a planned array of social, recreational educational, and cultural programs

Figure 3.1. CAS standards and guidelines for students services/development programs

- assessment of needs for special interest populations
- making appropriate referrals
- provision of individual advising or counseling support
- provision of student consumer information

2. Residential facilities that are clean, safe, well maintained, reasonably priced, attractive, comfortable, properly designed, and conducive to study.

   Functions associated with this goal include maintenance and renovation, equipment replacement, custodial care, energy conservation, and grounds care.
   - Maintenance/renovation programs should be implemented in all housing operations and may include (a) a preventive maintenance program designed to extend the life of the equipment and facilities, (b) a program designed to repair in a timely manner equipment and building systems as they become inoperable, and (c) a renovation program that modifies physical facilities and building systems to make them more effective, attractive, efficient, and safe.
   - Systematically planned equipment replacement programs should exist for furnishings, mechanical systems, maintenance equipment, carpeting, draperies, and kitchen equipment, where applicable.
   - Regularly scheduled cleaning of public areas should be provided.
   - Energy conservation efforts should be implemented through educational programs, as well as through timely renovation and replacement of inefficient equipment and obsolete facilities.
   - Grounds, which may include streets, walks, and parking lots, should be safe, clean, and attractively maintained.

3. Management functions including planning, personnel, property management, purchasing, contract administration, financial control, and, where applicable, conference administration.

   Financial reports should be available to all responsible offices and should be used to provide an accurate financial picture of the organization, and to provide clear, understandable, and timely data on which housing officers and others can base decisions and make plans.

   Representatives of the residence hall and family housing communities should be given the opportunity to comment on proposed rate increases and operating budgets. Rate increases should be announced and discussed well in advance of their effective date.

   Purchasing and property management procedures should be designed to ensure value for money spent, security for supplies and furnishings, and maintenance of proper inventories.

Figure 3.1.—*Continued*

> Clear and comprehensive communications and written individual housing agreements should be used to establish terms applicable to students and to the institution. There should be clear communication to students, other interested members of the campus community, and potential residents of the procedures and priorities for securing a room and/or board contract. Procedures for canceling, subleasing, or being released from a contract should be written and distributed, if there are provisions for such release.
>
> All service functions should be efficiently and effectively managed. Any off-campus housing referral or information service and any conference operation should be administered in a manner consistent with the mission and goals of the institution.
>
> 4. Food services, where applicable, which provide high quality, nutritious, and reasonably priced meals.
>
> Food services include provision of a variety of nutritional meals, secure and sanitary food storage, recipes that ensure appetizing food, good customer relations, pleasant dining environments, and safe and sanitary conditions (CAS, 1986, pp. 51–52).

Educational Goals of Residence Halls

Residence halls serve an important educational purpose, and they best serve the needs of the students and the university community when the educational goals of the residence hall program include the following:

1. The primary goal of residence halls is to assist students with their personal growth and development.
2. Residence halls should be appealing places to live. They should be places where students feel comfortable and at home. This means that not only should the physical facilities be comfortable and well maintained, but the social climate of each living unit also must be appealing and comfortable. Residence halls should be as free as possible from noises from other people's rooms, practical jokes, general disruptions, irritations, and distractions.
3. Students should be given as much freedom as possible in the decoration and control of their individual residence hall rooms. The need to have control over a territory is a basic human need. The residence hall room represents this territory.
4. Living in a residence hall should teach students tolerance for others, skills in group living, and a sense of responsibility to the community. Students should learn through the residence hall experience the ability to interact

with peers and to contribute as a member of a group. Residence halls should help students learn the necessary human relations skills to socialize and work with others. Students should have the opportunity to explore their own values in exchanges with other students, share ideas, and receive feedback about those ideas. Older students and the RA should serve as models for new students.

5. The focus of administration in the residence halls should be primarily educational. Managerial functions are necessary for a positive educational environment, but these functions should not become the focus of administration or the goal of the residence hall program.

Educational Skills RAs Need

To fulfill the educational mission of residence halls, you as an RA need to acquire knowledge and skills in the following eight areas:

Skills	Scope
Conceptual Application	This means a basic understanding of human development, including the concepts and strategies necessary to help students in their development and growth toward adulthood.
Counseling	These include listening, referring people for additional help, empathizing, and helping others resolve problems.
Basic Information	These include knowledge of the services and procedures on your campus, rules and policies of the residence halls, and knowledge of how to survive academically and socially on your campus.
Administrative	These include good organization, paperwork management, time management, and follow-through on projects started or assigned.
Teaching	Two types are required: educational programming skills and effective role-modeling skills. More traditional kinds of teaching skills may also be called upon as one may become an instructor for other RAs or for students.
Leadership	The leadership skills RAs need include how to set objectives, how to motivate others, and how to support others in becoming a leader.
Crisis Management	This is the ability to view a crisis situation and control it effectively. It requires self-confidence, remaining calm, assisting other individuals, directing resources, and knowing resources available to assist. It also involves good judgment, practice, and often good human relation skills.
Human Relationship	This includes an understanding of oneself and others and specific knowledge about such areas as motivation, sexuality, and behavioral problems. It requires the ability to react freely and communicate with others in a personal way that invites others to want to know you.

Summary

Four philosophical approaches to working with students in residence halls were identified in this chapter. The student services approach views residence halls as one of many student services provided to students on a college campus. The moral development approach is based upon the belief that by controlling the behavior of students one is able to train the student to accept a particular set of values held to be important by that college community. The student affairs approach holds that providing an enriched education for students means improving the overall quality of such things as educational programming, counseling, and the facilities in which students live. The final approach described was the student development approach, based on human development theory and focused on helping students identify and obtain goals consistent with their personal objectives and their stage of maturation.

These four philosophical approaches are not mutually exclusive. The more common pattern is a combination of the four based upon the history and traditions of the residence hall program.

A series of goals for residence halls were described to help accomplish the educational mission for residence halls and to enhance the quality of the facility in which students live. To accomplish the educational goals of residence halls, eight skill areas for RAs were identified.

Chapter 4
The Influence of Residence Halls on the Development of Students

Are residence halls influential in the development of students? Do they aid students in academic pursuits, help students integrate their personal values, and, in general, provide an environment that contributes to the students' overall growth toward maturity? Researchers have answered yes.

Comparisons between Students Who Live in Residence Halls and Students Who Do Not

One method of examining the effects of residence halls is to compare the students who live in them with students who do not. Arthur Chickering, in a book appropriately titled *Commuting Versus Resident Students* (1974), did this. He found that residence hall students did better in college, were more likely to succeed, and advanced more quickly. He summarizes some of these findings as follows:

> Residents, in response to immersion in a college environment, change most during the first two years. They decelerate and may even slightly regress after that, as they move back toward the home culture as graduation approaches. They change most quickly in the nonintellectual areas where the differences between high school and college are greatest. And change in intellectual areas accelerates as college courses and patterns of study become more challenging. In contrast, commuters' change is slower. They are constrained by internal conflicts and by pressures from parents, peers, and prior community. These constraints operate with least force for intellectual development, where the college experiences of commuters and residents are most similar. Thus the commuters more quickly approximate the scores of residents in the intellectual area. But because substantial differences exist, and persist, in the range of noncourse experiences and interpersonal relationships, nonintellectual changes occur more slowly. Beginning college with fewer advantages than resident students, commuters as a group slip further and further behind residents despite these changes. And, as a consequence, college has the effect of widening the gap between the have-not students and the haves (page 44).

Prior to Chickering's study, Alexander Astin (1973) conducted a national survey of both private and public colleges and universities for the American Council on Education. He compared students who lived in residence halls with students who did not and found at least six major differences.

1. Students who lived in residence halls were more likely to achieve a higher grade-point average than those students who did not live in residence halls.
2. Students who lived in residence halls were more likely to complete their baccalaureate degrees in four years and to apply for admission to graduate school than students who did not live in residence halls.
3. Students who lived in residence halls were more likely to major in an area of humanities (education, social science, etc.) or one of the arts, whereas commuter students were likely to major in business or engineering.
4. Students who lived in residence halls were generally reported to participate in more social activities, such as dating, going to parties, smoking, and drinking.

5. Living in a residence hall generally had a positive effect upon the student's self-image. The experience seemed to enhance self-confidence, public speaking ability, and similar measures of self-reliance.
6. Students who lived in residence halls reported greater satisfaction with their living environment than those students who did not live in a residence hall. Much of this satisfaction was due to the feeling of the resident students that they had greater contact with faculty and more opportunity to discuss their academic work with professors" (p. 206–208).

In a later study, Astin (1977) again compared students living in residence halls with students who did not. He concluded that "students who live in residence halls have more contact with faculty, interact more with student peers, do better academically, and are more satisfied with their undergraduate experience than are commuters" (p. 22). Astin goes on to say: "Perhaps the most significant impacts of living on-campus versus commuting are on achievement and career development. Living on-campus substantially increases the students' chances of persisting in college and of aspiring to graduate or earn professional degrees. Residents are also more likely to achieve in extracurricular areas, in particular leadership and athletics" (p. 220).

Smallwood and Klas (1973) compared three different forms of on-campus living with living off-campus. Students on-campus and off-campus entered the university with approximately the same academic backgrounds, grades, and other similar predictors. However, the students who lived on-campus performed better academically than those students who lived off campus. Smallwood and Klas found that the on-campus students also developed better study habits and were more involved in volunteer programs, social activities, and similar forms of university involvement. The students living in residence halls also reported a greater sense of community with the university.

Studies by Albrow (1966) confirm these findings and suggest that students who live off-campus feel more isolated from the college experience. Feldman and Newcomb's (1969) studies summarized the primary advantages for residence hall students as more social interaction and a better chance for academic success. These opportunities led to other developmental advantages, such as social and interpersonal skills, and generally provided increased academic motivation allowing students to use their academic abilities more fully.

Though it would be enough to say that residence halls help students achieve academic goals, provide more opportunities for social interaction, assist students in making career plans, and promote a greater satisfaction with the college experience, these studies do not answer how the individual is aided, develops, and matures. In 1975, Scott compared students who lived in residence halls with students who did not. He was particularly interested in the effect that residence halls had on student leaders, such as RAs. Scott chose to use the Personal Orientation Inventory (POI) to measure the differences between residence hall students and commuter students. This inventory is a standardized testing instrument designed to measure personal development or, more accurately, characteristics of self-actualization. The POI consists of 12 scales, as follows: time competence/time incompetence, inner-directed/outer-directed, self-actualizing value, existentiality, feeling reactivity, spontaneity, self-regard, self-acceptance, nature of man, synergy, acceptance of aggression, and capacity for intimate contact. A person scoring high on the POI is more fully functioning, has a more mature outlook on life, and leads a less inhibited life with greater personal freedom than does the average person.

Scott found that students who lived in residence halls achieved higher scores on the POI than students who lived off-campus or were commuting. He also found that students in leadership positions in the residence halls or who were RAs achieved higher scores on the POI than did other resident students. Scott reached the following conclusion:

> Based on the increase in self-actualization from the beginning to the end of the academic year, it was concluded that student assistants (also called resident assistants) and student leaders did differ from other students in their personal development and that these differences were related to their experiences in their position. Because an increase in self-actualization on at least twice as many scales of the POI occurred for residence hall students than for off campus students or commuting students, it was concluded that more development was fostered among students living in residence halls than among students living off campus or commuting from home (p. 218).

It is clear from these studies that residence halls have a positive influence upon the lives of students. Students who live in residence halls perform better academically, develop social and interpersonal skills more rapidly, and come closer to a level of self-actualization than students who have not had this experience. Residence halls do assist in the accomplishment of these important educational objectives. But how does living in a residence hall accomplish them? What is unique about this experience? Perhaps most importantly, how can the environment be shaped to increase, enhance, or ensure these important educational objectives?

Ways That Residence Halls Influence Students

Family Background

One of the key reasons residence halls accomplish more has less to do with the residence hall program or the staff than with the students who chose to live in residence halls. Newcomb (1960), in some of the early work on the development of college students, found that a student's background was the most important factor in determining a student's success or failure in college. Nothing the college can do inside or outside the classroom has as much influence on the student's ability to achieve as the experiences the student was afforded prior to college. Early childhood development, translated into opportunities to learn, prepares the individual for future learning—both emotionally and intellectually.

It has generally been the case that students who attend residential colleges and live on campus come from somewhat more affluent backgrounds than commuter students. These residential students are often afforded more developmental advantages prior to college, more often have parents who attended college, and more often associate with peers who plan to attend college. These background factors contribute to the overall development of the student, his or her motivations, and his or her ability to cope with an environment of ideas. The residential experiences further enhance these developmental advantages.

Leaving Home

As important as this background experience is to the student, the break with it when the student moves away from home is an important new step and a critical phase in the maturation process not experienced by those students who remain at home and attend college. The very act of moving into a new environment, free from parental influences and former friends, provides the student with new opportunities to learn. Meanwhile, the commuter student's environment remains relatively unchanged. He or she is not faced with the same challenges of adjusting to a new environment with a new pattern of social role expectations.

Peer-Group Influences

Of all the factors that influence a student's development in college, the student's peer group is the most powerful (Newcomb, 1960). Classroom instruction, course of study, and association with members of the faculty will not be as important to the student's personal development, values, career expectations, and desire to complete college or to go on to graduate school as other students with whom he or she associates.

In a residence hall, it is possible to predict who will make up a student's peer group—defined here as that group of students with whom the person commonly chooses to associate. A number of studies (Menne and Sinnet, 1971; Ecklund, 1972; Priest and Sawyer, 1967; and Martin, 1974) have shown that a student's friends, or what might be called his or her *primary peer group,* in a residential setting will be determined most by the opportunities that groups of students have to interact. Students who live in close proximity are generally afforded the most opportunities to interact with one another, and thus, one determinant of who a student's primary peer group will be is who lives close to that student.

Other factors obviously enter into friendship selection. Common interests, the size of the living unit, the location of a student's room in relation to the traffic pattern in the living unit, homogenity of the group, and isolation of the group all play important roles in increasing opportunities for certain individuals to interact and select their primary peer group.

Once selected, the peer group is critical in the student's development and growth. It carries so much influence because it acts as what Whittaker (1969) describes as the intermediate social environment between the family and society.

Peer groups take on almost a parental role by setting standards of expected conduct and holding the power to reward and punish. The rewards offered by peers consist mostly of emotional support and interpersonal esteem or influence within the group through acceptance. The punishments of the group are also emotional, based on actions such as ridicule, isolation, reprimand, or ostracism.

The residential experience heightens this peer-group influence. The similarity of backgrounds, the frequent and continual interaction by virtue of proximity, and similar academic and career goals contribute to the intensification of this influence in the residence halls.

As an aside, fraternities and sororities serve this same peer-support function. These organizations formalize the experience through rituals and ceremonies. The rituals serve as rites of passage into the organized group; however, most importantly, they serve to increase the commonality of experiences among the group members. Pledge pranks, hazing, and similar activities are used by the organization to solidify the group and to promote group trust, although hazing usually has the opposite effect.

Students in residence halls generally do not have formal rites, but they do have informal rituals that serve the same function. The experience of preparing for midterm and final examinations, of getting intoxicated together, of participating in intramural sports together, of undergoing the same social pressures for dating, of working together on a particular program or a student government project, and of simple physical contact through proximity and interaction serve the same function. Compare for a minute the experience of a practical joke played in a residence hall by a group of students and a fraternity prank. Both groups of students share in the same secretive adventure and undergo much the same unifying experience by selective inclusion into responsibility for the act. The difference between a group of students in a residence hall having a shaving-cream fight, "pennying" someone into a room, secretly discharging fireworks, or some similar activity within the residence hall is little different in function from the "kidnapping" of an active member of a fraternity or sorority by the pledge class, the stealing of a composite picture of a particular fraternity or sorority, or the painting of the fraternity or sorority's letters in prominent places about the campus. The action of the group, at the exclusion of others, promotes trust, confidence, mutual dependence, and community, further solidifying the group.

Roommate Influence

One element of influence in a student's peer environment is the student's roommate. During the freshman year, the roommate is a particularly important influence (Upcraft & Higginson, 1975). Heath (1968) studied the influence of roommates in a male residence hall and found that roommates forced individuals to become more tolerant, more understanding, more expressive, and either increased or retarded the individual's maturity. Vreeland (1970) went further, taking the position that freshman roommates who were also good friends could be identified as the primary force for attitude change in college.

Attitudes, values, and maturity are not the only things affected by a student's roommate. Murray (1961) found that a student's grades will deviate from predicted grades, either higher or lower, in the same direction the student's roommate's grades deviate. In other words, if one roommate does well academically, the chances are better for the other roommate to do well. Conversely, if one student in the room does poorly, chances are better that the other student in the room will also do poorly. Sommer (1969) provides one rationale for this observation in similar studying habits. He found that if one roommate was studying, there was a 75 percent chance that the other roommate would also be studying. Conversely, there was only approximately a 33 percent chance that the student would be studying alone.

Blai (1971) also looked at the influence of a person's roommate on academic performance when he experimentally assigned students in residence halls as roommates in an attempt to increase their academic performance. Roommate assignments were based on classification of the students as average, below-average, or above-average as indicated by their high school grades. Four experimental groups were formed. The results of the study indicated that the average students and the below-average students who were paired with high-ability students did better academically than their counterparts assigned with average or below-average students. This study confirms Murray's (1961) observation on grade influence.

The Influence of the RA

Another developmental influence in the residence hall is the RA. This was the conclusion of a study by Zirkle and Hudson (1975) at Pennsylvania State University. In this study, the researchers compared the influence of RAs who had been identified as counselor-oriented and RAs who had been identified as administrator-oriented on the development of maturity in freshman males. These students were randomly assigned to floors with either the counselor-oriented RA or the administrator-oriented RA. At the end of the academic year, the students were administered the "Perceived Self-Questionnaire," which is a standardized instrument measuring "overall maturity."

The researchers obtained some interesting results. They found a significant relationship between the RA's behavior and the development of maturity among these freshman males. Students who lived in a unit with a counselor-oriented RA had maturity scores significantly higher ($P > .001$) than those students from units with the administrator-oriented RAs. The researchers also measured the effect of not having an RA and found that those units with the RAs, whether counselor- or administrator-oriented, yielded significantly higher maturity levels than did units without an RA. Freshmen living in the units with the counselor-oriented resident assistant also had significantly ($P > .05$) higher grade-point averages than did students living in units with either the administrator-oriented RA or units without an RA. The students in the counselor-oriented units, as compared with the other groups, had generally more positive environments.

Zirkle and Hudson report that students who lived in this counselor-oriented environment

1. had more contacts with resident assistants concerning theft prevention, personal concerns, and informal matters
2. had lower assessments for physical damage to the unit
3. made more room changes within the unit and fewer requests to move out of the unit
4. had considerably more unit activities
5. felt they knew their resident assistant better, saw him more as a counselor and friend, and preferred to have him as their resident assistant again (page 32).

The researchers conclude by saying, "The behavior of the resident assistant has a significant effect upon student development. And this carries implications which are important to the role of the residence hall staff member and, more specifically, to the resident assistant in the total university educational program" (pp. 32–33).

These five important developmental factors—the student's background, the experience of moving into a residence hall, the student's association with a group of peers, the student's roommate, and the influence of the RA—must be viewed in the context of other environmental factors. These factors include the physical condition of the building, the predominance of students within a particular academic discipline; the composition of the residence hall as male, female, or coed; the rules, policies, and regulations of the university; the geographical location of the college or university; the selectivity of the institution; the size of the institution; and a number of other factors. These all contribute to the overall impact that the residence hall environment has on an individual student at a particular college or university.

Environmental Structuring of Residence Halls

Institutions have used this knowledge to design living environments that enhance opportunities for self-actualization, increase grade performance, and fulfill other developmental goals. Institutions have taken several approaches to shaping the environment. One category of approaches has attempted to increase students' academic performances by assigning students to live together on the basis of their academic majors or common course schedules. Snead and Caple (1971) assigned groups of students to live together based on their academic majors and the results of the environmental assessment technique at the University of Missouri–Columbia. In this study, students were first divided into groups by their academic majors and then by the environmental assessment technique, which defined six groups as follows: realistic, intellectual, social, conventional, enterprising, and artistic. Two small living units were used for this experiment—one male and one female. This environmental structuring resulted in higher than predicted grade point averages for the homogeneously grouped students when compared with other students.

In a similar study by Taylor and Hanson (1971) at the University of Minnesota, freshmen engineering students were grouped into two small residence halls. When the grade-point averages were compared at the end of three consecutive quarters, the researchers found that this arrangement, too, produced higher grades for these engineering students than for engineering students who did not participate in the special program.

Not all studies have shown that such special assignment programs work. Studies by Morishma (1966), Elton and Bate (1966), and Beal and Williams (1968) examining the same relationship between academic performance and assignment of students to residence halls on the basis of academic classification or major course of study have not been able to establish any significant causal relationship between grades and assignment within the residence hall. These researchers do, however, note that students in the special assignment programs do have a more positive attitude about scholastic achievement. It stands to reason that in time this attitude will have a beneficial effect on a student's academic performance and personal growth.

Research at Southern Illinois University by Duncan and Stoner (1976/77) on high-ability honor students assigned together shows that this particular form of assignment tends to increase the grade performance of these students in comparison with other high-ability students assigned at random. DeCoster, in two studies (1966, 1968) conducted at the University of Florida, earlier found this to be true when he grouped high-ability students together to compose 24 to 50 percent of a residential unit. When he compared the academic performance of these students with other high-ability students assigned at random, he also found that the homogeneously assigned honor students achieved grades higher than other honor students assigned at random. A two-year longitudinal study was undertaken by Blimling and Hample (1979) to determine the effect of a controlled study environment (controlled study hours enforced by the resident assistant in voluntary study units during prescribed hours) on average-ability students. After examining the grade performance of over 1500 students for the two-year period, the researchers concluded that the intervention of study-floor guidelines created an environment that facilitated academic pursuits and produced grade performances higher than those of students assigned without such guidelines.

It is evident from these studies that structuring the residential environment, either by homogeneously grouping students by academic major or academic ability, or by controlling the study environment, can positively affect the academic performance of students who live in residence halls.

Another major attempt to structure the residence hall environment has been through "living and learning" programs. The first program to draw national attention was at Michigan State University in the Case Hall program. Since that time, a number of research studies (Olson, 1964; Rockey, 1969; DeCoster, 1969,

1970; and Ogden, 1969) have shown that these special living and learning environments, in which students usually live and take classes together, have a positive effect upon

>   the student's satisfaction with the residence hall and the college

>   the student's cultural sophistication and aesthetic appreciation

>   the student's peer relationships

These living and learning programs appear to be particularly beneficial to new freshmen (Pemberton 1968). Newcomb (1962) suggests that the overlap of the residence hall and the classroom experience, as found in the living and learning programs, is one of the most viable means of using peer influence in academic matters.

Methods of Advancing the Growth and Development of Students Living in Residence Halls

Residence halls are the intermediate peer environment through which students are introduced to the university community. By living and working together in a residential situation, students are invited to membership in the university or college community. Residence halls do this formally and informally. This section examines eight methods used in residence halls to facilitate development in students.

Involvement

Students who live in residence halls become involved in other students' education. They are removed from the day-to-day pressures of living in a family and their original home environment, and are introduced to an environment that is part of the campus community. Astin (1977, 1985) and Mortimer (1984) both believe that involvement is a critical factor in student retention and student satisfaction. When students involve themselves in the college environment they are committing themselves to their own education. They have begun to become part of the community, to not only receive from the environment but to give back to it.

People are all more satisfied and more motivated to achieve when they feel part of what is trying to be achieved. Involvement requires commitment, and this commitment means that the participants become a stakeholder in its success. In this case, involvement in residence hall activities and in living with other students in the college environment is a form of commitment. Once students commit themselves, they are more likely to get more from their college experience.

Some studies (Huang, 1982; Rohner, 1974; Brandt and Chapman, 1981) have shown that one sign of a student's commitment in the residence hall involves the extent to which the student attempts to personalize his or her room. Posters on the wall, family pictures, and a relaxed environment all suggest that a student has accepted the residence hall environment as his or her own. In contrast, students who do not personalize their rooms convey a message of being transient. These students never feel as if they are at home or settled into a place. Without this type of attachment or sense of being settled, students are likely to remain uninvolved and act as if they are temporary residents. Residence halls are one method of involvement. They are an opportunity for students to separate from parents and define an environment. This type of involvement is a commitment to the institution and to the accomplishment of the goal of completing college.

Integration of the In-Class and Out-of-Class Experience

Residence halls also integrate the in-class and out-of-class experience. This is done to the extent that informal discussions about academic matters take place in the residence hall. It also happens through informal tutoring that occurs when an upperclass student helps a freshman or sophomore, or when political issues or major social issues are discussed in small groups in late-night discussions. These discussions can be some of the most rewarding and involving aspects of living in a residence hall.

These experiences help to join what takes place in the classroom with what takes place outside of the classroom. Students in these environments are called upon to defend their point of view and examine in-depth issues that for many years they may have taken for granted. Questions such as Does God exist? How do I feel about premarital sex? and Should I take drugs? are now approached on a rational basis as opposed to a prescriptive set of rules students have been taught to follow regardless of their rationale.

Living and learning centers—which are residence halls incorporating some form of classroom instruction and usually having a selection process for their residents—are good examples of a formal blend of the in-class and out-of-class experience available in residence halls. Mortimer (1984) and Boyer (1987) both describe living-and-learning centers as a key element in integrating the in-class and out-of-class learning experience.

Learning does not stop when a student leaves the classroom. It is the mulling over of ideas, the exploration of the implications of these ideas, and the application of these ideas to real-life situations that is reflective of learning. Because all of the students living in residence halls are focused on the same objective, academic discussions that enrich the classroom experience are a natural outgrowth.

Direct Intervention

Residence halls also provide the opportunity for direct intervention, such as counseling, with students. When a student is depressed, has a behavior problem, or fails to meet normal social expectations, RAs and other staff are available to counsel the student about appropriate behavior. Sometimes this counseling comes in the form of referring students for psychotherapy. This referral may give the student permission to confront some long-term personality problems that he or she has had.

Such intervention is a critical element in the person's overall education including both the student's intellectual development and his or her personality development.

Community

A fourth method used in residence halls to achieve educational objectives is the development of a sense of community in the residence halls. Community is the sense of mutual support and acceptance. It offers a safe environment for students to experiment with different roles and life styles. It also transmits a sense of institutional culture. This institutional culture represents those experiences and commitments that are valued in the community. Such concepts as academic integrity, tolerance for other life styles, compassion for others, honor, and trustworthiness are kinds of experiences and commitments that the educational community represents and that should be transmitted through the experience of working and living together in the academic community.

Optimum Dissonance

Sanford (1962) described the principle of optimum dissonance as the balance between challenge and support to meet that challenge. The educational environment presents many challenges for students. Competition for grades, fulfilling the expectations of one's parents and one's self, and financial stress, are just a few examples.

Associations students make in the residence halls through friendships and mutual experiences offer students the support in meeting the challenges of the environment. They provide individual students with feedback, a sense of acceptance, and nurture the student in his or her attempt to meet the challenges of the environment. When the student is stressed, has self-doubts, or has over extended himself or herself, support of friends give the student the opportunity to get reinforcement, get encouragement, and to expel their frustrations in the safety of mutually supported friendships.

Role Modeling

Your role as a resident assistant is another method by which students learn. You help set examples, give feedback, and help to mentor individual student growth and development. What you do and how you behave sets an informal standard for others in your living unit. Role modeling by the senior staff in your building is another way in which students learn what is appropriate and what is inappropriate, how to act and how not to act.

Adult Roles

Erikson (1968) identified four experiences people need in young adulthood to help them develop appropriate adult roles. These are

experimentation with different roles and life styles

freedom to choose activities and experience the consequences of those choices

involvement in what can be seen as meaningful achievement

time for reflection and introspection

Residence halls provide the opportunity for all four of these experiences. Because students are separated from parents, they can more easily become independent and experiment with different roles and life styles to determine what fits them and what does not. Residence halls also provide the opportunity to be alone and to do nothing. Students can reflect on what they want to accomplish and have an opportunity to examine their feelings.

When students make decisions, universities hold them accountable for those decisions. When these decisions are good, generally the student is rewarded. When the decision is bad, students receive counseling and can experience the consequences of those decisions. This kind of give and take helps the student to set reasonable boundaries for himself or herself.

The peer environment of the residence hall provides feedback to students. If students are being disruptive or have poor social skills, other students are quick to identify these deficiencies. There is no more critical judge of a person's behavior than a group of his or her peers. This feedback helps students gauge and refine their social interaction skills and their own standards for behavior.

A Synthesis of the Effects of Residence Halls on Students

When one statistically combines all of the research on residence halls (Blimling, 1989), it does not indicate that residence halls have a significant influence on students, compared with living off campus, in the intellectual areas of academic performance, study habits, or values. Although there are studies which do show residence halls have a positive influence in these areas, the sum total of research does not support this conclusion. Among the reasons for these differences in study findings is that students who choose to live in residence halls generally come from more affluent family backgrounds and are usually better prepared for college. Studies that control for initial differences generally do not show that residence halls have a significant influence on academic performance (Blimling, 1989).

The sum total of residence hall research does indicate that residence halls have a positive influence on students in the nonintellectual areas of perception of the campus social climate, participation in extra-curricular activities, likelihood of graduating from college, and personal growth and development.

One would expect the greatest degree of difference to occur between residence hall students and students living off-campus in those areas where the college experience of the two groups of students were most different. The college experience of residence hall students and off-campus students are likely to be most similar in the intellectual areas associated with the classroom activities and least similar in the nonintellectual areas associated with out-of-classroom activities. Chickering (1974) made this observation when he compared residence hall students with commuter students. He concluded that residence hall students were more likely to experience immediate changes in the nonintellectual areas because the differences between high school and college were greatest in these areas and that changes in the intellectual areas occurred more slowly because the experience of residents and commuters was most similar in these areas.

In 1989 Blimling synthesized 20 years of empirical research on the influence of residence halls on college students. This statistical synthesis revealed seven areas in which residence halls had a significant influence on students. These seven areas are

retention

participation in extra-curricular activities

perception of the campus social climate

satisfaction with the college

personal growth and development

interpersonal relationships

faculty interaction

Students who live on campus are more likely to graduate from college than students who do not live on campus. They are more likely to have greater expectations for academic achievement and are more likely to remain in college and graduate.

The residence hall environment also permits students to become involved in more campus activities. This is, in part, an issue of proximity. If a student lives on campus, it is simply easier for him or her to become involved in the activities that take place on campus. Through these experiences of working with other students, students gain important skills and experiences that aid the students throughout their lives. Skills such as working with others in small groups, managing a budget, expressing one's ideas in a formal committee meeting, negotiating with members of the administration, creating projects, following through on projects, and managing others are examples of what students learn through these experiences. These are "functionally transferable skills." This means that these skills can be applied to many different situations in both the work world and in a person's daily life.

Students who live in residence halls also have a better perception of the social climate. They feel that the campus environment is more comfortable, more academic, more supportive, and generally more enjoyable. Generally they are more satisfied with their college experience. They feel better about themselves, what they accomplish, and the quality of their education.

Living on campus also facilitates a student's personal growth and development. Students mature more quickly because they have more opportunities to grow and become independent. Because they are away from home, they must assume more responsibility for themselves. They are forced to meet more challenges and thus have greater opportunities to grow.

Residence halls also build stronger friendships. The interpersonal relationship of students who live in residence halls are strong because of mutual shared experiences in the halls. Living with one another allows residence hall students to have greater interaction with other students and make more and stronger friendships than students who live off campus. This finding merely reflects the opportunities those students have to interact. When you live with another group of students and see them regularly, you share more in common with them. These interpersonal relationships force students to develop a greater tolerance for different cultures and life styles. It helps to break down cultural biases that exist when people are limited in their experiences with people of other cultural heritages. The living environment helps breakdown these cultural stereotypes by forcing students to experience cultural diversity.

Finally, students who live in residence halls have more faculty interaction. This occurs partially because faculty are invited into the residence halls to meet with students and partially because residence halls are located on the campus and students can more easily mingle with faculty in informal situations. Residence hall professional staff also serve this faculty interaction role. Many hall directors are older, and some are married. Interaction with both faculty and staff provides for the opportunity for mentoring relationships, and for academic discussions and exploration of ideas.

Any discussion such as this cannot ignore that all residence halls are not alike. The architectural design of some buildings invite students into interaction with one another and have a warm and supportive atmosphere, whereas others seem to be sterile and institutional. The architectural designs of buildings do influence students. Research (Blimling, 1988; Heilweil, 1973) shows that satisfaction with the residence hall is inversely related to the size of the building. The larger the building—the more social density—the less satisfied students tend to be with living there. Long, double-loaded corridors also tend to isolate students and make them feel unwelcome. Highrise buildings, and buildings where more than two students are assigned to a room, also tend to decrease satisfaction. Ideal residential situations are those with suite living arrangements, shortened corridors, and buildings that have no more than four levels.

Policies in the residence halls can also help students to increase their satisfaction with the living situation. Environments where students are allowed to personalize their rooms and the residence hall living unit is allowed to personalize the common space (floor lounge, hallway) helps students feel more apart of the residence hall environment. The more a student can invest of himself or herself into the environment, the more likely the student is to feel comfortable in that environment.

There are natural limitations to all of these policies. It is unreasonable for students to so alter a room that it makes it unacceptable for future inhabitants. It is also unreasonable to believe that students should be able to endanger other students when personalizing their room or common space by including items that could create safety and fire hazards. Whatever policies are adopted within the institution to increase student satisfaction must be balanced by the need to maintain a clean and orderly building that is safe and secure for the current inhabitants and for those who will occupy that facility in the future.

Summary

Residence halls have a positive impact on the educational achievement of students who live in them and on students' personal growth compared with students who do not live in residence halls. Much of this academic and personal growth can be attributed to the family background, the decision to live in a residence hall, the peer group that exists within the residence hall, the student's roommate, and the influence of the resident assistant. There are methods that have proven to be successful for facilitating student growth and development in the residence halls. Universities can structure residence hall environments to enhance academic achievement and personal growth through special educational intervention programs that shape interaction within the residence hall environment.

Part Two

Understanding and Working with College Students

Chapter 5
  The Growth and Development of College Students

Chapter 6
  Common Adjustment Problems in College

Chapter 7
  Peer Counseling

Chapter 8
  Interpersonal Communication

Chapter 5
The Growth and Development of College Students

This chapter considers the biological, psychological, and social development of traditionally aged college students—those between the ages of 18 and 24. The focus is on what constitutes "normal" development during these years. *Normal* here means the average behavior changes, or those the majority of college students experience. If you think of a normal distribution curve, the term includes those responses that fall within one standard deviation above or below the mean for any particular group.

It is important to recognize that each person moves through development at his or her own pace. Maturation is influenced by individual differences that may accentuate or retard the process of development. Social factors, biological factors, and experience play roles in the pace at which one matures.

Biological Development

The years of young adulthood are a period of time in which men and women biologically are becoming adults. Women begin puberty somewhere between the ages of 8 and 13, and men start puberty approximately two years later—between the ages of 10 and 15. *Puberty* is the period when a person becomes physically mature enough to be able to reproduce. It involves developing secondary sexual characteristics associated with gender and with hormonal changes in the body.

Physically, women reach their full height at about the age of 17. Men lag behind and do not reach their full height until about the age of 21. Men and women grow differently during this period of adolescence. Mens' shoulders grow wider and their chest cavity expands, while their legs and forearms grow longer. Women grow wider in the pelvic area, ostensibly to enhance their ability to bear children.

Uneven Growth Patterns

Growth is not necessarily proportional throughout the entire adolescent period. Different portions of the body grow at different rates; therefore, some portions of the body may reach maturity faster than others. Typically the extremities, head, hands, and feet reach maturity prior to the legs, arms, and trunk of the body. This constantly fluctuating size lends to a decrease in motor skill coordination as the individual is learning to adapt to the changing size of his or her body. The description of the "awkward adolescence" is a reflection of this uneven growth toward maturity.

There is a trend toward the increasing size and earlier sexual maturity of recent generations. This trend is referred to as the "secular trend." Zastrow and Kirst-Ashman (1987) note that sons are likely to be as much as one inch taller and ten pounds heavier than their fathers, and that daughters will be between one half to one full inch taller than their mothers and approximately two pounds heavier. Menstruation is occurring in women of the current generation about 10 months earlier than it did for their mothers. The secular trend is worldwide. The reason for this trend appears to be related to better nutrition, better standards of living, and possibly the dominance of genes for tallness and rapid maturation. For the time being, this trend for increased size seems to have stabilized in the American population.

During college, men and women are approaching their physical prime. They reach their full muscular development generally between the ages of 25 and 30. Top physical speed, dexterity, and overall strength generally continue to increase until about the age of 30, when a gradual decline begins. Eyesight and hearing continue to improve and are best at about the age of 20 (Zastrow and Kirst-Ashman, 1987). For the most part, college students are in good health and generally have a high energy level.

Health issues that interfere with good health are heavy drinking, use of drugs, and stress. Each of these issues is discussed in chapters that follow. The major causes of death among college students are auto accidents and suicides. In a high percentage of cases, alcohol use is involved with both causes of death.

Psychological Adaptation to Physical Development

In 1950 Jones and Bailey conducted the first part of a longitudinal study on the influence of late and early maturation in men and women at the University of California. Mussen and Jones in 1957 contributed to this study. It showed that boys who matured early were viewed by others as more physically attractive, were treated more like adults, and were more likely to be chosen as school leaders. In contrast, late-maturing boys were viewed as less physically attractive, more tense, and more involved in attention-getting. But, they were also more flexible and more capable of confronting periods of uncertainty.

For women, the results are less clear. Early maturation does seem to be associated with some psychological benefits related to attractiveness and feelings of maturity; however, there is no noticeable negative effect associated with late maturation in women.

In 1981 Blyth, Bulcroft, and Simmons conducted a study in Wisconsin on early and late maturation. They found that boys who matured early had a higher self concept, were generally less satisfied with their overall physical development, tended to be more popular with girls, and participated in more school activities during high school. The same study found that early maturing girls were also less satisfied with their bodies than late maturers, were more often in dating relationships with boys, and may have had more behavior problems during middle school.

The short term implications of early and late maturation appear to affect self-concept and early identity formation. Early maturers generally had greater self-esteem, and there is some evidence (Peskin, 1967) that early maturers may have been pushed prematurely into decisions about identity. These differences appear to be short lived. By the age of 30 there are generally no significant differences in physical size, educational attainment, marital status, socioeconomic status, or in the number of children per family unit. One benefit to late maturing may be that late maturers are forced to deal with ambiguity in adolescence and to develop an increased tolerance for uncertainty. As a result they tend to be somewhat more flexible.

Psychological Development during the College Years

One of the most dynamic periods of psychological growth occurs during the college years. In this period young adults begin to integrate their identity, enhance their intellectual development, and internalize a personal set of beliefs and values. As people mature, they change. Sanford (1962) defines *change* as "a system that is altered from a previous state." There are two forms of change that take place as a person matures. The first is growth that Sanford (1962) describes as "an expansion of the personality by addition of parts or expansion of existing parts. The second is development that he defines as "the organization of increasing complexity." Both forms—growth and development—occur simultaneously throughout a person's life. Development is a continuous process; it is not a state that one attains. Development has an order and moves from general to specific and from mastery of simple tasks to mastery of more complex tasks. Development has characteristics associated with specific age levels, but it is influenced by individual differences such as heredity and the environment that may accelerate or retard the process. Development is not solely an internal process. It is the result of the interaction of the individual within the environment.

Development is driven by two forces: epigenesis and social role expectations (Erikson, 1968). *Epigenesis* is an internal evolutionary "clock" that biologically and psychologically pushes us towards maturity. Puberty is one example of this epigenetic clock or internal force which drives the individual forward. *Social role expectations* are behaviors that are culturally associated with a person's age and gender. As we grow older, society expects us to be increasingly independent, less impulsive, and more in control of our lives. When a person's current mode of behavior conflicts with the social role expectations for him or her at a particular age, the person experiences a developmental crisis. These crises are good. They force people to evaluate their current behavior and pattern of thinking, and to adjust it to meet new social role expectations. All of this simply means that society has come to expect more mature behavior from people as they grow older, and that society defines how people are expected to behave at different periods in their lives. The epigenic force is a factor that complements this process.

General Characteristics of Development

1. Development is continuous.
2. Development is a process, not a state.
3. Development has order.
4. Development moves from general to specific and from simple to more complex.
5. Development has characteristics associated with specific age levels.
6. Both heredity and the environment influence development.
7. Development occurs in the context of interactions between the individual and the environment, rather than through internal processes of maturation alone.

Development does not take place at random. It follows a logical sequence of stages. At each stage, people work to resolve the same or similar issues. These issues are referred to as *developmental tasks* and have a logic to their progression. For example, when children are very young, parents establish and enforce a bedtime. As a child grows older, this bedtime may get moved to a later time of the evening, but is still enforced. By the time the child reaches high school, typically parents no longer enforce any bedtime and leave this decision to the child. However, parents usually have established a curfew for the high school-aged child—the time when he or she must return home. As the child grows older, the curfew is generally withdrawn, and the time in which a single person may be expected back in the parents' home is left to the discretion of the young adult, with the understanding that there are some basic courtesies respected in the family home.

Rogers (1980) identifies these five characteristics of developmental stages associated with psychosocial development:

1. Development is sequential, but not invariant.
2. Development is cumulative, but not necessarily hierarchical.
3. Development is not universal, but it is influenced by social factors.
4. Development is qualitatively different.
5. Development is concerned with the "what" or content of development.

Development is sequential. It has an order, but this order may vary somewhat among individuals. The tasks accomplished at one stage do accumulate in such a way as to prepare the person for developmental issues at the next stage. Although there may be some hierarchical relationship, in that less-sophisticated issues are resolved in early years and more complex issues resolved in later years, this is not always true.

As you consider psychosocial development, try to understand the culture in which these factors are influencing the individual. Because cultures vary widely, different social influences may accelerate or retard different forms of development within any particular culture. Environment and social role expectations combine to influence development.

In the United States it is unusual to find a young man at the age of 16 or 17 living in a midwestern town who does not have a driver's license. Having a driver's license is one of the first symbolic representations of entering adulthood and provides the opportunity to have greater freedom. However, it is not at all unusual to find a young man from New York City, Queens, or Brooklyn who does not have a driver's license. Public transportation in New York City is such that a driver's license is not a necessity, and the environment does not demand that families own automobiles. Freedom may come earlier as parents permit their children greater liberty in the use of the subway system and other public transportation. Thus, the issue of autonomy can be advanced or retarded by the interplay of the social and physical environment and its influence on the individual.

Development is also qualitatively different, meaning that it is not simply an adding on of more responsibility; the complexity of organization increases as well at each stage in development. Psychosocial stages are also concerned with content issues. In part, what is being discussed (such as, dating, defining appropriate sex roles, marriage, and family) influences the stage of a person's development.

Two psychosocial theories are discussed here: the theories of Erikson (1968) and Chickering (1969). Although it may appear from some of the discussions that development is segmented in that one part of the person develops while the rest remains stagnate, this is not the case. Development is unitary; it involves the whole person. Elements of a person's personality develop in interaction with other characteristics of the individual. The process of change has order and develops a foundation for successive developmental changes.

Erik Erikson's Theory of Psychosocial Development

Erikson's theory focuses on how the personality develops as the result of the interaction between biological factors and social environmental demands. He describes eight stages of development based on Freud's phases of personality development. Figure 5.1 identifies Erikson's eight stages and how they correspond to Freud's psychosexual stages.

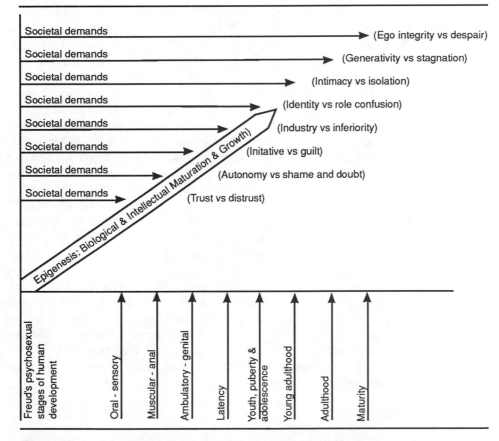

Figure 5.1: Erickson's eight stages of human development

Erikson believes that although development took place in stages, the personality was continually developing. A person does stagnate in the stage but constantly expands and enriches the dimensions of his or her personality. The stages that Erikson outlines are a representation of the parts that compose the whole personality. Maturation has a normal rate of growth and a sequence to this growth. The eight stages represent the sequence from birth through death. In each of eight stages there is a focus of concern, which Erikson describes as a *development crisis*. These crises occur as the person's current behavior comes into conflict with age-related societal demands. These conflicts must be resolved for the person to successfully move on to confront other conflicts. If they are not resolved at the stage in which they need to be, the person develops adjustment problems and may evidence maladaptive behavior in later life. At each stage, a person is drawn between two polar opposites. For example, children aged 6 to 12 must confront the crises of industry versus inferiority. Children who learn to master academic skills, peer relationships, and complex aspects of their environment develop an inner sense of industry or accomplishment. If they fail to master these activities, they feel perplexed by the environment, lack confidence in themselves, and develop a sense of inferiority.

The two stages of most concern during the college years are Stage 5 (identity versus role confusion) and Stage 6 (intimacy versus isolation). The period of time between the ages of 13 and 21 is when young people uncover facets of their personality in an attempt to define their personal identity. This is accomplished through a dynamic set of interactions between the individual and his or her social environment.

The internal need for autonomy is one of the driving forces behind this search for identity. It is coupled with the biological forces of sexual development and the replacement of the family unit as the principal reinforcing group with the person's peer group. Through a complex process of interactions, trial and error, failure and successes, the person begins to develop a concept of who he or she is. One's peer group is important to this process. It sets the standard for acceptable behavior and gives the person feedback. Parents, schools, and social mores that govern behavior in our society also give feedback to the individual.

Through the process of interacting in the community, the individual has the opportunity to experiment with different roles and life styles. The person must learn to manage the role of being a child in the family, a peer, a student, a boyfriend or a girlfriend, and perhaps that of being a part-time employee or a member of a sports team. Through these and similar experiences, people come to understand more about themselves, what they enjoy doing, and which aspects of each role are personally fulfilling. Some people mismanage the demands of these various roles and fail to integrate them by developing appropriate coping mechanisms to comfortably move among roles. If they fail, Erikson believes, people experience role confusion and will be uncertain about their identity. Table 5.1 summarizes Erikson's theory of the development of identity.

Table 5.1
Erikson's Theory of Identity Development

Concept	Process/related ideas	Characteristics/description
Erikson's ideas on identity	Revisiting the eight stages of the life cycle	Identity versus identity confusion (diffusion) is the fifth stage in Erikson's theory, coming approximately at the time of adolescence. Identity involves the adolescent's search for who he or she is as a person.
	Personality and role experimentation	An important aspect of identity development is the opportunity to try out different personalities and roles.
	Complexity	Erikson's concept of identity is complex, involving the following components: genetic, adaptive, structural, dynamic, subjective or experiential, psychosocial reciprocity, and existential status.
	A contemporary view of identity development	Identity development is a life-long process, although it is during adolescence that for the first time in development physical, cognitive, and social skills are sufficiently advanced for the individual to seriously inquire and investigate who she or he is as a person. Although some identity crises are cataclysmic, the majority involve gradual development over many years.
The four statuses of identity	Crisis and commitment	Crisis refers to the exploration of alternatives, whereas commitment is the extent to which the individual shows a personal investment in what he or she is doing.
	Diffusion, foreclosure, moratorium, and achievement	The adolescent who is diffused has not undergone a crisis or made a commitment; one who is foreclosed has made a commitment, but not undergone a crisis; one who is in moratorium is in the midst of a crisis, but has not yet made a commitment; and one who is achieved has both undergone a crisis and made a commitment.

Table 5.1—*Continued*

Concept	Process/related ideas	Characteristics/description
Developmental changes	Early adolescence	Most young adolescents are identity diffused or foreclosed, with the majority being diffused. Confidence in parental support, a self-reflective perspective about the future, and a sense of industry are important early adolescent characteristics that pave the way for the development of more mature identity later in adolescence and early adulthood.
	Late adolescence	It is during the post-high school years that the greatest shifts in identity are thought to occur, as many individuals move closer to identity achievement at this time. Some experts believe that college experiences promote identity exploration.
Sex differences	Vocational and interpersonal identity	Early research has indicated that a theme of vocational achievement is more characteristic of the identity of males, whereas interpersonal interests occupy the identity of females more, but more recent research in the late seventies and eighties suggests little, if any, sex differences.
Sociocultural influences	Culture	Erikson believes that cultural influences are very important in the development of identity. Sociopolitical climate, race, and social class are cultural factors that contribute to identity development. There have been few applications of Erikson's ideas to educational curricula, although some educational strategies reveal increases in identity exploration.
	Family and peer influences	Both family and peers influence identity development. In particular, a family context involving individuation and connectedness seems to enhance identity exploration.
Measuring identity	Problems and prospects	Identity is a very global construct, and like many such broad ideas, is very difficult to measure. The same problems associated with evaluation of self-concept apply to identity assessment as well. Nonetheless, a number of researchers are actively working on better assessments of identity—one such measure expands its measurement to interpersonal dimensions.

When the person resolves the issues at Stage 5, he or she progresses to Stage 6, that of intimacy versus isolation. This stage occurs during the young adult years, which might be defined roughly as ages 21 to 35. It is characterized by the desire to establish a permanent sexual relationship. Marriage and the establishment of a family often characterize this stage of development. It is important to note that in order to share themselves with their mates, people must first know themselves. Unless people have resolved the identity issues in the previous stage, they will have difficulty in the next stage. If people are unable to attain intimacy with another person during this period, they will feel isolated and alone.

Erikson (1968) identified four experiences that facilitate development of identity and intimacy. These experiences were identified in Chapter 4. They are

1. experimentation with different roles and life-styles
2. freedom to choose activities and experience the consequences of those choices
3. involvement in what can be seen as meaningful achievement
4. time for reflection and introspection

College provides the ideal opportunity to have these experiences. It offers students the opportunity to socialize with and model the roles of a variety of different life styles. Separated from parents, and in many ways on their own, students also have the opportunity to experience the consequences of their actions. The grades a person achieves and the successes and failures are owned by the individual. A college education is viewed by society as a meaningful achievement. Acquisition of a degree and working toward a career goal are consistent with a need to be involved in a meaningful experience. Finally, the college environment is ideal for providing time for reflection and introspection. Although many college students are pressed for time, there is no doubt that there is still the opportunity for most to have a large portion of unstructured leisure time available. This time provides the opportunity for reflection and introspection.

Residence halls provide an excellent opportunity for working on all four of these experiences. The interaction of students living together provides regular feedback to the individual, time for reflection and introspection, and late night discussions with other students. It also provides the opportunity to live alone or with a roommate in an environment controlled mostly by the individual. This environment allows a person to choose among a number of activities and to experience the consequences of choices made in this environment.

Chickering's Theory of Psychosocial Development in College Students

Arthur Chickering (1969) studied the psychosocial development of college students. His work drew heavily from that of Eric Erikson and Nevit Sanford, but he contributed an insightful look at the issues that confront college students between the ages of 17 and 24. Chickering based his research on his work at small colleges and the administration of a modified version of the Omnibus Personality Inventory to students from various types of institutions. His research revealed seven vectors of development that students worked on throughout the college years.

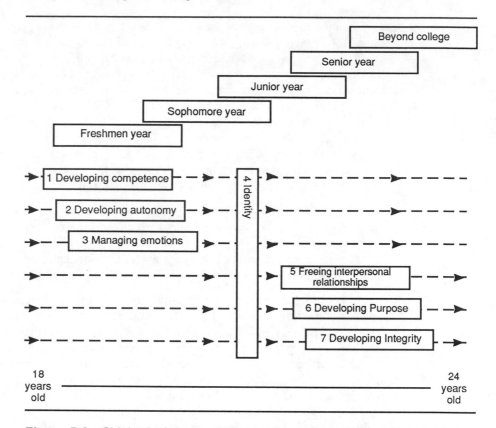

Figure 5.2. Chickering's seven vectors of psychosocial development in college students

A *vector* is a theme or a recurring issue that tends to drive growth and development in the personality. At certain periods in a person's life, societal expectations come into conflict with a person's usual pattern of behavior. The clash between a person's current behavior and new age-related role expectations causes a developmental crisis. This crisis creates an imbalance that the person needs to correct by adjusting his or her behavior and integrating this change into his or her personality. These seven vectors begin in early childhood and extend throughout a person's life. During college these are

- developing competence
- managing emotions
- autonomy
- establishing identity
- freeing interpersonal feelings
- developing purpose
- developing integrity

Developing Competence

When students arrive at a university, they are usually uncertain as to how they will fit into this new environment. It is an environment that they have yet to master and presents for them a number of uncertainties. The first thing that students must do is develop competence in the environment. There are three forms of competence on which students work. First is intellectual competence. Students must come to believe that they are intelligent enough to compete in the university environment. They do this by consulting with their peers, getting feedback from instructors, and measuring this progress by performance on tests. One response often heard from new students is, "It's not as hard as I thought it would be." This response is most likely the result of somebody who had high expectations for great academic demands and found that the students with whom he or she was competing and the instructor's demands were geared for freshman-level academic performance.

While working on intellectual competence, students also explore their physical competence. By this, Chickering is referring to whether students view themselves as though they are as strong as, as attractive as, as physically developed as the other students attending the university. This is an issue of fitting in, determining whether one possesses the same athletic skills, manual dexterity skills, and other normal physical skills which other students possess.

The third competency issue is social—interpersonal competency. Students need to feel that they belong. They need to develop confidence in their relationships with peers, develop strong social networks, develop dating relationships, and similar forms of social interaction that signify peer acceptance. Participation in clubs and organizations, election to residence hall government, and establishing friendship with roommates and others in the living unit give the person feedback about how he or she fits into the peer environment. Through this interaction, the person develops a sense of control or competency.

These three forms of competency—intellectual, physical, and social-interpersonal—have come to form an overall sense of competence or self-confidence. It is one of the first building blocks in the students' overall move toward the establishment of a working identity structure. The process by which these competencies are formed is the process of differentiation followed by a process of integration. First the individual examines how he or she is different from other students. In some cases this will mean that the person performs better than peers, and in other cases it means that the person is not functioning as well as peers. Through the process of trial and error, feedback, and comparison, a person begins to develop a concept of where he or she fits in relationship to others. As a person processes this information in relationship to other dimensions of his or her personality, it is integrated into one's overall self-concept, forming one element in the person's identity.

Managing Emotions

Two processes occur in the evolution of emotional development during the college years. The first is moving from controlling one's own behavior because of external influences to a process of controlling behavior through internal processes. As children we do what is right based upon external controls, generally through authority exercised by the school or parents. In adolescence, peer standards tend to control the same kind of behavior. What is right and what is wrong is often defined by the external source of peer norms. However, as we mature, we come to accept increasing responsibility for our actions. This is a shift in what is called *locus of control,* from external sources being responsible for our actions to an acceptance of ourselves as responsible for our actions.

The second process that occurs is a process of differentiation and integration. It is a four-step process: (1) awareness of one's emotions, (2) acting on emotions, (3) receiving feedback on actions, and (4) exercising internal control of actions. As an example, take a young man learning to control his aggressive behavior. First he becomes aware that he gets angry. He controls his anger principally due to external sources such as the social rules of school or the imposition of authority. At some point he acts on this emotion, perhaps by striking someone. He will receive feedback about this aggressive action. This feedback may come from friends or authorities who will reason with him about the propriety of this kind of conduct for somebody of his age. Peers may encourage or discourage this form of action. As a person grows older, this form of aggressive behavior is strongly discouraged, and punitive action is taken by society for those who are unable to control their actions. Eventually, through a process of reasoning, feedback, and having to confront the consequences of his action, the person internalizes appropriate responses to aggressive feelings.

During college, people come to confront a wide range of emotions, not as children but as adults. Emotions such as love, rejection, grief, anger, and lust are among those which a person must learn to understand and integrate. Most of us have heard the expression "he is not acting like himself." This is because people have a concept or definition of other people, and, when people do not respond as expected they are likely to get feedback about how the behavior has changed. In other words, others define for a person how he or she is perceived and how people have come to expect the person to act. This feedback process helps the individual maintain and establish identity and sets expectations for how one is to control his or her emotions.

The process of managing emotions is actually about increasing awareness of feelings and learning how to understand and trust these feelings. Young adults must come to recognize that they provide information. The only way this can be accomplished is by experiencing these emotions, receiving feedback on them, and integrating this information into the self-concept.

Developing Autonomy

The vector of autonomy is a recurring issue throughout life, as are the other vectors identified by Chickering. As early as the age of two, people constantly differentiate themselves from others and take greater control over their lives. This process consists of three elements. The first is developing emotional independence. When people become emotionally independent, they accept responsibility for themselves and lessen the need for emotional approval from family and peers. People come to realize that they are ultimately responsible for themselves and that although the recognition of friends and family is important, it is less important than what the people themselves individually believe is right. The second element of autonomy is what Chickering describes as "instrumental independence." Being instrumentally independent means that a person has become responsible for himself or herself and that the person has control of his or her environment. This usually involves being financially independent—employed—and having one's own residence. The integration of emotional independence and instrumental independence forms the third element of autonomy, which Chickering describes as "interdependence." This is a realization of independence.

For college students, the process of autonomy is a process of breaking away from parents emotionally and financially. College both helps and hinders this process. It helps the process, because it allows students to move away from home and therefore free themselves from parental control. Residence halls provide an excellent intermediate peer environment in the transition between parental control and total independence.

College also hinders the maturation process, because it is expensive and requires a substantial time commitment. Parents are usually involved in providing some financial support to students for college. This financial support inhibits the development of instrumental independence. As long as students are dependent on parents for the money to survive, the apartment or residence hall in which they live, and the cars they may drive, they cannot be truly independent. It is only after people become financially responsible for themselves that they can become mature to the point of interdependence.

Establishing Identity

Like the other vectors, establishing identity is a process begun in childhood. The college years are part of the period most critical to forming identity. The first three vectors—competence, managing emotion, and autonomy—form the framework for the establishment of an identity. They are necessary but not sufficient conditions for identity development.

The process of maturing and developing competence, understanding their emotions, and becoming autonomous helps people bring definition to their personality. For young adults to discover who they are, they must first separate or differentiate themselves from others. It is only by doing this that they can begin to integrate their successes and failures and develop a self-image or self-concept. Chickering describes identity as confidence in one's ability to maintain inner sameness and continuity. It involves a clarification of one's physical needs, personal characteristics, personal appearance, sexual identity, and the appropriate behavior symbolizing this identity.

Two issues central to establishing identity are developing an appropriate sexual identity and acceptance of one's physical appearance. Some research (LaVoie, 1976; Constantinople, 1969; and Toder and Marcia, 1973) has shown that men and women focus on different elements in formulating their identity. Both prior to and during college, men tend to focus on vocational issues, whereas women tend to focus on enhancing interpersonal relationships, intimacy, and developing a sense of attachment. Men press hard to demonstrate their competence and autonomy, while women have traditionally worked on developing shared dependence and group support (Constantinople, 1969).

Society defines acceptable roles for men and women. One rigid and highly masculine view of manhood is that to be a man one must have a great capacity for drinking alcohol, have frequent sexual interaction with women, be physically strong, show courage, and be a "regular guy." American males face varying versions of this "John Wayne" version of manhood. To some extent, all men compare themselves against this idealized standard. Role models within the academic community as well as outside the academic community help to soften this image and offer an alternative to students in the process of self-discovery. Students may discover a college professor, high school coach, or a favorite uncle who they admire and wish to be like. Through a process of differentiation and comparison, they come to emulate, copy, and generally model behaviors they believe are consistent with their idealized concept of how these role models would act in similar situations.

Neal (1981) identified nine beliefs males have about manhood in society. They are

- Men have greater potential than women.
- Masculinity is a superior endowment in the form of gender identity.
- Power, dominance, competition, and control are essential to proving one's masculinity.
- Vulnerabilities, feelings, and emotions are signs of femininity and should be avoided.
- Interpersonal communication emphasizing emotions, intuition, and physical contact are feminine, whereas rational and logical thought are masculine.
- Sex is a primary means to prove masculinity, whereas affection and sensuality are less valued forms of behavior because they are more feminine.
- Signs of vulnerability and intimacy with other men are to be avoided, because men must not be vulnerable with other men with whom they must compete and intimacy with other men implies homosexuality.

- Career success is a primary measure of a man's masculinity.
- Men are superior to women in career abilities and therefore their function is to be the economic provider of the household, whereas women's primary function is to care for home and children.

Women face similar gender identity issues. They too must find an appropriate role model. Roles for women have changed dramatically in our society. It was not long ago that there were strong social mores that inhibited women from working. During World War II women were called to work in factories as welders and machine tool operators. This was a significant departure from their historic role of homemaker. The transition was acceptable for patriotic reasons. They were needed to substitute for men who were in the military. However, after the end of the War it was clear that they were merely to be substitutes. Women were dismissed summarily at the end of the War only to be replaced by servicemen. The commonly held notion was that men needed the jobs more than women because they had a family to support.

Times have changed. Today there are more women earning bachelor's degrees than there are men. In 1985–1986, 501,900 women earned bachelor's degrees; only 485,923 men earned this degree. However, in Ph.D. programs and in professional degree programs (such as law, medicine, and dentistry), there were almost twice as many men as women earning doctoral and professional degrees. The number of master's degrees awarded for each was about the same (*The Chronicle of Higher Education,* 1988, p. 836).

Women do have many more roles today from which to choose. It is still acceptable for women to choose to be homemakers. It is also acceptable for them to choose to be doctors, lawyers, businesswomen, or hold a variety of other working positions.

Duberman (1975) identified some of the sex role issues that have historically shaped women's identities. These are

- to be passive, unassertive, and obedient.
- to be sociable, well-mannered, neat
- to inhibit verbal and physical aggression.
- to acquire better verbal skills, learn to speak sooner, become more articulate, and have better grammatical skills.
- to focus on developing harmonious interpersonal relationships.
- to be sexually passive.
- to be noncompetitive with males.
- to focus concern on popularity and seeking approval, to take a concerted approach to risk taking, and to confide intimately in others.

Duberman (1975) points out that unlike males, females are not forced to conform to prescribed sex roles throughout their early life. Women have generally greater freedom to experiment with different roles. For example, it is acceptable for a young girl to be a tomboy and receive little negative feedback on this sex role behavior. However, a little boy who demonstrates an inordinate interest in dolls or who appears to be acting like a "sissy" is likely to receive negative feedback from both parents and peers. Even in later life, females are capable of integrating certain historically male traits without being considered abnormal.

Acceptance of one's body and appearance is also an issue that requires integration into one's identity. If one is attractive, people are likely to treat that person in a certain way. Considerable research exists (Widgery and Webster, 1969; Knapp, 1978; Singer, 1964) that demonstrates that physical appearance affects the way we are perceived by others. People that are considered attractive are generally seen as more credible, better public speakers, more successful, more social, and happier. They are more often successful in interviewing for jobs and generally are able to command a higher salary level than similarly experienced competitors. The feedback individuals get about their relative attractiveness helps them develop positive or negative self-images.

A person's body type also contributes to this self-image. Parnell (1958) found that there were social stereotypes attributed to different body images. Overweight people are frequently judged as more gregarious, more sympathetic, more trusting, older, and less strong. Those with a muscular build are generally viewed as more attractive, adventuresome, independent, strong, and mature. People who are tall and thin tend to be viewed as frail, tense, stubborn, and difficult. One's height is also an influencing factor. Men are expected to be tall, and women are expected to be shorter than men. How closely one meets these body image, appearance, and height expectations is processed by the individual and comes to help shape that person's image of himself or herself.

Although objectively people know that being physically attractive does not mean that a person is more intelligent, more capable, more successful, better adjusted or happier than people who are less attractive, people react to stereotypes, not facts. The same is true with people of varying body types. Capability, sincerity, intelligence, and insight, are not reflected in one's weight or height. These physical appearance factors influence first impression. However, as people integrate their personality, the feedback they get from others and the constant press of the advertising media to obtain idealized states of attractiveness may cause an individual to doubt his or her self-worth. In truth, few people meet these idealized standards. What is important is not meeting these expectations, but developing comfort with one's self, and an acceptance of one's body and appearance.

Once a person has established a self-image and formed an identity structure, the person is prepared to move toward expanding and enriching this identity. During the college years and throughout the years of the twenties, a person works on resolving issues connected with the last three of Chickering's vectors: freeing interpersonal relationships, developing purpose, and developing integrity.

Freeing Interpersonal Relationships

As people come to know more about themselves, they feel more secure in relationships. Chickering observes that as people mature the depth and intimacy of their relationships are enhanced. People retain belief in fewer stereotypes, are generally more tolerant of the views of others, and have fewer superficial relationships. Friendships are based on greater trust, and there is more openness and freedom to express one's innermost feelings.

Women generally have had greater freedom to do this throughout their lives and have less difficulty in freeing their interpersonal relationships. The situation is different for men. Men are taught to be competitive with other men. It is difficult for them to share openly in friendships for fear that these expressions of emotion will be viewed as weakness. Men are generally much more selective about those with whom they share their most intimate feelings. Often this level of intimacy is reserved only for a special female companion with whom he feels secure, or perhaps one close male friend with whom he has shared many experiences.

People are not really prepared to participate fully in interpersonal relationships until they know themselves and feel secure in who they are. As this self-confidence and self-knowledge increases, a person becomes less vulnerable and more willing to take emotional risks by sharing parts of themselves with others.

During maturation there is a shift toward greater trust, independence, and individuality. People should become less anxious, more secure, less defensive, and more friendly. They are often more spontaneous and more respectful of other people. General cultural stereotypes are broken down, and there is an increasing tolerance for a range of different people.

As one becomes more trusting of members of the opposite sex, a person often develops a intimate relationship with a significant other. Although these relationships do not always lead to marriage, it is usually a consideration.

Clarifying Purpose

Career and vocational plans do not wait until the latter part of college. Most high school students and first year students in college wrestle with what they want to do with their lives. However, by the junior or senior year, career decision making is pressed by the rapidly approaching graduation date. Another way to express this is that the social demands of the environment create a crisis the student must confront. Wrestling with the crisis of a vocational choice forces the student to assess his or her strengths and to develop the beginnings of a commitment to a particular vocation.

By the time students are ready to graduate, most have chosen an academic discipline in which to major and have a general idea about how they might wish to earn a living. Graduate school, professional schools, and many entry-level positions are really an extension of initial thoughts about how these young adults wish to earn a living. It is an exploration; it is a determination of what fits and what does not.

As people make decisions about vocations, they are also enhancing their self-knowledge about avocational interests, the life style that they would like to live, and the things that they hold to be important—their values. If a person is committed to important social issues, such as the needs of the homeless, this particular value commitment may influence their career choice. If a person wants a high status position, high profile, luxurious life style, he or she may choose another kind of a profession. Some people are able to successfully integrate vocational, avocational, life style, and value commitments into an occupation. A person who is interested in being outside and working with nature, who enjoys backpacking and camping, might for example choose a career in forestry, as a conservationist, or perhaps with the U.S. Park Service. A person who is interested in animals and nature might, for example, choose a position as a veterinarian or as a zoologist.

The goal of this vector—clarifying purpose—in the college years is to integrate the four elements of purpose: vocational commitment, avocational interests, life style, and values, into an initial commitment for adulthood. As with identity and the other vectors, a person's purpose in life and overall career changes and matures as he or she develops. College is devoted to the integration of the initial commitment, and life after college is focused on exploring and confirming these initial commitments.

Developing Integrity

The last of Chickering's seven vectors is the vector of integrity. It consists of humanizing values and personalizing those values. Humanizing values is a process of making those rule-governed beliefs that guide society applicable to the human condition. It is a shift in how we view rule-governed behavior. It reflects a general liberalizing of values from a position where they are considered absolute to a position where they are considered to be relative. People come to learn that certain social rules may not always be consistent with the purpose for which they were designed. As people apply these beliefs and rules to their own lives, they come to accept or commit to those standards most consistent with the people's developing sense of values.

The humanizing of values also involves the internalization of these values. A person no longer considers them to be values to be held by others, but internalizes these values as his or her own. This follows a shift in what is called *locus of control,* a reflection of the increase in responsibility a person takes for his or her own actions, no longer holding others accountable for personal actions.

Personalizing values occurs as values are applied to one's own life circumstance. It is an integration of what a person believes with how a person acts. A person may, for example, believe that stealing is wrong but be arrested for shoplifting in the bookstore. This incongruence may reflect a failure to personalize values and integrate what one believes with how one acts.

Integrity is not something that a person achieves. It is a continuing process of moral growth and development. Although this is a continuing issue of concern throughout college, many of these value issues are not resolved until after the person has left college, begun a job, and developed family commitments. In part, the issue of integrity has to do with one's experience in being confronted with ethical dilemmas in which he or she must choose among different values. The extent to which one's behavior reflects personal values is a complex internal process. Research (Blasi, 1980) suggests that as a person's stage of moral development increases, he or she is more likely to act in a manner consistent with those values. In other words, moral development fosters greater consistency between beliefs and actions.

Cognitive Development

Two aspects of cognitive development are discussed here: intellectual development and moral development.

Cognitive development is concerned with increasingly complex structures or methods of reasoning. The characteristics of cognitive developmental stages are as follows:

- The stages form an invariant sequence. Issues at lower stages must be resolved in order to move to a higher stage of development, and it is not possible to skip from a lower stage of development to a higher stage of development without passing through the intermediate steps.
- The stages are arranged in a hierarchy. The movement is from simple to complex. In the early years, cognitive issues are resolved in a simplistic form. As a person gains experience, he or she may find more complex methods of reasoning and move to a higher stage.
- The sequence of cognitive development is universal. Regardless of culture or social issues, cognitive development follows a pattern or sequence inherent to the human life cycle. This is not to say that there are not some cultures or experiences that provide for more rapid advancement along the dimensions of cognitive development, or that certain educational experiences do not assist a person in advancing and retaining complex structures of reasoning. Social influences can affect the rate and the likelihood of reaching the high levels of cognitive reasoning, but absent these social, cultural issues, the potential to achieve the high stages is the same, regardless of culture.
- Stages are qualitatively different. This mean that there are different issues to resolve and new forms of reasoning to confront at each stage.
- Cognitive developmental stages are concerned with the structure or complexity of reasoning, rather than the content of the judgments made. It is not what answer a person gives to a question, but the reasoning or structure of the judgment used to reach an answer that is the crux of cognitive development. Cognitive development is the process of acquiring increasingly complex reasoning at each stage.

Many of the concepts in cognitive developmental theory come from the work of Jean Piaget (1952). Piaget was a Swiss psychologist who studied childhood intelligence. He worked with Theodore Simons, who helped develop one of the first intelligence tests. Piaget was interested in why young children made errors on intelligence tests. His study of these errors led him to the theory that cognitive development was structured into four major developmental periods. These structural stages were

1. sensor motor, ages 0–2 years
2. pre-operational thought period, ages 2–7 years
3. period of concrete operations, ages 7–12 years
4. period of formal operations, age 12 and up

Cognitive development occurs through *adaptation,* which is a process of change in order to adjust or fit into one's surrounding environment. It is composed of the process of assimilation and accommodation. *Assimilation* is the process by which one acquires and integrates new information into a thought structure. As a person gathers new information and experiences, these events are held not only in one's conscious awareness, but are also used to help shape one's thinking. As this information is accumulated, it is used as experiential information in resolving similar problem-solving situations.

Accommodation is the process of adaptation used when a person's perception and actions are changed to use a more abstract or higher level of reasoning. Assimilation involves taking in and storing information, and accommodation applies this information in more complex forms of reasoning.

Perry's Theory of Cognitive Development in College Students

William Perry was a counselor at Harvard University. In 1954 he began to study the thinking and reasoning process of college students attending Harvard and Radcliffe Universities. He was interested in how the reasoning of students changed as a result of their exposure to the classroom learning situation and the college environment. In assessing the reasoning of students, Perry used the Checklist of Educational Values, the Inventory of Beliefs, and an unstructured interview. The study, begun in 1954 and continuing through approximately 1971, used a variety of students. What Perry found was that the intellectual growth of college students closely followed Piaget's developmental criteria; stages were invariant, hierarchical, and sequentially ordered.

Through his research Perry found three major stages, each composed of three positions. He defined a position as a structure representing a mode or central tendency through which a person perceives the world at a given time. Figure 5.3 outlines Perry's nine positions.

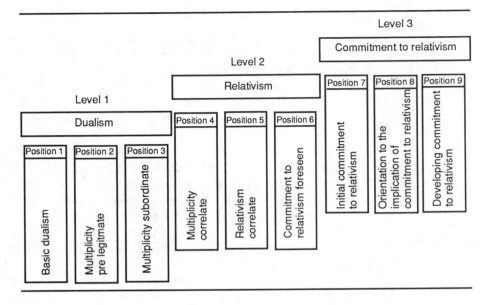

Figure 5.3. Perry's stages of intellectual and ethical development in college students

Dualism

Dualism is the first sequence of positions students encounter in their intellectual growth in college. In this stage, students see information classified as either right or wrong. They have little tolerance for ambiguity and attribute knowledge of "truth" to those in positions of authority. When two authorities disagree, one authority is usually seen as bad authority (Position 2) and later, when two good authorities disagree, a new category of "not yet known" is assigned to those areas where knowledge is uncertain (Position 3).

Although the Perry scheme does not examine behavior directly, certain behavioral patterns can be identified within each level of development. In dualism, Widick and Simpson (1978) characterize students behavior as

- stressful when uncertainty is encountered
- difficulty in resolving interpretative tasks such as essays
- instructors seen as knowing the truth
- disproportionate importance attached to evaluations

At this level, students believe all knowledge is known. Professors supposedly have the right answers. The role of a student is to study and learn from those who hold the truth. As a person develops in this stage of dualism, he or she moves from a period of uncertainty to a period of increasing acceptance that it is legitimate to feel uncertain about some events.

Relativism

Through the process of grappling with issues that have no right or wrong answer, a student reaches the stage where he or she is willing to accept that not all information is known and that it is legitimate to be uncertain. In relativism, the concept of absolute rights and wrongs—held in dualism—are replaced by the legitimacy of uncertainty (Position 4). Students are inclined to believe that people have a right to their own opinions and that no answer is any more valid than anyone else's.

In Position 5, knowledge is seen as certain only within context and relativistic assumptions of knowledge, and values begin to be linked to issues of self-identity. Knowledge and values are contextual and authorities are seen as ways to help a person reach his or her own decision as to what answers are correct. However, there are no absolute criteria for making these decisions.

In Position 6, students see the necessity for orienting themselves to make commitments where there is no certain right answer. They recognize that many questions have multiple answers and that authorities are useful in selecting among the alternatives. The important aspect of this position is that students have come to accept uncertainty and are willing to commit even when they are uncertain.

Widick and Simpson (1978) note that behaviors associated with the stage of relativism includes the following:

- an emphasis on intuition
- development of the capacity to perform complex analytic tasks with some skill
- more internalized learning
- a lessened concern with pleasing instructors

Commitment to Relativism

At the level of a commitment to relativism (Positions 7, 8, and 9) students focus on clarifying their place in the world by exploring careers, marriage, and life style. This level is characterized by self-discovery, commitment, balancing of priorities, and (in Position 9) a search or beginning of a synthesis in issues of ethics and integrity.

In Position 7 students make an initial commitment in some areas such as career, marriage, and life style. In Position 8 they experience implications of these commitments and explore the responsibility associated with these commitments. Finally, in Position 9 adults experience and affirm those commitments consistent with their identity and reassess or change commitments to meet that changing identity.

Perry acknowledges that Positions 7, 8, and 9 may be circular as opposed to linear. People throughout their adult life may reexamine these same issues as they fulfill other dimensions of their life. Thus, Positions 7, 8, and 9 may simply be a cycle created as people experience different issues of commitment throughout their later lives.

In 1981 Perry introduced a stylistic variation that is evident throughout the scheme, but is particularly important in Position 4. Students that appear to approach the stage of relativism by viewing authorities either as role models to be followed or as adversaries to be debated. Moore (1982) describes the different methods of cognitive adaptation as follows, "The adhering student struggles with the transition from being a dependent learner to becoming an independent one; the oppositional student struggles with the temptation to stay in the apparent 'freedom' of the 'do your own thing' perspective" (p. 7). Both groups of students depend on the authority figure, but in different ways—the adhering student for support and as a role model, the oppositional student for a challenge and for contrast.

Perry's scheme differs from many of the other developmental approaches in that it provides alternatives to development through escape, temporizing, and retreat. In retreat, a student confronted by too much challenge and not enough support may retreat to the security of basic dualism where there is certainty. Students who fail to make a commitment in the stage of relativism may "escape" into a relativistic way of viewing the world. They do not need to commit to uncertainty. Finally, some students "temporize" by remaining in a position because they are hesitant or unprepared to advance.

Conditions that tend to facilitate intellectual development include affective involvement, which involves empathizing with others and placing one's self in the role of another. Being confronted with new challenges, having the ability to process the encounter, and getting feedback as to issues of uncertainty assist with development. Other dimensions of personality such as ego style and identity formation may further enhance or retard intellectual development.

Kohlberg's Theory of Moral Development

In 1958 Lawrence Kohlberg completed his dissertation at the University of Chicago on moral development. His dissertation was based on research conducted with grade school boys in the Chicago area. His research blended the work of John Dewey and Jean Piaget into a new way of thinking about how people develop the capacity to make moral judgments. Kohlberg (1969, 1981, 1984) broke from the traditional view of moral development, which held that as people mature they absorb or internalize the cultural values around them. This view, sometimes referred to as *childhood socialization* or the *anthropological perspective,* continues to be supported by many viewing this issue today.

Kohlberg proposes that there are three levels of moral reasoning, each consisting of two substages. The three levels of moral reasoning are preconventional, conventional, and postconventional. Figure 5.4 illustrates the movement from Stage 1 reasoning to Stage 6 reasoning by showing the primary considerations

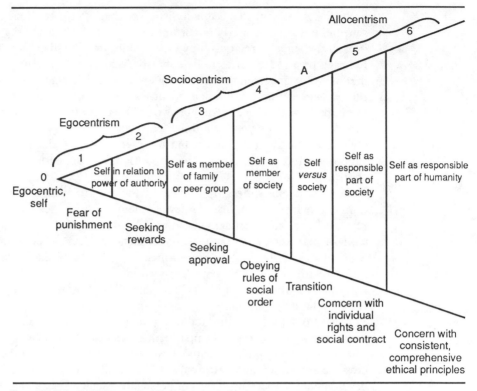

From Widick, Knefelkamp, and Parker (1980). Student Development. In Delworth & Hanson (Eds.) *Student Services: A Handbook for the Profession.* San Francisco: Jossey-Bass. Reprinted by permission.

Figure 5.4. The move from egocentrism to alleocentrism and the expansion of the primary consideration in moral reasoning in Kohlberg's model.

in making a moral judgment at each of Kohlberg's stages. The levels of preconventional, conventional, and postconventional reasoning correspond to egocentrism, sociocentrism, and allocentrism as considerations in moral judgments.

Preconventional Level (Egocentrism)

At the preconventional level, children are attentive to the cultural rules defined by their parents. They tend to interpret what is right by the physical consequences of their actions. Rewards and punishment tend to dictate what is right and what is wrong. Stage 1 is the "punishment and obedience orientation" (fear of punishment). In this stage the child is consumed with avoidance of punishment and defers his or her judgment to a parent or anyone with authority. There is no reasoning about the underlying moral order supporting this decision, only a response to authority and punishment.

In Stage 2, "the instrumental relativistic orientation" (seeking rewards), moral reasoning is based on self-gratification or hedonistic values. A person determines what is the morally correct decision based on issues of reciprocity, equal sharing, and quid pro quo.

Conventional Level (Sociocentrism)

At the conventional level of morality, a person relinquishes moral judgments to the expectations of the social group. Initially this is the family group, followed by the peer group, and finally some type of cultural or social order. Moral decisions conform to the social norm or model expectations in the particular social order regardless of the consequences. There is loyalty to the group, support for it, identification with it, and an internal justification for it. The conventional level of morality comprises stages 3 and 4.

Stage 3 is the "interpersonal concordance or good boy, nice girl orientation" (seeking approval). Morally correct decisions are decisions that please others. There is a concern with the stereotypes of what is good and what is bad or what the majority would do in a particular case. The focus is on being a good or nice person. There is an internalized standard of what a good boy or good girl would do in a particular situation. Such statements as "Nice girls don't" characterize the kind of judgments that would be made at this stage.

At Stage 4, "the law and order orientation" (obeying rules of social order), moral decisions are determined by fixed rules for the purpose of maintaining the social order. The correct decision is one that follows the rules, does one's duty, or upholds the social authority structure. As a member of the society, one has a duty to maintain the laws of the community because the law has been created by a legitimate order and is necessary for maintaining the social order.

Postconventional Level (Allocentrism)

In this level there is a shift to principled thinking and an effort to internalize and personalize values. Morally correct decisions are ones that conform to the individual's concept of justice. These decisions occur apart from consideration of the response to authority or the need to conform one's opinions to that of a group. Stages 5 and 6 compose this level of moral reasoning.

Stage 5 is the "social contract legalistic orientation" (concern with individual rights and social contract). Morally correct actions are actions that uphold individual rights as agreed upon in the society. There is an emphasis on the process by which decisions are made and an emphasis upon democratic decision making. Without this form of decision making, what is right is viewed as a matter of personal opinion or choice. When decisions are not made through the democratic and legal process, social contracts between individuals are the binding force of what is morally correct.

The highest stage of moral reasoning is Stage 6, "the universal ethical principle orientation" (concern with consistent comprehensive ethical principles). Morally correct decisions are ones that conform to one's own conscience, consistent with a valid set of ethical principles that are logically comprehensive, universal, and consistently held. Decisions are made on the basis of principles, not on the basis of rules. These decisions are based on deontic principles of fairness, equality, human rights, and dignity.

Another way to view these three levels of moral reasoning is a move from focusing on egocentric issues in early childhood (Stages 1 and 2) to a focus on the social environment (Stage 3 and Stage 4) to a focus on allocentristic or other directed values (Stage 5 and Stage 6). This shows development as a move from self-interest to interest in others. It is consistent with the developmental concept of moving from simple issues to more complex issues.

Moral Development in the College Years

Moral development in the college years has been described by Gilligan (1981) as a "shift from more ideology to ethical responsibility" (p. 155). The source of the shift is a realization of the relativity of moral values brought about by the wider exposure to ideas and influences in the college environment.

Most college students are in Kohlberg's Stage 3 of moral reasoning, in which what is right is determined by the peer group. If one's peers believe that a certain behavior is correct, for all practical purposes the person holding loyalty to that group will act accordingly. As the person moves away from dependence upon the peer group and comes to rely on his or her own judgment, there is a shift to adherence to moral judgments based on principles of law and order. This is Stage 4 reasoning. Most people in our society are Stage 4 reasoners. A greater exposure to education and the conflicting values in a college community presses many students to advance to consider moral judgments on the basis of ethical principles seen in reasoning at Stages 5 and 6.

The shift between Stage 4 (law and order) and Stage 5 (social contract legalistic orientation) is not a clean transition. This transitional shift is sometimes referred to as the "college transition" or the "Stage 4–Stage 5 shift" (Rodgers, 1980). The transition between Stage 4 and Stage 5 has three substages, as follows:

4 1/4 Moral judgments based upon personal and subjective choice

4 1/2 Moral judgments based on fulfilling hedonistic self-interest without consideration of consequence

5 3/4 Moral judgments based on personal choice which is subjective but which considers the consequences of whether or not the action will hurt someone else.

This transition is really a movement from the recognition of external sources of authority for moral decision making to an acceptance of one's personal authority and responsibility for moral judgments. It is a shift from letting others determine what is right and simply following those dictates, to accepting responsibility for one's own actions and acting in accordance with an internally held, valid set of principles.

One might question whether some of the students who seem to exhibit some of the most outrageous behavior in residence halls are making progress in their moral development. At one point, Kohlberg and Kramer (1969) believed that some students actually regressed after entering college. The research found that some students began making decisions based on hedonistic self-interests without consideration for others. Upon closer examination, Kohlberg (1973) concluded that it was not regression that some students experienced when they entered college, but a transitional period when some students experienced a conflict between the relativity of moral principles in conventional morality and a commitment to ethical principles based on social contracts in a legalistic orientation.

Heath (1978) suggested that freshmen reach a level of stability in high school and see themselves as self sufficient. When students enter college, they discover that to continue their growth they must become more allocentrically open and emotionally dependent on the influences of others. The consequences of this realization is a period of uncertainty as they begin to incorporate principled thinking.

This period of transition, marked by hedonistic behavior, has benefits. It permits students to increase their awareness of the concepts of equality and individual rights, their understanding of the collective functioning of humanity, and their knowledge and concern for the objective criteria used when making moral judgments (Turiel, 1974). It also allows a psychological moratorium that gives students the freedom to integrate conventional moral reasoning and establish a framework for Stage 5 reasoning based on ethical principles (Gilligan, 1981). Because students are still struggling with internalizing the principals to make ethical judgments, they substitute personal and subjective criteria to make these decisions. This makes it appear as if these students lack values or moral judgment. A more accurate description would be that they are in the process of developing principled thinking.

Social Development in the College Years

College influences students in two ways: formally and informally. Formal influences are those specifically designed by the university to inform or change a student in a specific way. A classroom lecture, a counseling session, or an orientation program is a formal method used by the university to influence students. Of equal importance in a college environment are the informal influences. These include informal interactions with faculty, discussions with friends in the residence hall, dating experiences, and the scholarly atmosphere of the institution. This segment of the chapter focuses on the informal influence of the college experience.

The process of influence is known as *socialization*. It is the system by which a person learns the social rules for interacting in the community. These rules of interaction, called *norms*, define acceptable behavior within the group and set standards for an individual who is seeking membership with that group. As a person comes to understand the social behavior associated with membership in a group, a person comes to accept these group standards so that he or she can gain group acceptance. The more the individual is integrated into the group, the more the person will conform to the normative standards of the group (Weidman, 1989).

The single most important developmental influence upon values, career aspirations, and overall adjustments is the student's peer group. It sets the standards for interaction, acceptable behavior, and approval. It also acts as a mirror to reflect the images that the student will create of himself or herself. Coelho et al. (1968) acknowledge that residence halls are one of the most important places for these peer groups to operate. Their research shows that friendships in college were most likely to form on the basis of physical proximity. These friendships formed in the residence halls help students meet new socioacademic demands, learn their way around campus, help combat feelings of loneliness, provide a tension relief as students talk about common concerns, and through informal discussions in the residence halls, provide orientation to classes, teachers, and types of courses to be taken (p. 338).

Part of the interaction in a residence hall is controlled by the physical environment. If the living unit is constructed in such a way as to form small isolated groups in the unit, chances are the smaller groups will form the initial peer groups for individuals. "The interior design and architectural arrangements concerning placement of living units and the nature of their location in relation to one another influences the choice of friends, the groups joined, and the diversity of persons with whom significant encounters can occur" (Chickering, 1974, p. 80). There is no question that one effect of residence halls is creating chances for students to have contact with one another. The day-to-day living situation of eating together, using the same washroom facilities, and other casual contacts gives students a chance to become acquainted and to influence one another's attitudes and beliefs.

Researchers (Priest and Sawyer, 1967; Case, 1981; Rubin and Shenker, 1978) all found that students who lived close to one another are more likely to form and maintain friendships than students who live further apart. These friendships are likely to be formed in college and to be maintained throughout college and beyond. Not all college students participate in a special clique; however, all are influenced to a greater or lesser degree by the general peer environment. Some students simply prefer to be loners. But most students identify with other students. Part of the reason for this may be that they believe that other students share their same personal values, interests, background, and experience (Sorenson, 1973). Friends and peer groups "give each other emotional support and also serve as important points of reference for young people to compare their beliefs, values, attitudes, and abilities. (Zastrow and Kirst-Ashman, 1987, p. 247).

There are a variety of different peer socializing agents within the undergraduate experience. The two that seem to exert the most influence are reference groups and primary peer groups. A *reference group* is a group with which the person wishes to be associated. In a college community this might be a fraternity or a sorority, a varsity athletic team, student government, or some other recognition group on the campus. The *primary peer group* may be the same as the reference group; however, it may be different. The primary peer group is composed of those people with whom the individual most closely associates. This might include an individual's roommate, persons in close proximity to this person's residence hall room, or students counted among the student's closest friends. Both the primary peer group and the reference group exert an influence on students.

Most students do not identify directly with the larger culture of the university. It is through intermediate social environments that students gain a sense of identification with the larger normative environment of the university. A student's reference group or primary peer group becomes the intermediate social environment through which he or she identifies with this larger university environment. This is why peer groups are so important during the college years. They are the bridge between the family as a controlling agent and the larger adult community.

A person's peer group tends to be most important in influencing beliefs, opinions, and dress. They are most likely to set normative standards for one's appearance, resolving school-centered dilemmas, and in seeking advice on dating relationships. They also help shape opinions about a variety of issues, including political candidates, academic courses, and popular school activities. However, family background and parental opinions carry more weight in making complicated moral judgments that have long-range implications. Marriage, career selection, family commitments, and sense of honor and duty tend to be values that a student keeps throughout his or her college career.

Residence halls provide a natural place for primary peer groups to form. Feldman and Newcomb (1969) were one of the first researchers to examine the influence of peer groups in residence halls. They described the peer group as the most important agent for change operating within residence halls. They summarized the ways in which peer groups influence students as follows:

- As part of the intermediate stage between the family and the larger postcollege world, the college peer group may help the individual student through the crisis of achieving independence from home.
- Under certain conditions . . . the peer group can support and facilitate the academic-intellectual goals of the college.
- The peer group offers general emotional support to the student; it fulfills needs not met by the curriculum, the classroom, or the faculty.
- The college peer group can provide for the student an occasion for and practice in getting along with people whose background, interests, and orientations are different from his own.

- Through value reinforcement, the peer group can provide support for not changing. Yet, it can also challenge old values, provide intellectual stimulation and act as a sounding board for new points of view, present new information and new experiences to the students, help clarify new self-definitions, suggest new career possibilities and provide emotional support for students who are changing.
- The peer group can offer an alternative source of gratification and a positive self-image, along with rewarding a variety of nonacademic interests for students who are disappointed or not completely successful academically. Friends and social ties may also serve to discourage voluntary withdrawal from college for other than academic reasons.
- College peer group relations can be significant to students in their postcollege careers—not only because they provide general social training but also because of the development of personal ties that may reappear later in the career of the former student (pp. 236–237).

Residence halls influence students by virtue of intensifying or defining the perimeters of the peer environment. Differences that exist between students living in different types of undergraduate residence halls are in part a function of the background characteristics of the student that are intensified as peer groups form within the structure defined by the hall's other residents.

Perhaps the most dynamic aspect of the residence hall environment is the potential it holds as a means of organizing the critically important peer environment. The power of this peer environment, as Feldman and Newcomb (1969) have shown, is to influence students, by helping to shape beliefs, career direction, and life style among other dimensions of personal growth and development. Newcomb (1966) observed that of the three major influences determining a student's success in college—family background, the peer group, and tutelage—only the student's family background was more important to the student's success than was the student's peer group. Once a student reached college, Newcomb found that the peer group was the major determinate of success or failure. It was more important than the information the student learned in the classroom. And, as Feldman and Newcomb (1969) discovered, the residence hall was an important component in determining how this peer group was formed and who composed it.

When one considers the potential that residence groups have for structuring associations by the mere assignment of students to live in close proximity to one another, and thus determining at least one level of the peer environment, the importance of residence halls to the overall influence of college on students takes on increased meaning.

Friendships are formed on a number of bases. Priest and Sawyer (1967) and Rubin and Shenker (1978) found that (1) proximity, (2) similarity of values, (3) reciprocity-mutual trust, (4) compatibility, (5) duration of acquaintanceship, and (6) admiration of the friend's good qualities were factors that significantly influenced the selection and maintenance of friendships. The frequency of shared interactions and of common experiences helps to maintain these friendships. Such interchange provides an opportunity to share relationships and to develop linkages of trust. These commonly shared experiences reaffirmed for students how they were similar and helped students develop a bond of mutual support and confidence. With greater confidence came greater trust and self-disclosure. Friendships of this quality last throughout college and beyond.

Chapter 6
Common Adjustment Problems in College

The Progression of a Student's Development in College

The theories of development reviewed in the previous chapter reveal a pattern of growth during the college years and beyond. In this chapter, developmental stages evident in each of the undergraduate years are examined in relation to adjustment problems students experience in college and the residence hall environment. As the overall scheme for this chronological development unfolds, it is important to remember that individual students vary in the pace of development.

The important fact to note from developmental theories is that the development of an individual involves a complex system of interrelationships and experiences based on physiological maturation, environment, and personality factors. Development is a continuous process and has no absolute starting and finishing points. It is a loose-knit, fluid interchange of events, circumstances, and developmental cycles. None of these developmental stages takes place in a void. No two people move through them at the same pace or with the same experiences. As an RA, it is important that you understand the types of development that are taking place.

Coons (1974) points out that the particular developmental task most in evidence at a given time defines much of the student's relationship to the institution. If you can identify which developmental task is most in evidence at a particular time, you should be able to anticipate the adjustment difficulties a student will be experiencing in the residence hall at that time. Your ability to recognize developmental issues and to understand the experience of students will help you respond appropriately to students experiencing problems.

Freshman Year

Attending a college or university for the first time is a threatening and frightening experience for many students. The familiar environments of home and high school are gone. In place of these is a new and formidable experience. Professors with doctoral degrees, maps to navigate around the campus, a library with hundreds of thousands of volumes, and thousands of new fellow students confront the entering freshman, who is thrust into this environment and expected to survive. This experience challenges the individual's personal security, need for acceptance, and need for physical comfort. Not only are the new students uncertain of this unfamiliar environment, but they are filled with doubt about whether they will be able to succeed in meeting the expectations of their parents, teachers, and friends, as well as the expectations they have for themselves.

Many students, upon entering the residence hall environment for the first time, project the attitude that they know everything there is to know about that environment. It is not easy to admit to other people that one is simply not knowledgeable about a new situation such as the residence hall, and freshman students often become a little frightened about the new experience. For men this seems to be especially true. Men, as defined by our culture, are supposed to be self-reliant, exhibit independence, and confront new tasks with little difficulty. It is often difficult for the freshman male to admit that he really does not understand all there is to know about what is happening. To ask simple questions such as "Where is the dining hall?" or "What do I do if I get locked out of my room?" is an admission that he is not in control of his environment. When one's ego is fragile and one's self-image is closely tied to the perceptions of other students, a person may be reluctant to ask simple and basic questions.

This new environment presents a major adjustment for students. Freshman year is often the first time they have been on their own away from their friends and families. They want to be accepted by their peers and want to make college a successful experience.

In these early days of meeting other people, students tell other people who they are through their past experiences and through what their parents do. Students use these reference points because their identity has been tied to these signposts for so long. Students who are dissatisfied with their background, dissatisfied with themselves, or feel a need to enhance their images will embellish their backgrounds and experiences when they describe them to other people. They may claim that their parents are much wealthier than they really are, that they were tremendous athletes in high school, or that they were heavily involved in some recognition group for intellectual achievement. By communicating this to other people, the student hopes to establish a more favorable impression and to gain the acceptance and approval of others.

Almost all students go through an adjustment phase when they enter the residence hall environment. Most are secure enough to adapt and establish an open and honest relationship with their peers. Some will rely on various forms of embellishment to bolster their identity and enhance their security. Sautter (1974) explains the trauma of the new freshman in making a transition to college this way:

> The transition to college is a real trauma for many freshmen. . . . The 17 or 18-year-old freshman probably does not have a very realistic idea about college. . . . The resident is probably self-conscious and a little confused, even somewhat home sick. . . . He or she does not understand the tremendous organization of the university or how to use the facilities available to him/her. The resident may have no friends. He/she does not know how to relate to upperclassmen, what activities to try to enter, or the meaning of the residence hall organization (pp. 5–6).

Transition to College

In this transition into college, students go through what Rossi (1964) has identified as an adaptation phase of somewhere between four to eight weeks. In this period, the student makes some major transitional adjustments to set a pattern for future interaction, values, and success in this environment. As Rossi concludes from his study:

Massive socialization effects occurred during the initial few weeks of entry into the institution in question, that effects were greatest among those individuals who were most oriented toward their peers, and that changes beyond the early weeks were relatively slight, as long as the individual remained in the institution in question. Indeed, the major shift in value emphasis occurred during the period between September and November, indicating that socialization to the normative system of the school occurred in a short period of time and involved changes of considerable magnitude. Changes of similar magnitude did not occur among upperclassmen, sophomore, junior, and senior classes being essentially alike in their value orientations (pp. 3–4).

Thus, most socialization takes place within the first few weeks (approximately six weeks) of entry into the institution. Students appear to come to college with a set of expectations that they were willing to change to conform to the prevailing group behavioral norms. The socialization process appears to be faster for female students than for male students and may at first influence academic performance by shifting grades downward.

Meeting the expectations of the peer group is an important developmental factor for the new freshman. In these first few weeks of adaptation to the new residence hall environment, freshmen learn to conform to the normative modes of interaction in the living unit and to emulate roles set by their peers. These patterns of interaction or models of how to cope with this new environment are set by upperclass students in the residence halls. The research of Coelho et al. (1968) explains the experience of the freshmen in college in this way:

Most students dealt with the perplexities of the new system by actively seeking information and taking cues from upperclassmen. . . . In effect, upperclassmen helped in learning new academic skills or improving standards of performance to meet institutional demands and personal level of aspiration. . . . Upperclassmen in the residence hall may also expose the adolescent to new aspects of himself by suggesting alternative acceptable uses of time and energy. . . . By actively using upperclassmen, the adolescent is free to experiment with role images of the developing freshman (p. 336).

Thus, the new student learns from the more experienced student how to act, what to say, and what to do. Freshmen conform to the group standard by emulating the behavior of the older and more experienced students. As these standards of behavior are set during the first few weeks, they come to form the expected role behavior within this new environment.

Another way of viewing this adaptation process of conformity or patterning is to view it as "habits." People are creatures of habit and soon develop a routine of studying, eating, sleeping, and socializing at predictable times each day. Much of a successful cafeteria operation is dependent upon this routine or habit. Probably the cafeteria manager at your institution can tell you with precision when the meal hour will be the busiest, approximately what percentage of the total number of students eating in that cafeteria will eat a particular meal, and even the approximate number of servings of each entree that will be requested for a given menu combination.

Students who develop the habit of studying between certain hours every evening and in a particular location every evening will tend to continue this pattern of behavior throughout the year. Likewise, people who exercise at a particular time during the day will tend to continue this pattern of behavior as long as their schedule permits. Once the pattern is established, it becomes difficult to break.

This has some interesting implications for what you as a resident assistant can do during the first few weeks after the new student enters the residence hall. If the environment the student enters is one in which studying is respected and offers a supportive community of openness and trust, it is likely that this will begin to form a pattern that will serve you and your residents throughout the academic year. Programs and other activities that help integrate the floor during these first few developmental patterning weeks would be very useful. Likewise, if noisy, disruptive, and otherwise prohibited types of behavior are allowed to go unchallenged during these first few weeks, it is probable that this will establish a pattern of expected behavior and create an entirely different type of living environment.

Residence hall living is likely to form important peer groups that significantly influence the development of students during their college years. Coelho et al. (1968) confirm the importance of the residence hall environment through their research with college freshmen. They explain this influence as follows:

> Friendships in the early period were formed usually on the basis of physical proximity. They were useful, especially to freshmen going to large universities, in preparing him to meet various new socio-academic demands and to learn his or her way around the campus maze. They help to combat initial feelings of loneliness, to provide tension relief as students talk about their concerns together, and to give orientation to classes, teachers, types of courses, through the impromptu bull sessions that arose in the dormitory unit (p. 338).

Part of the interaction in the living unit is controlled by the physical environment. If the living unit is constructed in such a way as to form small isolated groups in the unit, chances are that smaller groups will form the initial peer groups for individuals. Chickering (1974) explains that: "(1) . . . Friendships and memberships in various groups or subcultures influence development, and (2) . . . interior design in architectural arrangements concerning placement of living units and the nature of their location in relation to one another, influence the choice of friends, the groups joined, and the diversity of persons with whom significant encounters can occur" (p. 80).

Precollege acquaintanceships, similarity of attitudes, common interests, size of the group, the homogeneity of the group membership, and the relative isolation of the group all contribute both to the formation of the peer group and to the degree of influence it has on its members. The peer group is a significant influence in the lives of freshmen making the transition into college and helps set a pattern of behavior within the first few weeks that greatly influences their direction during the first year in college.

Tolerance

The new freshman is described by Coons (1974) as an authoritarian personality. Freshmen tend to view situations as either right or wrong. Students who have not learned to share, to compromise, and to accept other people's views will experience interpersonal conflicts. The residence hall is one of the best places for a student to learn to be tolerant. Learning to live with others in such close proximity, to accept the necessary inconveniences of noise, to adhere to regulated eating hours, and to cope with other people's annoying habits all contribute to helping the individual become more tolerant.

Tolerance is a necessary step toward maturation. Unless a person can learn to compromise, accept other people's views, and express his or her satisfaction or dissatisfaction with the behavior of other people, he or she will have difficulty moving to a level of maturity and personal identity.

Independence

As students adapt to their new environment through conformity with peer expectations, they begin to break with parents and enter a world defined by their peers. The establishment of independence from family is a necessary step in discovering one's identity. To be independent, one must establish an identity apart from parents and high school relations.

Coons (1974) explains that a typical freshman problem is a student who has become "bogged down in his attempt to resolve the child parent relationship. He will frequently complain bitterly of his overprotective, excessively involved parents who insist that he call home twice weekly and inform them of his every move" (p. 6). Although the individual undoubtedly has been testing his autonomy for some time, entry into college is often the catalyst necessary to sever the relationship with the parents and begin a new identity separate from theirs.

Powell et al. (1969) explain the cycles of this transition with parents as follows:

> Almost inescapable during the transition from high school to college is a change in perception of one's parents. It begins, generally, when parents are seen as having attributes such as usually being right, being somewhat different from other adults, and having some peculiar power and influence over one's behavior. Then uncertainties about the parents and their ideas arise—some ambiguity about how controlling or permissive they are going to be during the first year of college, some questions about dependence and independence relating to them. Parents are generally seen more and more realistically, feelings about them which were previously suppressed find expression, and the relationship changes from that of child to parent to that of adult-to-adult. The parents are perceived more objectively and compared with parents of close friends. The student's attitude toward them moves in the direction of understanding and acceptance in spite of their failures, weaknesses, and biases, which are now more evident than before (p. 102).

Freshman women often have more difficulty establishing autonomy than do men. Men are culturally expected to be more independent than are women, and they are usually given more freedom and more independence in making decisions at an earlier age. Females, on the other hand, more often are protected and sheltered by their parents, though this is changing as the role of women in our culture changes.

Independence carries with it new-found freedom. No longer does the student need to report his or her whereabouts to parents. No longer does anyone challenge or monitor the student's behavior. Freedom, independence, and self-determination are all dropped on the student in a relatively short period of time.

Students react to this new freedom by testing the boundaries of their freedom through trial and experimentation. Signs of this new freedom are observable. You will see it through declarations that they wish to have an apartment off campus, a car on-campus, and other visible signs that confirm their independence. An apartment, free from almost all control, seems to be the ultimate sign of independence. When they have their own apartments, students seem to make a declaration of true autonomy and independence.

Value Exploration

Students enter college with values most similar to those of their parents. Seeking a sense of belonging in their peer group, they explore the value systems of their peers and experiment with different beliefs and attitudes. College offers an opportunity to try different attitudes, beliefs, and values. This is the time of life in which to experiment with norms, to find those that fit and modify those that do not. This is a time when students reach out to discover what they believe.

In general, parental influences still prevail in the first year or so and tend to dictate the student's values in the more important areas of moral beliefs, social beliefs, and general behavioral standards. Peer influences tend to have a liberalizing influence on these values, but they have their greatest effect in more superficial areas, such as dress, dating, and politics. As Newcomb (1960) pointed out, the major influence on a student's success in college is the background the student brings to college. The peer influence and the tutelage that the student receives in college, although playing important roles, are secondary to the 18 or 19 years of moral and intellectual shaping that took place prior to college.

Most students have had experience making decisions for themselves that involve an assessment of their beliefs and values. These experiences force students to make decisions about why they believe the things they do. Some students have not had many of these experiences, and when they are placed in a new environment, apart from the security of their parents and home life, they often experience value conflicts. If the student is unable to understand the difference between what he or she was taught and the values being expressed by peers, the student can undergo a collapse of his or her value system. Coons (1974) explains it as follows:

> A student who has had no practice in listening, weighing, and discriminating may be overwhelmed. There is also the tendency to rebel against the authoritarian parents, and the possibility that the whole house of cards may come tumbling down about his ears is a very real one. The total collapse of the value system is a catastrophe of major proportions. The student may cease to function both academically and interpersonally within as short a time as forty-eight hours. The anxiety is intense, and he complains vigorously of a total loss of meaning and purpose and feeling "like an empty shell of a human being." "There is no purpose to getting up in the morning, going to bed at night, attending classes, or, in fact, doing anything" (p. 11).

One of two things could result from a collapse of the value system. First, the student may need to undergo psychotherapy and be removed from the environment until he or she has developed sufficient coping mechanisms to deal with the conflicts in values. The second alternative is for the student to seek a new value system and adopt it. Such students are drawn to some of the fundamentalist religious groups, special religious or cult groups, and charismatic groups in which they no longer need to make value decisions for themselves. The group prescribes what is correct and why it is correct, and it provides emotional support and a sense of belonging that reassures and reinforces the values offered by the group. Life becomes simpler, and the student is again able to function.

Social-Sexual Development

The social-sexual development of the student is the process by which the student comes to realize what it means to be a man or a woman. This is really a process by which the individual comes to establish an ego identity.

Our culture has one basic stereotype for masculinity. Men are supposed to be physically strong, sexually virile, daring, independent, and have the capacity to drink great quantities of alcohol. These attributes are looked to by young males seeking their own identities as men. Much of the freshman year is spent grappling with this issue of masculinity in an attempt to discover a suitable role model for the individual. Professors, a father, an uncle, and often older students serve as role models. The young man may find that he is more like the rather intellectual professor in his sociology class than the football coach. He may find this intellectual model more suitable for his particular blend of personal identity.

This process is gradual. Upon entering college, one does not start looking for role models. The process of developing a sexual identity has started much earlier than college; however, interaction within the peer group and the new independence in the relationship with parents pushes the individual into confronting these changes in life. At times like these, a person looks to others he or she would like to resemble and begins to model the behavior accordingly.

Among the demands placed on men in this stage of development is the rather inflexible cultural view of male sexuality. To be a man, our society defines that one must be heterosexual—not simply sexual but, specifically, heterosexual. Many young men experience a crisis because of demands placed on them to demonstrate their masculinity by having sexual relations with women. Take, as an example, a new freshmen who enters the college population for the first time in either the residence hall or in a fraternity house. He enters a situation where men are openly discussing their sexual experiences—both real and imagined—in great detail. A young man who has not achieved this level of sexual intimacy may begin to view himself in some way sexually inadequate. If he has not had these sexual experiences, as allegedly all of the other young men have, then there must be something wrong with him. Our society leaves him only one option—he must be homosexual. If a young man is more in touch with his feelings, more sensitive, and more easily given to signs of emotions, this sensitivity may lend to confirming for the student, and perhaps for others, the question of his homosexuality.

Frederick Coons (1974) writes about this dilemma of sexuality in describing the young college freshman or sophomore as follows:

> Our society plays a very dirty trick on its males by telling them that they must either be heterosexual or homosexual and they must make this choice at about age 16 or 17. The other assumption is that if one is not heterosexual, one must be homosexual whether [or not] there is any conscious awareness of sexual attraction toward the same sex. . . . The homosexual panic of the college freshman or sophomore usually arises in such a predicament. . . . On listening to a student, one hears nothing about overt homosexual behavior, or indeed, the predominance of homosexual fantasies. . . . He may confess some mutual sexual exploration with friends during adolescence, but no behavior identifying any homosexual adaptation. One is then in a position to point out his apparent heterosexual retardation and ponder with him whether he has not confused heterosexual retardation with homosexuality (p. 9).

Coons goes on to point out, "much of the college male's concern about homosexual feeling and behavior is a result of his confusion of intimacy and tenderness with genital sexuality. It seems that the American male is taught from birth that every time he begins to feel a warm glow and a desire for physical closeness with another person of either sex, he must have an orgasm if he is going to be a 'real man' " (p. 16).

Many young men in this period of discovering their sexuality may experience some homosexual contact. Kinsey (1953) and other studies have pointed out that homosexual experimentation and homosexual relationships are not unique and vary with both intensity and longevity. The problem is in making a number of unwarranted conclusions upon a solitary or infrequent experimentation with homosexuality and a person's sexual preferences. Chickering (1972) explains this danger as follows, "The danger is premature assumption that a homosexual affair signifies lasting homosexuality. Particularly where relationships with the opposite sex are difficult and anxiety provoking, such an experience and such an assumption may reduce still further the frequency of heterosexual contact and the possibilities for finding satisfaction in such relationships. Thus the unwarranted assumption sets in motion events which eventually make it valid" (pp. 84–85).

Female students experience virtually all forms of sexual behavior less frequently than do male students (Mussen, Conger, and Kagan, 1969). American society allows them greater latitude in defining their sexuality and in showing their sensitivity and emotions. Women have several roles that are legitimate options from which they may choose. A woman may choose a domestic career and find this a satisfying identity relative to society's expectations. At the other extreme, a woman may feel more comfortable taking on a somewhat more businesslike orientation and find that this sex-role is viable within the confines of the image identified with the more liberated woman. Mussen, Conger, and Kagan (1969) explain the sex-role stereotype option and resulting ego identification for women as follows, "There are more ways, even in adolescence, in which a girl can successfully establish a feminine ego identity than in the case with boys, although, not necessarily with less difficulty. For one thing, . . . the girl is permitted considerably more freedom as a child to engage in cross sex behaviors. There is also increasing evidence that the traditional feminine role is in a state of transition. This means that the girl may be exposed to conflicting social rewards and punishment" (pp. 692–693).

Women are given greater freedom in expressing emotions, sensitivity, and compassion toward one another. It is not surprising to see two female roommates cry with emotion and become very sentimental at the end of the school year. The same emotional behavior expressed by two male roommates would be viewed as unusual.

The basic needs to be comforted, held, and to express one's emotions are reserved in the male and relegated to heterosexual contacts. Dating behavior serves as the initiation for this establishment of satisfying heterosexual contacts. Initially, much of the dating relationship centers on having an appropriate personality interaction, being a "good date." Good conversation, the way one dresses, a nice personality, and other more superficial signs in the dating relationship are important in the initial stages. The dating relationship has a positive effect upon the individual's human-relations development. Specifically, it teaches such things as good interpersonal skills with members of the opposite sex; it develops social courtesies and skills; it aids in discovering more about one's own identity; it provides occasional sexual experience; and it fosters a level of intimacy that would not otherwise be available (Mussen et al., 1969).

Dating relationships, which begin in high school and seem to blossom in the first years of college, become a major influence in the person's development, self-image, and esteem. Dating relationships can be anxiety-producing situations for both men and women. Questions of physical attractiveness, personality, status, and other issues related to one's identity and image are drawn into question. Not having a date for the weekend can be a traumatic experience for both the man and the woman. Developing the self-confidence to request a date, with the possibility of being rejected, is sometimes difficult for the young man still developing his identity and self-image. Of equal difficulty for the woman is waiting to be asked for a date or not having socially acceptable means to make contact with a young man whom she would like to know better. At present, some of these stereotypic roles seem to be breaking down, permitting both sexes greater latitude.

Intellectual Development

Perry (1970) described the intellectual development of the college student as a move from basic dualism to a level where the student is able to accept a plurality of different views, interpretations, and value systems. In the initial transitional stage in college, the freshman and sophomore years, the student moves from this system of viewing things as either right or wrong to a stage in which he or she is able to accept a modified, dualistic view of the world.

The student comes to recognize that there is a plurality of answers and points of view and that people have a right to their own opinions. However, the plurality is perceived as an aggregate of discretes not having an internal structure of external relation, with the implication being that no judgments among opinions can be made.

Freshmen often develop an authoritarian and rigid view of the world. For them absolutes do exist. There are right and wrong answers. Freshmen are predisposed to accept "truth" from instructors based upon the instructor's authority.

Freshmen develop both academic skills and personal skills in this first year. Coelho et al. (1968) describe some of these skills as follows:

Academic Skills:

(a) to look ahead and see clearly what was expected of them so that they could organize a block of time;

(b) to distinguish between primary and secondary demands on their time, subordinating minor interests to major academic goals;

(c) to study for long stretches of time without feeling bored, imposed upon, or resentful, or to recover quickly from periods of negative effect, particularly through brief rewarding contacts with peers;

(d) to concentrate under difficult conditions or to rectify external conditions to improve their concentration efforts;

(e) to diagnose the interest and attitude of their professors;

(f) to formulate intermediate goals that were attainable within a sequence of long-range work responsibilities;

(g) to learn new academic skills and intellectual competencies required by the higher educational process.

Personal Skills:

(a) developing close and meaningful relationships, as well as productive work relations with one's peers;

(b) dealing with physical separation from one's family and regulating one's need for autonomy and relatedness to parents;

(c) extending one's heterosexual interests and feelings in preparation for courtship and marital decision (p. 331).

All students did not show all of these skills in the study, but each skill was evident in some student. The transition from high school to college places many demands on the new freshman. It requires him or her to balance the expectations of peers, college faculty, self, and parents.

Common Adjustment Problems in the Freshmen Year

The transition to college makes many adjustment demands on students. Each of the following discussions focuses on a common problem that freshmen experience and offers some suggestions on how you can help with their problems.

Self-Esteem Needs

Self-esteem is generally described as the gap between one's self-image and one's self-expectations. When one moves into a new environment, one's image and expectations often change. It is important in the transition to college that the person retain a strong ego-identity and a strong sense of self-worth. One's confidence can be easily undermined in a new environment in which basic security and self-esteem needs can be challenged by peers and the threats prevalent in the new environment. Students need to feel the comfort and support of other people to reaffirm their self-worth and positive self-image. You, as an RA, can be of assistance by adding support and encouragement to students. Opening up yourself as a friend and a supportive agent could be a critical step to students in helping them maintain a positive self-image and increase their self-concept.

Roommate Reaction

On the day freshmen arrive, students who have not specified a particular roommate get to meet the person(s) assigned to them as roommates. This can be a tense situation, particularly if the new roommate is of a different ethnic or racial background. Having parents present during this first encounter generally complicates any problem between the roommates. Students frequently are able to resolve conflicts within the first two weeks. Roommates often recognize that they share many of the same interests and many of the same apprehensions. They often become friends. This, however, is not always the case. Some roommate matches are just not as agreeable as others. Sometimes the life-style differences are too divergent, and the two students cannot reach an equitable compromise. In these cases, a roommate change is needed.

As an RA, you can best assist in resolving these situations by assuring all parties involved that the university will seek to reach a workable solution for everyone at a reasonable time after the move-in rush is completed. Undoubtedly, your institution has implemented a policy regarding these conflicts. You can be of great assistance by knowing the policies and following the procedures that the university has outlined. Most importantly, you need to know the rationale behind the policy. Parents and students will question you. Although it is likely that they will seek higher authorities to challenge any decision or interpretation you may make, you can lend credibility to yourself and to your superiors if students or parents approach higher authorities.

You can help the roommates become friends by involving them in common experiences (eating together, intermurals). Once the parents are gone, attempt to discuss the situation openly with the students. In the subsequent days, attempt to involve the students jointly in common experiences that can help them get to know one another. Athletic events, discussion groups, dining together, and other mutual experiences may reinforce their common interests and encourage the relationship.

If it is obvious that the two students are unable to resolve their conflicts, it serves no purpose to have them reside together. It is disruptive to them as individuals, to their development, growth, and possibly to the living unit as a whole.

Conflicts

Conflicts can arise naturally in any group situation, but they seem to be accentuated when groups of students are asked to live together in close proximity. The conflicts that arise between roommates are usually minor and usually show a difference in interpersonal communication style, life style, or personality types. Roommate conflicts and interpersonal conflicts with other students in the living unit are common for freshmen. The resident hall often is the first experience the students have had with small-group living. Often the lack of privacy and the irresponsible acts of a few individuals come into conflict with the need for privacy and the need to retreat from the stress and congestion of college. Group intensity infringes on territorial needs and the drive to maximize control over one's environment. As students develop greater tolerance and greater interpersonal skills, conflicts will be more quickly resolved among the students in the living unit. Patterns of acceptable behavior emerge naturally from the group as group norms become established in the living unit.

Academic Adjustment

Adjusting to the new academic environment with its demands for studying, more intense academic competition, and enhanced critical thinking skills is both frightening and anxiety-producing for students. The anxiety and apprehension surrounding the freshmen's first college examination can evoke stress, frustration, fear, and questions of self-worth. Such behavior as excessive drinking and disruptive actions are common. Other stress reactions, such as depression, panic, and avoidance, are also common.

Reaction to Freedom

The search for autonomy and independence can create a reaction to this new-found freedom. Students who have not had much freedom from parents may not have sufficient experience in disciplining their own behavior. As a result, such students abuse this freedom. Frequently, such behavior is disruptive to the living unit and/or personally destructive. As the RA, you can assist by being observant and by being available to students. If a student evidences negative social behavior, other members of the living unit will usually discourage it or at least bring it to your attention.

Evidence of students experiencing problems with this new-found freedom includes a decline in the students grades, poor time management, procrastination, and excessive socializing. These behaviors can be used as a basis for initiating counseling intervention to explore with students their current behavior and lack of self-discipline relative to their academic goals.

Problems with Parents

One of the most common problems for freshmen is the break in the child-parent relationship. This "break" is the result of the increasing autonomy of the student. It is a necessary part of growing up and self-discovery. To discover who he or she is, it is necessary for the person to separate from parents. This can be difficult for college students, because many rely on their parents for financial support. The lack of financial independence subjects students to some degree of control by their parents. As students mature and learn to handle greater degrees of freedom, they learn to respond on a more adult level to their parents. This does not mean that parents will respond likewise; parents also must learn to accept the new relationship with their children. The more protective and involved the parents are with the student, the longer this adjustment will take. Many students, however, are able to resolve this parent-child conflict by the end of the sophomore year. Some students and parents take longer. In either case, the resolution of this conflict is necessary to a student's growth and eventual maturity. As the RA, you may support students in establishing a more positive adult-to-adult relationship with parents by sharing with them your personal experiences and how you have progressed in this development.

Homesickness

Common to freshmen is a sense of loss or feeling of "aloneness" that has been termed "homesickness." It stems from an absence of attachment with the family. Depression can emerge as a reaction to this sense of loss. Though most students experience some homesickness, few students are willing to admit it. Students equate homesickness with a lack of maturity and with ties to the affirmation of the child-parent relationship. Most students are able to overcome this homesickness through a short weekend visit at home or through support of close friends at college. Those who are unable to cope with the depression of homesickness can develop a sense of complacency about college life and may need to return home until they are emotionally ready to make the break.

Extreme Introversion and Extreme Extroversion

Students having difficulty in establishing relationships may exhibit one of two common behaviors—extreme introversion or extreme extroversion. Introversion is a common reaction from the student who has difficulty establishing relationships with peers. The simplest solution, as the student may interpret it, is simply to remove himself or herself from the group. It is easy to do. The introverted student may limit contact with other students, spend time away from the living unit, watch television, or simply remain alone in his or her room. These students may feel insecure and perhaps somewhat frightened about the college experience. Some students simply take longer to establish positive peer relationships. They may be somewhat shy and retiring at the beginning of the school year but soon learn sufficient skills to interact with the other members of the living group.

Some students never seek this interaction. They are not afforded the opportunities to learn important social skills necessary for their development and maturity. Simple interactions, such as how to engage others in conversation, how to tell a joke, and how to participate in a group are all part of the social skills a person learns through contacts with peers. Perhaps most importantly, these students will not experience the support that peers can offer nor get the feedback they need for their own growth and development.

Extremely extroverted students are the other side of the coin. They wish to participate in the group so much that they try too insistently. Through their extroverted, sometimes compulsive, behavior, they force themselves on others to the extent that students begin to ostracize them. Often these students have what are best described as "awkward social skills," which causes them to do or say inappropriate things. Unfortunately, the harder these students try to become part of the group, the more apprehensive the group becomes. These students can develop a reputation for being overbearing and obnoxious and are left out of many group activities. Although a student may establish many contacts at the beginning of the year, as people get to know the extremely extroverted student, they move further and further away from him or her. As with the introverted student, the extroverted student has not learned an acceptable style of interaction within the peer group and overcompensates for the deficiency.

As the RA, you are in a position to observe both types of students and to assist them in developing skills that will benefit them in their interactions with others. All too often, the outstretched hand of the RA is clung to permanently by students with social-skill problems who have been ostracized by the group. They come to sit in the RA's room for prolonged hours, occupying much of the RA's time and inhibiting other students from making casual contact. Much of your free time can be consumed by these students because you are the one person who seems to care about them and who has extended a hand of friendship. By becoming their constant companion, you may not be assisting them in developing necessary social skills. Though they may acquire important skills by using you as a model, their close contacts with you may be an escape from establishing positive relationships with other people within the living unit.

In these situations, talk with the student about his or her interaction with other people. The discussion should center on ways in which the student might interact with the group. Suggestions related to group activities, informal discussions, and similar common experiences may be shared among members of the living unit and will increase contact for these students and assist them in developing better relationships. Some of these students may need assistance from a professional staff member. Do not be afraid to discuss the situation with your residence hall director and make a referral if needed.

Difficulties with the Opposite Sex

During this period of late adolescence and early adulthood, students are discovering their own sexual identity. It is not uncommon for a student to experience some difficulty with the opposite sex. The college social situation places an emphasis on dating and intimacy. Part of students' self-concept and self-esteem are defined by their relationships with the opposite sex. Because students at this stage have not usually solidified their identity, it is difficult for them to share themselves intimately with another person. It is not until young adults know themselves that they become capabable of sharing themselves with others in a deep and intimate way. Because students have not fully developed the capacity to achieve a compassionate relationship of personal intimacy, their relationships often lack the depth and emotional vitality that they are seeking. Students may substitute a number of brief, unsatisfying sexual encounters with members of the opposite sex, but these seldom satisfy the need for intimacy. In fact, these brief sexual encounters may trivialize intimacy and make it more difficult to achieve.

You will observe the stress and anxiety students have about dating. Some students will be confident in themselves and will date frequently. Others will consistently have difficulty establishing such contacts. These students may lack self-confidence, have a poor self-image, or have not developed good social/dating skills. Simply put, the student may not know how to meet somebody of the opposite sex or may not have occasion to meet someone of the opposite sex in a setting that could initiate a date. Prescribed social roles in dating for men and women compound this situation. On the one hand, a man may be reluctant to ask a woman out for fear that she may be dating someone else or that he may not have enough money to support the type of dating relationship that he believes is appropriate. The female student may be in a worse predicament. She may be reluctant to contact a man for a date for fear of seeming too forward.

You may be able to talk candidly with students experiencing difficulties in establishing social relationships. You can tell the student that deceptive tactics, witty "one-liners," and contrived schemes are often viewed as somewhat "corny." The open, honest and straightforward approach with an individual usually works best. Also, it is socially acceptable for the cost of the date to be shared and for women to initiate dates by asking men to social functions.

Fears of Homosexuality

Men in particular undergo a crisis in discovering their sexuality that often includes wondering whether they may be attracted to other males. Some may experiment with casual sexual contacts with other males, and some may overcompensate by continually declaring loudly and publicly how heterosexual their relationships are. Although the majority of students are able to establish a satisfying sexual identity, some students experience much anxiety in resolving this issue.

One view of the homosexual issue is to see the individual in terms of how satisfied the individual is with himself or herself. People are sexual: some people are heterosexual, some are homosexual, and some are bisexual. It would seem that the important factor is how satisfied students are with their sexual identities and how comfortable they are with the life style it presents. When there is a conflict between what the student believes he or she wants and what the student perceives he or she is, then there is a difficulty that the student must resolve usually through professional counseling.

By being an understanding listener, you may help the student better understand some of the questions surrounding sexuality. If, early in the year, you begin berating homosexuals or defending your own sexual identity to students in your unit, you may lose a student who needs to talk with you.

Suicide

The difficulty of handling autonomy and independence in college may cause students to cry out for help through attention-getting devices such as suicide. In a later chapter the issue of suicide in college is discussed. You should be particularly aware of this problem relative to the initial stage of settling in to the residence hall situation, though it is present among college students throughout their education.

Other Problems

Illness, family problems, financial difficulties, and general personal problems are always present among students. In today's high-pressure college environment, few students can afford to miss more than one week of classes and hope to catch up. These problems are not specific to freshman/sophomore years, but they may present special problems for students who have never had to cope with them independent of the support of their parents. Think back to the time you were first sick in college and your parents were not available to comfort you. It is rather frightening to be ill and on your own in school.

Financial problems are also frightening to new students. While at home, although you may have had certain financial constraints, you probably were never faced with worrying over whether you would have enough money to eat. The student who has irresponsibly spent his or her money in the first few weeks of the month—depending on the cafeteria eating arrangements at your institution—may not have sufficient money to buy food for the rest of the month. Though some students may be able to borrow money or to get additional funds from their families, some students cannot. Personal problems such as roommate conflicts, exams, a physical impairment, or having to spend a birthday alone for the first time can be a mild trauma for a new student.

Students will experience some of these problems in this initial stage of adjustment. You as the RA need to be sensitive to these needs and lend your support, assistance, and experience in guiding students through these difficulties.

The Sophomore and Junior Years

As students reach the end of the sophomore year and start the junior year, they should be well on their way to having defined a new relationship with their parents, established a sexual identity, and begun to examine questions of what they believe and what they value. They should have established some tolerance and the ability to interact with other members of the peer group. Intellectually, they should have begun to move into a less authoritarian frame of reference and a more open-minded acceptance of other points of view.

Students are now beginning to question what they have accomplished and what lies ahead. Most students are starting to study in their chosen major, having completed most of the core course requirements. They have successfully been able to stay in college until this point and have learned much about existence within the system, including such things as how to register, how to select classes, and how to use the college catalog and bulletin. Students should feel somewhat more comfortable with the environment and should have established a positive peer support group of friends on whom they may rely. If they have defined no other identity for themselves than that they are "college students," they have an interim identity that satisfies their need for the time being. High school seems far behind now, and there might even be some disdain toward those people who inquire what they did when they were in high school. Their identity and self-concept at this point is tied to the college. Many students have started to identitfy attainable role models in the educational community that they would like to emulate. Students are more confident in their abilities to cope with the new environment and more secure in what lies ahead and what they have already accomplished.

In this middle developmental period, sometime in the sophomore or the junior year, the student experiences growth in many areas and, in particular, emotional growth and identification and clarification.

Emotional Growth

As students come to understand themselves better, they increase their capability to move from responding only to their own wants and desires to accepting others in an intimate and sharing relationship. As students mature, they learn to free interpersonal relationships, enhancing their ability to share with others and to become less self-centered and more other-centered.

As a person comes to feel more secure in his or her relationships with the opposite sex and as interpersonal intimacy occurs, greater security and confidence in this relationship lessens the need for outward signs of physical affection. As Chickering (1972) points out, "although the interpersonal ties are stronger—again with persons of both sexes—they are considerably loosened and less binding. Couples do not have to walk with arms around each other or even hold hands. Public necking—that vehicle for personal declaration of attractiveness and likability—and mutually supportive commitments and assurances are no longer required. Physical intimacy plays its important part. But again, for most students the context is one of respect, commitment, and love. Sexual intercourse in the absence of such feelings is infrequent" (p. 105).

The development of this capacity for intimate contacts and a sense of loving between people carries a concomitant ability not only to love but to know how to accept love from other people. The student begins to accept other people in a common union of understanding and mutual commitment. People become more secure about releasing intimate and personal information about themselves. They learn to share their own life and experiences, desires, needs, wants, and frustrations with others in a union of caring and emotional support.

This period of emotional development takes time. The person moves from a level of self-commitment and self-exploration to a new level of personal acceptance. This state of intimacy is not an absolute, but it is rather a period of growth that may lead to marital plans.

Value Identification and Clarification

By the junior year students have confronted many of their attitudes, beliefs, and values. They have been forced to defend, question, abandon, or reevaluate many of the opinions about the world which they held on entering the college. In this period, the sophomore and junior year, students attempt to find a resolution to some of these value questions by sorting out what they believe and why. Vital issues of the day and questions about drugs, sex, religion, and politics take on increased importance in the late-night discussion groups as students attempt to sort out how they feel about given issues. Lehmann's study (1968) using instruments measuring beliefs, values, and dogmatism suggests that this period between the sophomore and the end of the junior year is a critical time in value changes and adjustment. Feldman and Newcomb's (1969) study confirmed this change in values from a conservative, authoritarian position to increased liberalism to an eventual melding of the two into a value system similar to that of the parents—with the important differences that by this time students have internalized the value system as their own. Though students emerge with a value system somewhat more liberal than that of their parents (Astin, 1977), overall it tends to be most similar to their parents' values.

Intellectual Development

As students move into this middle stage of development, they move toward making a conscious act of commitment to certain values based on the affirmation of values in a world viewed as relativistic. The student's ability to analyze and define problems, recognize important unstated assumptions, and draw valid conclusions is enhanced with increased exposure to college.

Students may become increasingly motivated by having the opportunity to explore areas of interest within their chosen academic major. By this time students have learned to balance academic demands with personal demands placed on their time. In essence, students have learned to function within the academic community in sufficient capacity to attain acceptable academic standards and maintain other personal needs.

Common Adjustment Problems in the Sophomore and Junior Years

Intimacy

The need to be loved and to love is an important factor in human relationships for the student in this stage of development. Problems that students often experience are those of intimacy. Students may experience great emotional trauma as a result of a conflict with a significant other. Breaking up with a boyfriend or girlfriend seems to be quite prevalent in this stage. Often, where the relationship had been satisfying at a particular interpersonal level, as the two students mature, one may find the relationship less fulfilling and meaningful than the other person. This leads to conflict and often a break.

As an RA, you will see many students experiencing these feelings of rejection. When the student is closely tied to another student by feelings of emotion, intimacy, and compassion, the break in this relationship can sever much of the student's self-esteem and sense of security. The loss and feeling of rejection can become all-consuming. It can halt the forward progress of an individual's development and bring the person into an emotional crisis that impedes functioning. Behavior common to these situations includes failure to attend classes, lethargic attitude about life, feelings of depression, feelings of loneliness, despair, frustration, and abandonment, and often feelings of revenge.

Your contact with the student in a counseling relationship may be the only assistance you can offer, other than referring the student to counseling with a member of the professional staff. It is important for you not to become an intermediary between the two parties. You will find this role untenable. It is too easy to be drawn into the controversy. You can be of the greatest assistance to the student by remaining objective, not taking sides, and helping the student think through the situation. Offer empathy but not pity. Offer support but not advice. And be very careful about agreeing with a negative appraisal of the other individual, no matter what your personal feelings are. Remember that the person did care for that individual at one time.

Sophomore Slump

Somewhere toward the end of the sophomore year, many students experience what is sometimes called a "sophomore slump." This is best described as a sense of depression or a questioning about being in college. With approximately two years of college behind and at least two more years of college ahead, many students question the basic worth of their education and what they wish to accomplish in life. One of the questions for many sophomores at this halfway point centers on the utility and application of material that they have already learned. They question the worth of some information they have acquired and seek greater control over their life. A feeling of impatience sets in. For students who are uncertain about completing college, this is a time of reappraisal and reevaluation.

Students usually resolve questions themselves. As an RA, you should not attempt to sell a particular point of view. Often the RA believes he or she is doing a student a service by attempting to convince him or her that he or she ought to stay in college. What might be best for a particular student is to be out of college for a time. Students occasionally "stop out" of college for a year or so after their sophomore year to experience other aspects of life. Many return; others find greater satisfaction in life outside of college. The important thing is for the student to decide. Each person must work through these issues. As an RA, you can help the student define the problem and offer perspective, support, and insight on how you have resolved these issues for yourself.

The Apartment Quest

Many colleges and universities have what is called a *two-year parietal policy* that requires students to stay in residence halls for the freshman and sophomore years—or until they achieve a given number of academic credits. There are two philosophies supporting this rule. One philosophy contends that at least two years of residential learning provides the basic foundation for social skills and other important developmental skills for the greatest majority of students. A second philosophy maintains that most of these skills are learned in the freshmen year and that the learning takes place primarily through interaction with upper-division students. Sophomores role model appropriate behavior for the incoming freshmen, who in turn pass it on the following year to the freshmen. The retention of the sophomores in the residence halls is a way of transmitting these skills from one generation of college students to the next.

In either case, by the end of the sophomore year many students are seriously considering a move from the residence halls into apartments. Though students justify their move by blaming the food in the cafeteria, the noise in the residence hall, or the belief that it is less expensive to live in an apartment than it is to live in the residence halls, the real issue is independence. There is nothing that seems to epitomize independence more than having one's own apartment. It presents a new freedom, a new life style, and a new experience heretofore unclaimed.

In the opinion of the authors, most students probably benefit from having their own apartment after the sophomore year. It offers them a new experience and demands of them the development of some new skills in working with people and meeting the demands of utility and telephone bills, food purchasing and preparation, and cleaning for themselves.

The one thing that may help retain students in residence halls is a sense of community in the living unit. Students who enjoy the experience of associating with other members of the living unit may envision the same type of interpersonal community environment the following year. If this is strong, they may choose to stay in the residence hall. Like most other things, it must be an individual decision. If a student has made up his or her mind to move off-campus, your greatest assistance may be in helping identify possible off-campus living arrangements. You may wish to invite someone to a floor meeting to speak about apartment living during the spring semester when most students begin their apartment search. Consumer protection agencies, the student ombudsman office, or the dean of students office might be good resources. There are important things that a student should know about contracts, leases, damage deposits, subleasing, pets, utilities, vacations, and landlords.

The Senior Year

As students complete their junior year and begin their senior year, they should begin to feel comfortable with themselves and be on their way to clarifying their values, accepting a sex role, establishing an adult-to-adult relationship with their parents and developing tolerance for different life styles. Intellectually, students should begin to relate to "truth" in the context of values and evidence. Students' critical thinking, analytical abilities, and abstract reasoning skills should all have increased. The end of four or five years of college by no means heralds the end of the search for identity, but students are usually not in crises about it. People continually discover new things about themselves and continue to learn and grow throughout their life.

Values

From the freshman to the sophomore year, the student moves from values of idealism to values of increasing realism. This increasing sense of realism is reflected in a decrease in rigid, inflexible views of the world. Lehmann (1968) found that one effect of college was that students became more flexible, less rigid, and less authoritarian. As students' experiences increase, they gain a better perspective and recognize the limiting variables in resolving complex issues. This might be described as a period of learning to accept the world around them with an increasingly realistic perspective.

Common Adjustment Problems in the Senior Year

As you might expect, most of the adjustment difficulties associated with the latter part of the junior year and the senior year revolve around career decisions and career anxiety. Upperclassmen are presented with what for most could be described as a threat to their basic security and identity. For many students, their entire lives for the previous four years have revolved around the university community. A student's identity is closely tied to being part of the collegiate environment. In the college years, students come to know the environment, to depend on the environment, to identify themselves with the lablel "college student," and to develop a sense of security within that community.

Facing graduation, students are confronted with a threat to their security. Within a period of a few months, they will be in some new location or environment. This challenge to identity is the catalyst for a developmental crisis. It is an opportunity for students to grow.

Career Planning

Much of the senior year is concerned with the selection of a career and life work. Students often enter college with a concept of what they believe they would like to do and use college as an opportunity to refine their general interests into a career direction. Super et al. (1957, 1963) suggest that career decision making can occur as early as age 14 and continues until around the age of 25. The exploration period Super describes is as follows:

1. crystallization of a vocational preference
2. specifying a vocational preference
3. implementation of the preference
4. stabilization in the chosen vocation
5. consolidation of one's status within the vocation
6. advancing in the occupation

The first step, firming up vocational preferences, occurs in high school and in the first couple of years in college. Specifying and implementing such preferences are usually concerns of the junior and senior years. The task of the senior year is implementing the vocational preference. Miller and Prince (1976) describe this process of career decision making as:

> Career planning includes examining the world of work, understanding the abilities, interests, and values that are needed in various occupations, synthesizing facts and knowledge about oneself and the world of work, and committing oneself to the career and beginning to implement a vocational decision. Finally, a plan for the future that balances vocational aspirations, a vocational interest, and family concerns must be developed along with a sense of direction to identify the next steps and make a tentative commitment to future plans (p. 13).

The careers and vocations people select are based on a combination of factors, one of which is the job market. Colleges and universities experienced an increase in the number of students interested in the sciences and engineering when the job market called for more engineers and scientists. A similar increase in the number of students entering the field of education occurred when there was a shortage of teachers in the occupational market. In the later 1980s, the interest seemed to be in accounting and functions related to management and business. The job market, then, plays an important role in helping someone select an occupation. However, of equal importance is how the students feel about themselves and what they believe they can accomplish. It is unlikely that persons who see themselves as shy and retiring will view themselves in an aggressive occupation such as sales and marketing. People come to make decisions about their vocations on the basis of many factors, including their self-perceptions, the availability of jobs, their status needs, other people's expectations of them, and previous role models with which they have identified.

Many students enter college with the impression that college is designed to teach a vocation. As students experience college,they come to recognize that college is not about training for a specific occupation. It is about becoming an educated adult—both intellectually and personally. Lehmann (1968) found in his research that a proportionally larger number of seniors, in comparison to their views as freshmen, no longer believed that the major aim of college was to prepare them for a vocation, but to provide a liberal education.

As an RA and a student yourself, you are no doubt aware of the frequency with which students change academic majors. Astin (1977) explains that "These changes are more systematic than random; students who change majors or career plans usually change to related fields. Fields differ markedly in their retention and recruitment of students, with business and law generally showing the greatest gains and science and engineering the greatest losses in the undergraduate years" (p. 135).

Astin, reporting on a study conducted in 1974, found that 10 major career fields—business, college teaching, engineering, homemaking, law, medicine, nursing, teaching, scientific research, and social work—account for approximately 64 percent of the career interests of undergraduate students, excluding those students who have undecided majors.

Job anxiety is an extension of career decision problems. The anxiety is centered around pending decisions of other people. Will a student be offered a job with a particular company or be accepted in graduate school with an assistantship? Will he or she need to take a job of lower status or attend a graduate school of lower status? Job anxiety mounts even for students who have been offered positions or graduate assistantships at their choosen institution. Often they are reluctant to accept these offers, hoping that something better will come along. The anxiety, stress, and tension mount as the year progresses and the jobs appear to be fewer and fewer. The news media often carry stories about how many college students will be out of work this year; at the same time, one begins to hear about friends who have acquired responsible positions. This is a difficult and stressful time for all. Many students are gripped with a type of panic that affects other students as the anxiety of one student feeds off the anxiety of others.

Often, students view their entire success or failure in college in terms of their ability to find employment in a particular occupation. This can be especially threatening for a humanities or social sciences major who may have been more interested in acquiring a liberal education than in pursuing a specific vocational interest. Fears of getting into graduate school—especially law school and medical programs—tend to raise the stress and anxiety among seniors.

Students in other fields opting for a limited number of positions in business management and related areas may become very competitive. Reports abound of students violating university procedures in the placement office to ensure a scheduled appointment with a favored firm. The anxiety preceding and following interviews creates stress. As you know from your own experience, people have a tendency to relieve this stress and anxiety through heightened reactions to situations and people. Interpersonal relations among people in these stressed situations can be aggressive, competitive, and difficult.

Fear of the Adult World

Most students who are completing college find their college experience generally satisfying. They recall with nostalgia their freshman days, their first date, and memorable moments on campus. After all, for the past four years much of their lives have been directly related to the campus environment. It has been their home. They feel warm and comfortable and very good about the college environment as a whole. They may question different aspects of their education, disdain the administration, and curse some of their instructors, but most will look on their time in college with very fond memories.

The student begins experiencing a sense of loss in leaving this comfortable, warm environment and may experience apprehension about his or her future. Many will suddenly be plunged into entirely new situations that will challenge and test them in new ways. Some students may feel a sense of relief in finally leaving, but most seniors feel a sense of loss as they depart from close friends and recall their college experiences.

Self-confidence

The anxiety, stress, and emotional involvement in departing from college can attack a person's self-confidence. The student's self-image, self-esteem, and status needs, as well as other people's expectations of him or her, all seem to come together at one time. If the student has had many positive, reinforcing strokes from interviews and friends, this may have a tendency to accentuate his or her self-confidence and encourage him or her to go beyond. Often, however, the opposite is true. The student may have one or two very stressful job interviews, parents are calling with questions about what he or she will do after college, relatives and friends have expectations of the student's success, and the student has expectations of what he or she should be able to do. His or her self-confidence is laid on the line. If the self-confidence is overly attacked, the student may retreat from situations and question his or her own self-worth. Depression often sets in. Students in this period need emotional support to make it through some very anxious situations.

Marital Plans

Some students plan marriage immediately after college. Much of a person's emotional dependency and security is tied to completion in this area. A traditional pattern for men and women is to get married and start a family. The anxiety surrounding the decision to get married, compounded by the job experience, compounded by the probability of relocating, plus general difficulties in completing the senior year in college and successfully graduating can unduly complicate a person's life. Commitments, plans, studies, and a myriad of other tasks all seem to need to be completed at one time. The graduating senior faces many decisions. It is a real trial of his or her emotional stability and coping mechanisms.

Other Problems

Stress and anxiety are self-perpetuating. When one or two individuals in a group become stressed and anxious, they often release this stress and anxiety toward other people. Thus stress and anxiety can become contagious and trigger similar feelings in other people. As an RA, you need to be cognizant of the pressure that is confronting seniors and to make yourself available to them for emotional support as well as for counseling. You have to be careful in assessing when it is appropriate for you to inquire about the decisions that may be confronting them at that particular point in their lives. Often merely asking questions can produce heightened anxiety. Having to disclose a lack of success in job placement to other people is difficult for many people.

Perhaps the best things that you can do are to make yourself available for assistance when students need it and to show your concern and interest. Make these students aware of the counseling opportunities on campus and of any career planning and placement workshops that may be available to assist them with some of these decisions. They will need your support and friendship and your positive reinforcement during this time of stress and anxiety.

As an RA, you need to be aware that you too will experience some of these same anxieties and crises as you move into your senior year. You will find that your interest and maturity level exceed those of many of the students in your living unit. So it may be very easy to lose patience and become intolerant of certain activities. Be careful not to take your anxieties and tensions out on the students in your unit. You will need to find some personal coping mechanisms and support among the other RAs. Some schools do not permit graduating seniors to assume the position of RA for this very reason.

The best way to decrease anxiety about job placement and other related graduation plans is to plan early. Put together a resume, contact the placement office, and do your job search and review early. These steps will help ensure some confidence for yourself as you approach job interview situations. As other people's anxiety mounts, you will be able to maintain confidence in your preparation and will have a "jump" on many late starters.

Chapter 7
Peer Counseling

Many RAs join a residence hall staff expecting to become full-time counselors. There are a few hall directors who also believe this. RAs do some counseling in the form of active listening. They do some advising in the form of providing information, and they do some referral counseling to help students seek assistance from a professional counselor or psychologist. RAs do not do psychological analysis or clinical counseling. It is unfortunate that many psychology majors view this helping relationship as an opportunity to try their ability to diagnose and assist troubled students. The skills necessary to do this take many years to develop. An RA is not expected to do this—and it should not be attempted.

The RA is best viewed as a peer counselor, a helper, or a skilled listener. Many of the skills needed to perform this counseling role cannot be taught in the short time most students remain in the RA position. For this reason, RAs should be chosen on the basis of their human relations skills. Sensitivity toward others, an ability to work in groups, an accepting personality, and a desire to help others are the qualities needed to fulfill the counseling responsibilities of the RA position. Every RA must have these qualities to some degree. A person can always be taught the operational procedures needed to manage the residence hall, to report emergencies, or to apply first aid. However, in the short time that a person holds the RA position, he or she cannot be taught to develop a personality that makes other students want to know him or her and the sensitivity to work compassionately with another student in a time of emotional crisis.

If you did not possess these qualities, you would not have been chosen as an RA. However, having these qualities is not enough. The key is knowing how to transform these qualities into skills. This chapter will help you do this by providing you with some counseling techniques, some counseling strategies, a counseling model, and some tips on counseling.

Complaints about Counseling

The most common complaints heard from RAs about counseling are (1) most students contact the RA for relatively trivial or routine things like unlocking doors or asking other students to turn down their stereos; (2) RAs are not always certain when they are counseling a student and when they are simply having a good discussion; and (3) RAs believe they are given too much theory and not enough practical information. These complaints are supportable.

Most of the requests that an RA receives are for routine tasks, like opening doors or giving information. These requests are important. How you handle them can either demonstrate to students that you are available to help or that you would prefer not to be bothered. It is easy for students to assume that if you are too busy to help with little things, you are too busy to help with something major. It is a matter of trust. You must demonstrate to students that you are interested in them as individuals. If you fail to do this, it is unlikely that you will have students interested in contacting you for any assistance.

Although it is not really very important to define the specifics of a counseling contact as it differs from a discussion, many RAs need to establish parameters for defining these situations. For this discussion's purposes, a *counseling encounter* is an act of helping another person cope with an emotion, a personal problem, stress, or a crisis by assisting the student in decision making and helping to return the person to an improved emotional state. Counseling contacts will come from one of three sources: (1) the student will initiate the contact; (2) you will observe behavior in a student that indicates the need for some form of counseling intervention; or (3) a resident of your living unit or another staff person will inform you of behavior that indicates the need for counseling intervention.

The third complaint heard from RAs is that they are given too much theory and not enough practical application. A modification of this complaint is that the techniques they have been taught are superficial, simplistic, and artificial. Some of this is probably true. It is difficult to teach people how to transform personal qualities into skills until they have some basic understanding of exactly what it is they need to do. On the other hand, a review of major counseling theories and counseling approaches is best reserved for those who are interested in counseling as a profession. It is easy to become bogged down with conflicting theories and schools of thought on counseling; yet there needs to be a pattern or model to follow.

The helping-skills or counseling model we will use is composed of three phases. The first phase is to become aware of your own feelings, motivations, values, strengths, and weaknesses in preparing yourself to help others. The second phase is to establish yourself with the residents in your living unit in a way that will encourage students to contact you for your assistance with their personal problems. The third phase is a five-step helping-skills model. In the last two sections of this chapter, the model is modified to suggest a method for giving advice and for making a referral for professional counseling.

An Overview of Helping Skills

Most problems students experience in college reflect maturation, adjustment to a new environment, or normal stress. Few of these require the assistance of a professional counselor. General depression, anxiety, stress, disappointment, rejection, and grief are the kinds of feelings that you, as an RA with skills in helping, should be capable of handling. These problems will be brought about by many of the same experiences you have had. Even though a problem may stem from feelings of inadequacy, difficulty with class assignments, problems with parents, money, or a member of the opposite sex, it can usually be discussed and some method of coping with it usually can be uncovered.

Most of these problems can be resolved alone or with the help of a friend. Simply talking about the problem with another person can be all the help needed. There is something special, a type of emotional catharsis, in sharing a problem with another person; it is almost as though one no longer carries the burden alone. The sympathy and understanding expressed by another can usually help a troubled individual cope with the problem.

Although you can help with most problems, not all students will share their problems with you. Though individually you may never be confronted by a student who is contemplating his or her own death, the probability that this will occur in your unit is higher than you may realize. It is quite probable that one of your residents will experience some type of serious emotional problem during the year as a result of breaking up with a boyfriend or a girlfriend. Your ability to respond to these situations may be crucial to the student's ability to function. Many of the skills you develop through your RA training will be used daily. Some, however, are really preparation for the one or perhaps two times that you may be called upon for some serious counseling during the year. These one or two times might make the difference between life and death for the student involved.

Preparing Yourself to Help

Confidence

The very nature of the helping relationship in counseling places you in a position of authority. The student comes to you seeking assistance with a problem. Many undergraduate RAs, not having previously been exposed to this degree of responsibility, feel a sense of ambiguity. They lack the basic self-confidence to enter into an exchange with the student for fear that they may say or do something that will make the student's situation worse.

This is a reasonable reaction, but, for the most part, unfounded. There is very little that you, as a reasonably prudent RA, could say that would do irreparable harm to the student. Most of the situations that you will encounter will be situations within your frame of reference. The types of problems that students experience in college are similar to the types of problems that people experience in all walks of life; most of them are not unique, special, or overly serious. It is important that you keep perspective, recognizing that by virtue of your position and training, students have confidence in you.

However, there will be situations that you may encounter during the year for which you will not have the necessary skills. As you come to recognize your ability to help students, you must also recognize your limitations. Later, this chapter discusses conditions under which you should seek the support of a professional counselor in making a counseling referral. For now, remember that you can help students most of the time. In situations in which you are uncertain, ask the hall director for guidance.

Attitudes, Beliefs and Values

As an RA, you are in a position to influence the attitudes, beliefs, and values of students during a critical time in their lives. In a counseling encounter, the influence is magnified by virtue of the counseling relationship, in which you are viewed as a person with the ability to help. It is for this reason that you must accept one of the basic canons of counseling—do not judge other people's values by your own.

RAs are selected in part on personal skills, motivations, and values that coincide with the institution's approach to working with students in residence halls. Except in the case of some religiously affiliated institutions, RAs are not chosen to teach beliefs or values. Though RAs may reflect their values in their day-to-day interactions with students, they generally do not have the responsibility to advance a particular set of beliefs.

To enter into a helping relationship with a student, you must first become aware of what you believe, not superficially, but what you really believe. Issues such as sex, religion, politics, interracial dating, and similar topics will confront you in many forms through your contacts with students. If you do not approve of interracial dating for example, you are entitled to this belief, just as other students are entitled to theirs. When students come to you for counseling, they are not coming to you to have you judge behavior. They are coming to you to receive help with a problem. Consider the following example. A woman in your living unit becomes pregnant and believes she wants an abortion. You personally find abortion unacceptable. How can you best help her? Will it help her if you condemn her for what she is contemplating or if you try to prevent the abortion? You have two choices. First, you could try to remain as objective as possible and facilitate the student's own decision-making process, helping her consider the choices available to her and their ramifications. Second, you could tell the woman that you personally have some strong feelings about this decision and refer her to a person who could be more objective.

Either of these approaches is acceptable. Sometimes people have such strong feelings about a particular topic that they cannot be objective. They sometimes cannot free themselves from values that judge the right or wrong of other people's actions. In these situations, the only option is to be open about feelings and tell the person that they cannot be objective enough to help with the decision.

The counseling relationship should be as value-free as possible. You can never free yourself from your values, but you can refrain from expressing them and judging others by them.

It is not always easy to remain nonjudgmental. Sometimes you may think you are helping people when you are actually attempting to push your view of the world. Perhaps the classic example of this is presented in a counseling encounter with a student who is contemplating resigning from college. When the student comes to the RA to discuss the issue, the RA takes the position of trying to convince the student to stay in school. This position is based upon the premise that it is better to attend college than not to attend college and that it is bad to drop out. This may or may not be true. Undoubtedly, the RA sets out on a well-intentioned quest to help the student stay in college. The person who should be making this decision and who should be in the midst of the evaluation is the student, not the RA. Not only is it presumptuous of the RA to assume that he or she is more capable of determining what is best for the student, but it places the RA in the position of assuming responsibility for the actions of the other person.

If you are to help other students with their personal problems, you must know yourself and know what you believe and how strongly you feel about these beliefs. Becoming aware of yourself is a continual process and may require you to participate in some self-discovery workshops with other staff members and students. Once you know what you believe, you can work to control these beliefs in your counseling encounters.

Motivation

What is the motivation to help another person with a personal problem? Ideally, it is associated with a basic sensitivity to others, the desire to alleviate suffering in others, and perhaps the knowledge that the other person trusts you enough to share his or her problem. It is ego-satisfying to help others with their problems and to have knowledge that they wished to share something of themselves with you.

Sometimes RAs find that they want to help so much that they come to assume responsibility for trying to solve students' problems. They cross the line between helping the student make his or her own choices and telling the student what they believe the student should do.

The helping role of the counselor is primarily one of an understanding, often sympathetic, facilitator of the student's own ideas. Many times you will feel as though you could simply dispense your wisdom on the particular topic and resolve the student's problem. Seldom will this be acceptable.

It is easy for an inexperienced RA to confuse the role of counselor with that of problem solver. There is much ego satisfaction in resolving other people's problems. However, this is not a useful method of helping a troubled student who is left with the solution to a particular problem and not the skills to resolve similar problems in the future. One of your goals as a counselor must be to help students develop these skills for themselves. If they do not, they will contact you with every problem that arises. Though some RAs may find that this enhances their personal esteem, it does not best serve students' needs.

Remember, it is always simpler to give advice than to stimulate ideas in others. If you find yourself falling into the role of guru, consider who is receiving the most benefit from the relationship—you or the students.

Objectivity

There are many demands placed on your time as an RA. If you are liked and trusted by your residents, they will bring you a number of their problems. People who are sensitive to the needs of others are also susceptible to falling into the trap of accepting other people's problems as their own. If you are to remain a viable resource for students in your hall, you must remain objective and retain some degree of emotional detachment. You can never accept responsibility for someone else's problem or someone else's decision. It is each student's responsibility to resolve his or her problem, not yours. Most people do not have enough time or emotional fortitude to accept responsibility for the problems and actions of an entire living unit of college students. You will be of help to your residents only so long as you can be objective and assist them with their own decision making.

Think about these questions carefully before you enter into a counseling relationship with a student. It is important that you understand yourself, your strengths and limitations, your values, and your motivations. Recognize that you are capable of helping students with most of their problems, but that you should not try to solve students' problems for them. Help them work through their own problems, recognizing that not all problems have a solution. You will be of help only so long as you retain some emotional distance from the problem.

Establishing Yourself with Your Residents

No matter how well you have prepared yourself to help students with their problems, unless students are willing to discuss their concerns with you, you may not have an opportunity to use those skills. The opinion that your residents have of you is important to your success in counseling. If they view you as a person solely concerned with the enforcement of college policies, concerned only about yourself and your friends, or concerned only with the prestige and authority of the RA position, this will affect their willingness to share their concerns with you.

First Impressions and the Start of School

What happens during the first few days of the academic term is critical in establishing yourself with your residents. The first impression you make on your new residents will have a lingering effect; it will either lay the foundation for further contacts or create barriers to them. Some RAs begin this process during the summer, before the school year, by contacting each of their residents by mail. Although this is a time-consuming process, the early expression of concern may pay off in improved relationships later.

Make an aggressive attempt to contact your residents as they arrive. Within the first week, you should have met and learned something about each resident. Many RAs make a list of the residents' names and room numbers on a floor diagram and keep it with them until they have committed it to memory. The list can also be used as a check to ensure that you have met each of the residents. By the time of the first floor meeting, you should have met and talked with each person in your unit, if only briefly.

In the following few weeks, you should make a point to stop at each student's room for a few minutes to become more familiar with them. People like to talk about themselves and what they do. Share things about yourself. Tell them about your hobbies, your interests, your college major, and anything else that interests you.

Part of what you do in establishing yourself is to develop a sense of belonging among the members of your floor. You do this by finding ways for people in your living unit to interact. Dinner is always a good opportunity to have a group of your residents get to know one another. Make certain, especially during the first few weeks, that you invite some of the new residents in the unit to have dinner with you and any of the other residents with whom you usually dine. It is important that you make an effort to establish all residents in your living unit as part of the group.

Once you have made the initial contact, follow up with each student. If a resident tells you that he or she is taking a math class or is trying to locate a particular building, make certain that you ask about that particular topic when you next see him or her. You really have several goals to accomplish during these first few days. First, learn the names of your residents. Second, learn their backgrounds. Third, learn something unique about them as individuals. And, fourth, learn something you can follow up on later. This follow-up is an important way to demonstrate that you care about the students.

These initial contacts will be important in helping you establish the respect of your residents. This respect can be more easily lost than acquired. Continual contact, recognition, reinforcement, and similar forms of support will be necessary throughout the academic year.

Establishing and Enforcing Policies

Students are not compelled by college policy to contact you for assistance, to respect you, or, for the most part, to follow your directions. Your residents do not report to you, and you do not have supervisory responsibility for them. Instead, your authority in the living unit is derived primarily from the authority that the students are willing to give you. To the extent that your residents respect you, recognize your competence, and come to you for information and assistance, you have authority in your living unit. It is true that you can make a disciplinary referral, but chances are that any other student at your institution can make the same referral.

Perhaps the case for not having authority is overstated. You do have some authority by virtue of the responsibilities assigned to you and the fact that the institution recognizes your authority to intervene in certain situations. The point is that your effectiveness in the RA position is dependent on how students view you in that role. If you attempt to present yourself as perfect, unapproachable, always correct, and puritanical, it is likely that few of your residents will come to you with their concerns for fear that you will condemn them or at least lose respect for them. On the other hand, if you conduct yourself in a drunken, rowdy, and slovenly manner, it is likely that students will feel that you are unable to handle your own problems, let alone theirs.

The respect of your residents is an important element in performing your job. It is not always easily gained, but it is easily lost. Being respected and being liked can be separate, but they do not need to be.

The issue of being liked and being respected always seems to play a critical role in the area of policy enforcement. Some RAs confuse being liked with being lenient about the enforcement of policies. Once you have explained the policies, the rationale behind them, and the institution's instructions to you on their enforcement, you have taken the first step in establishing the expectations for enforcement of these policies.

One good way to undermine your credibility is to inform your residents of the institution's policies and then add your commentary on the policies with which you agree and those with which you do not agree. "The university told me to enforce the marijuana policy, I personally disagree with it, but I have to enforce it." You are sending out a dual message to your residents. You have told them that you are doing something in which you do not believe. This is a difficult position for other people to respect. An easier position to respect is "The university has this policy; the reason for this policy is. . . ." If somebody asks you if you agree or disagree with the policy, your stock answer should be, "My personal beliefs about these policies are not an issue" or, "Yes, I believe in this policy and I have found it to be supported by most of the other staff." The fact that you agree or disagree with a particular policy is not really the issue. If you have accepted the responsibility of the job, you have accepted the responsibility to carry out the policies.

During the first few weeks, some students may feel a need to challenge your enforcement of policies. This is a testing period. Students will try to determine how strict you are, how sincere you are about enforcement, and what the real behavioral boundaries are. This testing is like testing the enforcement of the speed limit in a new town. The speed limit may be posted at 55 mph, but chances are good that one will not be arrested until traveling 60 or 65 mph.

Some students need to determine the tolerance limits of behavior. If you allow "Frisbee" wars in the hallways at the beginning of the year, or allow people to shoot golf balls in the hallway, play soccer, play their stereos loud enough to rattle the bathroom fixtures in buildings two blocks away, flood the hallway with water, or to throw toilet paper from the bathroom windows, then be prepared to permit this kind of behavior throughout the year. It is much easier to set reasonable limits at the start of the year than to stop excessive behavior once it has begun.

It is more important that people feel that you treat everyone equally, that you are consistent, and that you are fair than to have them believe you are doing them a favor by letting them do what they want. What needs to be communicated to your residents is that a small group-living situation carries with it special duties to respect the rights of others. This means some restrictions on personal freedom. In a community living situation, people simply do not have the personal freedom to play their stereos as loud as they wish until whatever hour of the morning they wish. There will be some students who are selfish and will not want to acknowledge these limitations on their freedom. Chances are that your relationship with them will become somewhat strained as you help them develop this understanding.

Availability

Being available to all of the residents of your living unit is a complex task. If you spend the majority of your time with a small clique of people, you run the risk of alienating other segments of the unit. The same applies to spending most of your time with other staff members, as is often the case. It is not easy to balance your personal needs of comradeship with the needs of your residents.

Students are sensitive. If they continually see the RA in the company of other RAs, they begin seeing the RA as a member of an elite club in which they cannot participate. This is difficult for RAs, who often find that their closest associations are with other RAs. It is equally difficult for the hall director, who wants to establish a spirit of unity among the staff yet wants to ensure that the needs of the building residents are met. If all the RAs congregate in one or two of the RAs' rooms, it is apparent that they are not spending their available time with their own residents. The RA will then be viewed as an outsider who only comes to the living unit to deal with problems, to change the bulletin board, or to enforce regulations. The RA must become part of the living unit, a part of the team. It is not an easy job. It takes time and continued effort.

Confidentiality

Confidentiality is essential. There is probably no quicker way to lose the respect of your residents and to ruin any opportunity to help students with personal problems than to begin sharing a person's personal problems with other members of the floor. Although the individual to whom you are speaking may feel good about the fact that you have taken him or her into your confidence, he or she will be wondering if you share what he or she tells you with others.

Inevitably, if you violate a student's confidence, it gets back to that student. Not only will that person probably never trust you again with any important information, but chances are that that person's friends will not trust you either.

The only person with whom you should legitimately share these confidences should be the hall director. Occasionally some information may be shared with other members of the RA staff, but only when there is a legitimate reason for them to have this information. The indiscriminate sharing of information can quickly generate a lack of trust among the residents in your unit. This is another reason why continual association with the other RAs in the building helps engender a feeling among the residents that the RAs are an exclusive group who get together and share information about their units. No one wants his or her personal feelings, beliefs, or confidences shared with large groups of people. If students chose to share information with you, they do not necessarily choose to share it with every other person on the staff.

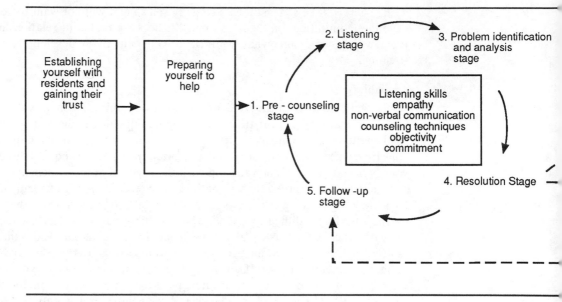

Figure 7.1. Counseling model

Again, if you require advice about a shared confidence, consult the hall director. There may be no need to share certain confidential information with the hall director, but the confidential information that you receive should be considered available to your hall director. You do not keep secrets from the person who hired you, has responsibility for your actions, has trained you, and who is interested in achieving the same objectives you are. If you do not believe that you can share certain confidential information with your hall director, either you should not have agreed to accept the information or you have a problem in your relationship with your hall director that must be resolved.

The best way to establish yourself with residents in your living unit is to be yourself. After all, one of the factors that gained you the position was your personality and your ability to get along with other people. Let that come forth. Be sincere and honest about yourself. Do not try to assume any superficiality about your job, what you will be doing during the year, or your authority. Be open, be yourself, and be available.

Remember that not everyone will like you, but this is not your goal. Your goal is to let everyone know that you care and are concerned about them as individuals, that you are willing to help, that you have information and training that can help them if they choose to take advantage of it, and that you are available to them.

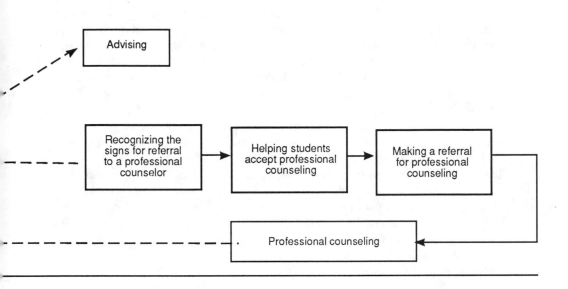

Counseling Model

The goal of all helping-skills encounters is to help students make positive, self-directed choices about their own lives that aid the students' development and return them to a state in which they can again cope with the college experience. There is a five-stage model you can use in bringing about this goal. The five stages are: (1) precounseling stage, (2) listening stage, (3) problem identification and analysis stage, (4) resolution stage, and (5) the follow-up stage.

Precounseling Stage

This is the stage in which the student has either sought your assistance with a problem, someone has told you about a problem a student is experiencing, or you have observed something about a student's behavior that needs to be discussed. In the latter two situations, you will be initiating the counseling. In these circumstances, you will need to explain the purpose of your inquiry. These inquiries can be simple expressions of the behavior you have observed. For example: "John, I have observed that you have been very depressed and moody recently. Is something bothering you?" Or: "John, is everything going all right for you? I noticed that you have not been attending classes recently and don't seem to be acting like yourself."

These statements give students the opportunity to discuss a particular problem, if there is one. They also show that you care. When someone has told you about a problem that one of your residents is experiencing, it is appropriate for you to explain by saying something like, "I was talking with *X* the other day, and she told me that you and your boy friend broke up. How are you feeling about that? Is everything all right?" Or: "The hall director told me that you were not pledged by the sorority in which you were interested. I was sorry to hear about it. How do you feel about what happened?"

These questions enable the student to understand how you came to observe the behavior and what behavior you have observed. An open-ended question will invite more than a yes or no answer. If the person wishes to talk, he or she has the opportunity. In both these cases—observed and reported behavior—you can prepare beforehand. You can think of areas you may wish to explore with the student, and you can plan the time to contact the student.

If the student approaches you with a problem, you will not have the opportunity to think about the problem beforehand or possibly to set the time and place for the discussion. You do, however, have the right to request the student select another time. You may find yourself in the middle of an important class assignment, late for an important meeting, or so frustrated that you simply cannot assist the student at that particular time. You should not feel that every time a student comes to you with a problem you must drop everything and deal with it at that precise moment. You will quickly learn that some students will come and sit in your room and simply spend time procrastinating. This wastes both your time and theirs. There are other students who run to the RA with every petty problem they have. Soon you will find such students running to you to check the most minor issues to be a nuisance.

You can decide whether to see the student immediately or postpone discussing the problem until a more convenient time. Each decision needs to be made independently. It should be based on what you know about the individual, his or her emotional state at the time, how often he or she comes to you with problems, and how important the completion of your own work is at that moment. You must also assess some things from the person's tone and physical manner at the time. A woman who continually runs to you for emotional support, often crying, may not need your attention as much as a woman who does not come to you often and is somber and lacks much emotion. You must begin making some subjective decisions about the individual and how important the particular problem. Chances are that the first encounters will be the most meaningful. If a student comes to you for the first time with a problem, if at all possible try to see that student and help him or her with the problem.

Try using these general guidelines to make your assessments:

- Is this the first time you have seen this student, or does this student run to you with every type of problem?
- What is the observed emotional state of the student when he or she inquires about talking with you? Is this state out of the ordinary for this individual?

- How much time will the problem actually take to resolve? Is this simply a request for information that you can resolve in five or six minutes?
- What is your relationship with the person? Is it a positive relationship in which the person trusts you already, or is it one in which you are still attempting to establish trust?
- How serious a problem does the person believe it is?

It is appropriate, based on your responses to these questions, to inquire whether the student believes that his or her problem requires your immediate attention or if it is something that can wait until you have more time or are better able to assist. Remember that you will not be able to give your full attention to helping if your attention is focused on studying for an examination or completing a paper. You will be trying to get the problem resolved so that you can continue with what you really want to do. It is better for both of you to set a time later—the same day if at all possible—to discuss the problem. Most students will understand if you explain that you have something that must be completed.

There is no rule that your personal goals must always come second to the desires, whims, needs, or problems of students in your living unit. You will find that they usually do. However, there are times when you must recognize that you also have tasks that must be accomplished. The trick is to balance personal, academic, and job responsibilities. To turn people away from your door regularly will soon earn you a reputation of not caring about your residents. When you think it appropriate, based upon your evaluation of the situation and some inquiries, make the decision to talk with people about problems they are experiencing when there is a time acceptable for both of you.

Assuming that you decide that a student's problem is important enough to set aside what you have been doing, your first step in the counseling exchange is to make the person feel welcome. You would probably do so anyway, whether you had invited the student to your room to discuss an observed problem or if the student just stopped by your room. Making the person feel comfortable requires just a little more effort when the purpose is counseling.

Set the environment for the exchange. Close the door, physically push what you were doing previously aside, and sit directly across from the person. If another person is in the room when the student comes in and is not discussing an important problem with you, it is legitimate to ask the other person to leave. The visitor, understanding your role, will not be offended. In no case should you try to discuss a serious subject with a student in front of another person. If the telephone rings during the conversation or if there is a knock at the door, answer it but be very brief with the caller. Tell the caller that you have someone with you and that you will return the call. This is a way of reinforcing to the student with a problem that he or she is the central focus of your concern. There is probably nothing more irritating for a troubled student discussing a serious problem than to have the conversation interrupted by a telephone call and the person with whom he or she is sharing the information spend an extended time on the telephone. This conveys a clear disinterest.

Be conscious of the nonverbal clues you are sending. If you lie down on your bed and stare at the ceiling or sit behind your desk, you could be nonverbally communicating disinterest or placing a barrier to intimacy between you and the other person. The same applies to assuming any physically superior position relative to the student seeking help. If you sit on the desk or tower above the person, you are conveying a superiority that may further inhibit the student from expressing his or her feelings.

The proper counseling posture is to sit directly across from the student. Your posture should be open—meaning that neither your arms nor your legs should be crossed. Nonverbally, having your arms or legs crossed could communicate that you are closed off from the other person. Your eyes should focus on the other person's face. If you have trouble looking into the other person's eyes, try looking just slightly above them at the eyebrows. You may find this less intense. Try to project a feeling of being relaxed and open, yet attentive and interested in the other person. Your voice should be calming, tranquil, and soothing, but not a whisper. Your entire demeanor should convey acceptance, comfort, and understanding. This mode helps the person feel more comfortable with you and more willing to share his or her problem.

Listening Stage

This is the stage in which the student talks and you listen. It is an opportunity for the student to describe how he or she views the problem. You in turn are periodically telling the person how you are interpreting the situation being described. Although people describe clearly how they view what is happening, you are trying to understand the student's frame of reference in order to understand the view being described. It is not important whether you agree with the viewpoint being presented; the important thing is that you listen and understand what is being said. In this communication you need to determine what is seen as the problem, what is viewed as the reason or cause, and how the student is currently coping. To determine these things, you first must be a good listener.

Communicating is a difficult process. It requires the person sending the message to confirm that the message being sent is the one being received. It requires the receiver to confirm that he or she has received the message that was intended. Thus, good listening is an active process. Messages are sent, received, and confirmed by each of the parties.

To do this you must know how to listen. There is a difference between hearing what somebody is saying and truly listening to what is said. This two-way process means that you must check the meaning of certain words. If the student says his or her roommate hates him or her, that only tells you that the student perceives a conflict with the roommate. Appropriate questions for you to ask in this situation are "What do you mean by 'hates you'?" and "What makes you believe that?" Communication only takes place when you both understand and have a common meaning for the words, phrases, and situations that are being described.

Useful techniques in the listening process are as follows:

- Be yourself—be natural, be comfortable, be confident with yourself. Act naturally and express an interest in what the person is saying.
- Talk less and listen more.
- Ask questions that clarify the communicated message.
- Use open-ended questions that call for more than a yes or no answer.
- Help the student stay focused on the problem and away from tangents.

Being yourself means exactly that. Be natural about your actions and your relationship to the other person. Do not try to be psychoanalytic, try to use complex terms when they are unnecessary, or attempt to impress the person with your knowledge. The student is looking for a friend and someone who can help. He or she is not looking for a psychoanalyst. You should refrain from giving the impression that you are doing a psychological counseling session. Your goal is not to make a diagnosis but to help the person cope with the problem.

Talk less and listen more is a good rule of thumb. This is a chance for the student to paint a picture for you of what is happening and for you to understand. The student at this point is the teacher instructing you. You, in turn, are trying to understand the subject matter or the view that the student is painting. You can only do this if you give the student time to discuss the problem.

The amount of time, however, is not the issue. Some students will be able to paint a clear and accurate picture for you in a relatively short time. Others will need to add a quantity of elaborate and nonuseful detail. You have a right to help the student move through the explanation with questions such as, "How does that particular event affect the problem?" Or, "Yes, I am familiar with that area, go on."

One of the important techniques to learn is to ask questions that clarify. This is a simple technique, but it is an important method of communicating to students that you are understanding what they are saying. Feed back the information that has been given you. Some stock questions you should make part of your listening vocabulary are "What I hear you saying is . . . ," "If I understand you correctly, you are saying . . . ," "Did you say . . . ," "What do you mean by . . . ?"

These are questions that clarify and, most important, give the student information on what you are perceiving. Sometimes this is enough for the student to gain perspective on the problem. You are asking questions that help the student clarify the situation by feeding back or reflecting what he or she has said. This reflection of ideas and perceptions is important in gaining a mutual understanding of what is being said as well as establishing a different viewpoint for the student.

The use of open-ended questions is a good technique to help the student elaborate in more detail areas you do not understand or areas in which you feel the student has made some incorrect assumptions. The difference between an open-ended and a closed question is that closed questions can be answered with one or two words. Open-ended questions need a more complete response. For example, if you ask a student, "What is your major?" the student may easily respond, "My major is. . . ." You could ask that same question and receive more information by asking, "Why did you choose your current major?" Open-ended questions are best for follow-up information. Follow-up questions are ones such as, "Could you tell me more about . . ." or "How do you believe the situation would have been different if you would have . . .?" Remember, most of the counseling session will be spent with the other person doing the talking and working through the problem. You will be asking appropriate questions to help clarify the problem.

Be careful not to deviate from the subject being discussed. It is appropriate for you to help the student keep to the problem at hand. When you ask questions, ask only those that directly relate to the problem. This will help eliminate diversion and help the student focus on the problem.

While talking with the student, you must have good attending skills—those nonverbal or subverbal indications by which you let a person know that you understand. Good attending skills are essential. They confirm that you understand what has been said. The following are some attending skills that you use in counseling.

- Nodding your head communicates that you understand and are soliciting more information or that you are giving approval to the individual. To see this technique work, sit down across from a friend and, while he or she is talking, nod casually throughout the discussion. Part of the way through, simply quit nodding and only look at him or her. Your friend will either begin going into more detail or may ask you if you understand what he or she is saying. In our culture, we need reassurance or confirmation that the other person hears and understands what we are saying.
- Supporting hand gestures, such as the rotation of one hand in a certain way, expresses the feeling of approval.
- Facial expressions, smiles, frowns, and similar expressions are also ways of expressing to the person that you understand and approve or disapprove. It is not necessary to say anything, just show the appropriate facial expression to get the person to continue talking.
- Subverbals such as "uh huh" or another similar form of subverbal humming sound in our culture communicates understanding.
- The open accepting posture discussed earlier conveys interest and sympathy.

If used appropriately, these techniques will aid in the communication process and facilitate listening. If you are acknowledging the receipt of information and asking questions of clarification, you become an active participant in the listening process. As a participant, you contribute as well as receive by confirming the information that is given. This interchange is essential to effective listening.

Problem Identification and Analysis Stage

Once the student has had the opportunity to explain his or her perception of the problem, what he or she believes to be the cause, and how he or she plans to cope with it, and you understand and believe you have a fairly accurate picture, you can then begin to analyze the elements of the problem. In this stage you will be helping the student direct attention to specific elements of the problem. The basic techniques used are questioning and sharing of personal experiences.

There are four steps to be accomplished in this problem identification and analysis stage:

1. Restate the problem as you understand it.
2. Analyze the problem to determine if the student's perception is accurate.
3. Develop options to managing or resolving the problem.
4. Determine student's expectations for the ideal and the realistic resolution to the problem.

First, you should reiterate or review the problem as you view it with the student. Establish your perception of the problem, confirming with the student the three basic elements of the cause, the perception of the problem as the student sees it, and how the student is currently coping with it. You are trying to confirm that you are talking about the same problem and that you understand.

Second, you analyze the problem to determine whether the student's perception is accurate. This should be done through a series of questions and confrontations.

Through questioning and answering you attempt to have the person acknowledge realities that may be in conflict with the person's perception of the event. Never assume that you know more about the problem than the student does. You do have a base of personal experiences on which to draw, and it may be appropriate to point out that what the student is experiencing is not abnormal and that many people have expressed similar problems.

Be careful, however, when expressing views about comparable problems that you do not minimize the student's problem. An example is students who receive poor grades on their papers. The students may feel that their professors have always had bad feelings toward them, so the students may try to shift the responsibility for poor performance to the professor. Questions you might appropriately ask would be, "What makes you believe the professor picked on you specifically? Have you spoken with the professor about the situation? Do you personally feel that this is the best example of your work? Do you feel that the paper could have been better than it was? Have you had an opportunity to see anyone else's paper? Are you certain that no one else has received a similar grade for a similar performance?"

Use confrontation to point out inconsistencies in what the student has said. Such statements as "On the one hand you have said . . . , but on the other hand you have also said . . ." are attempts to establish a consistent line of reasoning. Such comments help students gain a clearer perspective on the way they are viewing the problem. You have the advantage in that you have some distance from the problem and can be more objective. When students become emotionally involved in a problem, they can lose perspective and not always realize the inconsistencies in their reasoning. In the example of students who receive poor grades on a paper, you may have inquired earlier how such students had previously performed and found that they had done well. You may suggest the conflict in logic as follows: "You have done well on all your past examinations and papers, yet you say that the professor is out to get you. Why is that? Does that seem consistent to you?"

In analyzing the problem, there are three possibilities: (1) the student may be relaying accurate information and is perceiving the problem correctly, (2) the student may be relating distorted information and has a distorted perception of the problem, and (3) the student may have related accurate information but may have misperceived the problem.

Once you help the student analyze the problem, the next step is to develop options for managing or resolving the problem and to explore consequences of these options. In analyzing options, there are five elements to establish.

- Does the student have any control over what is happening? Often he or she does not. A good case in point might be the student who is experiencing frustration and anxiety because of financial problems created by the late arrival of a financial aid check. The student has little control over the cause of the problem. However, he or she may have alternatives that you could explore.
- Is any action on the part of the student necessary or indicated? Sometimes the best course of action is to do nothing. This is always an alternative.
- If some action could be taken to help the situation, what types of action are possible? If a student experiences financial problems because of not receiving a financial aid check, other courses of action might include a part-time job, a loan from another source, or an extension on payment the student needs to make.
- What are the resources the student can bring to bear on the situation?
- What are the consequences of the alternative actions proposed? What is the worst that could happen, the best that could happen, and the probability of each?

When discussing options with the student, you may make suggestions, but most suggestions and alternatives should be analyzed by the student. Do not fall into the trap of trying to answer the questions, "What do you think I should do?" or "What would you do if you were me?" The student is asking for your advice and for you to make a decision. This is usually inappropriate. Your response should be, "The question is what do you think you should do, not what I think you should do." Appropriate questions are, "Now that we are at this point, what do you believe you can do about the situation? What alternatives do you see available? What resources do you have to deal with it?" Suggestions that you might make could be derived from your experience within the institution. Such suggestions as, "Have you considered trying to get an emergency student loan from the Dean of Students Office?" Or, "I know there are part-time jobs available in the cafeteria; have you considered working there?"

The last step in the problem identification and analysis stage is to determine with the student what he or she believes to be the ideal outcome and whether this outcome is realistic. Specifically, what would it take to achieve the ideal resolution? Because what is ideal is not always realistic, it is also important to establish the likelihood of the desired outcome. Does the student have the resources to achieve it? Is it actually within the realm of probability?

Counseling Tips

1. Develop the skills of empathy, acceptance, attending behavior, and reflection.
2. Be confident in your ability.
3. Learn to listen to what the person is actually saying.
4. Never take notes.
5. Make the person feel comfortable.
6. Learn to ask open-ended questions.
7. Learn to give feedback responses.
8. Develop skills in confrontation and assertiveness.
9. Care about the person with whom you are talking.
10. Share personal experiences when appropriate.
11. Be authentic and sincere about your emotions and express them to the student.
12. Do not act shocked or upset.
13. Observe the person's body language and learn to be a good observer.
14. Keep confidences.
15. Do not make decisions for the individual.
16. Show acceptance of the individual.
17. Do not give advice except when called upon to do so.
18. Help the student to understand that feelings are normal.
19. Acknowledge responses that the student makes, such as crying.
20. Keep in mind that counseling is not a substitute for discipline.
21. Help students develop responses to assist them in dealing effectively with their emotions.
22. Apply these goals to most counseling situations: (a) help the student learn and grow from the experience; (b) assist the student in developing positive coping mechanisms; and (c) return the student to a state of previous emotional stability or improved emotional stability.

Resolution Stage

In the resolution stage, you want to have students reiterate the alternatives, to plan how they intend to implement action if necessary, and to develop a time-frame in which the action will be initiated. You confirm with students the action that will take place. When students leave your room, they should feel that several alternatives are available and that they have a definite course of action. This is the ideal situation. Sometimes it will not be possible to reach this desired end. Students you counsel should feel that they have worked through their own problem with your help. Make sure that students understand that you have a continued interest in what happens. Invite the students back to talk with you after they have taken the action proposed. What you wish to do is establish a foundation for the follow-up stage.

Follow-Up Stage

Use the follow-up stage as a check to ensure that students attempt to implement the course of action they identified during counseling sessions. Confirm with students again that you care and have a continued interest. This follow-up should be informal and might be accomplished by stopping by the students' rooms. However, you are the one who should make the effort. That may mean asking students to have dinner with you or making a point to ask them to stop by your room for a few minutes.

The follow-up need only be a one-time encounter for most situations. For some students who are having prolonged difficulties, it may be necessary to continue these follow-ups. This applies particularly to people who are under severe emotional strain, such as might occur when students break up with boyfriends or girlfriends they have been dating for a long time. Your continued support and interest will be helpful. Be careful, however, not to reinforce that depression or sorrow. If students find that they get attention for depression, it may reinforce the behavior. If enough people reinforce negative emotional states, students may become more depressed.

Many of the emotional problems that students undergo simply take time for them to work out. If you observe in your follow-up that a student is not coping with the problem effectively and that it is impairing his or her ability to function, you should initiate a counseling discussion with the student for purposes of making a referral to a professional counselor or professional staff person. Professional counselors or therapists should be able to give students some additional help in coping with their situations.

Related Counseling Issues

RAs occasionally have difficulty responding to students' crying. With men, the emotion is viewed as unmasculine, because our society tells men that they must withhold these emotions. Society permits women to express emotion through crying more openly and freely. If a student begins to cry when explaining a problem, do not be embarrassed or ignore what is obvious to both of you. Offer the student a tissue and some consoling words to confirm that this expression of emotion is acceptable and is nothing about which to be embarrassed. Crying is a natural emotion for many people and can be a healthy way of relieving the tension and anxiety of a difficult situation.

Listen carefully to what a person says. If you listen, you will find that most people tell you exactly what is troubling them. It is usually not necessary to look for hidden meanings. This, after all, is not the real reason that the person came to talk with you. Being a good listener and a sympathetic friend as an RA are the key elements of helping.

Learn to empathize with the student. Empathy is an important medium of support. It not only helps you understand what the person is experiencing, but confirms for the student your concern. Many counseling tips simply involve learning to empathize with other people.

Be confident in your ability to work with the student. You were selected to be an RA because of your skills in working with people and with groups.

Do not evaluate how well you are liked on the floor by how many people come to you with personal problems. The occasion to help a student with a personal problem may arise only a few times within your living unit in an academic year. It is important that when it does arise, you are trained and confident in your ability to handle the situation.

Remember that most problems students experience are normal, everyday difficulties related to depression, fear, anxiety, stress, lack of self-confidence, interpersonal relationships, and rejection. Each of these could be a crisis for an individual. People learn and grow from solving crises in their lives, and the ability to solve and handle one's crises helps one to handle future problems. These crises represent development and growth in the individual.

Be aware of your feelings about a student you counsel. Hostility toward the person, recent problems you have had with him or her, or stereotypes you have about the individual will color your perception of what the individual tells you. Try to erase these images and listen to the student. This will help enable you to see the picture that the student is painting for you.

Helping a Student Seek Professional Counseling

A referral to professional counseling should be made when it becomes apparent that the student is experiencing a severe emotional problem with which the student cannot cope. Behavior that you observe, that is reported to you by another person, or that the student describes may indicate such a referral is required.

Your goal in working with a student who has apparent need for professional guidance or who is experiencing an emotional crisis with which you cannot assist is to have the student agree to see a professional counselor and actually keep the counseling appointment. Many students are reluctant to seek professional assistance for fear that they may be viewed as "mentally ill." Although this label serves no purpose within the context of a helping relationship, it may be one of the greatest barriers you will need to overcome in having the student seek professional counseling.

There are three steps to making a referral for professional counseling: (1) recognizing the signs that particular students need referral, (2) helping the student recognize and accept the need for professional counseling, and (3) making the referral.

Recognizing the Signs for Referral

As noted earlier in this chapter, students are able to resolve most of the difficulties they experience with the assistance of a friend or with some help from you. There will be, however, some students who need professional help with their problems. It can be particularly difficult within the college environment to identify these students, because the college environment naturally lends itself to the acceptance of behavior that in another environment would be out of the ordinary. Students are experiencing conflicts and crises in both their identity and their values. Some of the common signs of emotional problems, such as erratic sleep patterns and eating habits, are difficult to interpret within the college environment. Following are some of the signs people use to signal a need for assistance. This list is not meant to be definitive or the only criteria on which to base a decision to make a referral. The behavior listed is intended solely to assist you in developing a common sense approach to identifying signals for help in the unique environment of the college residence hall.

- *Poor emotional control* can be exhibited in different forms. Open hostility and belligerence toward people for no apparent reason, exaggerated outbursts of emotion disproportionate to the event, and uncontrolled crying or laughter at unexplained, inappropriate times are some common signs of poor emotional control. The repeated or prolonged occurrence of these incidents over a several-day period may signal the need for help. This is especially true when the behavior deviates radically from the person's normal personality or is tangential to or follows a difficult emotional time—such as the loss of a parent or rejection by another significant person.
- *Excessive moodiness* or worry is another sign the person may be experiencing a problem. Anxiety, stress, and depression are normal outlets in a person's emotional cycle. A person who is anxious and feels under stress during final exam time may be expressing a very normal emotion. It is natural to worry occasionally. Extreme cases are people who spend an inordinate amount of time worrying about very trivial or insignificant matters, such as whether there will be enough forks in the cafeteria line. Preoccupation with or unnatural attention to detail is often a sign that the person needs assistance.

- *Sleeping and eating habits that change dramatically* are also a sign that the person is not coping well with some problem. A student who suddenly begins sleeping 18 hours a day and missing classes is probably experiencing some difficulty. The opposite is also true. The student who develops insomnia and begins taking catnaps during class or at other times also may be experiencing a problem. Eating can be another sign—either excessive or continual eating or abstaining from food for prolonged periods of time. Some erratic behavior may occur naturally. The student who has been studying or partying for three days may need to get some additional rest. The person who is crash-dieting may not eat for several days. It is important for you to recognize this behavior within the context of the surrounding situation and in relation to the individual's normal patterns.
- *An unnatural preoccupation with personal health* may be a sign of needing help. The person who constantly complains about the most minor ailment and continually seeks pills and medical advice from other residents may have emotional, rather than physical, problems.
- *People who express a universal mistrust or paranoia about others* may need help. This is a form of insecurity in which people claim that others are continually talking about them or are plotting against them, or similar unsubstantiated claims. These people need help.
- *Persistent and continued depression*—for more than one week—is generally not normal. This could be serious if the person stops talking about the future and begins viewing life as holding only more of the same joyless existence. A student reaching this state of depression is in serious need of attention and is possibly suicidal.
- *Students who talk openly about suicide* are signaling a need for professional help. Such discussions are to be taken seriously and are a call for help and support.

Questions to ask yourself:
- Does the behavior that the student exhibits seem out of the ordinary?
- Do you believe you can deal with the particular problem, or do you believe it is beyond your skills at this time?
- Is student's behavior getting worse, less frequent, or better?
- Does the behavior place anyone, including the person in question, in a life-threatening situation?

Use these questions to help analyze a referral situation. If the answer to any of these questions indicates that the student needs help, make the referral. Always include your residence hall director in the information you have about the student and his or her behavior. Share with the residence hall director your perceptions and evaluation and gain the director's assistance in helping you to work with the student. Remember, the psychological health of students and their active progress toward growing and accomplishing both academic and personal goals are the main purpose for which both you and your hall director are working.

Helping Students Recognize and Accept Professional Counseling

Make two facts clear to a student in making the referral. First, the student needs to understand that seeking assistance from a professional counselor is not an indication of mental illness. To overcome the student's reluctance to see a professional counselor, you may need to reassure him or her that all counseling records are confidential and protected by federal law. The institution will not remove the student from school, nor will it record on any of the student's transcripts that he or she has seen a counselor. A common fear is that a decision to seek help will become public and that the student will subsequently be viewed as unstable. It is a breach of professional ethics for a counselor to discuss a student's problem with anyone other than another professional counselor, unless the student seems likely to harm himself or herself or others.

The second fact the student must accept is that he or she needs assistance. If you can help alleviate the stigma of seeing a counselor by communicating the first fact well, you will have a better chance of getting the student to acknowledge need of professional assistance.

Listen to the student with interest and empathy. Do not encourage the person if he or she talks of bizarre or strange events that are taking place or bizarre actions that he or she may like to carry out. Your goal in listening is to determine a frame of reference from which to help the student reach a decision about seeking additional help.

Specifically, question the student about the behavior that he or she has exhibited. Inquire as to whether he or she feels satisfied with what is taking place and if it could be better. Never argue with the person or in any way try to convince the person that your perception of reality is correct and his or her perception is not. Confront the student only with logic and understanding.

You are not attempting to diagnose the cause of the problem but trying to help the student reach a decision about seeking further help. The same techniques of confrontation, open-ended questions, and questions related to the student's goals are appropriate. Reiterate the behavior the student exhibited and ask how he or she feels about the behavior. During this questioning, you attempt to have the student acknowledge a willingness to seek additional help.

If you believe that professional counseling help for a student is needed, talk over this perception with your hall director. In most situations, your hall director should be involved, if only by confirming the institutional referral procedure or suggesting a particular counselor to whom you may make the referral.

Making the Referral

Once the student has accepted the idea of seeing a professional counselor, have the student state the specific action he or she will take. In most situations it is the student's responsibility to make contact with the counselor. There may be some occasions in which you assist the student by literally accompanying the student to the counseling center, but for the most part you want the student to take the necessary steps in making the appointment and going to the counseling center.

One technique to confirm the agreed-upon behavior of seeing a counselor is to have the student state the specific behavior he or she will accomplish and the time-frame during which he or she will accomplish it. For example, "I will call Dr. Smith for an appointment to discuss my problem tomorrow morning, and I will attend the counseling session we agree upon." Have the student repeat this in exact terms. This becomes a kind of verbal commitment or bond between you and the student.

You will need to follow up with the student to ensure that he or she has kept the commitment. If he or she has not, the follow-up reinforces this verbal bond and may prompt the agreed-upon action. Sometimes this follow-up offers the student the needed opportunity to share with you the events of the counseling session. You can supply some feedback to the student and simply listen to what the student has to say about the counseling session.

Contact with the counselor, once the referral has been made, is generally not a good idea unless the counselor asks you for your help or feedback about the student's behavior. What transpires between the student and the counselor should remain limited to them, unless the student chooses to share the information with you.

Advising

Advising is the act of giving information and suggesting a specific course of action for an individual to take. There are times when you, as a resident assistant, will do just this. Advising should be infrequent, but there are some obvious times it is necessary.

It is appropriate for you, as a resident assistant, to advise someone when he or she comes to you with a request for specific information. An example might be when a student asks you where to get financial assistance. You can advise the student of any emergency loan programs the university has, job opportunities, and financial aid. You can share other types of information, such as not to take an overload of academic hours in the spring quarter when there are many activities. Other areas in which you might advise are directly related to personal safety, such as not walking alone at night in dimly lit areas or not keeping large sums of money in the room. These are appropriate areas in which advice is worthwhile.

As a general rule, advise only when the student requests specific information, when the person's safety or security is at stake, when the issue is of no emotional consequence, or when the results of your advice cannot injure or harm the individual. The following general rules about giving advice may help you analyze when it is appropriate and how to give it when asked:

- Do not give advice to people who do not seek it or who do not want it. Often your interjection of "What I would do if I were you . . ." is not at all welcome. It is better to wait until your opinion is asked and then to give it only if it is appropriate.
- If a person does ask for advice and it is appropriate to give it, do so in confidence. This allows the person to disagree and does not make the person feel as if he or she is following directions.
- Never give advice using such words as *don't* and *shouldn't*.
- Present advice as suggestions. Use phrases such as, "Have you ever thought about trying . . ." or "You might try. . . ."
- Use personal experiences in making suggestions. This provides the listener with a base for your authority in making the suggestions, and it reveals some personal information about you so the conversation is less one-sided.
- If you choose to give advice, give it cautiously and sparingly. Remember, no one likes to be told what to do or how to do it.

It is interesting to note that people are always ready to give advice, yet few people are willing to accept it. Even though many people solicit advice and suggestions, people seldom put them to use.

Chapter 8
Interpersonal Communication

Most of your skills in working with students stem from effective communications. Whether this communication takes place in a counseling framework or in a disciplinary encounter, it is based on your ability to verbally express yourself in a way that accurately transmits your thoughts to another person. Communication is a process by which ideas, concepts, thoughts, emotions, and feelings are shared with another person through the use of verbal and nonverbal symbols. The primary function of communication is to control one's environment to realize physical, emotional, economic, or social rewards. This definition does not imply that communication is exclusively for self-interests. Counseling, for example, is done for the purpose of helping others.

Three Levels of Communication

These are three levels of communication: cultural, sociological, and interpersonal. Most communication is noninterpersonal. People most often communicate either at a "cultural" level or a "sociological" level. Cultural communication refers to forms of communication defined by our culture, such as formal greetings at initial meetings, talk at parties with strangers, and ceremonies. Our culture provides a standardized or formalized way of communication at these functions. By living in this culture, you internalize these communication patterns. Topics of conversation with a person you do not know usually starts at the cultural level with things you share in common with others: Weather and sports are topics that might be discussed at this level.

Communication at the sociological level is communication defined by a person's membership in a particular social group. Social groups are defined by characteristics such as socioeconomic status, race, education, geographical region, religion, and the interaction of these and other factors. These social factors are combined to make up subcultural groups. Subcultural groups have accepted patterns of communication behavior just like those at the cultural level. Communication at this level is a function of increased knowledge about the beliefs, attitudes, and behaviors of the person with whom you are communicating. Cultural-level communication and sociological-level communication are two forms of noninterpersonal communication that demonstrate people's varying abilities to predict and understand the communicative exchange with another person. If the only knowledge you have about a person is on a cultural level, then your ability to predict that person's behaviors, attitudes, and beliefs for the purpose of sharing common experiences through the symbols of language is lessened. On the other hand, if you share with that person membership in a particular subcultural group, you increase your ability to predict the extent to which you can share your thoughts and ideas through mutually recognized symbols based on commonly shared experiences.

The third level of communication is interpersonal communication. In actuality, very little communication falls into this category. It is the most intimate level of communication, in which predictions in the communicative process are based on knowledge of a particular individual's learning experiences and commonly shared understandings. You can distinguish noninterpersonal communication from interpersonal communication on the basis of whether the communication is based on your understanding (or prediction of the person's verbal response) of the other person on a general group level or on an individual psychological level.

Interpersonal communication is the act of sharing personal, intimate, and valued experiences with another person. It differs from interpersonal relationships, in that interpersonal communication is the process by which one person provides personal information to the other. An interpersonal relationship, however, involves both individuals exchanging information on a personal level. An interpersonal relationship is characterized by shared trust and intimacy. It fulfills an emotional need to be close to other people and serves to help you define yourself, explore interests, and receive feedback from a person with whom you share trust and closeness. Some people argue that all forms of communication should attempt to move to the interpersonal level; others suggest interpersonal communication as an alternative form of communication and not as a goal in itself. The latter view is more realistic. Interpersonal communication is not required for successfully communicating in all interactions with people.

Establishing Interpersonal Communication and Relationships

Interpersonal communication is most gratifying when it is part of an interpersonal relationship. It is rare to move into interpersonal communication with a person whom you have just met. Exceptions might be going to a psychologist to talk about a problem or a dating relationship characterized mutual attraction when both parties engage in learning about the other. Although the establishment of an interpersonal relationship is not necessarily a prerequisite to interpersonal communication, it is the most appropriate and satisfying vehicle for the sharing this information.

The residence hall is an environment that lends itself to the establishment of interpersonal relationships. As students spend more and more time sharing the experience of living together, attending classes together, and participating in the academic and social events that occur throughout the year, the students increase trust in one another and gradually move to a level of sharing on an interpersonal level. The more interaction students have with one another, the more information they acquire about each other and the better they understand one another's behavior.

Encouraging Interpersonal Relationships

Interpersonal relationships in a residence hall—given shared space, frequency of contacts, and similar experience—are stimulated during periods of personal crises. When students experience crises with parents, dating relationship, or classes they are most likely to seek someone that they trust and with whom they can share their feelings. When presented with a crisis, people feel vulnerable and need the support of others. Although the RA is sometimes consulted because of his or her position and because of positive past contacts, most often students seek the counsel of other students with whom they share mutually rewarding relationships. Other students often lend support and shared experiences, providing comfort and acceptance to the student in crisis.

Interpersonal deprivation is another crisis that stimulates interpersonal communication. People have an optimum number of stable friendships they need to maintain in order to feel comfortable. When a person enters a new environment, such as moving into a residence hall for the first time, this transition usually alters the number of stable relationships, and the person seeks to reestablish this optimum level by increasing interpersonal communication to establish new friendships.

Consistent with the observation that people have an optimum level of friendships, it is interesting to note how students associate in small groups of five to six students who tend to spend the greatest amount of time together. One might characterize the typical residence hall living unit as a group of groups. New students transferring into the unit midway through the academic year often find it difficult to enter into these small groups because of the level of stable relationships maintained by the group. These groups are generally based on factors mentioned earlier (time, shared space, frequency, proximity of rooms, and so on). The students become friends, support one another, share mutual experiences, and influence one another's beliefs and attitudes.

If the RA can win the confidence of one or more of the students in these groups, the RA can more easily win a similar relationship with other members of the group. One way to apply this information is to analyze your living unit in terms of these groups and target some of your energies into maintaining positive relationships with key individuals within each group.

Interpersonal Communication Skills

Although most interpersonal relationships come about naturally, you can make an interpersonal relationship happen. A direct approach, in which you approach people with whom you have limited contact and inform them that you wish to establish an interpersonal relationship, usually is not successful. Such behavior is viewed suspiciously, because it violates our cultural expectations of how relationships are formed. You can stimulate these relationships, however, by showing interest in other people, what they do, and what they say. People generally appreciate being asked for advice. This is a rewarding process, acknowledging that other people's opinions have value.

People tend to remain in relationships they find rewarding. If the relationship is not rewarding, people leave the relationship. Thus, the stimulation and maintenance of a relationship is based on giving and receiving rewards through communication. These rewards take various forms, depending on your knowledge of the individual. Many of these rewards are intangible. The acknowledgment that you are in some way important, and that this person enjoys your company may be the total sum of the reward expected or needed in maintaining the relationship.

In sum, interpersonal relationships and thus interpersonal communication are most likely to occur when the quality of your relationship with another person is mutually rewarding. The relationship is sustained through the period of time in which it is mutually satisfying and serves a common need. Relationships dissolve or are modified when they cease to become rewarding.

Empathy

The ability to empathize with another individual is closely associated with interpersonal communication. Empathy takes place when two people share in the same sensory experience at an emotional level. Empathy requires the ability to attune yourself to the sensory and verbal cues expressed by another person to the extent that you experience someone else's feelings as your own. You do this by projecting yourself into the experience of the other person. The ability to empathize is based on the ability to understand and accurately read cues individuals give about their internal state. Verbal symbols and expressions of emotions are cues to interpret how a person is experiencing a particular internal issue. Of equal importance are nonverbal cues. Nonverbal cues such as eye movement, body language, voice inflection, and key word phraseology provide a deeper understanding of another person's communication.

By accurately reading a person's body language, a trained therapist can determine whether the person is suppressing information, is afraid, is sad, embarrassed, or happy. Having this information aids in interpreting and responding accurately to the experience of another person. The more information one has about a person, the more accurate the understanding of the experience being communicated.

There are two steps to empathizing. First, you must be able to predict and understand the motives and attitudes of the other person. The prediction is based on understanding the individual, and what rewards, behaviors, and experiences this person has had and finds satisfying.

The second step is learning to communicate what your understanding of what the person is saying. This feedback has the quality of reaffirming what you are hearing and seeing. Not only must this communication provide understanding, it also must be rewarding. The reward comes from knowledge that the other person understands and shares those feelings. This means that if the person is relating a sad, stressful situation, the person empathizing with that experience may feel a similar emotional state. He or she also may show depression, cry, or get angry. It is at this psychophysiological level that the deepest empathy takes place.

Interpersonal Relationships and the RA

As an RA you may find that some of the relationships you have with students in your living unit are not of the quality you would like. It is difficult for RAs to establish interpersonal relationships with students with whom they live. Students often feel that to get close to the RA is a form of seeking favoritism. Other students may discourage this behavior by teasing the student who is attempting to establish a close relationship with his or her RA. If you do not establish these close relationships in your living unit, the problem may not be with you but with your position.

One of the common responses to this void in close personal friendships RAs sometimes feel in their living unit is that they seek these relationships among the other RAs on the staff. This has some good and some bad aspects. On the positive side, RAs receive support from other RAs and may develop close personal friendships that are maintained beyond college. The negative aspect is that if all of the RAs spend all of their time together, students may view them as an exclusive clique. In some cases this can develop into a "we–them" mentality about working with students in the hall that lessens students' willingness to approach RAs for assistance.

Often RAs become so consumed with being an RA that they neglect their own needs for recreation and escape. You should develop friendships in your living unit and among the RAs, but also outside of the residence hall. These friendships may help you maintain some objectivity on what it is that you are doing and can provide a much needed retreat for you from the subtle pressures of living, eating, and sleeping residence hall work.

Part Three

Confrontation and Crisis Management

Chapter 9

Behavior Problems, Confrontation, and Counseling

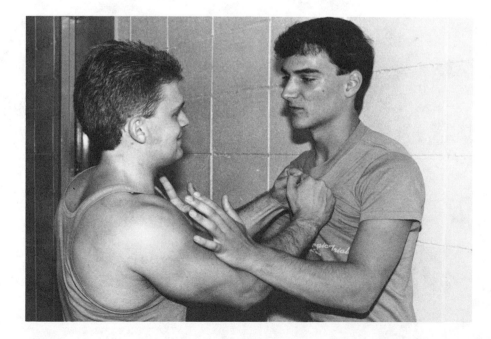

Counseling is never an excuse for discipline, yet the way you approach a disciplinary situation can still be within the framework of a counseling model. Some students have a need to challenge college policies by breaking rules or infringing upon the rights of others. As an RA, you have an obligation to the institution and to other students in your living unit to enforce the policies that the college community has agreed upon to guide its interaction. It may not always seem that a particular policy you are enforcing is helping students adjust to the responsibilities of college. Experience has shown that learning to interact within a residence hall environment aids students in both accepting accountability for their actions and in developing respect for rights of others.

Types of University Policies

Historically universities had a caretaker, or *in loco parentis* (in lieu of parents), philosophy about the relationship between students and the institution. Educators perceived their responsibility to students as one of making rules and regulations similar to those that parents may institute when educating their children. The federal courts agreed with this educational philosophy (*Gott* vs. *Berea College,* 1913) noting specifically that a duty of the college was to act in place of the parents while students were away from home.

Some institutions still retain in *loco parentis*-based rules and regulations; however, the majority of colleges have abandoned most of these in favor of policies based on a community standard of behavior in five major areas: (1) regulations related to the health, safety, and well-being of the college community; (2) landlord–lessee policies; (3) federal, state, and local laws: (4) regulations designed specifically for the unique situations provided by a small group living situation within a residence hall; and (5) regulations related to the academic mission of the institution.

Health and Safety Regulations

A college has a responsibility to protect the health, safety, and well-being of students, faculty, and staff. This is a special obligation that must be ensured for the institution to fulfill its educational mission. Policies in this area relate to security within individual buildings, possession of dangerous weapons on campus, state health codes, state fire regulations, and similar security or safety precautions. The rationale behind the prohibition against hot plates in student rooms, as one example, is probably determined by fire code regulations, and the policy prohibiting animals in the hall is probably determined by health code regulations.

Most residence halls have operational policies that require outer doors to be secured at a certain time each evening, that visitors of the opposite sex be escorted by a resident of the building, and that prohibit students from making duplicate keys for their rooms or exterior doors. These policies concern the security of people in the building. In the past few years, a number of colleges and universities have reported rapes occurring within the residence halls themselves.

Thefts of private and college property are not uncommon in residence halls where there is little or no security. It is simple to see why institutions must enforce these regulations.

Landlord–Lessee Regulations

The second category of regulations are landlord–lessee regulations. These are provisions of the contractual relationship between the student and the institution that a student signs when he or she requests a room. Such regulations as not permitting students to keep animals in the residence hall may be both a health regulation and a contractual obligation that the student assumes when entering the residence hall. Other landlord–lessee policies include students paying for room damages or damage to public areas, check-in and check-out procedures, contract periods of the room (such as requiring that the room be vacated during academic vacation periods), and the right of the institution to inspect rooms for the purpose of enforcing health and safety regulations. Most policies in the landlord–lessee relationship may be considered extradisciplinary, meaning that institutions have chosen to regard them not as disciplinary violations, but as contractual violations that may carry the imposition of a fine. Noncompliance with the regulations could mean termination of the contract or a similar penalty.

Federal, State, and Local Laws

Educational institutions generally accept responsibility for enforcing federal, state, and municipal laws through various means and with various degrees of dedication. Major crimes such as theft, battery, possession of dangerous drugs, extortion, and similar violations are usually enforced by institutions.

State universities have an obligation to reflect the standards of the citizenry of the state, the interests of the alumni, and the interests of the faculty, as well as the needs of the students. All of these groups play a part in the total university. The state has an interest in the university because of the funding it provides and because of the type of education that the people of the state want to see provided. The alumni have an interest in the university because its reputation reflects directly on the public's view of the degrees that the alumni received there. The faculty have an interest in the university because their professional careers are influenced by the reputation of the institution. And, of course, students have an interest in the university, in that it is the education at that institution that they are purchasing and the reputation of the institution that their degrees will represent. Most state and private institutions declare that these and similar behaviors are in opposition to the best interests of the institution and the students.

Laws regulating the use of both alcohol and marijuana have undergone dramatic changes. The drinking age has been lowered in many states to 18 and raised again to 21. Marijuana has become a socially acceptable drug among some groups.

Institutions are placed in a paradoxical situation. On the one hand, they do not want to place the RA in an enforcement role within the residence hall; on the other hand, they wish to provide an environment that is educationally sound and that reflects the basic educational interests of all members of the university community. This is a difficult task. Some college administrators believe that the strict enforcement of alcohol and marijuana regulations provides the type of living environment that is most conducive to the educational goals of students. The reasons given for the enforcement of these regulations are:

1. The institution must comply with its obligation to the state, the alumni, the faculty, and future student generations.
2. Not to enforce these policies gives tacit approval for the violation of institutional policy and the law.
3. Failure to enforce policies related to drug use encourages such behavior and promotes an environment that is not conducive to the educational interests of the institution and the students as a whole.
4. The university must stand for certain values both in theory and application.
5. Nonenforcement of laws related to marijuana and other drugs encourages the introduction of more dangerous behavior connected with drug trafficking and the influx of undesirable elements into the campus community.

Occasionally administrators take an opposing philosophy. They assert that it is not the institution's duty to monitor an individual student's behavior and that there are more important concerns of the institution than victimless crimes such as the use of marijuana or alcohol. These administrators argue that:

1. Marijuana and alcohol are socially acceptable drugs to many college students.
2. The purpose of the RA is counseling and not the enforcement of state law.
3. RAs are not trained as police agents; therefore, they should not involve themselves with the identification of and enforcement of law violations, except to protect the immediate well-being, safety, and security of residents in the unit.
4. The use of alcohol or marijuana is a victimless crime in which no one suffers.
5. The use of these substances is a personal choice that a student must make independently.
6. The university cannot enforce such rules and regulations, because it does not hold police power or have the technical or legal capability of enforcing such policies.
7. Because students are adults, it is the duty of police agents to enforce such laws as they would for any other adult members living within the community at large.

Small-Group Living Regulations

The fourth area in which institutions make regulations is in small-group living (that is, residence halls, cooperatives, fraternities, and sororities). This unique style of living requires regulations to help maintain an environment consistent with the mission of the institution. Policies regulating quiet hours, conduct in the hallways, noise, and similar environmental concerns are designed to enable all students to benefit from the environment without infringing upon the rights of other students. This is the area in which most of an RA's time is spent—helping people cooperate and learning to live together. Some students believe that they have a right to express themselves, even to the point of infringing upon others' rights. This does not necessarily mean that the RA must personally confront each violation. Other students live there too. RAs are not employed to fight all the battles. Students should ask offending students directly to comply with some reasonable noise or conduct level. Only when this course of action has failed should the responsibility fall to the RA.

Academic Regulations

The last area in which universities make rules and regulations concerns the educational mission of the institution. Academic rules and regulations seldom come under the purview of the RA. They include academic dishonesty, cheating, plagiarism, falsification of information, disregarding lawful directions of college officials, or failure to comply with rules related to the process or function of the institution.

Goals of Disciplinary Counseling

The process by which the university community educates students who violate the community standards is through disciplinary counseling. The goals of disciplinary counseling are as follows:

1. To educate the student by explaining the reasons for the community standard
2. To bring the student's behavior into compliance with the community standard
3. To have the student maturely accept accountability for his or her behavior
4. To help clarify the student's values as they concern their behavior in question
5. To assist the student in making future choice that will enable him or her to assume later adult roles
6. To help the student consider in advance the consequences of his or her behavior
7. To determine with the student the reason for the misconduct

These seven goals provide a framework for the disciplinary encounter. Through a dialogue, using techniques similar to those used in counseling, the RA attempts to accomplish these goals.

Confrontation Skills

There is no set of exact rules to tell you how to respond to a particular disciplinary encounter. You can, however, develop skills in confrontation that will be of assistance to you in many of your personal interactions. RAs find the first few confrontations with students difficult. They gain self-confidence in their ability to handle these situations with experience. Few ever feel comfortable or enjoy the actual exchange.

One way to feel more comfortable is to develop your assertiveness. Assertive behavior is behavior that confirms individual rights in a nonthreatening, nondefensive manner. It is open, honest, direct, and nonaggressive, and it communicates a person's beliefs or opinions. Assertive behavior does not require other social skills such as compassion, empathy, or persuasion. It is most simply viewed as a statement of the individual's rights, beliefs, attitudes, feelings, opinions, and similar forms of personal expression.

Assertive communication is different from aggressive or passive communication. Aggressive responses attack the other person or in some way infringe on the other person's rights. Passive communication permits another person to take advantage of your rights. To be put-upon, to be compelled to do something through a sense of guilt or to be taken advantage of is to be passive. It is acceptable to let people take advantage of you if you are willing to accept the sacrifice of time or duty.

If somebody inconveniences you by asking you to perform a special favor, being assertive does not mean necessarily that you must refuse. It only means that if you feel that it will impose an inconvenience on you, to the extent that you do not wish to comply with the request, you state this and do not comply with the request. It indicates that you are in control of your own life and that you are not compelled to perform special services for individuals that unreasonably infringe on you.

Because you are an RA, there are certain duties that you are expected to perform; some may inconvenience you. The acceptance of these duties is not being passive. It is simply following through on the expectations of your position.

Assertive Confrontation

There are three assertive techniques that you should make part of your disciplinary counseling skills. The first is called the assertive confrontation (based on a model by Lange and Jakubowski, 1976). It follows a simple four-step pattern, as follows:

1. Describe the person's behavior in objective terms.
2. Describe how this behavior affects you or others within the unit.
3. Describe how you feel about the behavior.
4. Describe what you would like to see the person do to correct the behavior.

Some examples of this are as follows:

"John, your stereo is very loud. The noise is preventing people on the floor from studying. I feel the stereo is too loud, and I would like you to turn it down."

"John, I saw you put glue in the lock of another student's room. Unless it is cleaned out before it hardens, a locksmith will be called to repair the lock at your expense. I do not believe you have a right to damage university property or to inconvenience this other student. I would like you to clean out the lock and ensure that it is in working order. I will discuss this situation with the hall director for possible disciplinary action."

Commitment Confronted

Another form of assertive confrontation is the *commitment confronted technique.* It emerges when a student has made a commitment for a certain type of behavior and then does not comply with the commitment. This may follow a discussion that you had earlier with the student about his behavior. Examples of this confrontation would follow a very similar format, as follows: (1) statement of the behavior observed, (2) statement of the student's commitment, (3) presentation of contradiction, (4) statement of how you feel, (5) statement of behavior you would like to see take place, and (6) statement of steps you will take. An example of this form of confrontation would be as follows:

"John, I observed you smoking marijuana in the floor lounge. The last time this took place, you gave me your word that it would not happen again. I do not understand why you gave me your word if you did not intend to follow through. I am angry that I cannot trust you and accept you at your word. I feel disappointed that you are unable to comply with your commitment. I would like you to get the marijuana out of the residence hall. I intend to discuss this situation with the hall director and to refer you for disciplinary action."

These two forms of assertive confrontation can be useful in your exchanges with students. They can also be useful in other interpersonal exchanges in which you feel that your personal rights have been infringed upon.

Broken Record Technique

A third assertive technique is called the *broken record technique* (based on a model by Fensterheim and Baer, 1975). It is the simple assertion of your belief, opinion, or request. Your response to any remark is the same until the person complies with your request. Simply put, you repeat the same demand or request over and over and over in a broken-record type response. An example of this is as follows: (Paul is the RA. John is the student.)

The RA says, "John, I see that you have furniture in your room from the floor lounge. You know that this furniture should not be in your room. I would like you to take it back now, please."

John says: "I need it in my room for studying."

"Unfortunately, there is not enough furniture for everyone, and the lounge furniture is to be in the lounge. Would you please take it back now?"

"I am studying right now," John replies. "I will do it later."

The RA responds, "I understand. I would like you to take it back now, if you would, please."

"But the furniture makes my room look so much better."

The RA repeats, "Take it back now, please."

"I would really like to keep it."

"Take it back now, please."

The exchange shows that the RA is requesting over and over that the same action be taken. Eventually, John will probably comply with the request, or the two will reach a compromise in which John may take the furniture back after he has completed studying. One thing the RA could try is to offer to help John take it back. The goal, after all, is to get the furniture returned to the lounge and to make John aware that the furniture did not belong in his room. If the RA could accomplish this by offering to help John carry it, this might accomplish the same end.

Disciplinary Counseling Model

Students are more likely to respond cooperatively or to avoid a confrontation when they respect you and your position. It is difficult to confront people with their behavior and to refer them for disciplinary action. Unfortunately, it must be done if the residence hall environment and the rights of others are to be ensured. The approach you take to accomplish this is important.

The model used for a disciplinary encounter is similar to the one used for the helping-skills form of counseling discussed in the previous chapter. The major differences are in the dynamics of the disciplinary exchange and the student's perception of you. In most disciplinary encounters, there is a confrontation involving some alleged violation of regulations, and the student will probably view you as an adversary. Figure 9.1 illustrates the disciplinary counseling model. It has five steps: (1) collect the facts, (2) approach the student, (3) listen to the student, (4) take the necessary action, and (5) follow up.

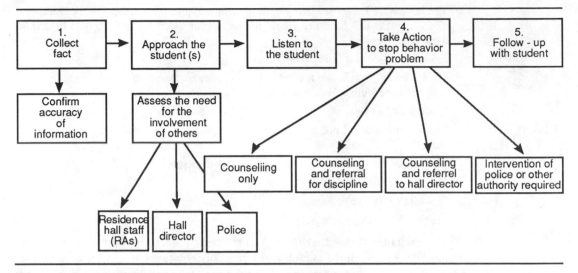

Figure 9.1. Disciplinary counseling model

Step 1: Collect the Facts

Before accusing anyone of violating university regulations, make sure your facts are accurate. Often a student who relates information about the behavior of another student will not want it known that he or she provided this information. There is an interesting attitude in our culture that it is somehow more honorable to protect people who have violated the law than it is to hold these people accountable. Terms such as "informer" and "stool pigeon" are labels attached to those who provide information about people who break the law.

Although some students will report other students and follow through with the charge, what is more often the case is that you will receive the information third-hand with the proviso that you not reveal your source. There are some circumstances in which you may wish to accept information under these conditions, but, in general, you should be reluctant. As a rule, when a student tells you he or she wishes to share some information with you with the understanding that you will not pass it on to anyone else, you should tell him or her that you cannot offer this guarantee. After all, he or she may tell you that his or her roommate just robbed a bank or is selling drugs out of their room. Should you be approached with the provision of the information secrets, tell the person that he or she will need to trust your judgment about whether this information will need to be passed on to someone else.

Even though a student has asked you not to tell the source of information, you can still talk with the student who allegedly violated the regulation. However, it means that the credibility of your facts will be in question. It also means that you will have insufficient information to make a referral for disciplinary action to a college official. Neither of these points preclude you from approaching the alleged violator with the information you do have. This person may be very open about the situation and admit his or her involvement. If the person does not, you have had the opportunity to discuss the behavior, a step that may have some positive benefit.

You may at this point like to read ahead to the section on How to Confront an Intoxicated Person. Note particularly the need to assess your own feelings about the person and the suggestions on when to confront a person about his or her behavior.

Step 2: Approach the Student

Approach is a better word for this action than *confront*. It is an issue of your perception. If you approach the student with the attitude that this will be a "confrontation," you develop a mindset that may be counterproductive.

One of the factors in a productive exchange is to engage the student in a meaningful dialogue concerning the alleged incident. If other people are present, the dialogue can become a group discussion or an audience debate. Neither of these multiperson interchanges is productive; it is a losing situation for both you and the student. If you cannot isolate the student and must approach him or her while others are present, deal only with terminating the offending behavior (such as yelling, playing the stereo loud, or damaging property). Do not attempt to go beyond this point until you can find some opportunity to engage the student in a one-to-one discussion about the behavior.

Having said this, take a look at what you can expect from students when you approach them with an alleged violation.

The Big Lie

One response students use is to claim that the event never took place, to deny that they were involved, and to challenge you to prove in some legalistic framework that they are responsible. This is the "big lie" response. The student is often aggressive, hostile, and somewhat threatening. You can only relate the information you have and attempt to bring the issue to a level of common understanding. You may tell the student that you cannot resolve the situation at this point and that you will refer it to someone who can. This is probably the only course of action available to you.

When students use the "big lie," you may become aggravated. Usually there is sufficient information to catch the students in their lie. Unfortunately, you will not have the opportunity to resolve the situation and will need to refer the student for discipline.

Misdirection

Students sometimes attempt to change the subject or minimize the consequences of their actions. This response is used to divert attention from the issue at hand. Students may try to lead you into a discussion about the general correctness or incorrectness of a particular institutional policy. Keep the discussion on track. Bring students back to the issue if they react philosophically.

Third-Degree Questioning

A version of the big lie is the third-degree questioning. In this response, the student challenges the information you received and your observations. Such questions as "How do you know that?" or "What makes you believe that?" or "Can you prove that?" are raised. Some students want to examine every element of the information and to place you on the defensive by demanding that you explain to them in detail every aspect. They will attempt to refute and argue with you over every minor point. Do not argue over "nit-picky" details that are probably irrelevant to what took place. You are only trying to determine the violator's view of what actually occurred.

The Hostility Response

You can expect personal hostility from some students you approach. Students may become hostile and challenge your motives for questioning their behavior. They may suggest that you have singled them out because of some personal hatred. This defense technique is intended to change the subject and to delay the issue at hand. Do not feel that you must justify your actions or your motives. Simply relate the behavior that you observed and question the person on why the behavior took place. It is enough to deny an accusation of personal dislike once, and it does little good to engage in a verbal exchange about past events or your perceptions of them.

Contrition

Admission of guilt and a true act of contrition are other techniques. Some students will openly confess their involvement in some type of negative behavior and tell you they are sorry that they caused any problem. Their goal here is that you should accept their true act of contrition and not make any further disciplinary referral. Although in minor situations, and based upon your perception of the individual, this might be appropriate, it can create a situation in which students may feel that all that is necessary after repeated offenses is to admit guilt and say they are sorry to evade accountability for their actions. Because students say they regret their actions does not necessarily mean that you should not make a referral. Admission of guilt is not the goal of disciplinary counseling.

Remember, it is the process that is educational. Part of this process is an examination of values and the decision making process which lead to the behavior. Sometimes the process of a disciplinary hearing—including waiting for the hearing—is one of the most educational experiences a student may have.

Shifting Guilt

Students who admit guilt sometimes plead with their RA not to make a referral to higher authorities. This is an attempt to make the RA accept some guilt for doing his or her job and making a disciplinary referral. Remember, you are not doing anything to such students. They have brought the referral on themselves.

If a student commits a violation serious enough to demand some type of disciplinary action, do not place yourself in the position of determining guilt or innocence or of giving dispensation to a person who has violated the regulations. It is important that students who attend your institution be treated fairly and consistently. Some of the realizations about the encounter can best be achieved through a session with a professional staffperson who will help the offending student examine the values that led him or her to make this inappropriate decision.

Step 3: Listen to the Student

Establish a meaningful dialogue with the student. This is as much a goal as it is a technique. You want to reach a point where the student is willing to discuss the situation with you. Given the circumstances—a disciplinary encounter— establishing a meaningful dialogue can be difficult. You can do this, however, if you approach the student as an equal, as an adult peer.

Students do not want to hear a lecture from you, nor do they want to be chastised or criticized. The approach you should use is the same approach you would use with a friend. You are not the students' parent and should not give them parental commands. The establishment of a meaningful dialogue means exactly that: a dialogue, an exchange of ideas with a give-and-take response.

You need to listen to the student's explanation of what took place. You use the same general listening techniques you learned in the earlier chapter on counseling. You want the student to tell you the truth about what actually took place. This may not be easy. Students may fear reprisal in the form of a disciplinary referral for the violation, or they might be afraid that you will lose respect for them. Defense mechanisms are common reactions. *Defense mechanisms* are attempts to explain behavior that cannot be excused in any other way. They are used by a person who feels threatened or insecure. Defense mechanisms help people protect their self-image or egos. Examples of defense mechanisms are repression, anxiety, departmentalization, compensation, rationalization, and projection. The latter two, rationalization and projection, are probably the most common defenses used by students in a disciplinary encounter.

Rationalization is the attempt to justify one's behavior with excuses that offer a more acceptable motive for the behavior. The person denies accountability for the action, contending that it was justified because of special circumstances. For example, the student who is discovered to have stolen a book from another student may say that he or she was only borrowing the book for a short time to prepare for a test.

Projection is another way a person may reject responsibility for his or her behavior. In projection, the person attempts to justify his or her behavior by attributing the same actions to everyone else. The all too-common excuse of "everyone else does it" is offered as justification for the behavior. Apparently, if everyone else is violating a particular policy, it must be acceptable. The truth is probably that a few other people do violate the policy, but when their actions come to the attention of the staff, the offenders are held accountable.

Your objective is to help students understand the faulty reasoning in offering these justifications. Willingness to accept responsibility is related to the student's maturity. As students' values mature and as they develop personal ethical standards of conduct, their willingness to accept responsibility for their actions increases. If this will mean that the student may be arrested, suspended from school, or subject to some removal of privilege or payment of fine, chances are less that the person will be willing to accept responsibility.

Your role is to help students better accept responsibility for their behavior. Your objective is to assist them in sorting through what took place and reach an understanding about their future behavior. You are the facilitator of the student's own review of the situation and an objective guide to help keep the student on a productive tract.

Step 4: Take Action

If it is clear that the student is in violation of a regulation of such a nature that it is necessary for you to make a disciplinary referral to a college official, inform the student of your decision. If you are not able to determine the facts of a situation and there is a discrepancy between what you believe to be true and what the student is willing to admit, make a disciplinary referral to resolve the disparity. It may not be necessary to make a referral for a first-time violation of a minor college regulation, but it is important that you discuss the violation with the offending student and inform him or her that such conduct is not acceptable and that continued violation could lead to disciplinary action.

A disciplinary referral is regarded as punishment by most students. Realistically, it is the method that colleges use to educate students about their behavior. True, the student might be placed in some probationary status or perhaps suspended from school for a period of time. These actions, however, are educational. They state to students that their conduct is not acceptable in the college community. When students do not achieve academically, they "flunk out" of school. Similarly, if students fail to abide by the regulations set by the college community to guide behavior, they have not fulfilled this aspect of their education.

By making a referral to the appropriate official at your institution, you are indicating that a particular student's conduct needs to be reviewed to determine if it is consistent with the expectations of the college community. If it is not, the college official, through whatever institutional process the school has adopted, will help the student bring his or her behavior within acceptable limits. If residence halls are to be part of the educational process and a student's conduct violates the reasonable standards agreed on to guide conduct within this small-group living situation, then there is every reason to believe that the student has failed this part of his or her education and should be held accountable.

Step 5: Follow Up

If you make a disciplinary referral, chances are that your relationship with the student involved will be strained. You have two choices: You can continue to perpetuate the animosity, or you can make an effort to discuss the difficulty in the hope of reaching some common understanding. The only acceptable choice is the latter. After all, you will still probably be living in the same unit, and it is better to get feelings like these out in the open and discuss them. The longer you wait to deal with the conflict, the more hostility will build up between the two of you.

Although it is easy to say that students should not take the referral as a personal affront, most students do. How you handle this followup can help appease the student's ego and help you remain above the immaturity and petty bickering that is likely to follow.

One of the more difficult aspects of a disciplinary referral is remaining objective. Your responsibilities are to bring alleged violations to the attention of the appropriate staff person, to assist students in understanding the reasons for referral, and to help students accept accountability for their behavior. This is where your involvement ends.

If students are found to be in violation of a regulation but very little action is taken, you should not feel betrayed. Students may believe they have beaten the system or beaten you. You may feel that you lost and the student won. If you let yourself get caught-up in this "win-lose" philosophy by becoming ego-involved in the outcome, you defeat the purpose of the educational process. Remember, it is the "process" that is educational.

Students returning from a disciplinary hearing usually need to reestablish themselves with their peer group in the living unit. They may allege that nothing happened to them, that they "beat" the system, or that in some other way they "won." There will probably be some attempt to minimize any action that was taken. You must maintain the confidentiality of any information you have about the hearing. This may be difficult, especially when you know that the student is lying about his or her case. You must remember that students have the right to disclose whatever facts about themselves they choose, and you do not have the right to disclose any such facts about them. Although you may feel that your credibility is at stake among your residents, in truth your credibility and personal integrity would be compromised more by sharing confidences and bringing yourself to the level of engaging in petty bickering.

Disciplinary encounters may place you in a defensive position. Try to remain above the personal attacks that you may receive or the practical jokes that may follow a particular disciplinary referral. Chances are, if you accomplish your task well, the student will feel that your actions were justified and will respect you for taking the action. This can only be accomplished if you do not make the encounter a personal confrontation but rather deal with the situation objectively. The goal is not to see the student punished, but to help the student develop mature behavior.

How to Confront an Intoxicated Person

Almost every RA will be confronted at some point with a resident who is intoxicated. It is predictable on weekends. Intoxicated students often return to the residence hall and start trouble. The manner in which you confront an intoxicated person can make the difference between a quiet agreement and a physical brawl.

First, consider the intoxicated person. His or her judgment is impaired, physical coordination is diminished, and the person is more unpredictable, possibly more aggressive, and generally less inhibited. The person will probably resent interference and will question the authority or motive of any person who confronts him or her. If the person is with friends, he or she will probably be concerned that his friends view him or her in the most favorable light, which may mean that the person becomes defiant. If your past relationship with the student has been strained, the alcohol could bring to the surface any hostility harbored against you.

Confronting anyone is not easy. Confronting a person who is drunk is more difficult. So, when possible, avoid confrontations with people who are intoxicated. If a student returns to the residence hall after drinking, is a bit loud but presents no real problem, do not confront the student about the behavior. It is only necessary to confront an intoxicated resident if (1) the person disrupts the living environment, (2) the person is damaging or destroying property, or (3) the person physically injures or threatens to injure himself or herself or another person.

When one of these latter situations presents itself, intervene. Start by assessing your present emotional state. Are you angry, upset, or frightened of the other person? It's acceptable to react in any of these ways. You just need to be aware of your reaction before you make the confrontation. If you are angry, it is acceptable to express your feelings to the other person, but it is not acceptable to demonstrate your anger through inflammatory remarks.

Once you have assessed your feelings, gather all the necessary information on what took place. If the person's stereo is too loud and other residents have asked him or her to turn it down, get the facts from these people before confronting the resident. If another student saw a student damage property, make certain you have the details of what the witness did and did not see.

If the gravity of the situation, your past relationship with the student, or your assessment of your feelings suggests that you should not handle the situation alone, do not hesitate to ask for assistance from your hall director, another RA, or possibly the campus police. However, these situations should not be escalated, unless, in your judgment, failure to involve other people would be worse.

The last step before actual confrontation is to stop and consider exactly what specific behavior you wish the person to stop, change, or alter. What is it you want the person to do at this particular time? Can the confrontation wait until a time when the person is not intoxicated? If the person is disrupting the environment, the goal of your encounter is obvious—to return the environment to its previous state. If the person is fighting with another person or is about to initiate a fight, again the goal is obvious. If, however, the person has damaged property or left beer bottles strewn throughout the corridors of the residence hall, there may be very little you can do by initiating a confrontation at this particular time. The person will need to be held accountable for the behavior, but the best time may be the following day, after the person has sobered up. The student may be more reasonable and less confrontational when sober.

At this point, you have assessed your own feelings, have the necessary facts about the situation, have made a decision as to whether to involve another staff person, know what behavior you wish the person to modify, and have decided whether to initiate the confrontation of this behavior now or wait until the person is sober. Assuming that you believe a confrontation is needed immediately and that you will handle it yourself, you must now confront the person.

Your first task in the confrontation is to make sure the person knows who you are. If the student is not one of your residents, it will be necessary for you to identify yourself as a resident assistant. Once this is accomplished, try to isolate him or her from friends or any spectators. Ask the person to step into your room, or into his or her own room, if that is the most isolated place you can find. If at all possible, avoid discussing the situation in front of other people.

In approaching the person, do so in a nonthreatening way. Remember, your goal is to return the environment to its previous state or to prevent some injury. It is not to moralize, lecture, condemn, evaluate, or in some other manner demean the person's behavior. Be sincere in your emotions and in what you are saying. Avoid accusations or inflammatory remarks. Use an approach that will elicit a feeling on the student's part that he or she is cooperating. Ask for the student's cooperation; do not demand it. Use techniques and skills of assertiveness that you learned earlier.

Never become physical, unless it is to protect yourself, and then only to protect yourself—not to retaliate or demonstrate your force or anger. Grabbing, pushing, or restraining the person may lead to unnecessary problems.

If the student chooses to escalate the situation by failing to cooperate or if you are threatened in some manner, do not hesitate to involve other members of the residence hall staff or the campus police if it is appropriate. Whatever your college pays you, it is not enough for you to place yourself in a position of imminent physical harm. Though physical altercations between students and staff are rare, they do happen. Many of these could be avoided if people would exercise more discretion.

Confront only specific behavior that the person has exhibited. Do not make value judgments about behavior. It is enough to say that the disturbance is creating difficulty for others or that it is presenting some other problem. If you are disturbed by the situation or if you were awakened because of the disturbance, express your anger. It is not necessary, however, to lecture. Use questions that require more than a simple yes or no answer to clarify the situation. Questions you might ask include, "Why are you yelling?" or, "Why is your stereo that loud?" or, "Why are you acting this way? How do you feel about your current behavior?" In any case, communicate clearly. Ask the person to explain or clarify behavior. Do not threaten; instead, clearly and calmly explain how the behavior is affecting others.

Remember always that your goal is to get the person to cease the behavior that is causing the disturbance. If you can do this by asking him or her in a friendly and cooperative tone to change the behavior, you will have a better chance of accomplishing the goal. Depending on your personal judgment, the degree to which the student has disrupted the environment, the student's history of similar behavior, and what your institutional policy considers customary in these situations, it may be necessary for the student's behavior to be reviewed by an administrator to determine whether formal disciplinary action is necessary. If, in your judgment, such a referral is necessary, it is appropriate that you indicate during your confrontation that this referral will be made. It should in no case be used as a threat. Rather, you should present your decision in such a way as to inform the student without it appearing as a punishment in and of itself. You might say something like, "I will be discussing this incident with the hall director for possible disciplinary action. I would like to talk with you about it again tomorrow."

Tips on Disciplinary Counseling

Many students want to discuss problems or information regarding a situation only if you promise not to tell anyone else. "I'll tell you if you promise not to tell anyone." What the student is really saying to you is, "I trust you, but not your judgment." What is more important is that this type of confidentiality can place you in a very awkward position. What if the student reveals a very dangerous situation? Or what if the student confesses involvement in a crime? What do you do then? Do you withhold this information from the appropriate college officials and thereby become party to the violation, or do you breach the student's trust in you by promising to do one thing and then doing another?

The only response you can make is to tell the student that you will need to decide what you will be obligated to pass on and what you can retain as confidential after you have heard the information. To accept information under the promise of withholding it as confidential places you in a losing situation.

Be familiar with the college regulations and with the rationale behind them. This information can only be received by discussing the rationale for various policies with the people making those policies.

Never openly discuss your objections to policies or regulations with the people with whom you are expected to work in an enforcement capacity. You may have objections to certain policies; most people do. The appropriate forum for discussion of these objections is not in floor meetings or with residents of the floor, but in discussion with staff and the people who can effect change. To share your personal concerns about policies with other students may make you seem hypocritical when you are obliged to enforce these policies.

Never tell your residents that as long as you do not see them violate a policy, it will be all right to do it. This often occurs in institutions where RAs are expected to enforce marijuana and alcohol policies. RAs often say that it is all right for the residents to smoke or drink in their rooms as long as they, the RAs, do not know about it. This communicates to students that certain behavior is approved as long as they are not caught. You will find that this position will defeat your credibility in the unit when you are obliged to enforce the policy.

Do not withhold information from supervisory staff. If it is determined that you had information about certain events and made promises not to release it, this could be a justification for removing you from your position. Remember, you are not a student advocate whose function is to defend students against the college; you are an employee of the college whose function is to help implement its goals, policies, and philosophies. There is an appropriate place for dissension, but it does not include leading groups of your residents to disobey policies.

Enforce policies and regulations consistently throughout the year. Do not, however, earn the reputation of being a "supersleuth." Be flexible and understanding, but clearly outline the boundaries for acceptable and unacceptable behavior.

Remember that the immediate goal of a disciplinary encounter is to terminate the violation. If the goal is to end a fight, deal with ending the fight and move on from there. Every time you have an encounter with a student because of his or her behavior, you do not need to make a referral. Referrals are made for situations in which, in your opinion, or by university policy, such a referral is called for.

Keep a personal log on students who continually have minor problems of a disruptive and irritating nature but that are not sufficient to merit a referral. If you must talk with a student about specific behavior (such as loud stereo, smearing shaving cream on the floor, or any number of other minor actions that do not merit a referral to a disciplinary officer), make a record of the time, date, event, and the fact that you spoke to him or her. If a referral at a later time becomes necessary, this information will help establish for others that you have been performing your duty and that you are not referring the student for a single small infraction. Too often, RAs become so fed up with a student's behavior that they make a referral in an "I finally got you" mood. They expect a disciplinary officer or a hearing committee to punish the student strongly, but if the student has had no other violations and you are not able to establish that you have had continual problems with him or her, chances are that only the individual situation will be considered and not past events. Some committees refuse to examine past events that are not substantiated by a hearing; however, most committees and disciplinary officers will listen to your statement of specific disciplinary encounters related to the student's behavior. The opportunity to introduce such statements in a hearing depends on how legalistic your particular hearing group wants to become.

Do not become ego-involved in making referrals and in the outcomes of those referrals. A referral is not a "win-lose" situation. It is not important that the student be found guilty or that he or she receive a harsh punishment for a violation. There is no contest between you and the student. Your role is to provide information and to bring disruptive misconduct to the attention of officials who will help the student overcome the problem.

If you must make a referral in a threatening situation involving students who are intimidating or a situation in which you know there will probably be a disciplinary referral, make certain that you have the assistance of another staff member or at least someone else who is willing to support your statements. In a hearing, you will be given some degree of credibility; however, you too will need to substantiate or support your assessment of the situation and of how you conducted yourself.

If you are forced to confront students who are hostile and possibly violent, get help from your hall director or campus police. Avoid getting into a physical altercation. If it looks like this is possible, get assistance before you get involved.

Finally, remember that behavioral limits in your living unit are set the first few weeks. If you allow students to be disruptive and violate college policies the first few weeks of the semester, you can expect to be confronting these problems all year. Put a stop to these problems early in the year, and you will save yourself and your residents much time and aggravation throughout the year.

Chapter 10
Conflict Resolution

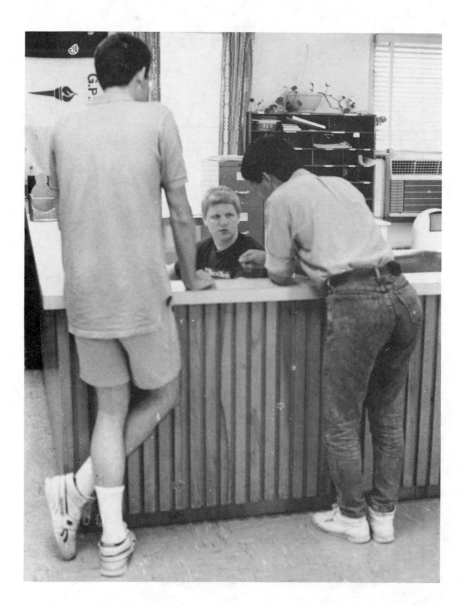

Defining Conflict Situations

As an RA, you will be confronted by many conflicts. Most will involve disagreements between a person and a policy or between two individuals. A conflict exists when two parties perceive that they have mutually exclusive goals—that is, that the satisfaction of one goal is incompatible with the satisfaction of the other.

Many people have misconceptions about conflicts. They often believe that all conflict is bad and should be eliminated. This is not true. Conflict can be productive and can lead to increased understanding. A conflict can stimulate the examination and resolution of many problems. It stimulates curiosity, creativity, and an exploration of personal values. When conflict is viewed in a positive framework, it can be an enjoyable exchange of ideas. It enables people to use their capabilities to the fullest to defend and augment their interests and to explore their own ideas. Through conflict people shape their values by having their attitudes and beliefs challenged. A positive conflict situation can foster respect and can consolidate groups of individuals.

Conflict can be positive when all participants are satisfied with some part of the outcome. It is not positive if the participants leave with hostile attitudes or mistrust and defensiveness toward one another. Thus, a constructive conflict situation is characterized by (1) constructive spirit and friendly attitude; (2) trust; (3) open, honest communication; (4) sensitivity to similarities; (5) a nonthreatening atmosphere; and (6) some satisfaction for all parties (Cunningham and Berryman, 1976). A destructive conflict is characterized by behavior, such as distrust, defensiveness, hostility, lack of communication, maximized differences, and general competitiveness.

Conflicts are not usually the result of individuals misunderstanding each other. Usually, the parties understand the other's position but disagree with it. The most common causes of conflicts are (1) value differences, (2) life-style differences, and (3) interpersonal communication breakdowns. Of these, value differences probably create the greatest number of conflicts. One person may require a neat and orderly environment, whereas another person needs the freedom to be disorganized and sloppy. This difference can lay the foundation for a roommate conflict over the degree to which their room will be cluttered or kept clean.

Some of the fiercest conflicts come in discussions of politics, religion, sex, and other value-loaded subjects. These are areas in which conflict and discussion can be very positive. It provides an opportunity for students to express and explore their values and to deal with other people's views. Such a conflict assumes the context of a potentially positive encounter.

The conflict that arises, however, between a boyfriend and girlfriend in which one wishes to express his or her sexuality while the other wishes to protect his or her virginity is another form of value conflict. The discussion revolving around why each person believes the way he or she does can be a positive exchange.

Life-style differences are common among residents of any living unit, because people come from different cultural, economic, and educational backgrounds. People are usually most comfortable with other people who are most like themselves and least comfortable with people who are most unlike themselves. When people from different backgrounds are placed together in a living unit, the foundation is laid for conflicts based on differences in life-styles. For example, if a roommate who likes classical music is placed with a roommate who likes hard rock, often the result is a life-style conflict. Such a situation, however, also provides the opportunity for each to learn something about the other's background and life-style and, perhaps, to alter or at least reevaluate his or her own values. The outcome depends on how the people involved perceive it. If they understand that different life-styles exist and talk about the differences in their backgrounds, why they believe what they do, and how they were raised, chances are that many negative conflicts can be avoided.

A lack of appreciation for, or understanding of, other people's human needs lays the groundwork for other conflict situations. If people feel that they are not being treated fairly, or if they believe that their ideas are discounted or devalued, they will feel rejected and may lash out at others. Such conflicts are created by poor interpersonal communication and the inability of one person to accept the other without being judgmental or evaluative. Conflicts of this type are common, but they often require the attention of a skilled observer to discover the reason why one person is reacting negatively to another.

Management Model for Roommate Conflicts

As an RA, you will deal with two general categories of conflict: conflicts between people and conflicts between a person and institutional policy. In the first conflict situation, you will serve as mediator or moderator (facilitator). In the second conflict situation, you may find that you become an agent in the conflict itself as a representative of the institution. This section examines first, the second type of conflict, between an individual and a policy. As an RA, you are asked to confront a student who has violated a policy. Your role in this encounter is that of arbitrator. In these situations, always remember that the conflict is not between you and the student, but between the university policy and the student's behavior.

Roommate conflicts are probably the most common type. Most of the time roommates can resolve their problems without outside intervention. Roommate conflicts are a little like family feuds; outsiders are not always welcome. Occasionally a roommate conflict may affect other residents in the unit. When this happens, you will be compelled to intervene in some manner. On other occasions, one or both of the roommates will come to you for advice, suggestions, or mediation in the conflict between them. When you enter into this type of situation, bear in mind that the student is not coming to you for a judgment on whose behavior is correct and whose is incorrect, but for assistance in working through the conflict.

Grant E. Miller and Steven D. Zoradi (1977) developed a simple behavioral approach for roommate conflict resolution. It is based on a seven-point model often used for resolving marital conflicts. The roommate model is as follows:

1. Problem recognition. RA calls roommates X and Y into their room for a conference to urge a discussion of the conflict.
2. Problem definition. RA listens alternately to both roommates' stories, using frequent paraphrasing to achieve full understanding.
3. Commitment. RA asks both X and Y if they are willing to solve the problem.
4. Highlighting pleasing and displeasing behaviors. If both roommates agree to attempt to resolve their conflict, specific pleasing and displeasing behaviors are obtained about each roommate from the other in each other's presence. Pleasing and displeasing behavior must be observable (that is, not statements such as "X is sloppy," but rather "X never washes his jeans").
5. Negotiation. Roommates trade and negotiate specific behaviors to satisfy the needs of each. For example, X will allow Y to smoke in the room if the window is open.
6. Contracting. A contract is made using the specific likes and dislikes of each roommate. After X and Y come to an agreement, they cosign a contract that will be posted conspicuously in their room.
7. Follow-up. New contracts are made weekly. Intervention by the RA is terminated as soon as possible.

Using this model, Miller and Zoradi conducted an experiment in two residence halls with approximately 600 students. In the experiment, half of the RAs were trained in the conflict-resolution model and half were not. In most of the conflicts in living units where the RAs were trained to use this model, the RAs used it to resolve conflicts. In the living units where the RAs had not been trained in the use of the model, conflicts were handled by using whatever other resources were available to the RA, along with his or her individual skills. At the end of the semester, the number of roommate changes in the living units where the conflict resolution model was used was compared with changes in the other living units where the conflict-resolution model was not used. Almost twice as many roommate changes occurred in living units where the conflict-resolution model was not used.

In using this model, the RA serves solely as a mediator. He or she does not sit in judgment over who is right and who is wrong. The goal of the model is to help the students work through their own problem. No attempt is made by the RA to resolve the conflict by a determination of right or wrong.

Analyzing Conflict Situations

The negative elements of conflicts—competition; mistrust; defensiveness; impaired communication; maximized differences; reduced alternative courses of action; and threats, coercion, and deception—are identified closely with nonconstructive conflicts between individuals. It is possible to analyze the conflict interaction between two individuals. If you happen to be an agent in the exchange, it is still important that you stop and analyze the conflict situation.

The first thing to look for is *defensive communication*. People become defensive when they feel threatened and attempt to dominate, impress, or assert they are correct. Characteristics of such defensive communication are an almost total lack of listening or understanding, and attacking, aggressive, and hostile behavior. Defensive communication is not conducive to the resolution of the problem.

Hostile communication is another form of conflict behavior characterized by direct verbal assaults. A person criticizes, ridicules, or makes fun of the other person. Hostile communication is often a prelude to overt action such as physical violence.

Manipulative communication often takes place in conflict situations. One person tries to interpret or reshape the circumstances of the conflict. That participant may try to misrepresent the facts, draw unfounded conclusions, or claim understandings not supported.

Avoidance is a way of changing the subject to avoid confronting a topic that is threatening. A person in a conflict may not respond to specific issues, or may change the subject to unrelated matters.

Evaluative responses of the other person's message is another approach that some people use when they attempt to discuss conflicts. One person makes a statement, and instead of responding directly to the statement, the other person evaluates or judges it. An example is saying, "That remark is childish."

People in a conflict situation often hear only what they wish to hear or expect to hear. This is called *selective perception*. They are not listening.

These communication exchanges are typical in conflicts. They are characterized by confrontation and by each person trying to win the support of the other person or of third-party nonparticipants. As a mediator or facilitator in the resolution of the conflict, you can employ two communication approaches to intervene in helping the disputing individuals resolve their differences.

Six Rules for Conflict Mediation

1. Never take sides. This means that you should never become the decision maker. Never side with one individual against the other. Never defend one person's point of view. When necessary, you may ask questions for clarification or feed back your perceptions, not to devalue one person's position but to bring to attention of both parties what was said.

2. When possible, employ a strategy of win-win to resolve conflicts. It is almost always possible that each person can walk away feeling as though he or she has won at least part of the conflict.

3. Help to ensure that each person's personal integrity is maintained. It is never acceptable to have one person feel debased or humiliated. This lays a foundation for greater hostility and is not an adequate resolution to any conflict.

4. Get conflicts into the open. If people are arguing back and forth about a particular situation, as mediator you may be able to assist them in defining their conflicts. It is better to get a conflict in the open where it can be confronted rather than react negatively to each other without adequate explanation.

5. Be aware of barriers to conflict resolution. Defensiveness, put-downs, judgmental reactions, gamesmanship, manipulation, discounting, aggressive attacks, and similar types of behavior are barriers to communication and play a counterproductive role in the resolution of conflicts.

6. Do not escalate conflicts by involving more people than necessary. Resolve conflicts at the lowest possible level between the individuals who are directly involved. When too many people are involved, people become concerned with maintaining loyalties and saving face. Too often things are said for the benefit of others, which are counterproductive to the conflict resolution.

Metacommunication

The first communication technique is called *metacommunication*. It means talking about what has been communicated. For example, you can make such statements as, "What I hear both of you saying is . . ." or, "I don't believe you are actually hearing what student X was saying," or "Could you paraphrase for us what you just heard student X say?" In this way you are establishing a common understanding of what is actually being transmitted. The real difficulty in communication is conveying one's thoughts and feelings through the abstract symbols of words. Words do not always accurately convey what people are trying to say. Words and phrases have different meanings for different people. When life-styles are in conflict, different words and phrases frequently carry different cultural meanings. It is important, when you discuss the differences between disputants, that you emphasize an understanding of what each person is saying. Metacommunication can help you do this. As a mediator you can comment on both what is said and the way it is said. Pay particular attention to nonverbal communication including body posture, facial expressions, and gestures. Comment on what you observe. Ask the students to talk about the meaning of words, and the meaning of their nonverbal communication. An example might be, "You look sad when your roommate said she was arguing with you. What makes you sad?"

Empathy

Empathy is the second skill that you can employ as a mediator. Although you should not take the side of one person against the other, you can empathize with each person's situation by showing concern. Be careful, however, that the students do not focus on trying to win your support for their particular point of view. Your goal is to have the students exchange ideas about how they feel about one another, not to convince you that one is right and the other is wrong. So, although you show empathy for each person's problem, you must also remain objective. This means that you must be able to empathize with each student and show compassion and caring for the resolution of the particular problem. You should try to feel what each student is feeling. Most importantly, you need to help each party understand what the other is feeling. Help each to empathize with the other person's view or perception of the situation.

To prevent threats, coercion, deceptions, and hostile types of conflicts, attempt to maximize the similarities between the differing points of view. Concentrate not on their differences, but on their similarities. Define the differences and help each of the participants understand why the differences exist. It is not productive to the conversation for one person to condemn or judge the other person's behavior; rather, he or she should express personal feelings about that person's behavior. It is important that one party does not devalue or discount the other person's views and that each listens actively and asks questions for clarification and meaning.

Chapter 11
Suicide Intervention

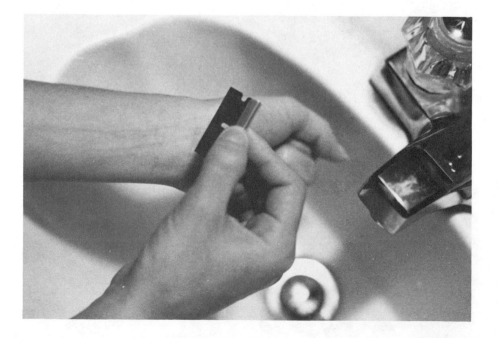

Suicide is the third leading cause of death among college students. In the decade of the 1970s, there was a 66 percent increase in suicide for this same age group (National Center for Health Statistics, 1983). One study (Kraft, 1983) showed that 70 percent of some 100,000 college freshmen surveyed had recently thought about suicide; however, less than 1 percent had made an attempt.

These statistics may represent only a portion of the actual number of people who kill themselves. Because of religious and social stigma attached to the act, families are quick to cover up suicides. Many deaths attributed to automobile accidents, as one example, may actually be suicides. Because of the poor reporting of suicides, it is estimated that the actual number of suicides in the United States may be three to four times higher than reported. Klageburn (1976) estimates that there may be as many as 200,000 to 400,000 suicides annually.

Few campuses have been spared the tragic occurrence of a student committing suicide. The pressures of college life and the difficult transition from adolescent to adult roles while balancing the pressures of academic work, parental demands, financial problems, and competition for grades all too frequently culminate in suicide. At institutions in which academic pressure and competition for grades are rigorous, there is increased potential for suicide.

Causes of Suicide

The causes of suicide are many. Binstock (1974) attributes many suicides to cultural pressures placed on individuals that prohibit them from freely expressing their aggressive feelings. In childrearing practices and other forms of interaction in our society, Binstock feels that we repress natural feelings of aggression through an emphasis on guilt as a source of control. In support of her contention, Binstock points out that suicides are highest among people with better education, artistic and professional people, and generally people who fall into the upper-middle class. Repressed feelings of anger among these individuals, she explains, encourage some of them to escape from this inner anger and pressure by suicide.

Cantor (1972) suggests that the combination of sex, sibling position, and family composition during the developmental years in early life make some people more prone to attempting suicide. In studies by Balser and Masterson (1959), firstborn females with younger brothers were found to have the most difficulty with the sibling relationship and tended to be more competitive, anxious, submissive, and dependent. These factors, the researchers hypothesize, provide a way of viewing the world that may permit the individual, at some point, seriously to consider taking her own life.

Pretzel (1972) attributes suicide to the combination of increased stress beyond what an individual considers tolerable and the recognition of an inability to cope with this stress. Coleman (1972) attributes the cause of suicide to an interplay of (1) interpersonal crisis, (2) failure in self-evaluation, and (3) loss of meaning and hope. These factors create a sense of despair beyond the individual's tolerance. Suicide becomes the means of escape, a final solution to the problem.

Santrock (1987) suggests that suicide should be thought of as the result of long-term experiences and situational short-term circumstances. Family history, depression, self-esteem, and low impulse control are long-term experiences that lay the foundation for suicidal behavior. Highly stressful situations such as a loss of a boyfriend or girlfriend, an unwanted pregnancy, or expulsion from college may be a proximal trigger for suicide. The combination of these two factors, long-term and short-term experiences, may lead to feelings of despair, depression, and worthlessness culminating in suicide.

Symptoms of Suicidal Behavior

People who are suicidal have some characteristics in common. Shneidman (1969) identifies four of these characteristics as follows:

- Depression. The person's feelings shift from external to internal sources, and he or she becomes increasingly concerned with his or her own emotional well-being. Different sleeping and eating patterns and a general withdrawal from other individuals usually follows.
- Disorientation. A person may experience misperception of reality and difficulty in developing a frame of reference.
- Defiance. In an attempt to reestablish control over their environment, suicidal people react negatively to other people and are defiant of authority, rules, regulations, and other constraints placed on them.
- Dependence/dissatisfaction. People who feel dependent on somebody else and are unhappy about this condition may feel despair over their inability to change things.

Engal (1968) identifies five other characteristics associated with suicidal people:

- Giving up—feelings of helplessness or hopelessness.
- A depreciated picture of oneself.
- A loss of satisfaction from personal relationships or from one's role in life.
- A break in one's sense of continuity between the past, and present, and between the present and future.
- A recollection of memories of earlier periods of giving up on life.

These are some characteristics common in people under severe emotional strain that may culminate in suicide. They are recognizable in a counseling situation or in discussions with the individual. A trained observer may identify these characteristics as silhouetting a suicidal person; however, a casual observer or an RA may not.

Some of the more obvious symptoms are such things as giving away prize possessions, living alone, a radical change in a person's life style, the loss of something very important (home, money, parent, and so on) (Benensohn 1976).

Continual loss of sleep, stress, anxiety, depression, and the loss of a sense of identity indicate a person's dissatisfaction with the current state of affairs and may trigger suicidal thoughts.

Lee (1978) divides the signs and symptoms into three general categories, which she identifies as (1) emotional, (2) behavioral, and (3) physical. The symptoms are as follows:

- Emotional signs include a dull, tired, empty, sad, numb feeling, with little or no pleasure derived from ordinary enjoyable activities and people.
- Behavioral signs include irritability, excessive complaining about small annoyances, inability to concentrate, difficulty in making decisions, crying, and excessive guilt feelings.
- Physical signs include a loss of appetite, insomnia or restless sleep, weight loss, headache, and indigestion.

These are signs you should be able to observe through your daily interaction with the students in your living unit. Reports by a roommate or other people in the unit can also be indications that a person is experiencing some problem. Most people indicate that they plan to take their own life prior to the actual commission of the act. In essence, the person is asking for somebody to help. Through nonverbal signs, such as severe depression and anxiety, or by talking about the act of suicide itself, the person may be signaling for assistance.

One may group the symptoms of suicidal behavior into two major categories: (1) those that relate to depression, and (2) those that relate to ambivalence. These are the two major components or characteristics of the suicidal person. Although not all persons who are depressed are suicidal, almost all people who are suicidal are depressed. Weiner (1980) states that depression is the psychopathology found most often in the deaths of adolescents 15 to 19 years old. As Lee (1978) points out, "Unrecognized and unrelated depressive illness all too often leads to suicide or at least attempted suicide. Anxiety, agitation, apprehensions, and a pervasive feeling of worthlessness are the components of a depressive state that could lead to suicide" (p. 201).

The feeling of ambivalence is analogous to a feeling of hopelessness and a loss of caring about the future. It is characterized by no longer thinking in terms of the future. Once a person has reached the decision to end his or her life, the person may exhibit a feeling of elation. This occurrence of "good spirits" is often interpreted as an improvement in the person's psychopathology. In reality, this improved sense of well-being may be a signal that the person has made the decision and is now relieved that finally the pressure and stress are lifted and that there is a resolution to the problem. The ambivalent attitude of not caring what happens is also a typical sign that summarizes many of the symptoms discussed previously.

Suicide Myths

One of the main difficulties in understanding the suicidal person is the amount of misinformation and myth that surround the subject. Following are common myths about suicide.

- Myth: Suicide is an inherited characteristic that passes from generation to generation. Children who have parents who commit suicide are more likely to commit suicide themselves.
  Fact: There is no research to support this finding.
- Myth: People who talk about suicide do not follow through.
  Fact: Stengel (1964) has shown that 70 percent of all people who commit suicide clearly announce their intentions within three months prior to the act.
- Myth: Once a person has tried to commit suicide, he or she will not try again.
  Fact: Approximately 12 percent of those who fail an attempted suicide try again within three years (Schochet 1970).
- Myth: People who commit suicide have an intrinsic death wish.
  Fact: Most suicidal people are actually gambling with suicide. Generally, suicidal people will leave themselves a way out. On the one hand, they want to take their own lives; on the other hand, they are still not sure that they really want to die.
- Myth: Women are more likely to commit suicide than men.
  Fact: Although more women attempt suicide, approximately twice as many men actually succeed in killing themselves. This is due to men choosing methods of suicide more lethal than the methods women choose.
- Myth: The decision to take one's own life is a sudden decision generally triggered by some traumatic or immediate crisis.
  Fact: Most suicides are the result of a long period of stress, crisis, depression, and poor self-image.
- Myth: Only mentally ill people commit suicide.
  Fact: Though many who commit suicide are unhappy and emotionally upset, most people are not mentally ill when they commit suicide.

Counseling Potentially Suicidal Students

Whatever the causes of suicide, the key problems for you as an RA are how to deal with the crisis when it occurs and, most importantly, how to recognize a suicidal student. The possibility of a suicide occurring within your living unit is real. As a counselor and helper, you need to know the signs of suicide and the appropriate responses. Because of your close contact with students in your living unit, you are the person with the greatest likelihood of recognizing the symptoms of a suicidal student, and the one most likely for the student to consult.

Before you consider working with a suicidal student, it is important that you understand your own feelings about the suicides. If you have strong religious beliefs about suicide and view the taking of one's own life as a violation of moral law, as Emmanual Kant did, or if you view life as a form of vital existence, as William James did, you must be sensitive to how this will affect your ability to help a student accept the intervention of a trained professional. The opposite is also true. You may believe, as David Hume did, that an individual has the right to commit suicide or that suicide is only an abandonment or denial of the will to live, as Schopenhauer believed.

You must also be prepared to work with the student who has attempted suicide and has returned to live in your unit. This person may continue to be suicidal. Your ability to recognize and understand your own feelings about the subject and to help the individual will influence your ability to be effective and nonjudgmental.

Remember that the student is in charge of his or her life and is ultimately responsible for its course. Develop some objectivity and psychological distance when you work with suicidal students to protect yourself psychologically from feeling guilt about decisions the student may make regardless of how well you have done your job. Kennedy (1977) explains the importance of maintaining a psychological distance in work with a potentially suicidal person:

> It is hard for counselors to realize that they are not God and that although they approach their task with sensitivity and dedication, they neither prevent nor postpone suicide or any other unhappiness in life. It is a sad but true axiom for psychology that a person who wants to commit suicide will eventually be able to do so no matter how we may try to prevent it. Counselors need a sensible approach to their own mental health in these circumstances. They cannot make demands on themselves that they cannot possibly meet. They cannot take responsibility for all the things that their clients do. We say yes to life for our clients, but we must be prepared for the fact that some of them will say no.
>
> The capacity to be realistic in the dangerously unpredictable circumstances connected with suicide actually frees a counselor to be more sensitive and responsive to troubled individuals and their families. There are many good things counselors can do, but there are things they cannot achieve in the way of controlling the decisions of others. The counselors' ability to balance these considerations determines their success in managing their own stress (p. 247).

Counseling suicidal people is a difficult, complex task. No RA can be asked to master the necessary skills. Professional counselors spend years learning to understand and help people through the personal crises that precipitate suicide attempts. Your responsibility as an RA is to be a supportive guide to the individual in crisis, and your goal is to have the student seek professional assistance with his or her problems.

Do's and Don'ts for Working with a Suicidal Student

The first rule in working with a suicidal student is to recognize your own skills and limitations. Remember, you are not in this alone. You have the support of a professional staff and the guidance of other people at your institution. It is imperative that these people be kept informed and involved in the ongoing discussions with the individual student through this time of crisis and stress. Your assistance in bringing about a realization on the part of the troubled student that he or she needs additional help is the greatest service that you can render. If you are confronted with a student who is discussing suicide or perhaps a student who has recently attempted suicide, the following are some things that you should and should not do.

Don'ts for Counseling the Suicidal Person

- Don't dismiss or discount any suicide threat.
- Don't argue with the individual about whether he or she should live or die. This is not the time for a philosophical discussion about the pros and cons of living. The only discussion should center around the person living.
- Don't make statements like, "Oh, go ahead and do it, I dare you." Such challenges and shock statements may be all the impetus the student needs to commit the act.
- Don't be afraid to ask the person if he or she is considering suicide. This may be the opportunity the student is seeking to discuss the subject. Most people do not really want to commit suicide and are looking for people to help them find reasons to live.
- Don't overreact or panic when a person begins to talk about suicide.
- Don't argue with the person by making such statements as "This isn't going to make things better. Suicide is a mortal sin, and you will go to hell."
- Don't try to cajole a person out of suicide by changing the subject and trying to make light of a situation by being overly humorous. The person intends you to take this situation seriously and does not need you to be overly cheerful.
- Don't be overly cool about the crisis. Show concern and care, not ambivalence, about the person's crisis and stress.
- Don't try to analyze and interpret the person's behavior. He or she does not need a psychoanalytic session with you. The student needs you to listen and to be supportive.

Do's in Counseling

- Do take every suicide threat seriously. Sometimes a person who is only making a suicidal gesture to get attention may accidentally injure himself or herself seriously enough to cause death.
- Do be aware of information regarding drugs and how they may be lethal. Kiev (1975) found drugs to be involved in over one-third of all reported suicides.

- Do use questions that force the student to concentrate on his or her positive resources and on contributions that he or she has made. Such questions as "I know that there have been many things that you have enjoyed about life; what are they?" Or "You must have considered the reasons for living as well as dying. What reasons did you consider for living?"
- Do seek support and help in a crisis situation by sending others for assistance.
- Do stay with the person if he or she has attempted suicide.
- Do be willing to listen. Do be sensitive, empathetic, and attentive.
- Do be supportive and offer your continued help to the student in the future.

Model for Suicide Intervention

One course of action for working with a potentially suicidal person is outlined here. This model is intended to apply to a student who is contemplating suicide. It is not designed to be used with a person who may be in the process of attempting suicide. Obviously, this is an emergency situation that calls for the involvement of professional staff and medical personnel. Should it happen that someone has taken an overdose of drugs or is in some way threatening to kill himself or herself, send for help and continue talking with the individual, in a calm, soothing voice about reasons for living.

Suicide Intervention Model

1. Assess the immediacy or severity of a student's potential for committing suicide.
2. Assess the availability of others to help.
3. Discuss with the student coping mechanisms he or she has available to deal with the problem.
4. Help the student determine a course of positive action by helping him or her assess the problem, brainstorm alternatives, consider consequences of each, identify a specific alternative, determine a timetable, and schedule a second session.
5. Get the student to agree not to kill himself or herself for a stated period of time as a suicide contract. If the student refuses, immediate help is necessary.

This model is designed to help you in counseling a student who may be contemplating suicide. If you panic and run for the telephone to get a professional staff member to handle the situation whenever there is a mention of suicide, you may be overreacting. Many people contemplate suicide at some point in their lives, and it is all right to think and talk about it. This model is designed to help you assess the seriousness of the situation, as well as to help you in your discussions with the individual. Any attempt or discussion with a student about suicide should be taken seriously. Although the person may be asking only for support, or attention, you are not in a position to second-guess the motive. If a student is unable to get attention in this manner, he or she may take additional steps to get this needed attention.

Step 1: Assessment

Kennedy (1977) reports a lethality scale used by the Los Angeles Suicide Prevention Center to assess the immediacy and severity of a person's crisis by assessing the potentiality of suicide. A modification of this scale appears below for you to use in assessing the suicide potential of a student in crisis.

- Sex—The potential is higher if the person is male or a first-year female student.
- Symptoms—The potential is greater if the person cannot sleep, expresses feelings of despair, or has dramatically altered sleeping or eating patterns within the past few weeks.
- Stress—The potential is greater if the person is under stress from exams, pressure from parents, competition for admittance to graduate school, and other such stresses.
- Suicidal plan—The potential is greater when the plan is more detailed, where the victim has access to a means (guns, drugs), and where the method is highly lethal.
- Family and friends—The potential is greater if the person is a loner in the living unit and has no family or close friends.
- Past history—The potential is greater if the person has attempted suicide previously. It is particularly high if this attempt has occurred within the past year.
- Communication—The potential is greater if the person has few outlets for communicating with others about his or her problems. If the person tends to internalize his or her problems and seldom shares them with others, the potential is greater.
- Medical problems—The person suffering from a terminal illness has a greater likelihood of taking his or her own life.

You make these assessments by asking fairly direct questions, such as, "How are you planning to take your own life?" or "Have you ever attempted suicide before?"

Step 2: Determine Availability of Others to Help

Once you get some basic information about the suicidal person's background, and how serious the person is, the next step is to assess the availability of others who can assist in preventing the suicide. These include the student's roommate, any friends he or she has, and members of the professional staff at your institution.

Discuss these options with the individual, expressing your availability and the availability of the professional staff to assist. Whenever you have a discussion like this with a student, you should discuss your observations with your hall director and follow up with the student.

Step 3: Determine Coping Mechanisms

In your discussion with the student, focus on coping mechanisms the student has available to deal with the problem. One method of doing this is to begin by helping the student focus on what he or she sees as a problem. By doing that, you are helping the student clarify the problem.

Step 4: Determine a Positive Course of Action

Ask the student the causes of the problem, what he or she has done about it, and what can be done about it. Together with the student, brainstorm some alternatives and possible solutions. It is important that most of these solutions come from the student. Examine the consequences of these alternatives and identify specific steps the student can take. Do this within the framework of a timetable so that the student will have goals to accomplish and something to look forward to tomorrow and the day after. Schedule a follow-up meeting to check on the student's emotional well-being.

Step 5: Suicide Contract

In various discussions, where the student claims that he or she is seriously thinking about suicide, it may be possible for you to get the student to agree to make a contract with you. In a contract of this type, a student agrees not to harm himself or herself for a specified period of time. This might be an hour, a day, or a week. In making such a contract, it is necessary that the student clearly understand that you are concerned about him or her and that you expect the student to honor the contract. Ask the student directly if he or she intends to honor the contract and to repeat in detail the agreed-upon commitment, such as, "I agree not to harm myself in the next 48 hours, to talk with you at the end of the 48 hours, and not to break the contract for any reason." This gives you time to get the professional staff involved and to give the student time to rethink alternatives. This permits the student to retain the power that he or she needs and a reason to continue living—a personal commitment to you.

Suicide contracts work often, but not always. If a person seriously wants to take his or her life, there is very little you can do about it. Your responsibility is to help the student with the crisis, help analyze the severity of potential suicides, keep senior staff members at your institution informed, recognize the signs of a person who is potentially suicidal, and to lend emergency crisis intervention whenever and wherever possible. If you can do these things and do them well, you increase the likelihood of a student making a positive decision to continue living.

Chapter 12
Crime on Campus

College campuses are not havens void of crime. Rape, burglary, assault, drug violations, and armed robbery happen on college campuses just like in the rest of society. In 1988, *USA Today* surveyed 698 campuses and found that in 1987, 285,932 crimes were reported on the 698 campuses surveyed, which represents approximately 1/6 of all colleges and universities in the United States. Among the crimes disclosed were 653 rapes, 22,170 burglaries, 13,079 assaults, 3,366 drug violations, and 1874 armed robberies in 1987 on college campuses. In total, this represented a 5.1 percent increase in crime on campus between 1986 and 1987. The results of this study showed that at the institutions surveyed:

- One in four students had been a victim of a crime.
- A violent crime (rape, robbery, assault) occurred on campus once for every 500 students.
- Eleven percent of surveyed students have been confronted by an assaulter, and 3 percent have been confronted more than once.
- Almost 30 percent of the surveyed students believe their campuses are not safe, and 42 percent of the women surveyed said they do not feel safe walking on campus alone at night.

Crime is a problem on campus and in the residence halls. This chapter focuses on three areas of crime. First is the issue of battered women. Increasingly, boyfriend and girlfriend relationships on college campus include physical violence. It is possible you will be involved with a resident who has been assaulted or who has assaulted someone. A second issue on campus is the issue of rape, both stranger rape and acquaintance rape. The chapter discusses causes of these assaults, what to do when one of your residents is raped, and precautions which can be taken to prevent rape. In the final segment of the chapter, the issue of campus theft and security is discussed. This is a continuing problem in all residence halls and one you need to discuss with your resident.

Battered Women

According to Zastrow and Kirst-Ashman (1987) there are approximately 1.8 million battered women in the United States, and over one-third of all women murdered are killed by a husband or lover. Men batter women for a number of reasons. Some men were abused children and have internalized this abusive behavior. When they become angry, they express their anger through violence— the way they learned as a child. Others believe they have the right to dominate women because they are men, and women are to simply do as they are told.

Young men in the stage of discovering their sexual identity may overreact to the need for power and control. When they encounter a problem with their girlfriend, some become possessive and act out their feelings by attempting to control or dominate their girlfriend. This may involve physical abuse.

Part of the reason men physically abuse women may be due to low impulse control, low self-esteem, and the belief that their behavior is controlled by the actions of women. A typical response from a man who has battered his girlfriend is "she made me do it." The idea that someone else is responsible for one's behavior is a problem in locus of control. These people rationalize their behavior by attributing it to the control of others.

Why do women stay in relationships with men after the women have been abused? There are several theories. Some women have low self-esteem and come to believe that they were responsible for getting hit. They believe they "deserved" it. Insecurity about the relationship and fear of losing a boyfriend who has offered them some kind of security are other reasons. Having a boyfriend who takes you places, involves you in the social life of college, and who makes you feel important presents a form of security. Women sometimes fear that if they break off these relationships they will be alone and will lose access to the social life of college.

Through dating people sometimes develop a love-hate relationship. They love intently, and they fight intently. They are so emotionally caught up with one another that both lose good judgment. The script that they write for the relationship progresses to the point where outrageous physical behavior becomes acceptable.

After a woman has been battered, she may feel guilty or embarrassed about what has happened. She may not know with whom to share this information and may fear reporting it to campus authorities or to her parents. This fear may be associated with concern over her parents' reaction or fear that the boyfriend will seek revenge.

Factors that contribute to men physically abusing women are alcohol usage, stress in college, immaturity of both students in the relationship, and a conspiracy of secrecy that surrounds a violent episode. These contributing factors make it difficult for you as an RA to intervene. You may notice one of your female residents returning from a date frightened and physically abused. A roommate may disclose to you in confidence that the girl she rooms with has been battered by her boyfriend. When this happens, it should be treated seriously. Assault is never acceptable, and it is not part of a normal relationship. If the violence is not confronted the first time it happens, there is no reason for it to stop. Although it is unusual, there have been instances on college campuses where the intensity of the relationship between a boyfriend and girlfriend has been so strong that a man in a fit of rage, jealousy, or revenge kills his girlfriend. Take each incident seriously.

The first thing that needs to be done is to assure the battered woman that she will be protected. If you have guest hours in your residence hall, generally the boyfriend can be kept out of the building. If you live in a coed residence hall or one without limited guest hours, this may be more difficult. In either case, you should report the incidence to the hall director, and the hall director should consider what other steps need to be taken. Usually the man who assaulted the woman is either referred for disciplinary action or arrested. These may appear to be punitive measures, and the woman may not want her boyfriend to get into trouble; however, if something is not done, there is no reason for the abuse to stop. If the man is not confronted with the consequences of his behavior, there is no way to help him stop and get the help he needs to control the unacceptable behavior.

Universities can and do have ways to compel men with these problems to get help. Mandatory counseling, a criminal trespass notice prohibiting the man from entering the woman's residence hall, and suspension or expulsion from the institution are options that the university has at its disposal to ensure the safety of a female resident. None of these steps can occur unless those people charged with managing these responsibilities at your university are informed about what is happening. Somewhere the conspiracy of silence must be broken.

Your role in working with a student who has been battered is to see that she talks to authorities at the institution about the incidence. You should do what is necessary to help her feel secure. It may be necessary for her to temporarily move to another room in the residence hall or in another building. If she is injured, medical treatment and possible counseling will be necessary for her to overcome the trauma and to once again feel comfortable with men.

Your residents need to know that violence does happen in dating relationships and that it is not normal. They need to know that the institution will protect them, help their boyfriend who cannot control his behavior, and ensure their safety. Students should feel comfortable in coming to you as an RA to discuss their concerns in this area. At a floor meeting or through an educational program, you should introduce your residents to the topic of violence in dating relationships.

Men need to have this information just as much as women. Although most men understand that assaulting anyone is wrong, some men excuse their behavior by claiming they have a "temper." This is not an excuse. The truth is that the man is unable to control his anger and goes into a violent rage, the result of which is that other people are injured. This is unacceptable. The consumption of alcohol is almost always associated with these episodes of violence. Because alcohol allows men to become less inhibited, they are more inclined to act impulsively. When they become angry or irritated, they disproportionately express their anger by destroying property or hurting others. Often their anger is not about anything their girlfriend has done. It just so happens that she is a convenient and safe outlet for the accumulated anger.

Talking about these issues helps. Men who batter women need therapy. It is not something that disappears by itself. Psychotherapy is effective in helping people change this behavior. Men who do not get help continue this violence until they are made to stop by police or university authorities. Unfortunately, the incident that finally triggers the intervention of authorities may leave a woman seriously injured, hospitalized, or even dead. Men who batter women have an emotional problem. If you know of men in your living unit who have this reputation or who have confided this problem, help them by getting them into counseling. It is not a problem they can work through by themselves. Professional guidance is needed.

Rape

Rape is a forced sexual encounter against a person's will. In 1986 there were 90,434 forcible rapes reported to the FBI (FBI Crime Statistics 1987). This represents a 43 percent increase in rapes since 1977 (Brothers, 1987). The majority of rapes happen to single women between the ages of 14 and 24, but it can happen to anyone regardless of age, personal appearance, or social economic level. The vast majority of rapes involve men raping women. There have been increased reports of homosexual rapes. The victims in these cases are usually children or adolescents. Although cases of homosexual rape have occurred on college campus, they are clearly the exception. The rapes discussed in this chapter concern women who have been raped by a stranger or women who have been raped by their dates or acquaintances.

A rape can occur at any hour, but evening hours, between 9:00 PM and 2:00 AM and weekends are when most occur. During the summer months rapes increase. Over 30 percent of all rapes occur outdoors, and approximately 25 percent involve more than one attacker. One-half of the victims know their assailant at least casually.

Myths about Rape

- Myth: Victims cause rape.
  Fact: Victims range from babies to women over 90 years old.
- Myth: Rapists are mentally ill.
  Fact: Most rapists are married men with families. They come from all educational backgrounds, occupations, and racial groups.
- Myth: Rapes are for the assailant's sexual gratification.
  Fact: Rape is an expression of aggression and dominance. Sexual gratification is not the primary concern.
- Myth: Women secretly enjoy being raped.
  Fact: Rape is a violent crime, and women do not enjoy rape any more than they enjoy a car accident or being beaten.
- Myth: If a woman wants to, she can prevent rape.
  Fact: Over one-half of all victims are threatened with a weapon or the use of a weapon in rape.
- Myth: Women invite rape by dressing seductively.
  Fact: Victims do not cause rape. Police believe that in stranger-rape, the rapists tend to look for women who are frightened, easily intimidated, or daydreaming.
- Myth: Rape is generally spontaneous.
  Fact: Almost 71 percent of all reported rapes involve some planning by the rapists.
- Myth: Men tend to rape women of a different race than their own.
  Fact: Most rapes are by a person of the same race or ethnic group.

Adapted from: National Crime Prevention Council (N.D.a).

Rapists can be any age, but most are between the ages of 20 and 30. They have a need to dominate and degrade women. For them, the excitement of the rape is the sense of power and control. Most enjoy the violence more than the sexual experience. It is the act of forcing one's will over another, that the other person is helpless and at their mercy, that is the emotional charge for rapists.

Many rapists were sexually abused as children. Some were also physically abused. Men who rape are people who are out of control. They enjoy the violence and need it to assert their masculinity. Rape provides them with a feeling of power and control, which often are missing in the rapists' daily lives. Rapists are often contributing members of society, living normal family lives. A person who rapes once will likely rape again.

Reaction to Rape

There are two major stages in the victim's reaction to rape. The first is the acute phase. This involves her initial emotional reaction. Women who have been raped are angry, afraid, and may feel guilty. They blame themselves, reasoning that they must have done something to bring this upon themselves. They are afraid of encountering this man again and ashamed of what has happened. Having been degraded and humiliated in this way, they may fear facing both family and friends.

Sometimes this fear of the rapists is generalized to all men. Victims never quite feel safe with men. They also report feeling dirty. They feel unclean and violated. The natural reaction that a woman has after being raped is to shower and clean her body.

The second phase of a reaction to rape is the *rape trauma syndrome*. Victims express a fear of being left alone and a fear of men. It may be months before they feel comfortable being around men and even longer before they feel comfortable in engaging in sex. Because they have been so dominated by another person, they have a need to gain control of their lives. This control is sometimes equated with having power to protect themselves. A common reaction is for women to obtain a handgun or move into a building with increased security.

Depression, feelings of low self-esteem, spontaneous and uncontrolled crying, and a feeling of being isolated are part of the psychological trauma that the victims of rape express. They fear what other people think of them. They may believe that others fault them for what happened or that others believe that they could have done more to stop it. Victims recall the rape scene over and over again in their mind. They will try to reason all of the things they could have done to prevent it or to have stopped it. Each time they discover what they consider to have been a viable alternative, they may condemn themselves for not having been smart enough or alert enough to apply that option.

Women who are in dating relationships or who are married often find it difficult to sustain their relationship. The boyfriend or husband may also find it difficult. Men often do not know how to respond. Some may even question whether the victim could have done more to prevent or stop the rape. The men too have anger about what happened. People are possessive about relationships and care about what happens to a loved one. Because there is no reason for what happened, there is nowhere for them to channel their anger.

The rape trauma syndrome may last for a year or longer. Sometimes a rape so influences a person that she never totally recovers from the psychological trauma. A woman may continue to avoid going out at night or be alone with men, and she may always feel somewhat insecure and vulnerable.

Reducing the Risks of Becoming a Rape Victim

Female students need to be made aware that they can be a victim of a rape. College campuses often lure young women into a false sense of safety. Because they see other students on campus their same age throughout the day, they assume that they are safe to walk through the campus at night. Women need to be made aware that most college campuses are no safer than the streets of the community in which it is located. Although security may be good in your particular residence hall or on your campus, it is not so good that it can prevent strangers from sneaking onto the campus, hiding in the parking lots, or hiding in unlighted areas of the campus.

Rapes occur in residence halls just as they occur in apartments off campus. When there are few people on the floor, women should keep their doors locked. Women should not walk on campus late at night unless they are with a group of other women or with a male escort. Many campuses provide night escort services. Unfortunately, 84 percent of the women surveyed in one study (*US-Today,* 1988) did not use the escort services.

While walking, women should be alert to the surroundings and the people they pass. They should remain in well-lighted areas and in areas where there are a number of other people. When walking alone on a street, women should walk close to the curb to avoid doorways, bushes, and alleys. They should respond carefully when people stop and ask for directions, not getting too close to the car. If a female student suspects she is being followed or is concerned about a particular area, she should walk to the nearest building and get help.

Every woman's residence hall should have a program about campus safety that includes a discussion about rape. It should include not only the issues related to rapes on campus, but also the issues of rape in the community or city in which you live.

What to Do If Attacked

There is no one correct answer to the question of what to do if you are attacked. The National Crime Prevention Counsel (N.D.a & b) recommends the following:

- Keep your head. Stay as calm as possible; think rationally and evaluate your resources and options.
- It may be more advisable to submit than to resist and risk injury or death. You will have to make the decision based on the circumstances. But don't resist if the attacker has a weapon.

- Keep assessing the situation as it is happening. If one strategy does not work, try another. Possible options in addition to nonresistance are negotiating, stalling for time, distracting the assailant and fleeing to a safe place, verbal assertiveness, screaming to attract attention, and physical resistance.
- You may be able to turn the attacker off with bizarre behavior such as throwing up, acting crazy or picking your nose.

Acquaintance Rape

In a three-year study of 6200 students at 35 colleges and universities throughout the United States financed by the National Institute of Mental Health, Mary Koss, a psychologist at Kent State University, discovered the following: 90 percent of the women knew their assailants and 47 percent of the rapes were by first dates or romantic acquaintances. More than 90 percent of the women did not report the rape. One out of 12 men admitted to having fulfilled the definition of rape or attempted rape, yet none identified themselves as a rapist.

In another survey, out of 6000 students at 32 colleges, one in six female students reported being the victim of a rape or an attempt. Most of those fell into the category of acquaintance rape (McMillen, 1988).

Estimates of the number of women who have been involved in acquaintance rape run as high as one in five (Leo, 1987). One of the reasons acquaintance rapes are not reported is that women feel responsible for what happened. Many do not consider the incident technically to be rape. They usually describe the act using other terms such as "he forced himself on me" or "he forced me into having sex with him." Most acquaintance rapes happen to young women inexperienced in dating relationships. High school seniors and freshmen are most often the victims, but it can happen to any woman. Usually the rape involves some type of physical restraint. Occasionally slapping or hitting is involved, and rarely is a weapon involved. Acquaintance rapes do happen on the first date and sometimes with blind dates, but most date rape situations occur on the second or third date after the initial discomfort of the first date is resolved.

There are several theories about what causes date rape. Some claim that it is motivated by the need to dominate, to express anger toward women, or to simply inflict pain. Another theory is that acquaintance rape is a result of misread social cues in the dating relationship. In some circumstances, men and women may misinterpret each other's signals. It has been argued that when a man hears a woman passively say no to a sexual encounter she may simply be acting coy by showing an appropriate degree of token resistance (Leo, 1987). There has been some research that shows that men who commit acquaintance rape may be more sexually active than other men and more likely to have a history of antisocial behavior (Leo, 1987).

Smith (1988) believes that alcohol and sexual promiscuity are two of the major reasons for campus acquaintance rapes. The limits of acceptable behavior are simply not as clear when the "norm" is sex on the first or second date. Alcohol is a compounding problem. It impairs judgment and in dating situations can lead to aggressive behavior, including acquaintance rape.

Whatever the cause(s) of acquaintance rape, it is legally and morally wrong. Women need to take precautions not to place themselves in situations that might lead to unwanted sexual attention, and men need to know that "no" means "no." Acquaintance rape most often happens when both parties have been drinking alcohol and return to either party's residence hall room or apartment. The two end up in the room after drinking, sitting on the bed and talking. What starts as an innocent kiss turns into heavy necking and petting and possibly forced intercourse.

Female RAs need to make their residents aware of the following (adapted from the National Crime Prevention Council (N.D.c):

- Women have the right to set limits, and when they are not sure about a sexual involvement, they have the right to stop and discuss these limits.
- Women have an obligation to communicate these limits to their date. If their date begins touching them in intimate places, if only by accident, they need to say no and mean it.
- Women need to be assertive in what they say. A man might misinterpret a soft or passive no. The response should be direct, clear, and firm.
- Women need to be aware that their nonverbal actions send messages. If they flirt, touch men in intimate ways, and generally try to "turn him on," they should be aware that they probably are communicating nonverbally the desire to have sex.
- Women need to be conscious of what is happening in the situation. A locked door, drinking, and heavy petting are signs of where this situation could be leading.
- Women should trust their intuition. If they think they are being pressured into having sex, they probably are.
- Women need to avoid excessive use of alcohol and drugs, and should avoid intimate social circumstances with men who have been using alcohol and drugs.

Men must bear responsibility for their own behavior. A woman may flirt with him, be seductive, or be in a vulnerable position but when she says no she always means no. No matter how "turned on" a man gets, he has no right to force his sexual desires on a woman. Male RAs need to make their residents aware of the following (adapted from the National Crime Prevention Council (N.D.b):

- Men need to know their sexual desires and limits and communicate them clearly.
- Men need to understand that when a woman says no to sex it is not a rejection of them. It is simply an indication that the woman does not have the desire to have sex.
- Men must accept the woman's decision. Sex must be mutually agreeable.

- Men cannot assume that previous sexual encounters with a woman grants them permission to have sex with this person at their discretion. Because a woman has said yes once does not indicate that she is going to have sex whenever the man wants.
- Men need to avoid excessive use of alcohol and drugs when dating. It impairs good judgment and may lead to acting on emotions without thinking.

Acquaintance Rape: Ways to Fight Back

Although each acquaintance rape situation is different, the National Crime Prevention Counsel (N.D.b) recommends the following ways for women to fight back:

1. Be assertive. Say no firmly, even if he tries to make you feel guilty or unpopular.
2. If no doesn't work, be rude!
3. Make noise. Talk loudly, scream, honk the car horn, cry rape, or cry fire.
4. Turn him off by acting crazy, saying you have a venereal disease, or threatening to throw up.
5. Try to get away and call your parents or a friend to come and get you.
6. If all else fails, resort to physical resistance, a swift jab to the throat or eyes, or a solid kick between the legs.

What to Do If One of Your Residents Is Raped

Rape is a traumatic experience for any woman and for the other women on campus. It sends a shock wave of concern throughout an entire campus. Residents respond with heightened anxiety, and rumors of rapists circulate throughout the campus.

Your concern as the RA is to see that if a young woman on your floor is raped, she is seen by the police or campus authorities. If one of your residents has been raped, your hall director or other campus officials should immediately be notified. The police or a rape crisis center should also be contacted. If a person has been attacked, the first thing she needs to do is get to safety and make a report. Do not let the resident shower, bathe, douche, or destroy any of the clothing she was wearing at the time of the attack. This is evidence and is needed by the police and/or campus officials. If the assault occurred in the student's room, do not disturb anything in the area until after an investigation has been completed. Police and other officials have been trained to preserve physical evidence for use in court.

The resident should be taken to a hospital emergency room for medical care. The doctor should be informed that this is a rape and that he or she should record any of the injuries. The doctor has been trained to handle these situations. He or she should also assess the risks of pregnancy and venereal disease. Bring a change of clothes for the student so that she may change at the hospital. The police may want to retain the clothes the student was wearing when attacked for evidence.

The student should not be left alone. If a rape crisis counselor is not there, you should be. Either you or the student's roommate should stay with her throughout the night.

As soon as feasible, the university's counseling center or a rape treatment or crisis center should be consulted. The student will need to have the support of someone who understands the experience of being raped and will need to begin therapy to deal with the anger, fear, and guilt that she will be feeling about the event.

Police will interview the student and will gather information about the assailant's description. If she relates any of this information to you, make note of it and share this information with the police or the campus authorities working with the police. Hospital personnel will use a special kit to gather evidence to be used in court. The physician will perform a gynecological examination, take a sperm specimen, take tissue samples from underneath the victim's nails, will take pictures and notes to document injuries, and will keep clothing and undergarments as evidence.

Some students do not want to report rape to the police. They are afraid of the reaction of their parents and friends. They are embarrassed by what happened and may feel responsible. In all cases, you should take steps to see that the student does report it to the police. In all cases you should immediately contact your hall director and let him or her help the student in making this decision.

Counseling Students Who Have Been Raped

As you know, your primary role is to help the student who has been raped enter therapy with a trained counselor. Even though the student may enter counseling, she will need your help. When you counsel a student who has been raped, supply warmth and support. She will usually want to talk with another woman and may feel that having other women present makes her feel more secure and protected. Do not try to cross examine or force her to relive the episode. Detailed descriptions of this sort may trigger other reactions that you are not prepared to confront. Thinking about or focusing on the issue will be an emotionally traumatic situation for the person and is best left to a professional counselor. Keep information about the rape confidential. The student should get support from persons whom she trusts, and she will determine in whom she wishes to confide.

If the victim does not drop out of school after having been raped and chooses to return to the residence hall, be sensitive to the crisis that she has experienced. Work on building her self-confidence and helping her reestablish personal relationships. She may feel awkward and as if everyone is staring at her. Anything you can do to dispel this feeling will help her. Some students find it best if they can return to the routine of studying as soon as possible while continuing their therapy to deal with the anger and fear related to the rape.

Other Crimes on Campus

Between 1986 and 1987 Laird (1988) in a survey of 698 U.S. colleges and universities found a 7.9 percent increase in burglary, a 6.1 percent increase in theft, a 2.8 percent increase in assault, and a 5.3 percent decrease in armed robbery. Twenty-four percent of the 2470 students polled on 50 campuses across the nation reported that they have had something stolen on campus at least once. And, 12.8 percent reported that they have had possessions stolen two to five times. Of respondents, 62.1 percent never had anything taken, and 1.1 percent had possessions taken five or more times. Most students (39.4 percent) in this survey believed that access to their residence was very easy, and that more campus lighting and better residence hall security would make their campus safer.

Theft has been a problem in college residence halls for years. Money, records, compact disks, and stereo equipment frequently come up missing. An unlocked room is an invitation to any dishonest person walking down the hall.One of the reasons that residence halls tend to make students so vulnerable is that they present a false sense of security. Students know the other students in their living units and often leave their door open or unlocked when they walk to the hall bathroom or when they visit a friend's room down the hall. Although people are usually aware of strangers in the hallway, if they are college-aged students, few people show much concern. It is easy for a student to walk the corridors to find open doors and simply step-in and take anything that looks valuable.

Students who live on the ground floor of a residence hall can be particularly vulnerable. Frequently they leave their windows open, and it is easy for a thief to cut the window screen and enter a residence hall room while the student is away.

As an RA you need to be particularly careful about any special keys that you have been issued. If these keys are stolen from your room or if you lose them, you jeopardize the security of every student whose room your master key will open. If an RA loses a set of master keys, generally the building or the living unit has to be rekeyed. This is usually a very expensive process and one that will make the residence hall staff quite angry with you.

There are some steps that you can take to help your residents take better care of their property. Tell them not to leave valuables such as wallets, checkbooks, and jewelry lying about their room. If they have a large amount of money in their room, they should put it in the bank. Items that can be easily stolen such as televisions, stereos, and computers should have the student's social security number etched some place on the item. This identification helps the student recover property in the event that the item is stolen. The student should also make a list of any serial numbers, model numbers, and descriptions of his or her property. One way to do this is for the student to take a photograph of the item in question and record on the back of the photograph the serial and model number of the item.

Doors and windows should have working locks. If the locks are broken, the campus physical plant should be contacted to repair them. If a student loses his or her key to the room, the door lock should be changed. Usually the university has a procedure to bill the student for the cost of this lock change.

Broken windows, doors, and lights should be repaired. If students prop doors open that are to be secured at night, some type of buzzer or alarm system should be considered to alert people to the opening of this door. Talk with the students about the need to keep these doors secured to keep unwanted visitors out.

Many of the thefts on campus are bicycles. Most residence halls are not designed to have bicycles inside the building. Although some students would like to put their bicycles in their rooms, most state fire codes prohibit bicycles in the room because they could present an obstacle when a person is attempting to exit in the event of fire. If students bring bicycles to campus, they should record the serial numbers, photograph the bicycles, and put them in a secure location. Most importantly, they should purchase a heavy duty lock. Inexpensive cable or chain locks are an ineffective means to secure bicycles. College campuses are known targets for bicycle thieves who often come on campus with a truck and simply load bicycles into the truck and drive away. It only takes a bolt cutter to cut most of the locks securing expensive bicycles. Bikes should be secured to a nonmovable item. Simply putting a lock on a bike and sitting it against the wall is an unsatisfactory solution to the problem of theft. Residents should be informed that whenever they see unusual behavior around the residence hall, burglary, vandalism, or somebody creeping around automobiles in the parking lot, they should report it to you and to campus police.

Any valuable item that is not marked in a student's room is vulnerable to theft. Within recent years, inexpensive burglar alarm systems have been developed. These systems usually consist of a motion detector or an infrared detector and some type of sound device. Students with valuable property in their room might consider one of these inexpensive detectors. No matter what time of the day or night, residence halls usually have somebody in them. The alarm alerts people that something is going on and people will come to check. Usually, this is enough to discourage or frighten away any person who has entered the room illegally. Sometimes a parent's homeowners policy will cover the theft of property from a residence hall room; often it does not. Many colleges and universities offer students an insurance policy through a commercial vendor to cover theft and damage to personal property in the residence halls.

Although there has been a decrease in the number of armed robberies on campus between 1986 and 1987, nevertheless there were more than 2000 that occurred on college campuses in 1987 alone (*USA Today,* 1988). It would be helpful to have somebody from your campus police department come and talk with your residents about residence hall safety and personal safety on campus. Your residents should know that, if someone tries to assault them on campus, they should think rationally and evaluate their resources. They should consider their options, including escape, use of self-defense techniques, negotiation, screaming to get attention, or acting disgusting or crazy. If the person is armed, the National Crime Prevention Counsel suggested that it may be more advisable to submit than to risk injury or death. The student should try to get an accurate description of the assailant's appearance and a license number of a vehicle if a vehicle is involved. This information should be given to campus police as soon as possible. If a person is robbed, threatened, or raped, campus police should be immediately notified. This notification may save someone else from becoming a victim.

Some actions that you can take in addition to bringing in a speaker are to set up a role play of a potentially dangerous situation with your residents and discuss the possible responses. A role play issue such as what to do if you return to your residence hall room and find somebody stealing your property is useful preparation. You can establish a sort of "neighborhood watch" in the residence hall. When strangers enter the hall, everyone should be observant of what the stranger is doing. It is not inappropriate for you to ask a visitor to your floor if you can be of assistance. If he or she is there for the purpose of mischief, your direct contact may discourage it.

In your floor meeting and in your staff meeting with the other RAs, talk about the issue of residence hall security. Spend some time thinking about ways in which the residence halls could be made more secure. When lights are out, see that they are replaced. If doors are broken, see that they are repaired. If there are bushes that provide concealment for people to break into ground floor windows or that allow people to hide for the purpose of robbing passers-by, have your hall director talk with your physical plant personnel about trimming these bushes. If cars in the parking lot adjacent to your building are being vandalized or items are being stolen from them, see that these occurrences are reported to the police. Police have plain-clothes "stakeouts" of high-crime areas. They will sometimes station police officers on top of buildings for the purpose of watching these areas. Some campuses have installed closed circuit television monitors to monitor these areas. When you see something suspicious, or whenever any of your residents sees something suspicious, it should be reported.

Every resident in the building has a responsibility to every other resident to help keep the environment safe. As an RA you need to help convey this to the students living on your floor. The best possible security occurs when everyone looks out for one another. It should be everyone's duty to make sure that doors are locked, that windows are secured, and the strangers are not left to wander the buildings unchallenged. If you have a serious problem in your residence hall with security, have your hall director invite the director of housing/residence life, the director of physical plant, and the chief of your campus police to a meeting with the RA staff and with students. There are some things that can be done in most residence halls to make them more secure. These things include removing shrubbery or replacing shrubbery with natural barriers, such as holly or bramble bushes which people will not want to encounter, installing better lighting, replacing poorly fitting doors with new doors, and purchasing electronic locking systems for exterior doors for use at night.

Part Four

Information on Contemporary Social Issues Confronting College Students

Chapter 13
  Substance Abuse

Chapter 14
  Sexuality

Chapter 15
  Cult Activities on College Campuses

Chapter 16
  Cultural Diversity:
    Race, Gender, and Sexual Preference

Chapter 13
Substance Abuse

Substance abuse is a serious problem throughout the world. It is not a problem exclusive to college students. It affects all of us in some form: personal experience, the experience of friends, or the effect it has on society.

This chapter discusses three commonly abused substances. The first section covers food abuse—perhaps the most commonly abused substance. This discussion does not encompass diet and health care, but rather the problems of bulimia and anorexia nervosa. These two forms of food abuse primarily affect women and occur most often during the college years. The next segment of the chapter is devoted to the topic of alcohol abuse. It discusses the behavior surrounding alcohol misuse and gives RAs tips for developing educational programming about alcohol and alcoholism. The last segment of the chapter is devoted to pharmacological substances or what is commonly referred to as *drugs* other than alcohol.

Food Abuse

Bulimarexia

Bulimarexia is an eating disorder characterized by a cycle of consuming mass quantities of food and then purging oneself of the food, usually by vomiting and/or the use of strong laxatives followed by fasting. It is a form of obsessive-compulsive behavior that is estimated to occur in somewhere between 5 percent to 25 percent of all college-aged women.

A person with this form of eating disorder has usually come to associate eating with emotions, so that not only hunger, but also emotions trigger the desire to consume food. The food is used to satisfy the emotion. This disease usually involves consuming foods used as desserts, like cookies and ice cream. The person feels guilty about the binging, usually for weight control reasons, and purges the food to alleviate the guilt.

It is estimated that approximately 90 percent to 95 percent of all bulimarexics are women. Most are from white, middle and upper-middle class families, with parents who are generally achievement oriented. Bulimarexic female students usually express fears of not pleasing their parents. This is coupled with low self-esteem and the high need for achievement. They often feel that they are being dominated by others and that they have lost control of their lives.

Many of these young women place an emphasis on an idealized romantic relationship and in doing so emphasize their physical attractiveness and sexuality. American women have been socialized by magazines, movies, and television to believe that thin is beautiful and seductive. To enter this idealized romantic relationship—in other words, to be loved—these women believe they must emulate this American sexual fantasy. They equate self-worth with how closely they approximate the slender ideal. Bulimarexic behavior is usually associated with low self-esteem resulting from unrealized love from parents and/or significant others. People with this illness believe that if they can become thin enough, others will love them more.

Physical Damage Associated with Bulimarexia

The binging and purging of bulimia sets up a cycle triggered by emotions. As these women purge their systems of food, usually by vomiting, it causes physical changes in the body. Vomiting reduces the potassium in the body system. It disrupts blood sugar and insulin levels, and influences the body's fluid and electrolyte balance. Continual vomiting removes the mucous membrane of the esophagus that acts as a protective layer in the throat and leaves the throat open to infections and the body open to illness. In some extreme cases, the person may develop a conditioned response to the consumption of food such that whenever he or she eats the body regurgitates the food. The nutritional problems inherent in this constant disruption of the system are evident. In extreme cases, people die.

Coping Mechanisms

One of the difficulties in confronting this disease is the embarrassment associated with the symptoms. It is not something people generally discuss. Usually, the purging is done in private, and the person experiences guilt. Sometimes in the residence hall, female RAs are made aware of this behavior as a result of discussions with residents, by observing a particular resident in the restroom, or by reports from the janitorial staff.

This substance abuse problem should be treated like any other substance problem. The goal in working with students with this illness is to get them to see a counselor who can begin a process of therapy that addresses their problem. As an RA, you are faced not only with the problem of identifying a bulimarexic person but also with the problem of confronting him or her with this disorder. Because these people are dealing with issues of low self-esteem, confronting them with the idea that there is something wrong with their behavior will not be easy. Many college counseling centers and health centers have recently developed brochures about bulimarexia. The realization of the physical problems associated with this disorder and the desire to regain control of one's life may help a student make the decision to seek assistance.

Therapy for bulimic students focuses on increasing personal self-esteem. It is usually done in group-counseling environments to help the students gain positive feedback from peers and to help them understand that their problem is not unique. In addition to the therapy, sometimes they are referred to a nutritionist who helps them design a weight management program as one step in beginning to regain control of their lives.

RAs in the residence halls may wish to consider doing some educational programming in this area if they have not already done so. Pamphlets and other materials should be made available in an inconspicuous and easily accessible place for students. If you have suspicions about a person who exhibits symptoms of bulimarexia, talk to your hall director about it. Together the two of you may be able to design a strategy for helping this resident.

Anorexia Nervosa

Anorexia nervosa is an eating disorder that may include bulimic symptoms. Again, it is a problem that almost exclusively affects women. Like bulimarexia, anorexia nervosa stems from a need for love and a belief that being thin—sexually attractive—will result in being loved. Low self-esteem issues, with an emphasis on approval from others as the determinant of self worth, characterizes this illness. One of the primary ways it differs from bulimarexia is that anorexia nervosa is a form of suicidal behavior. It shares with the disease of alcoholism the desire to die, the rejection of love, and a distorted sense of reality.

Anorexics actually develop a fear of food. They come to believe that if they eat any food at all they will put on weight. If they do eat anything, they are likely to force themselves to regurgitate. Anorexia nervosa is sometimes seen in women who have lost a considerable amount of weight through crash dieting, prolonged fasting, and other hazardous weight-reduction methods. Even when anorexics become so thin that they become emaciated, their perceptions of themselves are that they are still too heavy. Anorexics are never thin enough. They believe that once they reach the ideal thinness they will suddenly be loved by everyone. If this illness is left unattended, anorexics will die from malnutrition. They sometimes require hospitalization and force-feeding. Even this is not always enough to save their lives.

Again, the anorexic shares many of the same characteristics as the bulimarexic. Victims of this illness are usually white and from a middle to upper-class family background with affluent parents. They have low self-esteem, high need for approval from others, an idealized concept of romance, and an intense desire to be loved, which they believe can be realized by becoming thin.

You can identify the anorexic in some of the same ways you identify the bulimarexic. In addition, you can also watch for fainting spells, nutritional disease problems, and continual illnesses. The anorexic person usually is extremely thin, has an unhealthy look, continues to say he or she is still overweight, and turns down food or consumes minute portions of selected foods.

Anorexics require psychotherapy and medical health care. Because they want to die and their judgment is blurred, they are difficult to work with. They are unwilling, obstinate, uncooperative, and disbelieving. They reject help and by doing so force increased concern in others. Some anorexics require involuntary mental health commitments and court-ordered medical treatment. For these reasons, it is often not until the advanced stages of the disease that the person gets treatment. Sometimes the person has to be in a life-threatening situation, such as unconsciousness, to begin to get needed health care. A person who is anorexic should be viewed as a person who is suicidal and in immediate need of psychological care. It is possible, however, that a psychotherapist may have little or no effect on the person until the person is in an immediate life-threatening situation or is in a situation in which therapy is offered as her only alternative, as might be found in a court-ordered commitment.

Alcohol Abuse

The consumption of alcohol has become as much a part of college life as football. It has been part of the collegiate experience since the 1800s. Whiskey and ale played an important part in collegiate life in the 1800s with some institutions, such as Yale University, appointing a full-time faculty member as an ale tester. Drinking continued at most colleges and universities through World War II, even though most institutions had policies prohibiting its consumption on campus. After World War II, colleges and universities saw an influx in the number of older students due to the benefits extended by the GI Bill. Although most institutions still prohibited drinking on campus—which for all practical purposes meant in the residence halls or at football games—some authorities extended approval for students who were over 21 years of age or granted some form of tacit approval for students who had seen military service. This approval, it should be noted, usually came more as a result of lack of policy enforcement than as a result of any change in written regulations.

Throughout the 1960s, alcohol was still the drug of choice among students; however, it was not until after the 18-year-old age of majority was accepted by most states that colleges and universities began to permit the authorized use of alcohol on campus.

In 1986 and 1987 all states changed their alcohol consumption laws to permit only people 21 years old or older to possess or consume alcohol. This change in the law came as the result of strong lobbying efforts by such groups as Mothers Against Drunk Driving (MADD) with the U.S. Congress. Their concerns were the high number of drinking-related auto accidents, particularly by drivers and passengers who were under 21. Because some states maintained a 21-year-old drinking age and others an 18-year-old drinking age, young adults between 18 and 21 would often drive to neighboring states that had lower ages laws to drink. These young people would then drive home while intoxicated on interstate highways, creating a dangerous situation for public safety.

The U.S. Congress passed a law making the receipt of federal highway funds for states contingent on having a state drinking age of not less than 21. The millions of dollars states would lose prompted each state to change its drinking age to 21. Some states provided exemptions for people between the ages of 18 and 21 if they were drinking in a private club or a fraternity, and many "grandfathered" in those exemptions who were 18–21 years old when the law was enacted so that they did not lose a "freedom" that they already had.

Although the law has changed, 76 to 92 percent of all college students drink alcohol, if only occasionally. It is the drug of choice among college students as well as the rest of the American population. In fact, it is the most heavily used drug in America today—even more so than aspirin.

Problems Associated with Irresponsible Use of Alcohol

Nearly 33 percent of all college students experience some difficulty as a result of drinking during the academic year (Jessor and Jessor, 1975). One out of three students will fail an exam, destroy a friendship, commit some infraction of college policy, or violate the law as a result of drinking. The more serious criminal acts take the form of assault against another person, acquaintance rape, damage to public or private property, driving while intoxicated, or attempted suicide. The University of Massachusetts at Amhurst Student Health Services reported that as many as 17 percent of their weekend contacts with students, for selected periods in the spring, were alcohol-related (Kraft, 1979).

One study (Engs, 1977) sampling 13 colleges in 4 geographic regions found that the majority of the 1128 students sampled had experienced some problem as a result of drinking. Approximately 9 percent of these students admitted to damaging university property, approximately 4 percent had trouble with the law, and another 4 percent had trouble with college policies. A startling 1.8 percent of the students were arrested for driving while intoxicated. Considering that only a small fraction of intoxicated drivers are ever apprehended, this is a significant percentage.

Nationally, approximately 27 percent of people between 18 and 20 experience some problem (frequent intoxication, psychological dependence, physical dependence, or problems with friends, relatives, employers, and so on) as a result of drinking (Harris and Associates, 1974). The next highest frequency of problems related to drinking was for people 21 to 24 years of age, among whom approximately 18 percent experienced some problem related to drinking.

Perhaps the most serious and frightening abuse of alcohol occurs when a person ingests enough alcohol to kill himself or herself. This has happened at a number of colleges. The University of Nevada (November 1976), Alfred University (April 1978), the University of Wisconsin-Stevens Point (November 1976), Loras College (October 1978), and Georgetown University (January 1975), among others, have had students die as a direct result of the irresponsible use of alcohol (C.H.U.C.K., 1979). Other colleges have had students come near to death from ingesting too much alcohol or students have developed acute alcohol toxicity. An untold number of injuries and near-fatal accidents have occurred that are attributable to the misuse of alcohol.

Most of these deaths or near-deaths occurred when alcohol was irresponsibly used by the students, usually through the encouragement of their friends. Drinking games that require a participant to consume large quantities of alcohol in a short period of time were the cause of most of these incidents. In these games, the body does not have time to expel the alcohol from the system before it reaches a critical level. If people consume a large quantity of alcohol in a concentrated period of time, but not all at once as might occur in a "chug-a-lug contest," they usually pass out when the concentration of alcohol in their blood reaches approximately 0.3 percent. This is the body's natural way of ensuring that the person does not continue to drink. Vomiting is another way the body attempts to expel alcohol as a person reaches a critical level of alcohol poisoning. Death usually results when the blood alcohol level reaches 0.4 percent.

Causes of Alcohol Abuse in College

There are many reasons why people abuse alcohol. Depression, celebrations, and alcoholism are only a few of many explanations. College, however, presents a special set of demands during a period in which the individual is struggling with the transition to adulthood. There are four major explanations, other than chronic alcoholism, why so many students abuse alcohol in college.

Sex Roles

The heavy use of alcohol is part of the traditional sex role assigned to men (Zucker, 1968). Men use alcohol more often than women and in greater quantities (DHEW, 1974), although in recent years drinking among women has increased sharply (Rachal et al., 1975).

Drinking seems important for students during college because they are in the midst of struggling with their own identity to emulate behavior that confirms the appropriate sex role to themselves and to others. Wilsnack and Wilsnack (1982) explain it this way: "Masculine roles may encourage boys to drink: by selectively exposing them to situations in which unrestricted drinking is normally expected, by making it useful to drink as a means of showing adult manliness, and by creating internal needs and conflicts which drinking can assuage. . . . It is important to note also that traditional masculinity not only encourages drinking, but in contrast to traditional femininity, apparently does not impose any specific inhibitions on drinking behavior" (p. 11).

The traditional drinking role for women has been one of moderation or abstinence, but, as mentioned previously, this role appears to be changing. Park (1975), in a study of the drinking behavior of college women, found that the heavier use of alcohol was related to a rejection of the traditional feminine role in favor of the more contemporary role of a "liberated woman." As Wilsnack and Wilsnack (1982) summarize, "Traditional masculine and feminine roles may influence drinking behavior in four ways: by creating opportunities to drink, by creating normative obligations to drink (or not to drink), by creating needs and desires to drink, and by creating symbolic uses for drinking" (p. 4).

Peer-Group Influences

Closely associated with the fulfillment of students' perceptions of appropriate sex roles is the influence of peers. New freshmen who come to live in the residence hall, like most students, want to be accepted by the other members of the living unit. To do this, the freshmen emulate the behavior that they believe can gain them the acceptance of others or that the freshmen believe is expected of them.

Take the traditional male sex role as an example. A young man may consume a large quantity of alcohol to demonstrate to his peers that he is manly. A likely response from his peers is reinforcing the excessive use of alcohol. As the student's peers continue this reinforcement through laughter, joking, and often nicknames that reflect a past drinking episode, the student may continue or even increase his abuse of alcohol. Once a certain kind of drinking behavior becomes associated with the student, his reputation within the group can be dependent on that behavior.

As people mature, they become less dependent on outside approval; the importance of peer-group recognition diminishes. Interests broaden and role expectations change as students grow older. Behavior that was once socially acceptable eventually draws social disapproval and is usually curtailed.

Unfortunately for the RA, this need for peer approval is strongest during the first year or two of college—the years when the average student is most likely to be drinking the heaviest and most likely to be living in a residence hall.

The Search for the College Experience

Movies, books, television, and stories from friends and relatives about the wild and crazy things they did in college all contribute to a new student's expectation about what college will be like. Many behaviors exhibited as a result of drinking are built on myths about the college experience. A student enters college with the expectation that college is one of those unique experiences where freedom abounds, and students often involve themselves in dangerous or irresponsible acts for the assumed benefit of such experiences or their story-telling value. Sit with a group of students who are telling stories about their experiences in college and count how many times the stories include the phrases, "I was so drunk that . . ." or "I was so high that. . . ." The experiences that many students relate fulfill their preconceived ideas about college life and help to perpetuate the myths about it.

Many students believe that they must experience everything now. They are interested in immediate gratification. This orientation is different from past generations that were taught that some experiences were morally unacceptable or that certain experiences came only after a lifetime of hard work and perseverance. The current philosophy is not to be faulted. College is certainly a time to discover new things, but it is also a time to learn the responsibility that comes with the freedom acquired in adulthood.

Maturity

Freudian psychological theory proposes that there are three basic spheres that govern the psychological composition of the individual: the *id,* which is the base of the primitive instincts of every individual; the *ego,* which constitutes the reasoning abilities of the individual; and the *superego,* which comprising the ethical and moral principles of people in their society (Kendler 1963). When a person consumes alcohol, the higher-order nerve centers in the brain are anesthetized. In the Freudian model, this means that the superego and the ego are suppressed, and the more primitive instincts of the id begin to emerge. The longer a person has lived with social mores, expectations, and standards, the longer it takes to suppress these entrenched patterns of behavior. In short, a person's experience in life makes him or her somewhat more inhibited. Students who are 18 to 24 simply have not lived with these expectations as long as people who are older.

Alcohol effects these younger people more profoundly because they have less experience with the superego. They are already less inhibited, and the excessive use of alcohol allows the id to emerge, and they act out their feelings more freely.

Other Reasons

There are other reasons beyond the four just described why college students may choose to drink in excess. When students are asked why they consumed more alcohol than they should, the most common response is, "I didn't realize I was drinking that much." Other common reasons that students give for drinking too much are simply that they "like the taste," "like the effect that it gives them," or "like to get high occasionally." Whatever the reason, the person who drinks bears the obligation to drink responsibly.

Responsible Drinking

Responsible drinking does not harm the individual, other persons, or their property. This level of alcohol intake is appropriate to the social situation and is used to enhance the social experience.

Ways to Encourage Responsible Drinking

You can encourage the responsible use of alcohol by taking the following steps recommended by the Department of Health, Education, and Welfare (NIAA-DHEW 1974, p. 164):

- Respect the person who wishes to abstain.
- Respect the person who chooses to drink in moderation; do not be insistent about "refreshing" his or hers drinks or refilling his or her glass.
- Provide food with alcohol at all times, especially proteins such as dairy products, fish, and meats.
- Provide transportation or overnight accommodations for people unable to drive safely, recognizing that the host is just as responsible for preventing drunken driving as his or her guests.

Guidelines for Responsible Drinking

One of the best ways to encourage sensible drinking habits is to provide guidelines for responsible drinking behavior:

- Use alcohol as an adjunct to other activities and not as the primary focus of any particular activity.
- View alcohol as a beverage and not as a means to achieve a desired mood state.
- Avoid drinking games and other contests involving the rapid consumption of alcohol.
- Pace drinks to consume approximately one per hour.
- Do not use alcohol to impair social relationships or to degrade or humiliate a person.
- Never use alcohol in conjunction with other drugs.
- Know your limit.
- Plan ahead of time how many drinks you intend to have.
- Try not to consume more than four drinks in any one evening.
- Have a drink only when you truly want one.
- Eat something while you are drinking.
- Be careful if you consume unfamiliar drinks.
- Use mixers with your drinks.
- While you drink, occasionally switch to a nonalcoholic beverage, like plain soda or tonic water.

Party-Planning Suggestions for Responsible Drinking

Floor parties and similar gatherings are important socializing functions. New students coming to the institution need to share some common experiences, and planning and attending a party together can be one of these experiences. These gatherings aid students in developing social and organizational skills and in gaining a better understanding of themselves in social situations. Of course, parties also provide an acceptable vehicle for meeting new people and establishing social relationships with the opposite sex.

Laws requiring students to be 21 years old to drink have changed many institutions' policies regulating the consumption of alcohol on campus. Institutions have chosen to enforce these policies in several ways. Some institutions prohibit the possession or consumption of alcohol at all institutional social events, including parties in the residence halls. Other institutions permit the consumption of alcohol by those 21 years old or older, either by students bringing their own beverage to parties or by a system of students showing their student ID card to prove they are of legal age to drink. In states where drinking is permitted by people 18–21 only in private clubs, some institutions make provisions for drinking under these circumstances.

Whatever policy your institution has adopted, parties where alcohol is served—whether in apartments off-campus, fraternity houses, or in rented party facilities off-campus—are part of the normal social experience of people. Students need to have some information on how to host parties where alcohol is served.

Alcohol should never be the focus of a social activity. It can be an adjunct to a social gathering. To ensure that it remains an adjunct, here is a list of suggestions for planning a party:

- Serve an alternative beverage for the approximately one in five students who do not drink alcohol. They, too, should be made to feel comfortable at the gathering. An alternative beverage gives everyone a choice. If you choose to make a nonalcoholic punch, make certain that you keep it in a closed container. Sometimes inconsiderate people "spike" the nonalcoholic punch, thinking such a trick is funny or cute. Some people choose not to drink because they have a problem with alcohol, either medical or personal. Their rights must be protected. Alcohol added to a supposedly nonalcoholic punch may produce an unforeseen drug reaction that could result in convulsions or shock. Giving alcohol to someone who doesn't want it should be viewed with the same disdain as slipping somebody any other drug.

- Serve snacks. A party is more than drinking. Small amounts of alcohol stimulate the appetite, and people will be hungry when they begin drinking. Simple, inexpensive snacks, such as popcorn or potato chips, will satisfy this hunger and slow the absorption rate of alcohol. This should keep people more sober.

- Use a bartender at large parties. A bartender can control the flow of alcohol. He will also help prevent drinking contests and other disruptions that may occur at the party.

- Set a cut-off time for the party. Make sure that you actually stop the party at that time. This allows people to plan ahead and discourages people from staying around, drinking into the early hours of the morning.

- Use a moderate size glass or paper cup when serving from a beer keg. An 8-ounce or a 10-ounce cup is sufficient and will tend to limit individual consumption. It will cause guests to go to the bartender each time they want more and may have a subtle inhibiting effect.

- Purchase fewer beer kegs, not more. Take a rough estimate of how many people will be attending the party and divide this into the number of gallons of beer that the keg holds. Be conservative in this estimate. If you are afraid of not having enough beer on hand, it is better to purchase additional alcohol in cans or bottles. Use these only if all the beer in the keg is consumed. Too often people feel that they must empty an entire keg once it is tapped, claiming that they hate to see the beer go to waste. In some ways, it becomes a contest to empty the flowing fountain of beer. Anything you can do to discourage this will lead to the more reasonable consumption of alcohol at the gathering. The best way to avoid this whole situation is to not use kegs or have people bring their own beverage.

- Discourage people from pushing drinks. Talk to the residents on your floor and try to convince them that this practice is both immature and often obnoxious.
- Try to provide some form of entertainment. If the party is small, the conversation may be sufficient entertainment. If, however, it is to be a large gathering—such as the residents from an entire residence-hall floor—dancing or some other form of party entertainment should be planned. If the main focus of the party is on dancing or some form of party game, people will be less inclined to focus on the consumption of alcohol. People at dance clubs seldom get drunk because the main focus is the dancing. When people are active, alcohol becomes an adjunct to the activity and not the activity itself.
- Appoint one or two people to monitor the flow of guests into the party. Appoint people who are capable of making sensible decisions. These persons should inform uninvited guests that they are not welcome at the party. You can exert control over situations arising between residents of your living unit, but outsiders whom you do not know and with whom you have no personal relationship can present additional difficulties. If the party becomes an open public gathering, you put yourself in the difficult position of dealing with irresponsible behavior by strangers, in what might be a very negative and embarrassing confrontation in front of your residents. It is easier to prevent such problems than to confront them. A sign at the door saying "Invited Guests Only" helps to discourage roving bands of social marauders who search out floor parties in residence halls—sometimes for the purpose of creating trouble.

Short-term Effects of Alcohol

Alcohol is such an integral part of our society that it is difficult to realize that it is a drug, that its misuse can kill, and that it is the cause of one of the most serious diseases in America today. Many people believe that alcohol is a stimulant, because its moderate use increases the heart rate, slightly dilates blood vessels, increases appetite, stimulates the output of urine, slightly lowers blood temperature, anesthetizes higher-order nerve centers in the brain, and provides energy (DHEW 1972). Part of this energy surge results from the fact that alcohol is a food containing approximately 100 calories per ounce—a similar surge of energy is achieved by ingesting a candy bar or some refined sugar.

Although the moderate use of alcohol appears to have a stimulating effect on the body, alcohol is actually a depressant that affects some of the functions of the central nervous system. The degree of depression is related to the concentration of alcohol in the blood. Because the liver continually oxidizes the alcohol, and because some alcohol is lost through perspiration, the actual concentration of alcohol in the body varies. The rate and type of alcohol ingested also affects the percentage of alcohol in the blood.

Alcohol is absorbed directly into the bloodstream through the stomach walls and the small intestine, so its effects are felt rapidly. If there are other substances in the stomach, the rate of absorption is slowed. Some alcoholic beverages, such as beer and wine, contain nonalcoholic substances that also slow the absorption rate. As the concentration of alcohol increases, more of the central nervous system is anesthetized. In the brain, alcohol first depresses the higher-order functions and gradually moves to depressing lower-order functions. The stages that the alcohol follows in depressing brain functions are as follows (NIAAA-DHEW, 1972):

1. When the concentration of alcohol in the blood is less than 0.1 percent, a person feels relaxed, has some difficulty solving complex problems, and may become talkative, very active, or aggressive.
2. When the blood-alcohol level is between 0.1 and 0.2 percent, the person begins to lose motor-skill coordination. Reaction time is impaired, and judgment and coordination are lessened. Driving in this state of intoxication is very dangerous and in all states illegal.
3. When the blood-alcohol level is between 0.2 and 0.3 percent, there is severe impairment of motor skills, and general confusion and disorientation. Equilibrium is also affected.

As people's blood alcohol level nears 0.3, they may accidentally injure themselves by falling down or stumbling about. At 0.3 percent and above, people usually pass out. If someone is able to consume enough alcohol to reach a blood-alcohol level of 0.4 percent without passing out, coma or death is possible. This 0.4 percent level can be achieved by consuming a large quantity of alcohol in a short period of time. Such drinking games as "chug-alugging" or downing shots of alcohol one after another in a short period of time can produce this state.

Of course, individuals vary on how they react to exact concentrations of alcohol in their systems. The concentration of alcohol in the blood depends on body size and weight. For example, a person who weighs 200 pounds and consumes two drinks in an hour will not be affected as much as a person weighing 90 pounds who consumes the same quantity of alcohol in the same period of time. This assumes the same ratio of muscle mass; muscle and not weight alone affects drinking capacity.

Influence of Alcohol on Behavior

The following chart shows the general relation between blood-alcohol levels and behavior for a 155-pound moderate drinker who rapidly consumes 90-proof whiskey on an empty stomach.

Quantity	Percent blood-alcohol level	Resulting behavior
3 oz.	0.05	sedation and tranquillity
6 oz.	0.1	lack of coordination
12 oz.	0.2	obvious intoxication
15 oz.	0.3	unconsciousness
30 oz.	0.5+	death likely

A number of factors affect a person's reactions after using alcohol. These can be divided into two major categories—psychological and physiological. Physiologically, the following factors affect the body's reaction to alcohol (NIAA-DHEW, 1974):

- The speed with which alcohol is consumed. Normally a person can consume one-half ounce of pure alcohol, or what might be considered one shot of whiskey, per hour with very little effect. The liver can oxidize approximately this much alcohol per hour. Lingering over a drink or sipping a drink is a good way to minimize the concentration of alcohol in the bloodstream.
- Body weight. The greater a person's weight (muscle tissue, not fat), the greater the quantity of alcohol he or she can consume with fewer effects. Women physiologically—because their bodies have a higher percentage of fat—are not generally able to consume the same quantity of alcohol as men of equal weight. This, however, is a relative comparison and must be viewed in connection with other physical and psychological factors affecting the consumption of alcohol.
- Type of beverage consumed. Pure grain alcohol has the most immediate and dramatic effect. Practically 20 percent of the alcohol is absorbed immediately by the stomach, and the other 80 percent is absorbed by the time it reaches the small intestine. Other beverages such as beer and wine have the same effects; however, the rate at which the person becomes intoxicated is lessened because of other substances contained in the beverages.
- Whether the stomach is full or empty. If you are eating and drinking or have recently eaten a large meal, the absorption of alcohol into the system is slowed. Drinking after a meal or drinking in conjunction with any type of food are ways to slow the absorption of alcohol into the system—and thus remain more sober.

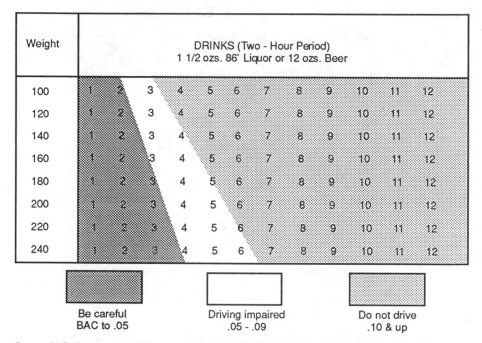

Weight	DRINKS (Two - Hour Period) 1 1/2 ozs. 86° Liquor or 12 ozs. Beer											
100	1	2	3	4	5	6	7	8	9	10	11	12
120	1	2	3	4	5	6	7	8	9	10	11	12
140	1	2	3	4	5	6	7	8	9	10	11	12
160	1	2	3	4	5	6	7	8	9	10	11	12
180	1	2	3	4	5	6	7	8	9	10	11	12
200	1	2	3	4	5	6	7	8	9	10	11	12
220	1	2	3	4	5	6	7	8	9	10	11	12
240	1	2	3	4	5	6	7	8	9	10	11	12

Be careful
BAC to .05

Driving impaired
.05 - .09

Do not drive
.10 & up

Source: U.S. Department of Transportation, National Highway Traffic Safety Administration

Figure 13.1. Influence of drinks in a two hour period on blood alcohol level (U.S. Department of Transportation National Highway Traffic Safety Administration)

Psychological factors also influence a person's reaction to alcohol. Some of these factors include (NIAA-DHEW, 1974):

- Why a person is drinking. If a person is drinking for the purpose of getting drunk, is depressed, or wants to celebrate, these psychological states will help determine how alcohol influences the person.
- Drinking history. A person who drinks regularly develops a tolerance to alcohol. An experienced drinker reacts differently to the same amount of alcohol than an inexperienced drinker of the same weight and similar physiological condition. This tolerance means that the person must increase the amount of alcohol consumed to produce the same effect.
- Body chemistry. Each person has a unique body chemistry that in part determines how alcohol affects him or her. Body chemistry is related to the psychological mood or state of the individual. The effects of body chemistry are most apparent in what is clinically referred to as the "Dumping Syndrome." This refers to how rapidly the stomach empties into the small intestine. The rate at which the stomach empties can be slowed or increased

by psychological conditions such as anger, fear, stress, euphoria, state of relaxation, and other factors. This is why a tired or upset person is more susceptible to the influence of alcohol.

- Drinking environment. Certain social situations encourage misuse of alcohol. If, for example, you are comfortably sitting with a friend and alcohol is used as an adjunct to this activity, the impact of the alcohol will probably be less than if you were drinking in a singles bar, at a cocktail party, or during a "happy hour" in what might be a stressful situation. Other people's expectations of how much you have drunk or should drink, or how you should act also influence your behavior.

Sobering Up

Once you ingest alcohol, the body must metabolize it in order for you to sober up. This process takes place primarily in the liver, although approximately 2 to 5 percent of the alcohol ingested is excreted through the urine, breath, and perspiration. The liver turns the alcohol into acetaldehyde, then into acetate, and into a variety of other compounds. Finally the body oxidizes the alcohol completely into carbon dioxide and water. The rate of metabolization is affected by a variety of factors, including body chemistry, but generally the liver can oxidize approximately seven grams of pure alcohol per hour.

At this rate, it takes approximately one hour to sober up for each alcoholic drink ingested. Coffee, oxygen, cold showers, and other home remedies have little or no effect on the rate at which a person sobers up. A moderate amount of exercise, however, increases the metabolic rate and thus aids the sobering up process, although it has a minimal effect on behavior and can be dangerous if the person is quite intoxicated.

Hangovers

Often the result of consuming too much alcohol is a hangover the next morning. Scientists are not certain what causes a hangover. Some researchers have hypothesized that it is caused by vitamin deficiencies or by oils that remain in the alcoholic beverage after fermentation; however, there are no conclusive findings to support either of these or other theories. The only known way to cure a hangover is time, bed rest, and solid food when possible. Aspirin can be used to ease the pain, but will not prevent or cure a hangover. Other home remedies, such as drinking a foul-tasting concoction of tomato juice, raw eggs, and hot peppers, does not work, nor does consuming "a hair of the dog that bit you" (some of the same type of liquor that got you intoxicated in the first place), vitamins, tranquilizers, oxygen, exercise, or any of the other traditional remedies for a hangover.

Alcohol Used with Other Drugs

Alcohol reacts with other drugs. One of the most dangerous effects of alcohol is when it is mixed with depressants or "downers." This combination causes a synergistic effect; in other words, if a person mixes one beer with a depressant drug, the combined effect will be greater than the individual effects of either drug when consumed alone. The effect could be the same as having consumed three or four beers. Combining alcohol with depressants can so rapidy intoxicate a person or shock the system that it can cause a coma or even death.

The second way that alcohol reacts with other drugs is that it *potentiates* them. This means that it can accelerate or change the effect of the drug. Such drugs as antihistamines, antihypertensive agents, anticoagulants, anticonvulsants, antidepressants, diuretics, sedatives, and tranquilizers, among others, are changed when a person ingests them with alcohol. Mixing alcohol with these drugs can cause negative side-effects.

Identifying the Problem Drinker

It is often difficult in the college years (ages 18–24) to distinguish a problem drinker from other drinkers. Students aged 18–24 are among the heaviest drinkers in the United States. During this period, they probably drink more than at any other time in their lives. Most of these people become moderate and reasonable drinkers. A percentage, however, become problem drinkers or alcoholics.

National statistics show that approximately 20 percent of all people who graduate from college eventually become alcoholics. This rate is higher than the rate among noncollege graduates. Interestingly, if you ask a group of college students if they know anyone who has a drinking problem who is currently in college, the overwhelming majority will admit to knowing such a person.

There is a good chance that during your time as an RA you will encounter one or more students who have a problem with alcohol. Some of these students may be alcoholics, meaning that they suffer from alcoholism. *Alcoholism* can be defined as "a chronic disease, or disorder of behavior, characterized by the repeated drinking of alcoholic beverages to an extent that exceeds customary dietary use or ordinary compliance with the social drinking customs of the community, and which interferes with the drinker's health, interpersonal relations, or economic functions" (Keller 1971).

Another way of defining alcoholism is through the behavior of the alcoholic. Generally, an alcoholic: (1) loses control of the amounts of alcohol consumed; (2) in some way damages himself or herself psychologically, emotionally, physically, economically, or in other ways; (3) comes to rely on alcohol as a panacea for all ills, turning to it during any time of stress or discomfort.

As an RA, you can watch for:

- Blackouts. This is distinguished from passing out. A blackout occurs when the person experiences a temporary loss of memory after drinking and cannot remember what happened during an interim as he or she drinks. Some alcoholics experience blackouts for several days. A person in the first stages of alcoholism may experience these blackouts for shorter periods of time— like one evening.
- A change in drinking behavior. The person begins drinking more often or continually, drinking in the mornings or early afternoons, or on a regular

basis. The person may also find that each time he or she begins drinking, he or she drinks until passing out. Either an increased frequency in the consumption of alcohol or the increased usage of alcohol in a drinking episode is an indicator of possible alcoholism.

- Avoidance. The person who avoids talking about his or her drinking behavior or is ashamed of discussing it probably has a problem with drinking. Hiding liquor in the room, carrying liquor to classes, and drinking before or between classes are signs of a person with a drinking problem.
- Chronic hangovers. A person who finds that he or she is sick almost every morning because of drinking has a drinking problem (Adapted from NIAAA-DHEW, 1976).

If you believe someone has a drinking problem, confront the student with the behavior that you have seen. Do not accuse the person of having a drinking problem or of being an alcoholic. He or she will be defensive, deny your evaluation, and possibly react negatively. You are not in a position to make this type of diagnosis. What you can and should do is discuss what you have observed with the person in a one-to-one dialogue.

If you have noticed the person not attending classes but instead staying in his or her room and drinking, this behavior could be pointed out. You might say something like, "I have noticed that for the past few days you have not been attending class and have been drinking all day. Do you find this is creating a problem for you?"

Questions like this can promote the helping relationship. It is very possible that the first time you bring this behavior to the person's attention, he or she will not respond. Do not give up. When you notice other or similar behavior, bring it to the person's attention again. Do this only if you are sincere and willing to help. If you are not interested or willing to help, then you may need to discuss alternatives with your hall director.

In this type of encounter with a student who has a drinking problem, your goal is to refer the person for professional counseling. If a person is an alcoholic and is experiencing problems because of drinking, he or she needs help. One of the most effective means of providing help is Alcoholics Anonymous (AA); its success ratio is higher than almost any other form of therapy available. Many college campuses have their own AA chapters. If there is not an AA chapter at your institution, try the local community. Almost every community has at least one chapter.

Note that heavy drinking does not necessarily denote alcoholism. There are other indicators, both psychological and physiological, that must be evaluated before any decision of this sort can be reached.

Alcohol Education Programming

Many colleges and universities have programs to help students drink more responsibly. These programs have grown from an increased concern for the behavior of irresponsible drinkers, the increased awareness of alcoholism, and the blatant abuses of alcohol visible on college campuses. The focus of the programs has not been on preventing students from drinking. Most students have made this decision prior to coming to college. It has also not been on the prevention of alcoholism; students seldom view themselves as potential problem drinkers or potential alcoholics. The most successful programs have focused on helping those students who choose to drink to do so in a manner that does not harm themselves, other people, or property.

How this concept is taught and whether it can be instilled as a popular attitude among students depend on many factors. Researchers found that simply providing students with information about drinking does little to change attitudes about drinking or drinking behavior itself (Engs, 1977). This was also true during the 1960s with drug-education programs. Researchers found that students who participated in drug-education programs had more knowledge about drugs, but the increased knowledge did not change their drug-taking behavior. In fact, in some instances, students with this knowledge actually increased their experimentation with different drugs (DeHaes and Schuerman, 1975).

A variety of approaches are required to change the drinking attitudes of students. Although having only one alcohol education program is better than not having any program at all, it alone will not change the drinking behavior of students. It takes a continuing program of information, value-oriented discussions, role modeling, and opportunities for students to experience the controlled use of alcohol to achieve the desired goal.

The potent peer environment in the residence hall plays a critical role in determining the standards of drinking behavior expected by students. If that standard encourages the overconsumption of alcohol, chances are, as the RA, you will spend a disproportionate amount of your time confronting behavioral problems created by alcohol abuse. However, if the acceptable standard of drinking is defined early in the academic year as moderate, and students are reinforced for this behavior, excessive drinking behavior can come to be viewed as a sign of immaturity. If you can accomplish this, chances are that you will have the opportunity to spend more time in the pursuit of other, more productive endeavors.

Following are a few program ideas that you can plan for early in the academic year. Additional program options are no doubt available through your residence life office or your counseling center.

- Distribute posters and pamphlets on alcohol abuse.
- Hold a symposium on alcohol abuse.
- Show films on alcohol.
- Invite experts on the problem as speakers.
- Distribute an alcohol use and abuse survey.
- Sponsor a bartending course (does not need to include alcohol).
- Have a speaker talk about liquor laws in your state.
- Print a newsletter that includes information about alcohol.
- Take a field trip to a distillery or brewery.

- Visit an alcohol detoxification center.
- Hold a poster contest on responsible drinking.
- Sponsor an essay contest, offering a prize for the best essay on responsible drinking.
- Organize students in your unit to do a service project for your local alcohol abuse center.
- Have a trivia contest about alcohol.
- Provide other programs in such areas as value clarification, assertiveness training, human sexuality, and interpersonal skills to help students mature and broaden their awareness.

Resources about Alcohol

Below is a list of resources provided by the National Institute of Alcohol Abuse and Awareness to which you can write for posters and more information about alcohol abuse.

1. The National Institute on Alcohol Abuse and Alcoholism maintains a state-by-state listing of most private and public treatment facilities currently available. For the appropriate list, write to

   National Clearinghouse for Alcohol Information
   P.O. Box 2345
   Rockville, MD 20852

2. Local Alcoholics Anonymous chapters and Al-Anon Family Groups (for the members of families of alcoholics) are also listed in virtually every telephone book. For further information, you may wish to contact the national headquarters:

   Al-Anon Family Groups Headquarters, Inc.
   P.O. Box 182, Madison Square Station
   New York, NY 10010

   Alcoholics Anonymous
   P.O. Box 459
   Grand Central Station
   New York, NY 10017

3. The following organization (formerly the North American Association of Alcoholism Programs) can provide a list of member groups that are the major state agencies concerned with alcoholism:

   Alcohol and Drug Problems Association of North America
   1130 Seventeenth Street, N.W.
   Washington, D.C. 20036

4. The following has a list of major nonprofit organizations in many cities that can refer clients to private physicians, as well as public and private

agencies providing treatment for alcoholism. Some of these referral organizations not only provide generalized information service but also have
individualized counseling and treatment services.

National Council on Alcoholism, Inc.
2 Park Avenue
New York, NY 10016

5. Any veteran who is eligible for VA medical benefits can receive alcoholism
treatment at no charge. Treatment of acute intoxication for alcohol-
related problems is available at any VA hospital in the country. Use the
following address to contact one of the number of VA hospitals that now
also offer special comprehensive treatment programs for the disorder:

Veterans Administration
Alcohol and Drug Dependent Service
810 Vermont Avenue, N.W.
Washington, D.C. 20420

6. Most facilities sponsored by The Salvation Army provide food, shelter, or
rehabilitation and take the form of halfway houses. In some areas, The
Salvation Army provides a broad range of other services. Contact the Salvation Army headquarters at

The Salvation Army
120 West 14 Street
New York, NY 10011

Drug Abuse

Drugs have a long history in the United States, dating back to morphine addiction among soldiers in the Civil War, the use of codeine in patent medicines
throughout the 1800s, and the use of amphetamines or "speed" by American and
Japanese pilots during World War II. Opium and heroin addiction in the United
States was not uncommon in the early 1900s. It is the decade of the 1960s, however, that is most often identified with the abuse of drugs in the United States.
During this period of social change that gave rise to a countercultural youth
movement, experimentation with drugs was viewed as a way of expanding one's
mind and enhancing one's abilities. Drugs became identified with a process of
self-discovery and as a way of making a statement in opposition to the established
social/governmental system that supported the war in Viet Nam.

As more people began experimenting with drugs in the hope of expanding
their minds or to identify with the countercultural movement of that decade, the
federal government moved to restrict the use of these new substances through
increased drug enforcement and more stringent laws. When popular drugs became
more difficult to obtain, street varieties or substitutes were developed to take their
place. The result of this has been a variety of different substances sold on the
streets as something that they are not. Suppliers of these drugs unscrupulously
"cut" or dilute the original drug with other substances, creating street varieties
that in many cases are very dangerous. As the drug supply in the 1960s increased

to meet the demand, possession and use of certain drugs in the college age community became socially acceptable and within certain groups was a status symbol. It was "cool" to be able to supply your friends with certain drugs. It became acceptable to use drugs at parties with almost the same freedom that one used alcohol. Drugs became readily available among college students, and soon thereafter, in the high schools and grade schools. The alarm that people felt over the visible sign of change within the American culture helped foster the emphasis on more closely monitored distribution of drugs, enforcement of drug laws, and research into drugs.

By the late 1970s, the predominant use of drugs among college students fell into three major categories: cannabis (marijuana and related substances), stimulants, and depressants. Though some psychodelics such as LSD were also used, they became less popular. Narcotics, such as heroin and morphine, though experimentally used by some college students in the '60s, never gained any degree of popularity in the general college population. The greatest change that has been seen in the 1980s has been the increase of cocaine among college students. Marijuana, amphetamines, and barbiturates are still in use by college students, with some evidence suggesting that they are becoming popular once again.

The National Institute on Drug Abuse regularly surveys high school seniors and college students on their use of drugs. In 1989, the Institute found that approximately 44 percent of high school seniors indicated that they used marijuana and that 10 percent admitted to using cocaine. The survey showed that casual drug use among high school and college students has declined by almost half what it was a decade ago. This reduced demand is the result of changing attitudes and social norms among high school and college students.

Snodgrass and Wright (1983) did a study of the use of drugs among college students attending a large state university in the southwest. They sampled 770 students and found that out of this group 16 percent of the males and 9.4 percent of the females used marijuana on a regular basis; 10.4 percent of the males and 9.2 percent of the females used cocaine on a monthly basis; 11.9 percent of the males and 9.8 percent of the females used uppers (amphetamines) on a monthly basis; and 6.5 percent of the males and 5.8 percent of the females used barbiturates on a monthly basis. In terms of popularity, alcohol was still the most popular drug, followed by marijuana, amphetamines, and cocaine, in that order. Men who lived off campus were more than twice as likely to use marijuana daily than those males who lived on campus. Among females, there was little difference between on- and off-campus use; however, those who lived off campus were almost four times as likely to use marijuana daily as to use alcohol.

This part of the chapter is divided into four subparts. The first contains information about drugs that are being or have been used among college students. It includes a brief discussion about each. It is not intended to be a definitive statement about each of these drugs nor to include all drugs that may be available. Pharmacological desk reference guides are available to give more in-depth discussions than are provided here.

The next subpart concentrates on ways to recognize individuals who are using drugs, and most importantly, those who may be having difficulty with the use of those drugs. The third subpart outlines appropriate emergency procedures in cases of drug overdose. The final subpart discusses the philosophy of helping students make positive, self-directed choices about the use of these drugs.

Before you read any further in this chapter, understand the authors' personal point of view about the use of drugs. From a purely physiological perspective, it is inadvisable for a person to ingest substances that alter the body chemistry without a clear understanding of the ramifications of using such substances. There is clear evidence that the introduction of any drug, unless prescribed for a specific medical purpose by a qualified medical expert, creates an effect that may not be beneficial to the body. Drugs are not only physically harmful to the individual, but they also may present major social adjustment problems. Students who are experimenting with drugs or who use drugs for recreational purposes inhibit their ability to perform at their optimum level of achievement. Having said that all drugs have negative side effects, we devote the next section to discussing the major drugs in use by college students.

Reference Section on Drugs

Cannabis

Marijuana: Marijuana is generally classified as a mind-altering drug with a low potential for overdose. Although it is generally believed there is no physical addictive potential in the use of marijuana, it is clear that the drug may be habitual—meaning that it becomes emotionally or psychologically addictive. Marijuana is consumed by either smoking it or ingesting it, usually through some food substance. A person under the influence of marijuana generally exhibits dilated pupils, impaired coordination, inappropriate laughter and rambling speech, increased appetite, and distorted sense of time or space. If the drug is used heavily over a prolonged period of time, fatigue and psychosis may result.

More has been written about marijuana than any other drug in the past 20 years. The country has moved from extremes of placing people in prison for prolonged periods of time for possession of marijuana during the early 1960s, to laws in the late 1970s that made possession a misdemeanor with small monetary fine as low as $5. Most of the marijuana sold in the United States is of relatively low potency, containing 1 percent to 3 percent of tetrahydrocannabinol (THC), the active drug agent, although some reports suggest that the potency of marijuana sold in the United States in the past few years has increased.

Marijuana is used primarily among 18 to 25 year olds with a clear trend toward use in the younger ages. In the 18 to 25 year age group, approximately 60 percent of college students report having used marijuana at least once. There is no significant evidence of any mental injuries from the moderate use of this drug, and there is no correlation between the use of marijuana and the need to advance to drugs of stronger potency.

The three principal dangers associated with the use of marijuana are that it is illegal in all states, that its frequent use may impair normal social developmental experiences needed for growth to maturity, and that smoking marijuana increases the potential for acquiring lung cancer. Research with adolescents and college students who use marijuana frequently shows that they often do not have the same type, frequency, or intensity of normal socializing experiences as those young adults who do not regularly use the drug. These socializing experiences help people grow and develop toward maturity. If much of one's life centers on the use of a particular drug that clouds perception and distorts reality, it is difficult for that person to internalize socially learned developmental skills that prepare him or her psychologically and emotionally for adulthood. Smoking marijuana presents a health threat. The inhalation of marijuana, like tobacco, is associated with a number of lung diseases, including cancer. Some researchers have argued that smoking marijuana may be more harmful than smoking cigarettes because with marijuana the smoke is held in the lungs for a prolonged period.

Some of the marijuana available "on the streets" is treated with PCP (sernyl or phencyclidine), also known as angel dust. This animal tranquilizer is a strictly controlled substance and is no longer available on the streets in any quantity. Derivatives or imitations of PCP are sometimes used to "enhance" the marijuana. Marijuana that has been mixed with these or other substances taste and smell like a strong chemical.

Hashish: Hashish is generally regarded as an hallucinogen with low overdose potential and no physical addiction properties, although again, it may be habitual. Generally it is either smoked or ingested in some food substance. Hashish is sold in grams or by the ounce. It is cut or broken into small bits and smoked. Like marijuana, it is sometimes mixed with liquid PCP or other fillers. Hashish is made from the resin of cannabis plants. Its effects are different from those of marijuana. Hashish is more hallucinogenic and less calming. A person using this drug acts very much the same as someone who has been smoking marijuana; however, the person usually becomes more irritable and more agitated. Historically this drug was used as an anesthetic for pain, but because it was slower than some modern anesthetics it was abandoned.

THC: THC is the active chemical of marijuana, pharmacologically known as tetrahydrocannabinol. At one time, drug dealers claimed to sell THC, and occasionally today people claim that a substance they are distributing is actually the chemical derivative of marijuana, thus giving the same effects without having to smoke the drug. Despite this claim, in actuality THC has never been available except to clinical government researchers. The synthetic processing is time consuming, very costly, and requires that the substance be kept at a very low temperature. Because of its highly unstable condition and its high cost, it has never been available on the street. Usually, the substance drug dealers are selling is some other substance represented as THC.

Table 13.1
Controlled Substances: Uses and Effects

Drugs	Schedule*	Often Prescribed Brand Names	Medical Uses	Dependence Potential: Physical	Dependence Potential: Psychological	Tolerance	Duration of Effects (in hours)	Usual Methods of Administration	Possible Effects	Effects of Overdose	Withdrawal Syndrome
Narcotics											
Opium	II	Dover's Powder, Paregoric	Analgesic, antidiarrheal	High	High	Yes	3 to 6	Oral, smoked	Euphoria, drowsiness, respiratory depression, constricted pupils, nausea	Slow and shallow breathing, clammy skin, convulsions, coma, possible death	Watery eyes, runny nose, yawning, loss of appetite, irritability, tremors, panic, chills and sweating, cramps, nausea
Morphine	II	Morphine	Analgesic	High	High	Yes	3 to 6	Injected, smoked			
Codeine	II III V	Codeine	Analgesic, antitussive	Moderate	Moderate	Yes	3 to 6	Oral, injected			
Heroin	I	None	None	High	High	Yes	3 to 6	Injected, sniffed			
Meperidine (Pethidine)	II	Demerol, Pethadol	Analgesic	High	High	Yes	3 to 6	Oral, injected			
Methadone	II	Dolophine, Methadone, Methadose	Analgesic, heroin substitute	High	High	Yes	12 to 24	Oral, injected			
Other Narcotics	I II III V	Dilaudid, Leritine, Numorphan, Percodan	Analgesic, antidiarrheal, antitussive	High	High	Yes	3 to 6	Oral, injected			
Depressants											
Chloral Hydrate	IV	Noctec, Somnos	Hypnotic	Moderate	Moderate	Probable	5 to 8	Oral	Slurred speech, disorientation, drunken behavior without odor of alcohol	Shallow respiration, cold and clammy skin, dilated pupils, weak and rapid pulse, coma, possible death	Anxiety, insomnia, tremors, delirium, convulsions, possible death
Barbiturates	II III IV	Amytal, Butisol, Nembutal, Phenobarbital, Seconal, Tuinal	Anesthetic, anticonvulsant, sedation, sleep	High	High	Yes	1 to 16	Oral, injected			
Glutethimide	III	Doriden	Sedation, sleep	High	High	Yes	4 to 8	Oral			
Methaqualone	II	Optimil, Parest, Quaalude, Somnafac, Sopor	Sedation, sleep	High	High	Yes	4 to 8	Oral			
Tranquilizers	IV	Equanil, Librium, Miltown Serax, Tranxene, Valium	Anti-anxiety, muscle relaxant, sedation	Moderate	Moderate	Yes	4 to 8	Oral			
Other Depressants	III IV	Clonopin, Dalmane, Dormate, Noludar, Placydil, Valmid	Anti-anxiety, sedation, sleep	Possible	Possible	Yes	4 to 8	Oral			

Category	Drugs	CSA Schedules	Trade or Other Names	Medical Uses	Physical Dependence	Psychological Dependence	Tolerance	Duration (hours)	Usual Method	Possible Effects	Effects of Overdose	Withdrawal Syndrome
Stimulants	Cocaine†	II	Cocaine	Local anesthetic	Possible	High	Yes	2	Injected, sniffed	Increased alertness, excitation, euphoria, dilated pupils, increased pulse rate and blood pressure, insomnia, loss of appetite	Agitation, increase in body temperature, hallucinations, convulsions, possible death	Apathy, long periods of sleep, irritability, depression, disorientation
	Amphetamines	II III	Benzedrine, Biphetamine, Desoxyn, Dexedrine	Hyperkinesis, narcolepsy, weight control	Possible	High	Yes	2 to 4	Oral, injected			
	Phenmetrazine	II	Preludin	Weight control	Possible	High	Yes	2 to 4	Oral			
	Methylphenidate	II	Ritalin	Hyperkinesis	Possible	High	Yes	2 to 4	Oral			
	Other Stimulants	III IV	Bacarate, Cylert, Didrex, Ionamin, Plegine, Pondimin, Presate, Sanorex, Voranil	Weight control	Possible	Possible	Yes	2 to 4	Oral			
Hallucinogens	LSD	I	None	None	None	Degree unknown	Yes	Variable	Oral	Illusions and hallucinations (with exception of MDA); poor perception of time and distance	Longer, more intense "trip" episodes, psychosis, possible death	Withdrawal syndrome not reported
	Mescaline	I	None	None	None	Degree unknown	Yes	Variable	Oral, injected			
	Psilocybin-Psilocyn	I	None	None	None	Degree unknown	Yes	Variable	Oral			
	MDA MDNA	I	None	None	None	Degree unknown	Yes	Variable	Oral, injected, sniffed			
	PCP‡	III	Serrylan	Veterinary anesthetic	None	Degree unknown	Yes	Variable	Oral, injected, smoked			
	Other Hallucinogens	I	None	None	None	Degree unknown	Yes	Variable	Oral, injected, sniffed			
Cannabis	Marihuana Hashish	I	None	None	Degree unknown	Moderate	Yes	2 to 4	Oral, smoked	Euphoria, relaxed inhibitions, increased appetite, disoriented behavior	Fatigue, paranoia, possible psychosis	Insomnia, hyperactivity, and decreased appetite reported in a limited number of individuals
	Hashish Oil											

United States Department of Justice Drug Enforcement Administration (N.D.)

*Scheduling classifications vary for individual drugs since controlled substances are often marketed in combination with other medicinal ingredients.

†Designated a narcotic under the Controlled Substances Act.

‡Designated a depressant under the Controlled Substances Act.

Psychodelic Drugs

LSD: Lysergic acid diethylamide (LSD) is probably the best known of the psychodelic drugs. It has a high potential for overdose, although no physically addicting properties. It is consumed in a variety of ways, including tablets, capsules, or in liquid form that has been put on sugar cubes or pieces of blotter paper. People under the influence of LSD have wide and varied mood swings, ranging from excitement and hyperactivity to lethargy. They can become anxious, panicky, confused, and out of control. Constricted pupils, glazed eyes, and a complete disorientation of space and time are some of the physical signs of a person using LSD. The long-term effects of the use of this drug involve convulsions, unconsciousness, psychotic episodes, increased delusions, and panic psychosis.

LSD or "acid" is pharmacologically called lysergic acid diethylamide. An LSD experience varies with the individual, the environment, and the amount of drug that has been ingested. Generally, the person begins to hallucinate and have erratic changes in emotions.

LSD was popular in the late '60s as a consciousness-expanding drug that promised to increase the user's activity and intelligence. The drug was originally developed by the U.S. Department of Defense to create disorientation and confusion in an enemy. LSD is the most potent of all psychodelic drugs with which students experiment. A small amount can produce dramatic changes in the brain chemistry and its functions.

Most of the LSD available today is produced in illegal laboratories. Because it is odorless and tasteless, it is difficult to detect. Like other illegally produced street drugs, LSD is often diluted with other substances such as speed to produce a "high." Two of the greatest harms associated with the use of this drug are having what is called a "bum trip," which is a bad emotional hallucinogenic experience while taking the drug and having flashback experiences when a user is not taking the drug. While having bum trips, people have been known to attempt to commit suicide. Some users who are psychologically unable to deal with the experience can remain in a permanent psychotic state. Flashbacks occur at unpredictable times—for some users, several weeks to several months after the ingestion of the drug. These flashbacks are spontaneous hallucinations or series of hallucinations produced without warning or additional ingestion of LSD.

There is evidence to suggest that the use of LSD produces damage to the user's chromosomes, the effect of which may be genetic defects in offspring. It is not known if this chromosome damage is permanent or temporary. It is clear, however, that if a person is currently experimenting with the drug or has taken it some time during the past 6 to 12 months, there is an increased probability of genetic damage in children conceived during this period.

PCP or Angel Dust: PCP is a tranquilizer-hallucinogen that has a high risk for overdose and a potential for physical addiction. A person who is under the influence of this drug will act drowsy, euphoric, panicky, confused, and uncoordinated and dizzy. PCP was originally developed as a horse tranquilizer, and pharmacologically is known as sernyl or phencyclidine. This substance is sometimess sprayed on marijuana or parsley and either smoked or ingested. The repeated use of this drug causes severe paranoia and damage to the central nervous system. The drug causes hallucinations, and users usually have bad experiences while hallucinating. One of the side effects of the drug is either temporary or permanent paralysis. The user may also become very panicky and violent when using the drug. This panic reaction may have lingering psychological effects, even when the chemical effects of the drug have worn off. PCP is distinguishable if used in marijuana or other substances by its heavy chemical odor and heavy chemical taste. This substance presents a serious risk to the person's life and other people's safety. This drug is becoming more difficult to obtain and, for all practical purposes, has been removed from the commercial drug market.

STP (DOM): STP is a synthetic acid originally developed for military use to instill terror in enemies. Users of STP have a high potential for overdosing; the drug creates a negative experience. STP (which stands for serenity, tranquility, and peace), also sometimes is referred to as DOM. It is virtually unavailable today. This drug creates long-lasting hallucinations of 8 to 10 hours. Like other psychodelic drugs, it is not physically addicting. Again, like other psychodelics, behavioral signs associated with someone using this drug include wide and varied mood swings, hallucinations, depression, rambling speech, and tremors. Long-term effects of this drug include psychosis and possible psychological dependency. The drug is generally distributed in tablet form, which is usually pink and cone shaped, but sometimes white, blue, or peach.

DMT: The effects of dimethylteryptamine (DMT) are similar to those of LSD. DMT is generally distributed in the form of liquid or colorless crystal and users have a high potential for overdose. It is most commonly consumed by spraying it on marijuana and then smoking it. One of the dangers associated with the use of this drug is that it causes a sudden rise in the blood pressure that can cause hemorrhages in the small blood vessels of the brain, resulting in death.

Psilocybine and Mescaline: Psilocybine is the chemical found in the *Stropharia cubensis* mushroom. This drug is sometimes distilled by boiling the mushrooms and making a type of mushroom tea. In laboratories it is possible to extract the chemical from the mushroom. The substance is ingested orally. A person under the influence of this drug acts excited, restless, anxious; the user also hallucinates. The person may become irrational at times, have rambling speech, increased perspiration, dilated pupils, and periods of insomnia. The effects of the drug, depending on the amount taken, lasts for approximately six hours. If the drug is taken over a prolonged period of time, the person may begin to have increased delusions and eventually exhibit a type of panic psychosis.

Mescaline, a drug developed by western plains Indians for use in ritual ceremonies, has similar effects.

MDA, MMDA, Ecstasy, and Designer Drugs: Methylenioxyampatepamine (MDA) is a synthetic chemical. It is a chemically based amphetamine drug classified here as a psychodelic because of its ability to cause hallucinations in the user. Other behavioral signs users exhibit include increased energy, panic, perceptual changes, anxiety, exhaustion, vomiting, and often psychosis. Continued use of MDA increases the hallucinations, flashbacks, and possible panic psychosis. This chemical was originally developed by the government as a weapon to tranquilize an enemy into submission.

MMDA is a similar organic substance whose users display the same general behavioral signs as users of MDA. MMDA is derived from myristic oil, a substance found in nutmeg. Both of these substances are difficult to obtain on the street, but often a combination of LSD and PCP is sold as MDA or MMDA.

Other drugs are developed from time-to-time; they have been called "designer" drugs. These are synthetic drugs that alter the molecular structure of a federally controlled substance to avoid the technical definitions of the controlled substance. It usually takes law enforcement authorities several months to get the new drug on the register of controlled substances.

Ecstacy or MDMA is one such drug. Ecstacy is an hallucinogenic amphetamine. It can be dangerous. One of the major problems of the so-called designer drugs is that no one can be sure what effect altering the chemical composition of these drugs will have on people. A related problem for all "street drugs" is that users and treatment staff never can be sure of exactly what someone who is only interested in profit has put into the drug. It is a significant risk to a user's health and mental well-being to ingest substances that alter the body chemistry without knowing what effect the drug will have. Physicians are often reluctant to prescribe medication, even when they know the effects of the drug, because any drug alters the system and most have some side-effects.

Stimulants

Amphetamines (Speed): Amphetamines, commonly referred to collectively as speed, are stimulants whose users have a very high potential for overdose and high potential for physical addiction. Amphetamines include drugs such as dexedrine, benzedrine, and methedrine. In many ways these drugs give a reaction similar to adrenalin—a hormone from the adrenal gland that stimulates the central nervous system. Amphetamines are usually distributed in capsule or tablet form and marketed among college students by such names as "black beauties," "white cross," "reds," and "uppers." Because they reduce the appetite in people taking them, amphetamines were commonly used as diet aids. The use of amphetamines as diet pills to decrease the appetite is no longer an acceptable medical practice. Other effects of this drug include hyperactivity, irritability, restlessness, anxiousness, euphoria, and irrationality. The speed user also tends to be much more talkative, somewhat paranoid, uncoordinated, dizzy, and poor in reflexes. Users' eyes have constricted pupils. The long-term effects of amphetamines include insomnia, skin disorders, excitability, and malnutrition. One of the real dangers to the users of this drug is that speed increases the heart rate and blood pressure, increasing the possibility the user will experience a stroke.

Speed is popular on college campuses during exam times. It has the effect of creating a state of total stimulation. Wide awake alertness is characteristic of this drug, and it was this property that caused its use during World War II and the Korean War by pilots on long bombing missions. Prolonged use of the drug creates significant damage to the body. Because of the acceleration of the user's metabolism, the liver and kidneys cannot filter the impurities fast enough and are forced to overwork. In a short time, they begin to disintegrate. The accelerated blood pressure, coupled with decreased food intake and erratic sleep, push the effects of many years of living into a short period of time. Irreparable brain damage, speech impairment, and other negative side effects have accompanied the prolonged use of amphetamines. A person who has been using the drug regularly for a period of time may have difficulty withdrawing from it. Though the withdrawal itself does not generally require hospitalization, the immediate "come down" after withdrawing from the drug can create significant psychological disturbance.

Metamphetamines: Metamphetamine is a stimulant chemically similar to amphetamines. The major difference is that metamphetamines have less effect on blood pressure and heart rate, but more effect on the central nervous system than do amphetamines. The slang terms for this drug include "speed," "crystal" and "meth." "Crystal meth" is one form of metamphetamine being sold on the street. It is usually smoked, but it can be melted and injected. Its relatively low cost and high overdose potential make "crystal meth" particularly dangerous.

Acute toxic effects of metamphetamines are similar to amphetamines. It includes irritability, confusion, aggression, deliriums, and depression. Long term use may result in toxic psychosis and abnormal mental states. Long term physical damage to the liver, the heart, and the brain may result from chronic use or overdose. Stroke or cerebral hemorrhage and death are also possible results of chronic use or overdose.

Imitation Drugs: Within recent years, imitation or "legal drugs" have been produced and marketed to college students. These are usually capsules that use many of the traditional names assigned to actual amphetamines, such as black beauties, yellow jackets, and white cross, but the imitations usually contain caffeine or some other legal substance. One of the dangers associated with the use of these imitation drugs is that they are sometimes confused with the real drug, and they set the precedent for the use of substances to meet certain demands of the individual. Although the use of caffeine or other moderately stimulating substances in low amounts may not in and of itself present a serious risk, concentrated or excessive dosages of the substances may. A person needing to study may decide to take a handful of the imitation speed drug and physiologically create some of the short-term effects of amphetamines.

Cocaine: Within the past few years cocaine has enjoyed a new popularity among the more affluent college students. It has come to be known as the "rich person's drug." Cocaine is a narcotic stimulant. Although its users have a low potential for overdose, cocaine does have the potential for addiction similar to the type of addiction found in those who use amphetamines. Cocaine is most often consumed by sniffing or snorting; however, it can be injected. When using this drug, a person is hyperactive, somewhat irritable, a little anxious, generally euphoric, talkative, and shows a distorted sense of time and space. If this drug is used for a prolonged period of time by snorting or sniffing, it begins to destroy the mucous membrane tissues of the nose. Some of the signs of someone who has been using the drug for a period of time are a red and runny nose, dilated pupils, and a rather hyperactive or anxious state of being.

Cocaine is an odorless, white fluffy powder. It is a stimulant that activates the central nervous system, producing constricted blood vessels and other physiological effects similar to those of amphetamines. Although the potential for overdose of cocaine is limited, it is possible—particularly if the substance is injected. The excess consumption of this drug may cause convulsions and death. The drug, originally developed as an anesthetic, causes an effect similar to that found in speed, but for a shorter duration. It is very costly, and its regular use can amount to thousands of dollars per week. Even though this drug is expensive, the National Institute of Drug Abuse found that between 1978 and 1981 the use of cocaine jumped from being the seventh most popular to the third most popular illicit drug in use, with the number of students reporting its use doubling from 6 percent in 1975 to 12 percent in 1980.

"Crack" is a hard rock-like version of cocaine. It is smoked in a pipe. It gives a short intense elevation in awareness, and is highly addictive. One or two uses of crack may be enough to cause a psychological addiction to this drug. The feelings of being "high" are followed by depression. Those addicted to the substance use it to alleviate this depressed feeling. The more often the drug is used, the shorter the length of time associated with the elevated euphoric feeling.

Depressants

Barbiturates is a category of depressant drugs commonly referred to as "downers." Their users have a high potential for overdose, particularly when barbiturates are mixed with alcohol. Physical addiction is possible with the use of this drug, as was seen with the rather liberal prescription of tranquilizers by some physicians in the past. Barbiturates may be injected; however, the most common form of consumption is by ingestion in tablet or capsule form.

People under the influence of this drug are drowsy, belligerent, depressed, irrational, often confused, and slurring in their speech. Users may begin laughing for no reason, and they have impaired coordination, dizziness, increased sweating, and constricted or dilated pupils. People who continue to take barbiturates over a prolonged period of time become excessively sleepy, confused, and irrational, and they experience severe withdrawal symptoms when they cease taking this drug. These symptoms include vomiting, tremors, hallucinations, hypertension, and seizures. Barbiturates are particularly dangerous for people who suffer from low blood pressure, heart defects, or depression.

The overdose of barbiturates in the form of tranquilizers and sleeping pills is often seen in suicide attempts. The overdose produces respiratory failure and cardiac arrest. If a person survives an overdose of barbiturates, he or she often experiences permanent brain damage.

One of the more foolish methods of abusing barbiturates is to consume them in combination with alcohol. This combination heightens the effect of each drug beyond the effect that the alcohol and barbiturates would create independently. This combination of taking barbiturates and alcohol is sometimes referred to as "loading." The combination of these two chemicals results in a multiplier effect. The result of this combined drug is known as a synergistic effect. It causes increased risk of overdose, brain damage, psychological damage, and related physical problems.

Qualudes, pharmacologically known as methagualone, are barbiturates that also possess some of the depressant characteristics of alcohol. One of the popular myths surrounding this drug is that it increases sexual pleasure. Because it is a depressant, it does probably lower one's inhibitions, making a person more relaxed. The drug may also produce a sense of euphoria.

The frequent use of the drug causes psychological dependency. If consumed in excess, like other barbituates, qualudes will result in coma, convulsions, delusions, and death. There is a withdrawal from the drug which is very unpleasant and may include severe nausea, liver damage, and temporary paralysis. When combined with alcohol, the effects can be lethal.

Narcotics: Heroin and Other Opiate Drugs

Users of heroin and other opiate derivatives, such as morphine, codeine, and opium, have a high potential for overdose and a strong physical addiction. Although these drugs are sometimes taken by inhalation or by sprinkling them on marijuana and then smoking it, the most common method of consumption is through injection. A person under the influence of heroin or other opiate derivatives appears drowsy, euphoric, and uncoordinated. He or she has depressed reflexes, constrictive pupils, and loss of appetite. If these drugs are used over a prolonged period of time, the user will show dramatic weight loss, lethargy, and temporary sterility and impotency. Withdrawal symptoms include cramps, sickness, and vomiting. Because a person develops a tolerance to the drug, increased dosages are required to maintain the euphoric effect.

Much has been written about opiate drugs. They are highly addictive, very dangerous, and are not usually found on college campuses. Though there is sporadic experimentation with these drugs on college campuses, their daily use so impairs users' ability to cope with college life that they leave college. Narcotics are usually difficult to obtain on most college campuses, although, like most other drugs, a person searching hard enough usually finds them.

This category of drugs is generally considered to be so dangerous that most college students consider its use to be a serious problem. Even the students who experiment with some of the other drugs that have been discussed thus far draw the line when it comes to heroin and opiate derivatives.

It is expensive and often dangerous to obtain opiates. The sale of this category of drug is scrutinized carefully by federal and state police agencies. Although police officers may be willing to overlook the use of other drugs, they seldom overlook students who use and deal in narcotics. Narcotics are not considered recreational drugs. Possessing even small amounts of these drugs can result in serious legal repercussions.

Counseling Students about Drugs

The use or possession of drugs in a residential environment is inconsistent with the goals of an educational environment and cannot be permitted to exist unchecked by the educational institution. The use of drugs in the residence hall presents major problems for the institution and students. Where drugs exist unchecked in the residence halls, use and distribution of drugs increases. There is no one more vulnerable to violence than somebody who is dealing in drugs. Students dealing in drugs have been beaten, robbed, and in several situations killed for their money and their drug supply. This kind of violence does not belong in any community, whether it be a residence hall or a city. Administrators have an obligation to create a safe living environment in residence halls. No environment where drug use is open and drug selling continues is a safe environment.

As mentioned many times throughout this book, the college years of late adolescence and early adulthood are a period in which men and women are subject to considerable peer pressure. The desire to conform is enhanced by a living environment such as a residence hall. In this environment where peer groups play such an important role in the development of students, the widespread use of drugs sets a peer standard that encourages the use of drugs. Students who under other circumstances may not consider trying drugs may be encouraged to do so when there is strong peer pressure. In an effort to gain the approval of their peers, students can easily be caught in a cycle of drug abuse that inhibits them from attaining their educational goals.

The use of the drugs clouds a person's perception and retards the ability to obtain important socially learned skills for maturation. One of the advantages residence halls provide is the opportunity to grow and mature in an enriched educational environment with other intelligent people pursuing academic goals.

Students learn from interacting with their environment, their peers, by handling crises, understanding their emotions, and by learning new social skills. If a person is under the influence of drugs, his or her perception is clouded and his or her emotions are artificially controlled. This important social development is never fully realized, and the person cannot obtain the full benefits of the educational experience the institution has to offer.

Because one of the goals of higher education is to help people realize their full academic and personal potential, students who have made the decision not to pursue this goal by choosing to impair their development through the use of drugs probably do not belong in college. Students who attend the university for the purpose of developing their character and their intellect are wasting their time and money, and the resources, and interest of the institution when they decide to inhibit this development through the use of drugs.

Educational institutions have a broad constituency. Their reputations affect not only students enrolled but also the faculty, the alumni, the community, and future students. Because these educational institutions enjoy the benefit of the laws of the communities in which they thrive, they have an obligation to uphold these laws. Institutions for higher learning also have a social responsibility to develop an educated and law-abiding citizenry through students who graduate from their institutions. No state institution of higher education can, in all good conscience, refuse to uphold the laws of the state that supports it.

Having said that colleges and universities should prohibit drug use in residence halls, the issue of how an institution goes about confronting the problem of drugs on campus through enforcement by RAs, the campus police department, or through drug counseling is a separate issue. The educators at some institutions see the role of the RA strictly as a counselor. These educators believe that enforcement of drug policies interferes with the primary counseling role of the student and is the responsibility of law enforcement agencies. They see the role of the RA as a friend, confidant, and counselor, believing that drug enforcement inhibits students from sharing their concerns about drugs or other issues.

At the other extreme are a few institutions who require their RAs to call the campus police whenever they suspect a violation of drug policies has occurred or is occurring. The role of the RAs in this case is clearly one of enforcement, which the residents of the floor understand to be an expectation of that RA at that institution.

Most institutions fall somewhere in the middle of these two extremes. The issue of enforcement of drug policies is usually handled internally within the institution's disciplinary system. At this point we need to draw a distinction between detectable drugs, such as marijuana and hashish that would be detectable outside the room by the odor, and what can be classified as the undetectable variety of drugs that the RA must physically observe in the room or must observe in the student as he or she experiences the effects of the drug.

Most institutions have established procedures for handling detectable drugs in the residence halls. Such procedures often result in a first warning and explanation that any future violation may result in referral to university disciplinary authorities. Any second violation of this policy regarding detectable drugs usually involves some type of confrontation between the RA and the student. Each institution establishes its own set of policies for handling these confrontations.

One technique that is commonly used is that the RA, accompanied by another staff member, knocks on the door and identifies himself or herself to the resident of the room, asking permission to enter. If the person does not respond within a reasonable period of time (usually three minutes), the RA is usually authorized to use a master key to enter the room to determine the cause of the odor of smoke for fire safety purposes. Upon entering the room the RA is able to stand and observe but not to conduct a search. Things that are observable include towels stuck under the door, the odor of marijuana or hashish, smoking pipes and related paraphernalia, fans drawing smoke to an open window, and any drugs that are in plain view. Depending upon the institutional policies, sometimes drugs are confiscated by the RA or a senior staff member. (Usually if there is a large quantity, the room is secured by the staff until the police can arrive.) The students are generally informed that they will be referred to the institution's disciplinary authorities.

To reiterate, each institution has its own set of policies. Some have selected a less confrontive method, which may or may not involve entering a student's room.

The discovery of students using other drugs, such as amphetamines, LSD, or cocaine, happens less often. Occasionally an RA is informed that a resident is using drugs, the RA may observe a resident who may be using drugs, or an RA may enter a student's room and accidentally see certain drugs in plain view. RAs are really not in a position to be detectives or supersleuths in the discovery of drugs. Although they many discover drugs, it is not likely.

Although there is a need to address this topic with residents and to confront the problem when it becomes apparent, RAs are not in the residence hall for the primary purpose of enforcing drug policies. It is realistically an element of their job, and it should be performed with the same efficiency as other elements of the job. When you as an RA believe there is a problem with the use of drugs by one or a group of your residents, particularly such substances as amphetamines, barbiturates, and narcotics, you should discuss it with your hall director or senior residence hall staffperson. These individuals have training, experience, and skills in handling these situations. They may have information about the student that has not been shared with you, or there may be special ways of treating these situations within your institution.

From time to time students may address the topic of drug use with you. Sometimes it will be in the context of what they did in high school, some experimentation they are currently doing, or the context of what friends of theirs have done with drugs. These discussions on the legitimacy of drug laws and the effects of certain substances can be as informative to a student as a college lecture. It is helpful if you have some facts about drugs and can relate them to students. It is also helpful if you can provide students with referrals to campus counseling services if they are interested. If such a discussion materializes, and it is likely that at some point it will, it should provide a good opportunity to invite a speaker on the topic of drugs, their legality, and their effects. Many city- or state-run detoxification programs have a public service program available on the topic.

You may learn of someone who is using drugs in your living unit. This information may come from another resident or the person with the problem may come to discuss it with you. Your role in these counseling situations is to support the person's desire to get assistance with the problem and put the issue of drug enforcement and policies aside for the more important goal of assisting the student with his or her personal problem.

People who have been abusing drugs for a period of time will need the assistance of a professionally trained counselor. They need to attend a detoxification program to handle some of the psychological and physical withdrawals. These individuals also need to build their own concepts of self-worth and discover new ways of coping with the stress of everyday life in college. This therapeutic change can be accomplished by working with a trained professional over a period of time in the right environment. You can be of greatest assistance in helping students to locate a professional person to help with their problem and then reassuring them that these matters will be handled confidentially, without involvement of the police, institutional disciplinary records, or any breach of confidence to parents, employers, or others outside the institution. Only in rare circumstances is it necessary to include the parents of a student, and this decision should be made by members of the professional staff in consultation with the student.

Drug Overdoses

Drug overdose occurs whenever the body is called upon to react to a substance beyond the body's ability to do so. The body reacts to substances up to a particular point, and then the body either damages itself or begins shutting off body systems. This may be life-threatening. If a person ingests too many amphetamines, the body begins pumping blood and increases respiration to the point that the body begins breaking down by causing hemorrhages in small blood vessels, which may cause death. Sometimes the body attempts to expel substances that have been ingested by vomiting, or at other times the body may simply shut down or become partially functional, as when a person becomes unconscious.

Many substances ingested in excess can be toxic to the body. Too much alcohol, too many aspirins, or a handful or two of salt can have a toxic or fatal effect on a person. The overdose potential is particularly high among the drugs discussed in this chapter. As a staff member you need to be familiar with the emergency procedures at your institution so that, should you encounter a drug overdose, you will know what to do.

Generally, if you confront a situation in which someone is unconscious and you find it difficult to arouse the person, your first responsibility is to stay with the person and send someone else for assistance. Follow this procedure:

1. Have the person call for an ambulance, the campus police, or the health center, whichever is the procedure at your institution.
2. Your hall director should also be notified at this time.
3. If the person is unconscious, check him or her for signs of breathing. If he or she is not breathing, first check to see if there is an obstruction in the throat.
4. If there is, clear the obstruction and administer mouth-to-mouth resuscitation.
5. Check whether there is any evidence of an accident, such as falling from a chair or being shocked by an electrical appliance. If the person has fallen, do not move him or her.
6. If the person has received an electrical shock, immediately attempt to initiate breathing by use of mouth-to-mouth resuscitation.
7. Check the pulse by locating the carotid artery in the neck directly to the right of the larynx (Adam's apple).
8. In the absence of any evidence of injury, convulsion, or accident, and the appearance of such things as drugs or any evidence that the person may have injected something, try to arouse the person. Try calling the person by name, placing a cold washcloth on the person's face, or shaking the person.
9. If the person is not unconscious but has taken a large dose of some drug (not a caustic or corrosive poisonous substance), attempt to have the person vomit by having the person put his or her fingers down the back of the throat or having the person drink a glass of warm salt water or a mixture of mustard and water.
10. Look around to see if you can locate any drugs in plain view. If drugs are present, give them to the medical personnel when they arrive. This will assist in determining an antidote for the drug.
11. If you are unable to find any drug in the room, question the person's associates to determine what the victim may have taken.

In cases in which a person has ingested some psychodelic drug and is not unconscious, but is simply experiencing the drug and is in a trancelike state, two options exist. First, you or someone else may stay with the person to help ensure that the person does not injure himself or herself or others. It is important to keep a tranquil atmosphere in the room and to keep at least two people in the room besides the person who has used the drug.

The second option is to contact medical personnel who can take custody of the person and assist the person should he or she become violent or experience a negative physical reaction. The latter option is a preferable method of handling students who are "tripping." Unless you are highly skilled in dealing with people who are on drugs and familiar with the behavioral effects associated with drugs, you run the risk of being injured by the student or bearing some responsibility for the student's possible injury.

This is particularly true if a student has taken PCP (angel dust). This animal tranquilizer is very dangerous. It can cause paralysis, brain damage, and in many cases excessive violence. The adrenalin surge is so strong in people using the drug that they may become disproportionately strong for their size. Because users are reacting to the drug and not thinking, unintentionally they may seriously injure themselves or someone else.

LSD can create fear, panic, and hallucinations from which the person will try to escape. Any person standing in the way may be injured. The excitement or need to escape may cause the person to smash through a window or jump from the top of a building.

It is preferable to get early assistance from medical personnel trained in handling these situations rather than to find yourself in the midst of a crisis and have to send for medical assistance at the last minute.

Chapter 14
Sexuality
By Jan Miltenberger

Jan Miltenberger, R.N., M.S. is Associate Director of the Student Health Center and Director of Student Health Promotion at Indiana State University

In the 1980s, college students became increasingly aware of a host of sexual issues. There was concern about AIDS, condoms, teenage pregnancy, date rape, abortion, right-to-life, adoption, chlamydia, homosexuality, drugs, alcohol, and caring or uncaring relationships. These problems did not go away as the population of our country increased and became more diverse.

Sexuality is part of one's total personality and involves one's sense of being male or female. It includes sex roles, self-esteem, family structure, schooling, dating, and a multitude of other complex, intertwining factors. There is no such thing as a "normal" sexuality. There are probably as many perceptions of what is "normal" sexuality as there are people on the earth.

RAs need information about sexuality among college students. Students, many living away from home for the first time, usually date more, drink more, and become more intimate with the opposite sex than they did living with their parents. Because society has a more open attitude toward sexuality than before the 1960s, each resident is confronted by recent changes in social and sexual issues. Students ask questions such as: How far will I go? What are my values? What risks will I take? What should I do if I have problems?

As an RA you must become a knowledgeable resource person about sexuality. To do this, you must first look within and assess your own attitudes, feelings, and values regarding various aspects of sexuality. Did you take a sex education class in high school or college? Have you attended seminars on sexual issues? Have you examined your feelings and attitudes about homosexuals, abortions, AIDS, premarital sex, and teenage pregnancy? It is your responsibility to be aware of your attitudes and values about sexual issues.

This chapter focuses on the main issues concerning sexuality and college students. It reviews topics such as contraceptives, pregnancy, abortion, AIDS and a few other sexually transmitted diseases (STDs), homosexuality, and quality relationships.

As an RA you need to be aware of resources on campus and in the community. You should be able to answer the following questions about your campus:

- Is there a student health center and/or student counseling center on campus? What do students say about these services? What services are available? Have you checked out the information for yourself? Rumors don't count!
- Are the health practitioners and counselors sensitive to the sexual problems of young adults?
- Can students get contraceptives and health information at the student health center?
- Is there a family planning or Planned Parenthood clinic nearby? Does the facility perform anonymous HIV testing?
- Is there a gay rights group on campus?

Contraceptives

Sexual urges and sexual activity are normal. If a man and woman are engaging in sex, they should expect pregnancy to occur if nothing is done to avoid conception. Some students believe they can be sexually active and not take precautions to avoid pregnancy and STDs. If you are sexually active and do not intend pregnancy, you should be prepared. Both the man and the woman have a responsibility to prevent unwanted pregnancies and sexually transmitted diseases from occurring. An unwanted pregnancy causes much emotional and physical anguish. Once conception happens, there are serious decisions that must be made. Preplanning, learning all that you can about contraceptives, and talking about sex and contraceptives with your sexual partner can prevent a lot of pain, especially for women.

Over 20 percent of women become pregnant during their college careers (Smith, 1988). Planned Parenthood reports that the average couple has been sexually active for nine months before requesting contraceptive information. Contraception is the responsibility of both individuals. Even though the woman has the most adjustments and decisions to make if pregnancy does occur, both individuals need to consider their options and the consequences. If the male partner is not willing to assume his part of the responsibility, women must. Women should be firm and clear about their decisions regarding sexual activity.

Abstinence from sexual activity with others has become more important lately due to the concern about AIDS. Abstinence is the only sure way to prevent pregnancy and STDs, including AIDS. However, realistically abstinence is not a viable alternative for the majority of college students. The surgeon general's 1987 Report on Acquired Immune Deficiency Syndrome advocates mutually faithful, monogamous relationships (only one continuing sexual partner) to help prevent the spread of this deadly disease. Unless you know with "absolute certainty" that neither you nor your sexual partner is carrying the HIV virus, you must use protective measures. Many college students do not think this includes them because they believe they are invulnerable: "It won't happen to me." The problem is, it probably will not while they are still in college. AIDS has a very long incubation period—the average length of time is about eight years from the time of infection until the person exhibits symptoms. Many college students, even though they know about AIDS, do not practice abstinence or use condoms with every episode of sexual intercourse. AIDS and other STDs are discussed in greater detail later in this chapter.

There are advantages and disadvantages to every contraceptive method. There is no way that an RA can be totally knowledgeable about all of the methods. However, it is important for the RA to be aware of the basic information regarding birth control pills, spermicides, diaphragms, cervical caps, the vaginal sponge, condoms, and so on. Students are usually interested in this topic, regardless of their sexual activity. Much is written today about what to use, when, and why. Some college health centers require women students to view a videotape

Table 14.1

Comparitive of Effectiveness of Contraceptive Methods

Method	Number of Pregnancies per 100 Women During One Year of Use*
Abstinence	0
Sterilization (male or female)	<1
Combination Birth Control Pill	2.5
Intrauterine Device (IUD)	4
Condom with Spermicides	10
Diaphragm with Spermicides	18
Sponge	18
Spermicides (jellies, foams, creams, suppositories)	20
Withdrawal	20
Fertility Awareness (natural family planning)	24
Chance (no method)	60–80

*Source: American College of Gynecology 5/87 "Methods of Contraception" - Planned Parenthood pamphlet (1987).

on the various contraceptive choices before discussing the best choice for the individual at specific times in her life. Most students are aware that there is no such thing as the perfect contraceptive with 100 percent effectiveness. The selection of the best contraceptive is a matter of individual choice, with consideration of the person's health history.

There is always new information about contraceptives. Educational programming on this topic can be an excellent way of meeting resource people on your campus and in your community. It is important that you seek knowledgeable, open-minded, sensitive people to be guest speakers for these programs. Sexuality and contraception are areas where some people are opinionated and biased. Good speakers might include a family practice physician, a gynecologist, a nurse midwife, a sex therapist, a health educator, or a nurse practitioner in gynecology.

Birth Control Pills

The birth control pill is the number one choice of college women who are sexually active and wish to avoid an unplanned pregnancy. There are over 20 different kinds and strengths of pills. It is especially important for the beginning user to consult with her health practitioner regarding any concerns or problems. Because most young women are on the low dosage of estrogen and progesterone, it is crucial that the pills be taken regularly at the same time every day and as directed. The birth control pills do *not* protect women against the virus that causes AIDS. Women who have multiple sexual partners during their reproductive years and who use the pill should also use condoms to protect against the HIV virus (Hatcher et al., 1988).

Some women are unable to take the pill because of health problems or family history. Women students should be advised to only take medication that is specifically prescribed for them. Smoking cigarettes and taking the pill can be dangerous. The nicotine in cigarettes can increase the risk of blood clots in women taking birth control pills. Blood clots can cause heart attacks or strokes, even in young people.

Condoms

Condoms are the best product for AIDS prevention in sexually active individuals. Condoms are the second most widely used reversible contraceptive in the United States after the pill (Hatcher et al., 1988). The RA should know about the availability of condoms on his or her campus. Condoms are frequently sold in the health center, the bookstore, the student union, and the residence halls. In 1988 over 200 college campuses had condom vending machines installed, although many were subsequently removed due to vandalism by students.

The AIDS issue has caused many campuses to evaluate their policies and procedures regarding sexual issues. Both men and women should be taking a more active and responsible role regarding contraception and health. With the exception of withdrawal, condoms are the only easily reversible method of birth control for men. The emphasis is also on prevention of STDs. In the March 1989 issue of *Consumer Reports,* an article entitled, "Can you Rely on Condoms?" appeared. The report, based laboratory results and surveys, explains which brands are most likely to protect against STDs. There is also a newspaper, *Condom Sense,* that is published by The Condom Resource Center, 5433 Manila Avenue, Oakland, CA 94618. It explains everything you ever wanted to know about condoms and more.

Approximately 2–3 million condoms are sold through mail-order companies. Many people find this a convenient way to purchase condoms. The spermicidal latex condoms with a reservoir tip offer the best protection against STDs. The natural membrane condoms, often called "skin" condoms, are not effective in preventing AIDS and hepatitis B. In the United States, at least 40 percent of condoms are now purchased by women. Gay men's organizations have become active proponents of condoms to make sex safer.

Five Good Reasons to Use a Condom

1. Prevent AIDS

2. Prevent Herpes

3. Prevent Gonorrhea

4. Prevent Chlamydia

5. Prevent Pregnancy

Many nurse practitioners and family planners recommend the use of condoms and spermicidal foam together. It is advisable for women to be prepared and comfortable with more than one contraceptive.

Vaginal Sponges

After more than seven years of research and development, the vaginal contraceptive sponge can now be purchased for about $1 each. It is a barrier contraceptive that can be bought over-the-counter. One size fits all. It is a small (less than two inches in diameter) pillow-shaped sponge with a concave dimple on one side that fits against the cervix and a woven polyester loop on the other side for removal. A spermicide is incorporated into the sponge during the manufacturing process. The spermicide is nonoxynol-9, which has been used in vaginal contraceptives for over 20 years with no apparent health risks.

The sponge is moistened with water and placed high in the vagina against the cervix, providing 24 hours of continuous contraception. It is not necessary to use each sponge the full 24 hours as long as it is left in place at least 6 hours after the last act of intercourse. Some of the advantages and disadvantages are as follows:

Advantages
- It is available in one universal size, so there is no need for a prescription or fitting.
- It is suitable for multiple-coital use for 24 hours, unlike the single-coital condom.
- It is both a spermicide and a barrier.
- It is easy to use, inexpensive, and generally unobtrusive when in place.

Disadvantages
- It is considered to be about 85 percent effective, so it is not as effective as some other methods.
- There have been complaints of odor developing if the sponge is left in place for over 18 hours. It must be left in 6 hours after intercourse.
- Some users have had difficulty removing and distinguishing the loop.
- About 2 percent of men and women are allergic to the spermicide and develop a local rash.

The Morning-after Pills

Some women may have heard of a prescription medication that can be taken within 72 hours of unprotected intercourse. These pills are not recommended by the U.S. Food and Drug Administration (FDA) and can have serious side effects. Since 1981 Planned Parenthood has endorsed the use of the "Morning-After Pill" in emergency situations only. The most common regimen is to take 2 OVRAL tablets within 72 hours of unprotectived intercourse and repeat the dosage 12 hours later.

The side effects can be nausea, vomiting, headaches, dizziness, and menstrual changes. These synthetic female hormones are available but are only used in special circumstances.

Contraceptives Summary

Students who have infrequent or unexpected sexual relations may prefer using a nonprescription method of contraceptive. The most effective is the condom plus a spermicidal agent, preferably the foam. The foam is more evenly distributed in the vagina. If used properly, the effectiveness of condom plus spermicidal is slightly less than the pill.

There are many excellent references about the specific aspects of various contraceptives. All students who wish to avoid an unwanted pregnancy and take precautions against AIDS and other STDs should know all that they can about the various methods. The more you know, the greater are your personal choices. The RA might want to have a floor program with a question and answer session regarding various contraceptives. Be selective in choosing a knowledgeable person who feels comfortable in a casual, spontaneous discussion situation. Some possible guest speakers are professors who teach human sexuality classes, nurses from the student health center, or personnel from a family planning agency. It is often a good idea to have students write down questions prior to the guest speaker's appearance.

Pregnancy

The most common sign of pregnancy is a missed menstrual period. Nausea and vomiting, breast tenderness, frequent urination, and tiredness can all be early signs of pregnancy. However, none of these signs always signifies pregnancy. Uncertainty and wondering are so agonizing that any woman who suspects she may be pregnant should go to a clinic, health center, nurse practitioner, or physician to have a pregnancy test done. Confirming a pregnancy as soon as possible not only relieves a woman of uncertainty but allows the health provider to discover any health problems that may endanger the life of the mother or the unborn child. The RA can serve a vital function if he or she understands the importance of having the pregnancy test done and can properly advise the possibly pregnant student or her boyfriend.

Women miss menstrual periods for all sorts of reasons, and a missed period does not necessarily indicate a pregnancy. Verifying pregnancy involves two procedures: a laboratory test that checks the urine for human chorionic gonadotrophin (HCG), a hormone produced by the developing embryo, and a pelvic examination by a health professional to check for relevant changes in the cervix and uterus.

The most common pregnancy urine test is the two-minute slide test, which is accurate within 12 days after conception (Hatcher et al., 1988). If it is absolutely critical that the person have the diagnosis of pregnancy confirmed, a more expensive blood test for HCG can be done.

The laboratory tests are said to be positive, negative, or inconclusive. "False positive" means that the test is positive for pregnancy, even though the woman is not pregnant. This is rare, but it can occur, even with experienced laboratory personnel performing the test. False positives can be caused by drugs such as marijuana, methadone, large amounts of aspirin, birth control pills, and some tranquilizers. "False negative" means that the test shows that the woman is not pregnant, when in actuality she is. False negatives are fairly common. In other words, the woman is pregnant, but the test results do not confirm the pregnancy. A false negative could be a result of urine that got too warm on its way to the lab; urine that was not concentrated enough; or contamination of the urine by soap, aspirin, or other substances in the specimen bottle. If the specimen is taken too early in the pregnancy, there may be an insufficient amount of the hormone to cause a positive lab test. If it is too late in the pregnancy, after about three months, the test may be falsely negative.

If the woman has a negative pregnancy test and her period does not start, she should return for another test in a week and continue using contraception, because if she is not pregnant and continues to be sexually active, she could get pregnant. After two or three negative tests, she should be advised to schedule a pelvic examination, as some pregnancies never get positive test results.

Given the effects of various drugs on a variety of laboratory tests, women students should not get upset when a health professional asks them about drug use. The professional needs to have factual information to make these important health diagnoses.

Home pregnancy test kits claim accuracy as early as nine days after a missed period. As one might expect, the accuracy of the test varies from person to person, depending on the woman's skill in performing the test and on individual hormone variations. Experts on pregnancy caution that women should be careful in depending on the home tests, which may delay seeking professional medical care during the crucial early weeks of pregnancy. The usual cost of a home test is about the amount one would pay to have the test done at a clinic.

If a student is pregnant, it is important to determine how far along she is in the pregnancy. Medical people calculate the weeks of pregnancy from the first day of the last normal menstrual period and not from the day conception may have occurred.

Early in the pregnancy the student has some time—not a lot—to make her choice about what to do. She can (1) continue the pregnancy and keep the baby; (2) continue the pregnancy and give the baby up for adoption; or (3) terminate the pregnancy by having a legal abortion at a medical facility. Usually this is a very difficult and personal decision for a woman to make. The important point is that she should be aware of all of the options available and not be pressured by parents, friends, or her sexual partner to do something she does not want to do, whether it be to have an abortion or to continue the pregnancy. The RA should be aware of agencies where the woman can receive proper counseling. Some of these agencies are the college health center, the college counseling center, the community mental health center, a local women's center, Planned Parenthood clinics, child and family services agency offices, or a religiously affiliated person or group. Antiabortion groups will provide information but will also try to persuade the student not to terminate the pregnancy.

The decision of whether to share the information with the woman's sexual partner is sometimes difficult. If she does not share the pain of the unplanned pregnancy, then she either allows her partner to avoid his responsibility or else prevents him from assuming it.

If the student is single and considers keeping the child, it would be advisable for her to talk with other single mothers about their experiences. Some of the groups just mentioned can help her realistically prepare for single parenthood. If the student is considering terminating the pregnancy, it is important for her to know that the earlier an abortion is done, the safer it is.

Abortion is one of the most controversial political, religious, and ethical issues of our time. Women choose abortion for various reasons. Proper usage of contraceptive methods cannot absolutely prevent unwanted pregnancies. Whether or not a woman feels she has the right to terminate a pregnancy, she definitely has the right to know what is involved in an abortion procedure.

Abortion

The abortion issue will forever remain a heated and controversial issue. Nobody really feels that abortion is good. Abortion may be an answer for some women in certain situations given the complex social issues of our multicultural world.

Many Americans believe in freedom of choice, but they are still confused about the issue of when life begins. People have argued for years about whether human life begins at conception, at the age of viability (considered to be approximately 20 weeks), or at the actual birth. Medical personnel know that many spontaneous abortions or miscarriages occur during the first three months of pregnancies. It is estimated that 40 percent to 60 percent of all fertilized eggs are never implanted and are sloughed off naturally in menstrual blood. Many Americans favor abortions in cases of rape, incest, or their own personal situation (*Newsweek,* 1989).

There are more than 6 million pregnancies annually in the United States, and half of these are felt to be "mistakes." As a result of mistakes, 1.6 million pregnancies end in abortions every year (Fraser, 1989). The Alan Guttmaccher Institute reports that 18- and 19-year olds have an abortion rate twice that of the national average (*Newsweek,* 1989).

College women have abortions for a number of reasons. In order to make a good decision, the woman has a right to professional counseling in a supportive, nonjudgmental setting. A woman should be able to make an informed decision after having the factual information explained to her in an understandable way.

Many articles and books describe in detail the recommended methods, procedures, risks, and possible complications of abortion. The RA should familiarize herself with basic information about how and when abortions are performed. However, actual counseling and assistance in decision making should be done by a professional counselor, nurse practitioner, or physician.

Legalization does not guarantee decent abortion services, which ideally should provide concerned safe care, counseling, good health education, and birth control services in an atmosphere that is accepting of the individual's sexuality. With such health care, freely provided, there would be fewer unwanted pregnancies and consequently less need for women to have to choose abortion at all.

For all women, abortion involves health issues of vital importance. Abortion is an operation involving the risks of blood loss and infection. Like other surgical procedures, it should be avoided if possible.

Because the decision to abort or complete a pregnancy is so great, many women feel isolated and alone in making their decision. Often only a student and her partner are aware of her pregnancy. They may both have feelings of guilt, confusion, and fear. They may both need emotional support and varying degrees of counseling.

The RA must be especially careful not to be judgmental of the pregnant student's final decision. A woman who has chosen to undergo an abortion needs emotional support and acceptance during this difficult time. In addition to expressing her concern and availability, the RA should be aware of the support services available on campus and in the local community to help a woman deal with any emotional problems resulting from the abortion.

After an abortion, a patient is given a few basic instructions that an RA should also know:

- Bleeding and cramps vary from woman to woman; some women have none, but most have both during the first two weeks after an abortion. Some women may have spotting for four weeks after surgery.
- The next normal period should begin in four to six weeks. If women take birth control pills, their period will probably start after they use the first packet.
- It is important to rest for one or two days after the operation and to avoid strenuous exercise.
- Women should be aware of possible complications: excessive bleeding, vomiting, fever, severe cramping, or a foul-smelling vaginal odor or discharge.
- After abortions, women must avoid possibilities for infection. They should use no douches, tampons, or tub baths, and they should avoid sexual intercourse for at least one week or whatever is recommended.
- Women should have a postabortion checkup two or three weeks after the operation and receive instructions in contraception.

Usually, it is a great relief for a woman to end an unwanted pregnancy. However, there may be mixed or confused feelings after the operation. The RA needs to understand that some sadness and a sense of loss may occur.

The RA may be involved with students who have repeat abortions. In this case a woman is more likely to receive censure from other students, because they may now view her as careless and irresponsible. The emotional feelings and reactions to a second abortion may be quite different from a first one. The RA may be quite challenged to work not only with the pregnant student but with others on the floor who are aware of the situation. Of course, no information should be shared by an RA about any personal, confidential situation.

The person who has almost been left out of the abortion issue is the woman's partner. If the man is thought of, it is usually with hostility and blame. The RA might lend a sympathetic ear to the male student who wants to talk about what a personal experience with abortion has meant to him.

In 1988, an antiprogesterone steroid called RU486 was in use in five countries by over 20,000 women who ended pregnancies up to three weeks after a missed menstrual period. This drug has been approved for use in France, China, Sweden, the Netherlands, and Great Britain. Women in the United States probably will not have access to it in the immediate future because of political issues and threats by abortion opponents to boycott pharmaceutical companies that distribute RU486 in the United States (Fraser, 1989).

The RU486 pill is taken orally under a doctor's supervision. When coupled with another drug called *prostaglandin,* RU486 is reported to be over 90 percent effective.

Homosexuality

Homosexuality is a controversial and emotional topic. Many college-age males are fearful, resentful, and reactive toward effeminate males, whom they stereotype as possible gays. Because many of these young males are struggling with identity, self-esteem, and developmental issues, it seems easier for them to make fun, harass, or intimidate possible gays than to take the time to learn and understand about differences in life-style choices. The RA may have difficulty with some residents, especially males, who discriminate against a possible gay student. In general, women students seem to be more accepting of gays and lesbians.

According to studies conducted by the Kinsey Research Institute, between 4 and 12 percent of the American population is primarily homosexual; about 50 percent is primarily heterosexual; and the rest fall somewhere in between (Bendet, 1989).

The AIDS epidemic has influenced attitudes regarding the homosexual population. Some heterosexuals feel like those who have chosen the gay life style deserve this deadly disease. Others are challenged to accept differences in people and have reached out to help young gays who are having to cope with devastating illnesses, death, and dying.

Many heterosexuals, especially males, do not view homosexuals as people with legitimate rights and feelings. Such fear results in *homophobia*—an irrational fear of homosexuals. Homophobic people believe myths about homosexuals.

Myths about Homosexuals

- Myth: Homosexuals look different than other people.
  Fact: Only 10 percent of all homosexuals could be viewed as "visible homosexuals." Most gays look and act publicly like everyone else.
- Myth: Homosexual males are effeminate and weak; lesbian females are masculine and physically strong.
  Fact: Sexual preference has nothing to do with body type. Also, no relationship has been demonstrated between occupational choice and sexual preference.
- Myth: Homosexuals seduce innocent children.
  Fact: More heterosexuals than homosexuals seduce innocent children. Either situation is intolerable, and we must help young children know that no one has a right to touch their private parts unless it involves medical care.

A student who is gay may have some difficulty dealing with some aspects of his or her choice and may be interested in discussing counseling options. Whatever the situation, the RA is challenged to assess his or her own knowledge, attitudes, and beliefs about homosexuality. You must be able to talk with a person who is homosexual and see the many aspects of his or her personality without focusing on sexual choice. You must be overtly and covertly nonjudgmental when you see certain people who portray the stereotype of male or female homosexuals.

It is your responsibility as an RA to honestly examine your feelings and attitudes regarding the homosexual life style. If you are prejudiced about homosexuality, it would be wise to read about the subject and work at being more tolerant.

Remember that you can learn about many differences in life without condoning the ideas or practices for yourself. AIDS has challenged many professionals, including physicians, nurses, and counselors, to closely reexamine their beliefs and values regarding human life and homosexuality. Everyone has to make sexual choices. These choices may be vastly different from yours, but each individual does have a right to be treated with kindness and respect as a human being.

AIDS

As an RA it is important to assess the available resources about AIDS on your campus. First, you need to evaluate the educational response of your institution to the AIDS issue. The AIDS problem crosses many disciplines and various departments. The American College Health Association is active in providing AIDS resources specific for the college age population. The American Red Cross and state health departments have pamphlets and educators available to address various groups.

Resources for Information about AIDS

To obtain more information about AIDS, you can contact the following groups:
Toll-free AIDS hotline: 1–800–342–AIDS

Office of Public Affairs
U.S. Public Health Service
Room 721-H
200 Independence Avenue, S.W.
Washington, D.C. 20201

The Gay Men's Health Crisis Education Department
Box 274
132 West 24th Street
New York, NY 10011

AIDS Project of Los Angeles
3670 Wilshire Boulevard, Suite 300
Los Angeles, CA 9001

San Francisco AIDS Foundation
333 Valencia Street, 4th Floor
San Francisco, CA 94103

National AIDS Information Clearinghouse
P.O.Box 6003, Dept. AAN
Rockville, MD 20850
1–800–458–5231

American Council for Healthful Living
439 Main Street
Orange, NJ 07050
STD/VD National Hotline
1–800–227–8922

On many campuses the current health issues have stimulated changes in student health centers. Many centers now employ health educators, nurse practitioners, physicians, and nurses who are wellness oriented. The emphasis is not only on treating illnesses and injuries but on helping students to be more knowledgeable and responsible for making healthy life-style choices. As an RA you should know the variety of resources and services provided by your student health center.

Precautions Against AIDS

The most important decision is to be responsible for your own health and take precautions to protect yourself against AIDS.

- Don't feel pressured to have sex before you are ready. If you and your partner have sex only with each other and neither of you uses needles, your risk of getting infected with the HIV virus is very low.
- Don't have unprotected sex with a partner.
- Know which sexual practices are considered safe, probably safe, and unsafe.
- Avoid the exchange of all body fluids, including semen, vaginal secretions, blood, urine, and feces.
- Avoid multiple sex partners. Choose your partners carefully.
- Never share an IV needle with anyone. It is best not to use any drugs unless prescribed by a clinician.
- Do not share razors or toothbrushes, because they could expose you to small amounts of blood.
- Anal sex is more dangerous than oral sex. It is felt that 99 percent of HIV transmission through sex occurs with intercourse—anal or vaginal.
- Do not mix alcohol and other drugs with sexual activity; this behavior impairs your judgment and may contribute to engaging in sexual practices that you would not ordinarily do.

HIV Testing

The HIV antibody test is *not* a test for AIDS. It tests for antibodies produced by your body in response to being exposed to the HIV virus that causes AIDS.

If you are considering being tested, you should ask the following questions of your health professional:

- What is involved in the testing? What will I learn?
- What are the credentials of the person who is doing the testing? In some states, registered nurses are certified as AIDS educators or disease intervention specialists.
- Is pre- and postcounseling done? This is recommended by the experts to help you know more about what the testing means.

- Is the testing confidential or anonymous? *Confidential testing* is done at some local hospitals. It means access to your medical record is limited to clinicians and personnel taking care of you. However, lab technicians, secretaries, and your insurance company may know. *Anonymous testing* means no one knows your real name. You are given a fictitious name or number. Some people never feel anonymous because someone might recognize them. Most experts recommend using anonymous testing unless proof of the test is needed for a specific job or foreign travel.
- Is HIV testing done at the Student Health Center? In the community? Where is the closest testing site?
- What should you do if the test is negative? Positive?
- What if you decide not to take the test?
- What if you are HIV positive and pregnant?

HIV testing is a very serious matter, especially if the test results are positive. Even if you think you can handle the results, supportive counseling during this stressful time is essential.

As an RA, if a student requests information from you, refer the student to the student health center, Planned Parenthood clinic, or an agency such as the State Board of Health. You have a key part to play in not disclosing personal information and not contributing to rumors.

The preliminary results of a survey conducted by the American College Health Association (ACHA) and U.S. Public Health Service on 20 college campuses in 1988 showed that approximately 3 out of 1000 college students are HIV positive. Many college campuses have already experienced situations involving individuals who are HIV positive. A positive test result does not indicate that person will develop AIDS Related Complex (ARC) (a related but less serious condition than AIDS) or AIDS, but that person is capable of spreading the virus. As such, the individual should take precautions to protect all partners with whom he or she may have intimate contact. The Centers for Disease Control predict that AIDS will be the number one killer on college campuses by 1991 (Smith, 1988).

If you have someone living on your floor who has ARC or AIDS, remember that AIDS is not spread by casual contact. AIDS is a devastating disease that can cause a person to have many serious emotional and physical problems. We all need loving and supportive friends. You need to be as compassionate toward the victim as possible.

AIDS has challenged many people to assess priorities and to be more responsible for sexual decisions. It is important to help young people think more about preventing something than to cope with the consequences. As an RA you can help students become more knowledgeable and encourage actions and behaviors that promote long, healthy lives.

Sexually Transmitted Diseases

Initially, it may appear that the RA would not need to know about sexually transmitted diseases. However, these diseases do involve the college population, so it is important for the RA to be knowledgeable and informed.

The STD problem is truly epidemic. Despite the seriousness and increased incidence of these diseases, the majority of sexually active people have little awareness of the risks and dangers involved in STDs. This section presents the facts on the major STDs of the 1990s.

STDs always involve at least two people, and any person who has a STD should assume the responsibility for informing partners with whom he or she has had sexual contact. Obviously, some people feel embarrassed to discuss it or fear the effects on a particular relationship. However, the consequences of undetected infection are so harmful that there is no excuse for not telling one's partners. If some students are afraid to tell their partners directly, the local public health services or college student health centers will do it for them, preserving anonymity.

Free diagnosis and treatment for STDs are available at public health centers and college health centers throughout the country. However, the infected persons must take the initiative by reporting the earliest symptoms. Ignoring the symptoms in hopes that they will disappear is very risky. Sometimes symptoms do disappear or seem to subside, but this does not mean that the disease is gone. With some infections, such as syphilis, it merely means that the infection may be entering a new stage.

At either the college health center or a public health center, the individual will be asked to describe the symptoms and to recall if he or she has had sexual contact with someone who may have had an STD. Patients will then be examined and laboratory tests done to determine if a disease is actually present.

Once the specific disease has been diagnosed, the recommended treatment will be instituted. Sometimes antibiotics are effective, and other times specific medications or treatments are prescribed. The examinations, tests, and treatments vary with the disease. However, reexamination is important to make sure the disease has been arrested.

Following diagnosis and treatment in a clinic, patients are asked who may have infected them and whom they may have infected. This information is confidential, and contacts will not be informed of the source of identification unless permission is given to do so. Usually the contacts are notified by means of a letter informing them that they have been exposed to STD and that they are required to go to a doctor or clinic within 48 hours. These people must be examined and possibly treated so they will not spread the disease to others.

Table 14.2
Sexually Transmitted Diseases

Disease	Symptoms	Diagnosis	Treatment	Prevention	Comments
AIDS (Acquired Immune Deficiency Syndrome)	Unexplained increasing and persistent fatigue Persistent fever, chills, and night sweats Unexpected weight loss Swollen glands Creamy white patches on tongue or mouth Persistent diarrhea Persistent, frequent dry breath Shortness of breath or lack of breath Pink or purple flat or raised blotches (not common in women with AIDS)	There is no single test for diagnosis. The HIV-test is used to test for antibodies (substances produced in the blood to fight the disease). This test measures exposure to the infection of the human immunodeficiency virus (HIV), which does not always lead to AIDS. Preliminary results show that 20%–30% of those infected with HIV develop AIDS. The diagnosis of a AIDS depends on the presence of "opportunistic disease." Anyone with an HIV-positive test is considered contagious.	There is currently no available antiviral drug to cure AIDS. Some success is being shown with radiation and surgery to treat various illnesses. The drug AZT has been used to extend survival and improve the quality of life of those who have AIDS.	Make careful choices about sexual partners. Avoid multiple partners. Unprotected sex is unsafe. Use condoms during sex. Do not engage in casual sex. Latex condoms provide the best protection. Use condoms with contraceptive jellies, cream, or foam for possible additional protection. Determine your partner's sexual history, knowledge of STDs, and awareness and practice of safe sex. Do not use IV drugs or share needles. Avoid using amphetamines (speed), recreational drugs, or any drug that can weaken the immune system. Be knowledgeable about sexual practices which are safe, probably safe, and unsafe.	The HIV virus is transmitted by infected body fluids mainly semen, blood, or vaginal fluids. Needles contaminated by the virus can also transmit the disease. Mothers who have the virus can transmit it to unborn children during pregnancy or through breast feeding. The virus is not spread through casual contact (such as hugging or handshaking). No family member of anyone with AIDS has been shown to have contracted the disease by living in the same household as the infected person. The time between infection with HIV and the onset of symptoms can range from six months to seven years.

Disease	Symptoms	Diagnosis	Treatment	Prevention	Comments
AIDS - Continued					There is no danger of getting AIDS from donating blood.
					Blood transfusion products are screened for HIV in the United States. Risk of contracting AIDS through donated blood is almost nil.
					There is no danger of contracting AIDS by living in a residence hall with a person who has AIDS.
					Tests for HIV are available through your student health center or through your public health center. Results of these tests are confidential and in some cases can be done anonymously.
					AIDS research is continuous. New treatments or a cure could develop in the near future.

Table 14.2 *Continued*

Disease	Symptoms	Diagnosis	Treatment	Prevention	Comments
Bacterial Vaginitis (Nonspecific vaginitis, *Hemaphilis vaginalis, Gardenerella vaginitis*); inflammation of the vagina	Grayish or whitish watery vaginal discharge Pain on urination Vaginal itching Painful intercourse Foul odor of discharge	Culture by health practitioner.	Oral antibiotics or other prescribed medications—oral Flagyl is the most common medication. Your partner must be treated at the same time, and you both must complete the full course of treatment to prevent reinfection.	Avoid multiple partners.	Sex is permitted as long as you use condoms for the duration of treatment.
Chlamydia (*Chlamydia trachomatis*)	Burning on urination Vaginal discharge Symptoms of pelvic inflammatory disease (PID)	Culture by health practitioner.	Oral antibiotics. Your partner must be treated at the same time to avoid reinfection.	Avoid multiple partners.	Potential complications: Untreated infection could affect a woman's fertility. With concurrent treatment sexual intimacy can continue.
Cystitis (Honeymoon cystitis)	Pain, burning during urination Frequent urination Foul-smelling, cloudy urine Lower abdominal pain Blood in urine Painful intercourse	Urinalysis by health practitioner.	Oral antibiotics and often Pyridium, a urinary anesthetic, to decrease pain and bladder spasms. Treatment of partner is only when needed. Drink 8–10 glasses of water per day. For length of treatment use condoms. Have a follow-up urinalysis 3–4 weeks after treatment.	Urinate often Wear cotton underpants—nylon underwear and hose hold in moisture that leads to increased bacterial growth. Good personal hygiene—wash genitals once a day and dry thoroughly. Drink cranberry juice—increases acidity of the urine and lessens chance of infections. Urinate after sex.	Potential complications include a recurrence of bladder infection.

Disease	Symptoms	Diagnosis	Treatment	Prevention	Comments
Gonorrhea (The clap, drip, *Neisseria gonorrhea*)	Female—usually no symptoms, some have puslike vaginal discharge, vaginal soreness, lower abdominal pain, painful urination Male—cloudy, puslike discharge from the penis, burning on urination; about 20% of men have no symptoms	Bacterial smear and culture of male urethea or female vagina by health practitioner (throat culture if oral-genital sex).	Penicillin or other antibiotics. Treatment of partner is essential. Any sexual partners must receive treatment. Special instructions: Refrain from oral-genital sex, avoid intercourse until treatment is complete and have follow-up evaluation by health practitioner.	Avoid multiple partners. Spermicides provide some protection. Use condoms.	If untreated, can cause inflammation, pain, and sterility in male and female. Can cause infant blindness during delivery if infant passes through infected birth canal. It is estimated there are 3 million persons affected yearly.
Herpes Simplex Virus II (HSV II, Type II or genital herpes)	Blisterlike sores on vulva, cervix, penis Painful intercourse Itching of vulva, penis Painful urination	Pap smear of lesions and culture by health practitioner. Physical examination of sores.	No effective known treatment, local analgesics. Oral acyclovir or acyclovir cream on sores can decrease symptoms. Active sores heal in 10–20 days. Special instructions: Report herpes to physician if pregnant, wear loose underwear, avoid intercourse if sores present.	Annual Pap smear Good personal hygiene Avoid oral-genital intercourse when sores are present.	Potential complications: About one third of victims experience recurrences. Herpes may be spread to newborn during birth, causing serious problems. It is estimated there are 3 to 5 million persons affected yearly.

Table 14.2 *Continued*

Disease	Symptoms	Diagnosis	Treatment	Prevention	Comments
Monilia (*Candida albicans,* yeast infections)	Female—thick, cottage cheese-like vaginal discharge, itching, burning sensation, redness of vulva, painful intercourse	Microscopic evaluation, gram stain, or culture by health practitioner.	Antifungal vaginal suppositories or creams (Mycostatin/Nystatin) are prescribed, usually for seven days. These are messy, so wear a minipad or shield. Complete the treatment even during menstruation. Treatment of partner—only when needed; yeast is rarely transmitted sexually. Special instructions: Wearing cotton underwear treatment may be needed for two cycles of the medication. Birth control pills and diabetic conditions increase the risk by creating conditions in the vagina favoring the growth of yeast. Antibiotics can decrease vaginal bacteria and a yeast infection can result. Don't use tampons because they absorb all the medication.	Avoid douching, because it can destroy normal bacteria in the vagina.	Potential complication: recurrence.

Disease	Symptoms	Diagnosis	Treatment	Prevention	Comments
Pelvic Inflammatory Disease (PID, salpingitis, or inflammation of fallopian tubes, endometritis or inflammation of the lining of the uterus)	Abdominal/back/pelvic/leg pain Fever, chills, vomiting Painful urination Painful intercourse Postcoital bleeding Excessive menstrual bleeding	Gram stain, culture, exam, and history by health practitioner.	Oral antibiotics as prescribed. Treatment of partner is not usually required. Special instructions: Use condoms during treatment, bedrest is essential until pain subsides. Avoid milk products if taking Tetracycline and watch for minilial flareups.	Avoid multiple partners. Use condoms. Avoid IUDs (intrauterine devices).	Potential complications: Sterility, chronic pain, and infections.
Pubic Lice (crabs, *Phthirus pubis*), tiny creatures not larger than a pinhead that under magnification look like crabs	Itching Lice in pubic hair	Lice or eggs in pubic hair.	Kewell shampoo—leave on 4 minutes, then rinse (crabs are not affected by normal soap). May need to repeat treatment. Also, RID is effective; should not be used by person allergic to ragweed. Follow directions carefully. Treatment of partner only when he or she is infected. Special instructions: Remove all visible signs of infection and wash infected clothing, bed linens, or sleeping bags	Follow good hygiene practices. Do not sleep in others' beds, wear their clothes, or use their towels.	No potential complications. It is estimated that 1–2 million people are infected each year.

Table 14.2 *Continued*

Disease	Symptoms	Diagnosis	Treatment	Prevention	Comments
Pubic Lice - Continued			and dry in dryer set on high heat. Crabs can survive 24 hours apart from host. Avoid inter-course.		
Syphilis (Loues, *Treponema pal-lidum* infection)	Primary: 3 weeks postex-posure chancre (pain-less sore) on penis/vagina/rectum/anus/cervix/mouth/throat Secondary: 6 weeks postpri-mary Rash on feet and hands Loss of appetite Fever and sore throat Nausea Painful joints Headaches Tertiary: 10–20 years—see comments	Dark field exam of fluid of chancre and VDRL (blood test) by health practitioner. This blood test is routinely done upon hos-pital admission, obtaining a mar-riage license, giving blood, joining the mili-tary, and be-coming pregnant.	Penicillin shot (stages 1 and 2). Treatment of partner is es-sential. Special instruc-tions: Use con-doms for 1 month.	Avoid multiple partners.	Potential compli-cations if un-treated include brain damage, heart disease, spinal cord damage, and blindness. An in-fected pregnant woman may pass syphilis on to her unborn child, giving the infant congenital syphilis. It is estimated that approxi-mately 400,000 persons are af-fected yearly.
Trichomoniasis (Trich, caused by a one-celled parasite)	Frothy, thin greenish vaginal discharge Vulvar itching/pain Frequent urina-tion May be asymp-tomatic	Wet mount, cul-ture, and Pap smear by health practitioner.	Oral Flagyl as prescribed—usually for 7 days. Treatment of partner is es-sential, al-though men usually don't have symp-toms. Both must complete the course of treatment or partners may reinfect each other.	Avoid multiple partners.	No potential complications.

Disease	Symptoms	Diagnosis	Treatment	Prevention	Comments
Trichomoniasis - Continued			Special instructions: Use condoms during treatment, avoid alcohol with Flagyl, repeat Pap test in 2–3 months if original was abnormal.		
Venereal Warts (*Condylomata acuminata*)	Dry, wart-like growths on penis, vagina, vulva, cervix Constant discharge Itching	Exam and possibly blood test (VDRL to rule out syphilis) by health practitioner.	Podophyllin ointment or liquid applied to warts every 3–4 hours. Treatment of partner is required only if infected. Special instructions: Several weeks of treatment may be required. Use condoms	Avoid multiple partners.	No potential complications.

Healthy Relationships

College students confront all types of relationships with family, friends, girlfriends, boyfriends, fellow students, teachers, and other adults. Some people are good at building satisfying and healthy relationships, whereas other young adults have difficulty. Good relationships do not just happen. They take time, patience and communication. This is true for all relationships, but particularly true of intimate relationships.

The ingredients of a healthy relationship include open and honest communications on each side. There is comfort in exchanges that are assertive, accurate, and clear. This level of communication requires trust and the ability to listen.

In a healthy relationship each person feels whole. Each person is not dependent on the other person. Each recognizes that he or she is responsible for his or her own well-being and happiness.

People who have a healthy relationship have friends outside this relationship. These other friends are important. Being isolated and feeling dependent on another person is not healthy. When a person in the relationship becomes jealous of these other friends, he or she is becoming possessive and is signaling that he or she is insecure in the relationship.

Healthy relationships provide opportunity for growth and the opportunity for mutual support. Because each person grows in a relationship, relationships change. Like people, relationships mature. Healthy relationships allow people to fulfill their potential. One person in the relationship does not try to hold the other back or try to compete with the other.

Another characteristic of healthy relationships is that the people depend on one another when things are good and when things are not good. There is commitment. There is support. There is a sense of being a team.

Work and play are shared in healthy relationships. Both share the responsibility for the relationship, the maintenance of the household if the two are living together, and the fun things to do.

In healthy relationships there is freedom—freedom to be honest without the fear of hurting the other person, to express one's emotions openly, and to tell the other person what you feel and what you need.

Other factors are important in healthy relationships. People learn from all relationships. Those that are not constructive help us to develop a perspective on what we need in a relationship and to gain insight into our own ability to function supportively in an intimate relationship with another person. Nobody needs to remain in an unhealthy relationship. As an RA you will talk with students about their relationships. You can offer perspective and help the student assess the health of his or her relationships.

Chapter 15
Cult Activities on College Campuses

It is estimated that almost 3 million young people between the ages of 18 and 24 are active in 2000 religious cults in the United States today. The 1981 Gallup youth survey found that, between 1978 and 1981 alone, there was an 18.1 percent increase in religious cult membership among teenagers. On campuses, it is estimated that approximately 1 in every 20 college students has turned to some form of nontraditional religious activity. As an RA, you have the greatest contact with new students. These students are the most vulnerable to becoming involved in destructive religious cults. The information provided in this chapter should assist you in understanding what a religious cult is, how its members recruit students on campus, the effects that membership has on an individual, and the early warning signs of someone experiencing problems with cults.

Defining Religious Cults

The distinctive features of a religious cult, as it is used in this chapter, involve a close allegiance to a charismatic leader, an inordinate preoccupation on the part of the group with the attainment of money, and the use of behavior modification practices and brainwashing techniques to convert and retain members. Cults are distinguished from the more traditional forms of religious groups by their highly syncretic beliefs and practices coupled with some form of separation from society.

Newspaper articles and scholarly books have referred to groups such as the International Society of Krishna Consciousness (Hare Krishna), Sun Myung Moon Unification Church, The Divine Light Mission, Church of Scientology, and the Children of God as examples of cults. However, there are hundreds of smaller groups that could also be so classified.

Cult Recruiting on College Campuses

There is substantial evidence that college campuses are among the primary targets for cult recruiting. In a study of 237 members of Moon's Unification Church (Galanter et al., 1979), almost half (42 percent) of the members studied were attending college at least part-time at least six months prior to joining the group, and nearly one-third (31 percent) were full-time students. Only 25 percent of the members completed college after joining the Unification Church, although 58 percent had begun.

Many recruiting techniques are used by cults on college campuses. Some organizations specifically target freshman and senior students because of their vulnerability as they experience uncertainty about their futures. Recruiters have used counseling centers at universities to find students in personal crises, either by waiting in the waiting rooms, or by standing outside the counseling centers to find students who are troubled. They befriend the troubled student for the purpose of gaining the student's confidence and inducing the student into eventual membership to the cult.

Residence halls have always been a favorite place to recruit students, particularly on the weekends, when recruiters can wander the corridors and find students who are alone, instead of with friends. Not even libraries are safe from the intrusive proselytizing of cults. Recruiters search the library stacks to find students who are exploring questions the cult recruiter can use to entice the person into taking the first step toward joining the cult organization. Other techniques that have been used by cult recruiters on campuses range from ads in campus newspapers for students to do "Peace Corps" type work, to starting student organizations with lofty principles designed to entice students into joining the organization.

Under the guise of situations like vegetarian cooking classes or yoga classes, or as organizations dedicated to world peace, institutions have recognized some of these groups as student organizations or have given these organizations permission to operate on campus. Using front groups to hide their actual identity, cults frequently lure students into organizations without students having full knowledge of the actual purposes of the organizations. Moon's Unification Church, as one example, is associated with over 140 different front groups. On college campuses it is known variously as the Collegiate Associate for the Research of Principles (CARP), New Educational Developmental Systems, and the Students for an Ethical Society, to name but three. Many students are deceived into membership in one of these groups only to discover the identity of the group some months later. Richard Delgado, professor of law at UCLA, described the problem with the recruiting practices of cults before a special U.S. Senate Committee in 1979, as follows:

> The recruiter . . . uses deception and concealment to forestall truth. Gradually, the recruit gains knowledge of the cult, its identity, its demands. This information is parceled out only as the cult perceives that he or she has lost the ability to assess it according to his or her usual frames of references. A convert thus never has full capacity and knowledge. One or the other is impaired by the cult design (p. 60).

It is important to understand that cults, through their recruiting process, attack people psychologically and emotionally, not intellectually. Everyone is vulnerable to the deceptive proselytizing of cult groups.

The Conversion Process

The conversion process, sometimes referred to as *mind control* or *brainwashing,* is based on two fundamental principles: (1) if you can get a person to behave in the ways you want, you can get him or her to believe what you want; and (2) sudden, drastic changes in the environment lead to heightened suggestibility and drastic changes in attitudes and beliefs.

Stages in Conversion

To grasp the conversion process, consider it in three stages: (1) unfreezing beliefs, (2) conversion or snapping, and (3) refreezing of new beliefs or indoctrination. The first stage is devoted to an unfreezing of the person's current belief system. This is where most of the mind-control or brainwashing techniques are employed. Organizations approach this differently; however, there are commonalities in the techniques employed to convert members. The foundations of the techniques of brainwashing were first advanced in the Chinese thought-reform camps during the Korean Conflict. New technology based on research on persuasion, propaganda, motivation, behavior modification, group dynamics, nonverbal communication, light, color, sound, texture, eye contact, and altered states of consciousness (Conway, 1979) used by the cults today are more effective than those used on Korean Conflict prisoners and produce profound changes in the individual.

In the initial stages of conversion (the unfreezing of beliefs), the new recruit is usually isolated from all but cult members. This often takes place at a weekend retreat or workshop but may also be seen when individual students are not left alone and are constantly in the company of cult group members. The new recruit is subjected to long, boring lectures, deprived of sleep, maintained on a diet low in protein, and sometimes required to chant or meditate for long periods of time. The recruit may also be subjected to tremendous peer pressure, guilt manipulation, personal confessions, and personal intimacy that promotes a sense of family through hugging, kissing, touching, and flattery.

Deprived of the opportunity to validate beliefs outside of the cult and maintained in a state of mental and physical exhaustion, the recruit becomes quickly absorbed in a world of new happenings and new experiences. Finally, the person's individuality and personal control slips away and the person enters a state not unlike a trance—a state of altered consciousness.

As the person's attention is narrowed, he or she undergoes what has been described as a sudden personality change. Conway and Siegelman (1978) describe it as "snapping." They define this moment as an "overpowering, holographic crisis of the brain." This period may temporarily energize or exhilarate individuals, but it has a devastating effect upon individuals' ability to function as they did before. It is as if a wall has been constructed to block the person's personality. With this accomplished, cult members begin the final stage of the conversion experience—indoctrinating the new recruit with the cult's particular set of beliefs and practices.

For a period of time immediately following this snapping experience, the person is highly susceptible to absorbing new information. It is in this period that the person is programmed or indoctrinated with beliefs of the cult. New beliefs become locked into the new personality and become the guide by which this person functions in the world. Examples of such beliefs are that parents are disciples of Satan, all people outside of the group are evil, thinking for one's self is bad, and the cult must be obeyed without question.

Mind Control Methods Used on Recruits

Robert Lifton (1961), a psychiatrist who studied the brainwashing process in thought-reform camps in China during the Korean Conflict, established eight principles used in mind control. These principles, coupled with some of the new information on mind-control techniques, are employed in the conversion of new members. The eight psychological themes are as follows:

- Milieu control. This is the ability of the cult to control the environment of the individual. The cult controls not only the physical environment, but usually communication as well by restricting the nature of the conversations. During workshops or retreats, cults control the person's life through the use of a detailed schedule that determines the nature and timing of each event throughout the day, even the most mundane events.

- Mystical manipulation. This form of manipulation uses every possible device the cult has available, no matter how painful or bizarre. Its purpose is to provoke "specific patterns of behavior and emotions in such a way that these will appear to have arisen spontaneously from the environment" (p. 422). The cult requires the recruit to trust it because it has a higher purpose. As the recruit gives more trust to the group, the group takes on increased importance. The recruit begins to feel that he or she cannot escape from the organization and begins to surrender to its will.

- The demand for purity. In most religious cults, there are absolute goods and absolute evils. People are either good or they are evil. Those who are in cults are good; those who are not are evil. This bipolarization provides the opportunity for the person to be good by joining the organization. The process used is to make the person feel guilty about all the evils associated with not being in the group.

- The cult of confession. Cults generally demand that people show shame and confess their sins to the group. These personal confessions are explained as purification, but are used as a way of exploiting the individual and as a way of enhancing guilt that the individual must feel for being part of the evil world of the outside as opposed to the good world of the cult members.

- The sacred science. No matter what cult group is discussed, each claims to have the "word"—the sacred science. There is something unique about the cult's truth; something divine about its approach, something special separating the cult from the rest of the world. This "special insight" is viewed as the final answer, the correct path.

- Loading the language. Language is a very powerful tool. It is the way that we understand and conceptualize. Cults have a system of making language value loaded. Common words are given special meaning by cults. This special ideological jargon soon becomes a way for the person to demonstrate membership involvement and participation in the group. The recruit is rewarded for using it, and is looked on as an insider in the use of it.

- Doctrine over person. The human experience of the past is always subordinate to the claims of the doctrine. No matter what one's practical knowledge and past experiences have been, it is not a substitute for the "truth," as explained by the dogma of the religious group. Thus, it is never possible to challenge the dogma or doctrine on the basis of human experience, no matter how foolish or how contrary it is to the person's past experiences.
- The dispensing of existence. Because only those in the cult organization are good, it follows that those outside the cult are bad. It also follows that good is better than evil, and good should exist, and evil should not. It is often upheld by the cult leaders that only those people who are involved in the group will be saved or have the right to exist. Those who are not part of the group do not have the right to exist or will not be saved. Somewhere in the cult doctrine there is usually the allegation that these people will be dealt with by a divinity who rewards people who are in the organization and punishes those who are not.

Reasons for Joining Cults

Why do people subject themselves to this kind of experience? On their intellectual merits, cults would probably recruit very few people. However, the process of conversion attacks the person emotionally and psychologically, not intellectually. College students are particularly vulnerable to the proselytizing of these groups. The normal developmental issues students encounter in the transition to adulthood leave them searching for identity, emotional support, and answers to complex questions of values and ethics. Cults, with their emphasis on community and a well-defined dogma, are enticing alternatives to students confronted with developmental issues that normally lead them to more complex reasoning and emotional maturity. The attraction of cults continues to grow as faith in the competing social institutions of education, church, family, and government diminish.

Psychosocial developmental issues encountered during the late teens and early twenties increase the vulnerability of college students. Earlier chapters discussed the developmental theories of Chickering. This theorist acknowledges conversion into a fundamentalist cult or religious movement as a path taken by some students to resolve the task of development toward adulthood. John Clark (1979), a professor of psychiatry at Harvard Medical School, states that about 42 percent of the cult members studied in his clinical work joined cults during this period of development toward adulthood.

Cognitive development in the late adolescent period is another developmental factor in the susceptibility to cults. William Perry (1970), the director of counseling at Harvard University, proposed a theory of the intellectual development of college students. He reasons that students initially think dualistically. In this dualistic scheme, young adults believe that absolute truths and falsehoods exist and are known to authorities. The authorities are usually professors, but others may also serve in this role. Students seeking absolute truths can easily be drawn to a charismatic leader of a cult as an authority who offers clear, absolute truths and falsehoods. In other circumstances, unresolved cognitive conflicts would push the student to more complex ways of relating to the world of ideas. The highly structured environment, limited personal freedom, and an impersonal atmosphere found in cults are environmental conditions that support this dualistic thinking.

Other reasons for the susceptibility of students to cults may be that institutions have grown so large and complex that a sense of belonging or community that once existed on campus has been replaced by a feeling of isolation by some students. Where the generation of college students of the late '60s and early '70s were drawn together by political issues and social causes, the generation of the late '70s and '80s was drawn apart by competition and an uncertain economic future. Harvard theologian Harvey Cox (1977) believes that it is this need for community or belonging that is the principal attraction of cults. If this is true, and students continue to become more isolated on campus, there is every reason to believe that the attraction of cults will grow stronger in the years ahead.

Ways That Cults Harm the Individual and Society

Persons who have undergone the conversion experience and who have been programmed as members of cults are sometimes distinguished by such characteristics as glassy-eyed stares, fixed smiles, and an almost programmed, zombie-like appearance. The new convert's speech may lose vocabulary and may acquire a memorized style that demonstrates a loss of the ability to think abstractly. Generally, these individuals have difficulty reasoning. Their I.Q. levels drop, and their ability to handle complicated situations and jobs is diminished. Other mental damage includes a reduction in cognitive flexibility, lessening adaptability, a narrowing and blunting of affection, and a regression of behavior to childlike levels. Possible pathological symptoms include disassociation, delusion, and similar mental disorders (Delgado, 1977).

Physically, cult members often suffer from poor diet, lack of sleep, severe stress, and emotional and physical exhaustion. Problems associated with these deprivations range from ulcers and scabs to untreated injuries. Nutritional anemia, vitamin deficiencies, tumors, and other diseases are not infrequently found among members of extremist religious groups.

Cults also harm society significantly. Their fundraising projects are seldom if ever for a worthy or philanthropic cause. Such projects are usually directed at supporting the wealth of the organization and involve everything from fraudulent street scams to quick money-change deals. One large cult group uses female members as prostitutes and has recently begun promoting the prostitution of young children associated with the organization.

Avoiding Cult Involvement

Many cults have specially trained recruiters whose sole purpose is to convince people to join their organization. These recruiters use deception, manipulation, high-pressure sales techniques, and anything else that works to get a potential recruit to take the first step. Recruiters know that if they can get the new recruit to take the first step in an environment the cult controls, they are well on their way to recruiting a new member. As an RA, you need to be aware of some of the approaches commonly used by cult recruiters, both for your own information and to disseminate to your residents. The Citizens Freedom Foundation (1983), a nonprofit organization dedicated to educating the public about destructive cults, makes the following recommendation to people about cult recruiting:

- Beware of people who are excessively or inappropriately friendly. There are no instant friendships.
- Beware of groups that pressure you because "everyone else is doing it." No one knows what is right for you except you.
- Beware of groups that recruit you through guilt. Guilt induced by others is rarely a productive emotion.
- Beware of invitations to isolated weekend workshops having nebulous goals. There is no reason to be vague unless there is something to hide.

Symptoms of Cult Involvement

There are signs that you can observe in others that may indicate that the person is involved or is in the process of being recruited by a religious cult. Some of the observable signs are as follows:

- A sudden and dramatic change in an individual's behavioral patterns. The student may stop going to class or spend inordinate amounts of time reading religious materials or begin behaviors that were not previously exhibited.
- A breakdown in communications with parents, old friends, roommates, and so on, when the person becomes more secretive and defensive.
- A sudden rush of new friends, particularly nonstudents, and an abandonment of old friends.
- The person expounding that society is evil and expressing a need for personal purification.
- Absence for long weekends, after which the person returns to the residence hall dramatically changed.
- A lack of rational ideas and an inability to discuss concepts without parroting dogma and scripture of a particular cult.

Through observation you should be able to determine some of these dramatic changes in behaviors, attitudes, and practices in your residents. It is simply not normal for a student to be a "normally functioning college student" one week, and after one weekend at a workshop or retreat return to the residence hall and begin sanctimoniously going about condemning people.

Intervention Methods

Intervening when a student has surrendered his or her personality and beliefs to the doctrine of a religious cult is difficult. If you observe some of the signs of cult involvement discussed in this chapter in one of your residents, it is appropriate for you to discuss it with a senior staff member. The alternatives that the staffperson will need to consider rest in part with your institution's policies and in part with the laws of your state. It is advisable for the staffperson to work with the student's parents, with a psychologist, and with people knowledgeable about cults.

Deprogramming is an effective method of helping the individual regain his or her personality. It is an intense process that focuses on helping people to begin thinking for themselves again. One of the characteristics of people programmed by a cult is that they have lost the freedom to think and act independently. Deprogramming helps people sever the dictates of the cult and invites them to begin thinking and making decisions for themselves. The earlier in cult involvement this deprogramming takes place, the greater the likelihood that the deprogramming will be successful. The longer a person remains in the cult group and functions at the will of the organization, the more difficult it will be for that person to regain control over his or her life.

Students need to understand that it is normal to occasionally feel alone, overwhelmed by decisions that need to be made, or as if things are falling apart. These are normal emotions and feelings that everyone experiences. Cults do not have the answers to these questions. They only cloud the student's mind so that it becomes impossible for the person to feel and to fulfill lifelong goals and ambitions.

Some states grant guardianship to parents of children trapped in cults. Once parents have legal custody, they may consider some form of psychotherapy or deprogramming. As an RA, you can be sensitive to the needs of your residents and to some of the behavioral signs associated with cult involvement. The earlier you are able to discover it, the greater the opportunity the student will have to fulfill progress with his or her life.

There is no question that destructive cults rob young people of the very thing that educational institutions are designed to impart. Whereas education expands the mind and enhances personal development, membership in a destructive religious cult closes off the mind and retards this development. Approaching this problem is not easy; it requires sensitivity, understanding, and the ability to help students understand options.

Chapter 16

Cultural Diversity: Race, Gender, and Sexual Preference

Most colleges and universities are heterogeneous environments in which students from wide and varied racial groups, nationalities, and social classes study together. This has not always been the case. Prior to World War II, most college campuses could be described as homogeneous environments, composed principally of white, upper-middle-class males. A number of important social movements and federal intervention programs changed the scope of higher education. Programs such as the GI Bill, which provided educational benefits to men and women in the military, the National Defense Student Loan Fund, and a number of financial aid programs greatly changed the demographic profile of American higher education.

This chapter examines some of these issues of cultural diversity. The first segment of the chapter examines race and ethnocentrism. The second segment examines gender issues. In this segment, the issue of violence against women is also reviewed. The final section deals with the issue of sexual preference.

Race and Ethnocentrism

Today's complex world forces each of us to categorize elements of our world. We define these categories based on what we have been told and what we have experienced. The more remote our experience, the more we rely on the perception of others and on cultural myths. This process of creating general classifications and attributing to them descriptive generalizations is called *stereotyping*. Stereotypes are a first element in differentiating our immediate social group from other social groups. It is one of the methods by which we define our social position and normative environment.

Unfortunately, the broad generalizations often associated with stereotypes are factually inaccurate. The idea that all black people are lazy, all Chinese are industrious, white people are smarter than other groups, and all Hispanics in the United States are migrant farm workers are factually inaccurate. Although stereotypes help us deal with abstracts, they presume that all members of a group operate similarly. These broad generalizations assume facts that are not true, and they enable us to ignore human qualities that do not conform to the cultural stereotype.

Stereotypes prejudge people based on their race, social status, gender, sexual preference, hair length, or life style. Prejudice is negative prejudgment. When one acts on this negative prejudgment by treating a group or a person unequally, this action is discrimination.

It is possible for people to hold prejudice without discriminating. They can harbor negative feelings and attitudes but also not act on these feelings and believe in equal treatment. But, people can also be prejudiced and actively discriminate or not be prejudiced and not discriminate. In many cases, people intellectually discount stereotypes as not having a rational base but emotionally harbor some negative feelings about a particular group. One example of this might be a person who recognizes that there is no rational basis for discriminating against an individual on the basis of race, but he or she disapproves of interracial dating and interracial marriage. This person may not discriminate in employment, performance evaluations, or social acquaintances but may discriminate in choosing not to date or befriend somebody from a different racial group.

Sources of Prejudice

There are three general sources of prejudice: psychological, social, and historical. Some people have a need to discriminate against other groups. The basis of this need may be feelings of personal inadequacy or inferiority. These people believe that their self-worth is enhanced when the worth of others is diminished.

Another source of psychological prejudice is using minority groups as a "scapegoat" for frustration and aggressive feelings. If something happens that is inconsistent with our preconceived idea of how it should have happened, we need to explain why our perceptions did not reflect reality. One of the ways to resolve this cognitive dissonance created by the gap between perception and fact is to attribute the reason to a particular minority group, making that a group scapegoat. A person who is passed over for a promotion which is given to a member of a minority group might easily channel his or her frustration and aggressive feelings toward the minority group. Minority groups may also become scapegoats in a broader sense when we are simply angry and frustrated and vent our anger and frustration on a minority group even though the group is not the source of the anger. The group might simply be a convenient and safe outlet for negative emotions.

Yet another type of psychological source of prejudice is found in people who have authoritarian personalities. These people are rigid, inflexible, intolerant of others, and have a need for others to submit to their will. Authoritarian personalities need for society to be well ordered and consistent with their view of how the world should function. They are likely to be very conventional and fundamentalistic. People with authoritarian personalities would view a minority group member as a person who is unconventional and who therefore does not fit into their ordering of the world. As such they would be likely to hold a low opinion of members in this group, discriminate against members of the group, and generally consider the group to have inferior qualities and characteristics.

Some feelings of prejudice are the result of socialization. Prejudice is learned from generation to generation by being a member of a particular group. Some of these prejudices may be ingrained into the group of which we are a member and thus become part of our view of reality. As children we learn these myths and stereotypes about ethnic groups. The family environment and the peer environment in which we live reinforce and validate these beliefs. This form of prejudice is developed in the same way that we develop feelings of nationalism, patriotism, and religion. The process is the same, although the feelings are markedly different.

Society also promotes prejudice through the competition in the workplace. For many years some groups have had control in certain industries or civil service positions. A classic example of this has been the Irish immigrants and their influence in the New York City Police Department. At one time, in New York City there was a predominance of Irish in civil service positions. When Italians and other minority groups began to vie for the same positions, there was some animosity and discrimination. The same competition for jobs and resulting animosity occurred when blacks were hired at the same wages as whites in construction work, civil service positions, and in the military. Competition for jobs and the idea that a person thought of as less skilled, less intelligent, and less capable was now employed in an equal position was threatening. It threatened people's economic survival and challenged them to reexamine their identities. If a minority member regarded as less qualified was placed in an equal position, then a person was forced to either upgrade his or her view of that minority group, of that individual, or to diminish his or her own self-worth. This process of social adjustment was another source of prejudice.

Historically there are many sources of prejudice. The clearest example is blacks who were held as slaves until the conclusion of the Civil War. For many years after the war, blacks were held in economic bondage and are still the subject of prejudice and discrimination. At one time, similar feelings were directed at native American Indians, whose culture was viewed as inferior to that of whites. Hispanics and other groups have suffered the same historic source of some of the prejudice and discrimination held against them today.

Minority Students and Cultural Differences

By the year 2000 the Carnegie Council estimates that the number of minorities attending colleges and universities in the United States will come to approximate that of white students (Carnegie Foundation, 1980). The average number of minority students (American Indian, Asian, black, and Hispanic) enrolled in colleges and universities in the United States is 17.9 percent (*Chronicle of Higher Education,* 1988 p. 20). This reflects a range of a low of 2.3 percent in Connecticut to a high of 66.4 percent in Hawaii. In the continental United States, the highest percentage enrollment of minority students is in New Mexico, with 35.4 percent, and the Washington, D.C. area, with 35.2 percent.

Large research universities provide inhospitable environments for all but the best-prepared minority students. Often minority students attending large, predominately white institutions feel culturally isolated. They have, or at least feel they have, a marginal status. Many minority students, who have not shared the same cultural and social background as the majority group, find it difficult to operate in a predominately white institution while they maintain associations in the minority community.

Language, social customs, and cultural differences tend to make the minority group members feel out of place. Some black students have described their experience on a white campus as similar to the way white students describe their experience attending a university in another country. Language, social customs, and backgrounds are different. It takes time to feel comfortable and to adjust.

Language presents a problem for some minority students. Hispanic students are usually bilingual. They are able to converse in both Spanish and what is called "standard English." Many white students who have had only one language throughout their life must adjust in college to a more sophisticated style of communicating. Books, lectures by faculty members, and discussions that they have with members of the academic community generally demand a greater degree of linguistic sophistication. All students must adjust to this demand for a more elaborated linguistic code, but students who come from minority groups that have a separate language must contend with this new elaborated linguistic code while maintaining sophistication in a second language.

Some students are bilingual, having two separate languages and being able to switch between the two; some black students may need to be functionally bidialectal. What has been called "black English" is a rich dialect with its own set of grammar and a special lexicon. Students who come from social backgrounds where black English is a primary means of communicating must enrich their language skills, as white students do, by improving their standard English. However, blacks usually are expected to retain linguistic sophistication in black English to communicate with other black students in certain social situations. Black English might be used with close friends at a party or to discuss music or just as a way to show common bonds and a sense of linkage or community with one's black heritage.

Cajun students may experience a similar problem. In rural communities in Louisiana, Cajun French is the language used in the family and in many social circumstances. In the rural community schools, standard English is taught, but some students retain a heavy Cajun French accent in the use of standard English. To be part of their Cajun French culture, students must be able to speak Cajun French but must also be able to develop the language sophistication for verbal and written communications with faculty in the elaborated linguistic code of college-level standard English.

These three examples serve to highlight the special demands placed on some minority students who function in predominately white, middle-class institutions. They are forced to develop not one, but two language systems and be fluent in both. This fluency requires extra effort. It contributes to minority students' feeling of being marginal and their apprehensions about the majority culture.

Cultural Separateness

Because campus environments strive for egalitarianism, does not mean that there should be no cultural differences. Each culture has qualities and traditions unique to its heritage. Ethnic groups, such as the Irish, Italians, Greeks, or Chinese, have a heritage that links them together and links them with their past. Membership in an ethnic group affects one's identity. It influences a person's self-concept and models for the person's gender and occupational roles.

Tradition and ritual are also defined by ethnic group membership. These play an important part in how one lives and in the associations one makes. It helps to reinforce one's ethnic heritage and helps to promote a sense of collective identity among members of an ethnic or racial group.

Membership in an ethnic group might also define who one marries, the age at which one marries, and the marriage ceremony. Although it is not the custom in the United States for marriages to be arranged, arranged marriages are common in some ethnic communities. Symbols of ethnic identity may include the way one dresses, distinctive accents in the use of English, choice of food, and religion. A language other than English may be spoken in the home and used with other members of the community.

Isolation is an important element in maintaining ethnic separateness. To the extent that the group can develop a community separate from that of the majority culture, that group can maintain its traditions and heritage without severance of these unifying links by the majority culture. In large cities such as San Francisco, Chicago, and New York, it is not uncommon to find ethnic neighborhoods (such as "Chinatown" and "Little Italy") with distinct identities from the majority culture.

Forms of Racial and Ethnic Interrelationship

There are three forms of racial or ethnic interrelationship between minorities and the majority culture. The first is *conformity* or *amelioration*. This is where the culture of the ethnic group is usurped by the majority culture. Members of the ethnic or racial group are integrated into the majority culture, and the distinction or heritage that linked the group together is abandoned in favor of conformity to the normative social environment of the dominant group.

The second form of interrelationship is a merging of cultures, what has been referred to as a *melting pot* approach. In this form of relationship, cultures are merged and the dominant culture adopts some of the characteristics of the minority culture and the minority culture adopts some of the cultural characteristics of the majority. The adoption of certain food or dress is an example of a superficial melding and appreciation of different cultures. Non-Irish wearing green on St. Patrick's Day and non-Italians celebrating Columbus Day are other signs of adoption and appreciation for different cultures.

Cultural pluralism is the acceptance of separate enclaves for different cultures. There is a common respect for different customs and a general pride in one's cultural heritage. Cultural pluralism is common in urban environments, such as the previously mentioned cities of Chicago, San Francisco, and New York, where there are a multitude of ethnic communities.

In the campus environment there is a merging of different cultures and in some a press to conform to the dominant Anglo culture. Some students maintain associations with students of the same ethnic or racial background through student clubs and organizations such as the Black Student Association, the Jewish Student Association, the Asian-American Student Association, or the Hispanic Student Association. These groups provide an opportunity for these students to reaffirm their ethnic, cultural, and racial heritage and provide a forum for these students to advance their political and social beliefs.

It is important for all people to develop associations with those with whom they share a common heritage. Such associations include participating in a fraternity or sorority, joining a particular type of political organization, or forming linkages with an ethnic or racial heritage. These associations can become the intermediate peer environments through which students relate to the larger normative social environment. They offer security, acceptance, and most importantly a collective sense of identity or security.

Cross-Cultural Communication

As noted in an earlier chapter, higher education has changed significantly since the early 1920s, when college students came from basically the same socioeconomic background and had similar kinds of social and cultural experiences. There were few international students and few minority students in higher education. As enrollment in higher education has grown over the years and become more egalitarian, institutions have moved from this homogeneous group to a more diverse student population. Within recent years, many institutions have purposely recruited minority and international students. It is not unusual on large campuses to find a wealth of students from different cultural backgrounds. This variety and richness of cultural backgrounds and experiences also present increased complexity in human relationships inherent in a group living situation. This is one of the important opportunities students have to learn from people of various backgrounds and experiences. In a residence hall, students are forced to interact at several levels. Outside of the residence hall or in their hometown community, issues tend to segment cultural groups and inhibit opportunities to understand and share an appreciation for what that culture has to offer.

Studying about a culture or learning its language is only one step in developing an understanding and appreciation for that culture. This is not to say that it will not be possible to establish an interpersonal level of communication with somebody from another culture, but only that such a bond requires a conscious effort at understanding the person's background and experiences. There is great value in developing an understanding and appreciation for another culture. It not only enables you to enter into what might be a rewarding interpersonal relationship with a person, but it also helps provide you with the skills to work with people from varied backgrounds.

Language is an integral part of both self-concept and psychological processes. Our view of the world and our relationships with other people rest within language and our ability to use it to control our environment. The development of one's own identity, one of the primary issues in the college years, is tied closely to the ability to use language to control one's environment. Success in being able to control the environment through language begets more self-confidence. Through language, students get feedback about themselves and are able to communicate their innermost feelings to others. If students must communicate in their secondary language or dialect to receive feedback and to control their environment, they bear an additional burden that can inhibit success.

Basil Bernstein, a sociolinguist (1975), identifies two forms of communication. One he describes as an elaborated code of communication that employs complex syntax, written rules of grammar, elaborate lexicon, and the use of complex sentences to express ideas. He identifies the second language code as a restricted code. This code is based on an understanding of commonly shared symbols and minimizes the use of complex and elaborate symbols. Standard English, that particular system of language heard on the six o'clock news and taught in high schools and colleges, is an elaborated code. Valley girl talk, street talk, and some forms of interpersonal communication are restricted codes. Such codes use many commonly shared symbols and mutually shared experiences that need little explanation. We typically use restricted codes within the family and with close personal friends. Anyone who is able to communicate has access to some form of restricted code. The use of elaborated code, however, is available to many, but not all, speakers within a culture. One code is not necessarily better than another code. They are separate tools and serve different purposes in our communication patterns.

Speakers of black English who also use standard English are considered to be functionally bidialectic, in that they can speak black English in situations appropriate to this communication pattern and switch to standard English when it is necessary to communicate in this dialect. It is sometimes assumed that black English is a substandard English form. This is not true. It is a separate linguistic system, with its own grammatical rules governing usage, a rich lexicon, and an intricate set of nonverbal and verbal intonational communication symbols. Black English is a separate language system or unique dialect. A student who is a competent speaker of black English enters the higher learning environment, which is predominated by the use of both elaborated and restricted forms of standard English. This student must communicate at a competent, sophisticated level both in black English and standard English. Native speakers of standard English who come from a traditional white middle-class background must also learn to improve their use of the elaborated form of standard English for use in the classroom; however, they are not required to switch between two separate dialects.

Other subcultural groups must also learn to accommodate the special demands placed on them in a situation defined by standard English usage. The Cajun French of Louisiana, as well as people coming from isolated low-income rural areas in Appalachia, must be able to shift to a new language dialect.

Language is one of the most evident signs of cultural difference in the melting-pot of cultures present in residence halls. When cultures vary, values, habits, hygiene, food preferences, social customs, and a host of other factors associated with a culture also vary. It is easy for Americans to sit in judgment of other cultures, using our culture as the standard. There is a tendency for us to ignore people who are different or to ostracize them because they do not share the same experiences. This attitude stems from a need to be in homogeneous groups, to be close to other people, and to develop an interpersonal relationship with others. We recognize implicitly that it is more difficult to establish these relationships when our cultural experiences are different. Although different, such relationships are not impossible, and, if they are achieved, can provide one of the most rewarding friendships a person can have.

There are some steps that you can take to improve cross-cultural communication on your floor. First, you must spend time with people from different backgrounds. This enables you to develop an understanding of each ethnic group's unique experience. With international students, you may wish to treat yourself to spending time learning about their countries, where they went to school, some social differences between their country and yours, and aspects in their culture that you value. Often a student will be interested in sharing these experiences with other students in the living unit who share an interest in the other culture. Holding a floor program on that particular country or inviting the international student to participate in late-night discussions are ways to obtain that person's participation in the living unit and to diffuse cultural prejudices and biases that may be building.

Second, when a student from another country exhibits some behavior you find to be questionable or seems to be particularly distraught over something, take the time to inquire. Males from Middle Eastern countries, as one example, are not reluctant to hold hands in public. In the American culture, two men holding hands suggests that they may be homosexual. In the cultures of the Mideast, it may only suggest that they are acquaintances. If you wonder about some type of behavior, religious practice, or other aspects, take the time to ask and understand. If the particular behavior is disruptive and causes conflicts or resentment in the living unit, this is a reason to talk with the student about the behavior. It is more than likely that the student will appreciate your inquiry and be interested in how the behavior is viewed in the American culture.

Never sit in judgment of another person's experiences or culture. Cultures are different; one is not better than another. Be sensitive to how you would feel if the situation were reversed and try placing yourself in the other person's situation.

You might feel alone in a different culture, using a language that you can speak but with which you still may have difficulty. Students can be very authoritarian, overly involved in themselves, and searching for their own identity. It is obviously not an easy situation to mediate.

This same cultural sensitivity applies not just to people from other countries, but also to people from other subcultures within this country. There are some experiences unique to the black community that are different—not better or worse—than the predominant white middle-class cultural experience of most campuses. Take time to know and understand this experience. Also understand that students may feel more comfortable in relationships with people from their own subcultural backgrounds. In the black community, sometimes students experience sanctions for participation or emulation of the dominant white culture of the university. This may also be true for some native Americans, Chinese, and Hispanic students.

Understanding the cultural differences and getting to know more about individuals will assist you in breaking down the cultural barriers and stereotypes identified with these groups. By diffusing these racial and cultural stereotypes, you may be able to avoid some of the bigotry and cultural conflicts that occur when people live together without taking the time to know one another. Part of a student's education in the institution should include developing an appreciation for other cultures. Each has something to offer.

Do's and Don'ts for Counseling Minority Group Members

As an RA you work with students from a variety of cultures. When students from different ethnic and racial heritages are asked to live together, one can anticipate some conflicts that arise as the cultural norms and expectations of one group come into conflict with those of another group. Common problems include taste in music, loudness of music, styles of conflict resolution, hygiene habits, frequency and type of alcohol use, and styles of holding parties. If you are a member of a majority group, be sensitive to some issues that may be unique to minority group members. Know as much as you can about their culture and show respect for the culture. Be available and treat minority group members as you do other students in the living group. Establish an accepting peer relationship. At all times, be yourself.

Don't try to adopt the language or dress of a minority group member or assume that you have the right answers to the conflicts that occur. Don't assume that you know what it is like to be a member of the minority group, have an appreciation for their feelings of marginal status, or represent a culture that they need to emulate. Do not say things that would violate their cultural norms. For example, preaching to students from rural Mississippi about the evils of hunting wild animals, when hunting and fishing is part of their cultural heritage, is unwise and condescending.

By working with students and encouraging appreciation of the diversity of cultures, you help students to develop tolerance for other life styles and an acceptance of the heterogeneous, culturally diverse environment in which we all live. If college is to prepare students to live in today's society, it is important that students understand that society is becoming increasingly pluralistic. Living and working together in the residence halls is a microcosm of what living and working in today's society is becoming. Acceptance, understanding, and appreciation now helps students develop the social sensitivity and cultural appreciation they need to work and function cooperatively in today's society.

Gender and Sexism

For generations women have been treated as second-class citizens. Historically they were regarded as chattel, the possession of their husbands, and were given limited freedoms. Their role in society was to bear children and maintain the home while the husband protected the family and provided its financial support. These traditional roles for men and women have promoted certain gender stereotypes, influenced how children are socialized, and impacted what students consider in developing their own self-concept.

There are differences in behavior between men and women. It is not clear if these are innate or environmental. Most likely, it is a combination of biological and social influences that result in certain behavior patterns that we identify with men and women. Research (Zastrow and Kirst-Ashman, 1987) shows that boys are more aggressive, children tend to prefer same-sex toys, and that as children boys and girls prefer to play with same-sex peers. Studies also show that girls are allowed more freedom in their gender behavior than boys and that children are inclined to imitate behaviors associated with their same-sex parent. During adolescence, the normative social environment of the peer group tends to socialize men and women toward accentuating certain kinds of behaviors. Forms of socialization include factors such as boys being discouraged from crying and girls being discouraged from being aggressive. Boys are encouraged to pursue competitive activities—like aggressive athletic sports, whereas girls are encouraged to pursue cooperative activities, like dance and music.

The effect of this socialization process has been offered as an explanation for why in later adulthood men view masculinity in terms of success and power and women view femininity in terms of grace and beauty (Zastrow and Kirst-Ashman, 1987). The socialization process for women also allows greater intensity in the relationships and greater freedom in disclosing personal feelings. The result of this is that women in college have a more in-depth and complex understanding of friendships and tend to be less demanding and more understanding in resolving conflicts than men are.

Browne, D. (1987). Hagar the Horrible. New York: King Features Syndicate, Inc. (World rights reserved). Reprinted by permission.

These advantages in knowing how to work in groups can have mixed results in the workplace. For example, female supervisors focus their concerns on their subordinates' expectations of them, as opposed to the expectations of their supervisor. Women managers tend to act more as counselors and confidants and thus sometimes find themselves in conflict between the interest of their supervisors and their subordinates (Marsh, 1988).

In male-dominated positions, women frequently find it difficult to be accepted by their male peers. This results in a lack of cooperation and strained personal relationships, which tend to produce greater stress for women because they place greater value on close peer relationships than do their male counterparts (Marsh, 1988).

Employment Discrimination against Women

Despite the increasing access women have to higher education, they still are over represented in what have been considered historically female positions. According to the U.S. Bureau of Census (1986), 98.3 percent of all secretaries are women, 98.2 percent of all dental assistants are women, 97.4 percent of all child care workers are women, 96.9 percent of all receptionists are women, and 96 percent of all Registered Nurses are women. In contrast, only 16.2 percent of all lawyers and judges are women, 16 percent of all physicians are women, 10.8 percent of all police officers are women, 6.2 percent of all engineers are women, and 0.7 percent of all fire fighters are women.

More than 50 percent of all women in the United States work; however, only 1 percent hold top-level corporate management positions, and less than 6 percent hold minimal management positions (Zastrow and Kirst-Ashman, 1987). They are also underrepresented in the U.S. House of Representatives, the U.S. Senate, and among the 50 state governors.

In higher education, more than 50 percent of the students attending college today are women, yet there are twice as many men as women in graduate programs. In addition to the traditionally aged students, 60 percent of the undergraduate students who are over 25 are women. Women students attending college are also more likely to be part-time and have family commitments, including the need for day care, special life-style and vocational counseling, and the need for more flexible schedules.

In many areas in higher education, women lack professional role models. For example, according to a survey by General Electric in 1988 (*Chronicle of Higher Education,* 1988), nationwide there were only 400 female engineering professors out of over 21,500 engineering professors nationwide. Similarly, in 1987, out of 4175 people who received Ph.D.s in engineering, fewer than 300 were women. Other areas such as the physical sciences, computer science, and the biological sciences have had the same difficulty in attracting women to this traditionally male field. Women who may have an interest in this area find it difficult to locate appropriate female role models who can mentor their progress and model an appropriate role for them.

Sexual Harassment

Sexual harassment involves some form of sexual submission as a condition of employment or education or as a way to affect employment, job evaluations, or letters of recommendation. Such harassment almost always involves some form of power relationship in which the male is in a supervisory position and has some control over a student's grades or employment status.

Sexual Harassment Defined

Sexual harassment is defined by the Association of American Colleges (Project on the Status and Education of Women, June 1978) as follows:

Sexual harassment may range from sexual innuendos made at inappropriate times, perhaps in the guise of humor, to coerced sexual relations. Harassment at its extreme occurs when a male, in a position to control, influence, or affect a woman's job, career, or grades, uses his authority and power to coerce her into sexual relations, or to punish her refusal. It may include:

- verbal harassment or abuse
- subtle pressure for sexual activity
- sexist remarks about a woman's clothing, body or sexual activities
- unnecessary touching, patting or pinching
- leering or ogling of a woman's body
- constant brushing against a woman's body
- demanding sexual favors accompanied by implied or overt threats concerning one's job, grades, or letter of recommendation
- physical assault

Reports of sexual harassment are extensive, ranging as high as 90 percent of women in some employment areas having claimed some form of sexual harassment (Deane and Tillar, 1981).

The most direct kind of sexual harassment involves an employer who solicits sexual favors from an employee under the threat of terminating his or her employment. On college campuses, a faculty member who suggests awarding grades for sexual favors is a clear case of sexual harassment.

Many less clear circumstances may constitute sexual harassment. Under certain circumstances, sexist language, sexist jokes, suggestive comments, and other demeaning gestures or comments by a faculty member in the classroom or by an employer may constitute sexual harassment.

Sexual harassment is prohibited by Title VII of the Civil Rights Act of 1964 and by the Equal Employment Opportunity Act of 1972, which expanded the authority of the Equal Employment Opportunity Commission (EEOC). This commission and the federal courts have the authority to enforce Title VII in the workplace and on college campuses. Most colleges and universities have developed their own sexual harassment policy. If you or one of your residents has been sexually harassed, you should approach your hall director, the dean of students, or a counselor in your counseling center to learn the correct steps to pursue the matter. Chances are that if a faculty member or an employer has harassed one student, he or she has possibly harassed others. Institutions as well as companies have an interest in stopping this behavior. It is detrimental to the teaching and educational process, and both harassed and nonharassed students should not be subjected to this abusive, unfair conduct.

In making a claim of sexual harassment, there is also a need to respect the rights of the person being accused. The accused person should be presumed innocent until it is proved otherwise, and he or she is entitled to due process in the investigation and disposition of the accusation. Allegations of sexual harassment are often difficult to prove. One of the factors an administrator will consider is how often these claims have previously been made against this same faculty member or employer. Whatever procedure the institution uses, it is important for you or your residents who may have been sexually harassed to report it to someone in authority. A staffperson can explain the process and advise you or your resident about how to proceed.

Confronting Sexual Harassment

Victims of sexual harassment have several alternatives available to them. Each has its own potential positive and negative consequences. Alternatives include ignoring the harassing behavior, avoiding the harasser, or asking the harasser to stop (Martin, 1984). The MSPB (1981) study found that ignoring the behavior had virtually no effect. Asking the harasser to stop, however, effectively stopped the harassment in half of the cases.

Avoiding the harasser is another option. A severe shortcoming of this approach is that the victim is the one who must expend the effort. The ultimate avoidance measure is actually quitting the job or dropping the class to avoid contact with a sexual harasser. This is the least fair (and potentially most damaging) alternative to the victim.

There are, however, several other suggestions to help victims confront sexual harassment. In many cases using these strategies will stop harassment. First, a victim needs to know his or her rights. A call to the Equal Employment Opportunity Commission (EEOC), the federal agency designated to address the issue of sexual harassment, is helpful. Many women can obtain necessary information about their rights and the appropriate procedures to follow for filing a formal complaint.

Many states also have state laws that make sexual harassment illegal. Such states often have agencies or offices that victims may call for help and information. For example, the state of Wisconsin has the Wisconsin Equal Rights

Zastrow and Kirst-Ashman (1987). *Understanding Human Behavior and the Social Environment.* Chicago: Nelson-Hall. Reprinted by permission.

Division to address such issues. Additionally, organizations and agencies also have specific policies against sexual harassment. Filing a formal complaint through established procedures is often an option.

Most victims, however, choose not to pursue the formal complaint route (Martin, 1984; MSPB, 1981). Some victims fear reprisal or retaliation; others don't want to be labeled troublemakers. Still others don't choose to expend the time and effort necessary in carrying out a formal process. Most victims simply want the harassment to end so that they can do their work peacefully and productively.

In addition to knowing your rights, the following suggestions can be applied to most situations where sexual harassment is occurring:

- Confront your harasser. Tell the harasser which specific behaviors are unwanted and unacceptable. If you feel you cannot handle a direct confrontation, write the harasser a letter. It is helpful to criticize the harasser's behavior rather than the harasser as a person. The intent is to stop the harassment and maintain a pleasant, productive work environment. There is also the chance that the harasser was not aware that his or her behavior was offensive. In this case, giving specific feedback is frequently effective.
- Be assertive. When giving the harasser feedback, look him or her directly in the eye. Look like you mean what you're saying. Don't smile or giggle even though you're uncomfortable. Rather, stand up straight, adopt a serious expression, and calmly state, "Please stop touching me by putting your arms around me and rubbing my neck. I don't like it." This is a serious matter. You need to get a serious point across.
- Document your situation (Farley, 1978). Record every incident that occurs. Note when, where, who, and what was said or done, what you were wearing, and any available witnesses. Be as accurate as possible. Documentation does not have to be elaborate or fancy. Simple handwritten notes including the facts will suffice. It is also a good idea to keep copies of your notes in another location.
- Talk to other people about the problem. Get support from friends and colleagues. Sexual harassment often erodes self-confidence. Victims do not feel they are in control of the situation. Emotional support from others can bolster self-confidence and give victims the strength needed to confront sexual harassment. Frequently sharing these problems with others will also allow victims to discover they're not alone. Corroboration with other victims will not only provide emotional support, but it will also strengthen a formal complaint if that option needs to be taken sometime in the future.
- Get witnesses. Look around when the sexual harassment is occurring and note who can observe it. Talk to these people and solicit their support. Try to make arrangements for others to be around you when you anticipate that sexual harassment is likely to occur.

Although sexual harassment is generally thought of as being an issue related to harassment against females, males may also be sexually harassed. These sexual advances may be homosexual or heterosexual. They may involve a female faculty member or employer harassing a male or female student or a male faculty member or employer harassing a male or female student. Under some circumstances, sexual harassment may also include a student harassing another student if a supervisory or power relationship has been established. Some campus policies are pervasive enough to cover language such as sexist jokes in sexual harassment. Such jokes may be actionable at an institution under its set of policies and guidelines.

Sexual Preference

People are sexual. Some are heterosexual, some are bisexual, and some are homosexual. A few people are asexual, meaning that they are not sexually involved with either gender. Heterosexuality is the accepted sexual preference in most areas of the world. This has not always been the case. In ancient Greece and Rome, and during much of the Middle Ages, homosexuality and bisexuality were viewed as simply other forms of sexual expression. For religious and social reasons attitudes towards sexuality changed to the acceptance of a Calvinistic view of monogamous, heterosexual relationships. Laws were passed to punish individuals for behavior that fell outside of traditional heterosexual relationships. There were strong social sanctions including mocking, ostracism, and physical attacks directed at homosexuals. Throughout much of America's history, homosexuals have been discriminated against in employment, in social contacts, and in other ways. The media and the movies, which help shape public opinions, have portrayed homosexuals as child molesters, poor parents, effeminate, and indiscriminate in their choice of sexual partners.

In the 1970s and the 1980s there was an increasing awareness of and acceptance of homosexuality. Local laws have been passed (such as in Washington, D.C. and San Francisco) that prohibit discrimination on the basis of sexual preference. There were gay pride marches and demonstrations, gays were active in lobbying Congress, and gay groups are recognized as a political force in the United States. There is a growing acceptance of homosexuality, although homosexuals continue to suffer discrimination and social sanctions because of their sexual preference.

When AIDS first became an issue of public concern in the mid-1980s, there was a strong backlash against homosexuals, because this community was one where cases of AIDS were particularly prevalent. Fundamentalist religious groups and groups with very conservative ideologies advocated extreme measures against homosexuals. There have been incidences of homosexuals being attacked and beaten merely because of their sexual preference. The federal courts have also failed to protect individuals from state laws that regulate the private sexual conduct between consenting adults, making some state laws illegal that prohibit homosexuality, sodomy, and similar sexual conduct.

The number of homosexuals in the United States is difficult to determine. Kinsey's (1948) early studies suggest that approximately one-third of all men have had some homosexual contact. Most of this contact occurs during adolescence and young adulthood. Approximately 10 percent of all males were exclusively gay for a three-year period in their adult life, whereas less than 4 percent of homosexual males were exclusively gay throughout their whole life. The most common pattern is varying degrees of bisexuality.

There are far more gay men than gay women. Kinsey estimates about two to three times as many men as women have had some homosexual contact. He estimates about 0.19 percent of all women have had some type of homosexual experience before the age of 40, but less than 0.03 percent remain exclusively lesbian for their whole lives having had no heterosexual experiences.

Reasons for Being Gay

One theory about why people are gay attributes the preference to biological sources. It is suggested that genetic factors determine a person's sexual preference. There is some research to support this view. In 1952, Kallman found a significantly high percentage of identical twins who were homosexual. In virtually every case that Kalman studied, if one twin was homosexual, so was the other.

Although this study presented some interesting findings, subsequent research (Zuger, 1976) has not been able to substantiate this research. Generally, the idea that homosexuality is the result of genetic factors has been discounted.

A second theory about why people are homosexual is a psychoanalytic theory. This theory suggests that if one grows up in a family with a dominant mother, a young male is unable to resolve the normal oedipal conflict. (Freud believed that young males had the desire to have sex with their mother, and this was resolved when they developed a fear of castration by their father. This fear resolved the oedipal conflict and they were able to channel their sexual impulses toward other females.) If the mother is dominant, there was no fear of the father and, therefore, no reason to resolve the oedipal conflict. In psychoanalytic theory, women become lesbians because of rejection or indifference by their mothers. The need for affection and attachment leads the person to engage in sex with other women.

One behaviorist theory of how homosexuality develops is through the reinforced pleasurable experiences one might have with same-sexed peers in early childhood and adolescence. Because these relationships are mutually satisfying, they reinforce closer contact. As intimacies increase between the friends, the natural progression of the friendship, reinforced by pleasure, leads to homosexual contact. To the extent that these are mutually satisfying and supportive and continue to be reinforced by pleasure, they are sustained. Essentially, this theory suggests that one learns how to be homosexual. This may come from watching the behavior of others, participating in a peer group that accepts or encourages this life style.

Yet another explanation is a sociopsychological theory about reasons for people being gay. Theories in this area suggest that we all have a need for close friendships and a need to be supported, encouraged, and nurtured. If these needs are not met as children, we seek them in adolescence and in adulthood. For men, if their fathers were frequently away from the family or did not know how to express love and affection, sociopsychological theories suggest that a male might seek this affection and acceptance in sexual relationships with other males. Another sociopsychological explanation is that, if a child learned early in life that women were very threatening (or for lesbian women, that men were very threatening), they may seek the security and comfort in same-sex relationships.

Other theories are advanced, such as ones that homosexuality is an issue of sexual confusion, hormonal imbalances, or that it is a form of mental illness. There is little credibility for any of these approaches.

It is probable that a number of factors contribute to a person's sexual preference. Close friendships, availability, learned experiences, curiosity, social acceptability, and early childhood experiences may contribute to why a person is homosexual. No one theory is likely to answer the question for every person.

The real issues regarding homosexuality are not why people are or are not homosexual. Sexual preference is not an indication of intelligence, trustworthiness, loyalty, or any other factors that might influence how people participate in our communities. Most males have had some homosexual contact in preadolescence or during adolescence. Sexual preferences tend to emerge as people become sexually active. This begins with puberty, and the preferences are shaped throughout adolescence and young adulthood. Usually this is the time when people experiment. As noted earlier, most homosexuals have had a number of heterosexual experiences. A person who has one or two homosexual experiences is not necessarily a homosexual nor bisexual. One homosexual experience does not a homosexual make, just as one heterosexual experience does not a heterosexual make.

Because of the social stigma, people choose varying degrees of disclosure regarding this issue. There are at least four general categories of homosexual disclosure. The first is being openly gay. The person does not attempt to hide his or her homosexual preference and lives openly in the community as a homosexual male or female. The opposite of this is what is referred to as a "closeted" gay person. This person may or may not be sexually active. He or she may be married or unmarried. The closeted gay's sexual preference is members of the same sex, but for reasons of social stigma, he or she is unwilling to admit publicly the homosexual preference. In the third category are people who are privately gay, meaning that they are open about being gay to selected close friends, but hide being gay from others. A fourth category includes those people who are openly gay and who are married. Some marital relationships allow for people to be in a married heterosexual relationship and at the same time engage in some homosexual conduct outside the marriage.

Coming Out

"Coming out" is slang used to describe the act of a person who has decided to publicly proclaim his or her homosexuality. Young adulthood is the time when this often happens. At this age people are in the process of discovering their sexual identity and separating from family, and they sometimes find a need to explain their sexual preference to their parents and their friends. This produces a more open and honest relationship but carries with it the threat of rejection. Coming to accept one's self as homosexual is an important element in one's self-concept and identity. There are life-style and life-direction issues that must be considered in openly declaring one's homosexuality.

Most homosexuals say that homosexuality is not an issue of preference. It is a part of who they are. They are simply expressing what is an inherent part of them. It is not that they are choosing a particular life style, it is that the life style has chosen them. Some homosexuals are sad about the social stigma that they have to endure and the likelihood that they will not have children or be part of what is considered to be a traditional family structure. They are saddened by what will often become a strained relationship with their parents and the friends that they will lose because their heterosexual friends fear that they may also be thought of as homosexual.

Gay Life Style

There is not one specific gay life style. Gays, just as nonhomosexuals, conduct quite diverse relationships, ranging from permanent, monogamous, gay relationships to gays who engage in sexual contact with many different partners. Most gays are indistinguishable in their behavior and mannerisms from heterosexuals. Some have acquired certain effeminate mannerisms; most have not. Effeminate behavior is not a characteristic of being gay. Transvestism is present in the gay community, but it is also present in the heterosexual community and is not a behavior that is specifically linked to homosexuality.

Traditional meeting places for gays have been gay bars. This developed because of the social stigma of being gay and the need to find places separate from the heterosexual community where homosexuals could feel comfortable. Gay bars are still a frequent meeting place for gay men and gay women. At one time, gay bathhouses were prevalent in large cities. Gay bathhouses were places where men would go and take a steam bath or relax in a whirlpool. These were also places which generally permitted open casual sex. With the increased concern about AIDS and venereal disease, many of these bathhouses have been closed by health departments.

Gays have developed communities of support particularly in large cities. In these communities there are counseling support groups, social clubs, religious organizations that support gay concerns, and all the other social structures found in any community. College campuses often have a student group of gay men and lesbian women who offer information and support to students who are wrestling with their sexual identity or who are gay. Near large college campuses there is usually a facility that provides a contact for gay students.

Most gay men and women are productive members of society. They live in monogamous relationships and have the same relationship problems that married couples do in heterosexual relationships. They are no less loving and no less caring for each other.

Homosexuality and the Residence Halls

Undergraduate men and women who are in the process of discovering their own sexual identity are often threatened by homosexuality. Heterosexual men seem to have the most difficulty accepting gay men. They are often insecure about their own sexual identity and believe that by ridiculing or abusing homosexuals they affirm their heterosexuality for their male peers. This fear of homosexuality is referred to as homophobia. The issue of homosexuality is a complex issue for young males because it is tied to the issue of power and dominance.

A gay student living in your resident unit can create concern on the part of the other residents. He or she may become the object of ridicule, practical jokes, and abuse. Students may feel uncomfortable in using the same restroom as the gay student and may have unfounded fears of contacting AIDS merely by living on the same floor with gay residents. Often other males believe that because they are male they are automatically the object of attention and desire of the homosexual student. This is one of the great myths surrounding homosexuality. Just as all heterosexual women do not perceive all males as potential sex partners or interested in developing some type of intimate relationship, homosexual males do not view all other males as potential sex partners or wish to enter into an intimate relationship with them.

Sometimes young heterosexual males who have certain effeminate traits or females who have certain traditionally masculine traits are labeled by other students as homosexual. No matter what they might say or do to deny these allegations, they may suffer the same ostracism, social stigma, and harassment that homosexual students suffer who are open about being gay.

If handled correctly, with education and support, in a mature environment it is possible for an openly gay student in your residence living unit to be accepted by the other students. This coexistence rarely exists in a traditional all-male residence hall, but this level of maturity is possible. In apartment-style living situations or in living units that provide isolation and single rooms, gay students, individually or as roommates, sometimes coexist with residents in the living unit with little difficulty.

Counseling Gay Students

College is a time in which people are coming to better understand their sexual identity. It is a period in which one discovers or acknowledges his or her sexual preference. It may be a time in which a young man or young woman may experiment with homosexuality. This is a normal part of sexual development and should not be misconstrued as having adopted a homosexual life style.

In the event that a person who is wrestling with this issue chooses to talk to you about his or her sexual preference, you have the opportunity to help that student think about his or her sexual identity. It is also likely that a student who is wrestling with this issue, may not discuss an issue as intimate as his or her sexuality with you because of fear of rejection and ostracism. If by chance a gay student does trust you enough to share such an intimate concern, there are some things that you should and should not do. First, talk with the student about the basis of the gay experience and belief that he or she is homosexual. Focus on the student's knowledge about the issue and the extent of his or her experience. This is not an opportunity for the student to graphically describe sexual conduct to you, but an opportunity for the student to think about whether the amount of experience justifies the belief that he or she is homosexual.

Second, talk with the student about his or her knowledge regarding the homosexual life style. Is the student aware of the sacrifices, what will be faced, and is he or she willing to confront these issues?

Third, remember that this issue is about the student learning or discovering his or her own sexual identity. It is not about you advocating a particular life style or being judgmental about a homosexual life style. The choice is up to the students.

You can recommend that the student speak with a counselor in your counseling center. This may help the student gain perspective, give him or her more information, or help the student become comfortable with whatever judgment he or she makes. Therapy is usually not successful in having a person change his or her sexual preference. For students who are still in the stage of shaping or who are uncertain, counseling may help them resolve some issues surrounding sexual confusion. But, if students are truly homosexual, they will know, and therapy might best be directed at helping them adapt to this life style.

Some students who are gay may talk with you about whether they should tell their parents. Again, this is an individual decision each person must reach for himself or herself. The advantage is a long-term, honest, and an open relationship with parents; the disadvantage is possible rejection and parental anger. Whatever decision the student reaches on this issue, he or she needs your support and probably the support of a campus counselor to reason through whatever decision is best for them.

Sometime during the academic year it would be helpful to sponsor a speaker on homosexuality as part of your residence hall program. Such a speaker can provide some information to the general student population, dispel some myths regarding homosexuality, and give some students the courage to discuss their own homosexual feelings. In the best case it may help to develop among the residents a more mature and accepting attitude toward people who are homosexual.

Part 5

Educational Outreach

Chapter 17
Educational Programming

Chapter 18
Community Development

Chapter 17
Educational Programming

Purposes of Programming

Programming may not be as easy as the professional staff in the office of residence life may tell you it is, but it is not nearly as difficult as some of your fellow RAs make it out to be. It does take time. It does take planning, and it is not always successful. The hardest thing about programming in the residence halls is getting your residents involved. The thought of sitting through another lecture or being expected to learn one more thing after spending a long day attending classes and studying is often too much to expect. There are days when all a student might want to do is vegetate in front of a television and escape. As the semester proceeds, stress increases, and it becomes increasingly difficult to stimulate interest in educational programs.

You might ask, why bother? It would save time for everyone if you weren't expected to do programming. And, in some ways you might be right. It would save you the trouble of helping others learn the skills of planning and organizing, and it would surely save effort for a speaker who might be asked to a program. However, it is always easier to run a dorm as a hotel than as a residence hall. One of the important differences between the two approaches is that residence halls are designed to contribute to the educational experience of the student. If college residence halls were in the business just to provide shelter, they would not need RAs and could probably contract with a hotel chain to do a better job of management.

Programming is one of the major vehicles available to you to make the experience of living in a residence hall part of the educational experience of college.

Education in college should be viewed as a total experience and not just as the 12 to 18 hours each week students may spend in class. As a total experience, all aspects of the environment must contribute to the students' education. Woodrow Wilson expressed it this way: "So long as instruction and life do not merge in our colleges, so long as what the undergraduates do and what they are taught occupy two separate, air-tight compartments in their consciousness, so long will the college be ineffectual" (Wilson, 1913).

In the residence hall, the formal manner by which instruction and life are merged is through various leisure-time programs that blend the common interests of individuals into shared experiences leading to new opportunities for self-discovery. Programming is teaching. It is the forum that you, as an educator, use to organize, with your residents, activities that make a positive contribution to the learning environment and the students' education. Programming is the tool that is used to change the impersonal atmosphere of a residence hall into an integral part of the educational environment. Without programming, residence halls are little more than shelter and the RA little more than a caretaker.

As students in the residence halls share programs, they are drawn closer together and open new media of communication. The interface of these common educational experiences creates a fertile atmosphere for discovery, creativity, and self-exploration. Programs can inform, give people the tools to develop, and bind people to one another in a sense of community.

The parameters of programming have been defined as narrowly as the interaction between two people and as broadly as the assembly of a theater audience. In the present context, this definition is relevant: *programming* is any organized activity designed to make a positive contribution to a student's education.

Goals of Programming

There are four basic programming goals in residence halls. They are:

- To develop a community.
- To educate.
- To involve students in their own learning.
- To provide an outlet for the release of emotions.

The development of community in a residence hall is enhanced when people have mutual respect for one another, respect one another's rights, trust one another, and have a commitment to the group as a whole. Programming that creates interaction among students on educational topics related to their common interests helps build understanding and acceptance within the group. As the group becomes mutually supportive and understanding of one another through personal experiences, a respect for the other person's positions and rights is gained.

Programming also serves the goal of educating. Through programming, people can learn new hobbies, develop new leisure-time activities, and explore new interests. A program on mountain-climbing may foster a sense of community and at the same time provide information to students interested in exploring this aspect of their potential. Skill-development programs for personal growth in areas such as assertiveness training, time-management, and value-clarification also serve to educate students. Parties, social exchanges, and dinners teach social and interpersonal skills that contribute to students' general education and may aid in the release of emotions.

Students who participate in residence hall government or arrange programs are involving themselves in their own learning. People who spend time in a group discussion on values or develop a workable study schedule are also involving themselves in their own learning. Programming brings about the opportunities for this involvement.

Programming also assists students in the release of emotions. Intramural athletics, aerobic dancing, any form of physical competition, canoe trips, overnight camping trips, and survival-training programs are examples of programs that can aid in achieving this particular goal. Participation in these programs helps students release aggressions, tensions, stress, anxiety, and similar emotions. The fun and excitement of the activity help students escape from the pressures of college and provide a legitimate time for students to revive themselves.

Types of Programs

Most programmers divide programming into eight general categories, described here.

Educational

Educational programs are generally information-oriented. Speakers, documentary movies, and group discussions centering on a particular current affairs topic are often categorized in this area of educational programming. A program that helps students explore career opportunities, or gives them information about a campus service (such as the student health center, study skills program, academic advising program) are other examples of educational programs.

Recreational

Recreational programs are entertainment-oriented. Such programs as movies, field trips, canoe trips, hiking, mountain climbing, parachuting, and other similar types of activities generally fall into this category.

Cultural

Cultural programs include concerts of various types, mime artists, art exhibits, and similar activities. Theater productions, opera, and similar activities are included in this category.

Athletic

Athletic programming includes intramural sports, interresidence hall athletics, and other athletic competitions.

Wellness Activities

Some of these activities might be athletic or educational or a combination of the two. A program that helps students design a personal exercise program or teaches them about nutrition are typical examples of wellness activities. A regular jogging program for members of your living unit or some type of aerobatics program are other examples.

Crafts and Hobbies

Programs that teach students a craft such as knitting or pottery fall into this category. Hobbies includes a diverse number of activities, from collecting baseball cards to gardening. Programs on these topics enable students to explore new areas of interests and to acquire new skills. Some of these may lead to a job after college or to the continuation and refinement of knowledge in the area for personal enjoyment.

Developmental

Developmental programming is considered skill development. It concentrates on such topics as assertiveness training, time management, workshops on overcoming self-defeating behavior, and career- and life-planning workshops. These programs help people develop important personal skills that assist them in their growth toward maturity. Participation in group counseling, some form of encounter group, or biofeedback training are also developmental.

Social

Social programs are those activities that join people together to teach social skills, to have fun, and to release tension, anxiety, and frustrations. Parties, dinners, and most gatherings for the purpose of socializing are activities classified as social programs.

How to Program

Programs that are presented early in the fall term help establish the expectation for more programs. Students quickly come to accept programs as part of the natural order of life in residence halls. Many RAs who have programming requirements wait until the last minute to plan their programs. Their motivation often is to meet job requirements. If they were truly interested in the development of their residents, they would set the expectation of education in the halls by having programs in the first month of the school term when habits are set. If you have ever attended one of these last-minute programs, you will recognize it immediately: speakers on information or educational-oriented topics brought in during the last part of the year. When this is the first attempt at programming, it is usually doomed to fail.

If a good foundation for programming is laid early in the year, students will anticipate attending programs. Programming will become a normal part of the environment and the routine of college life.

There are two ways to arrange programs—the spontaneous way and the organized way. The spontaneous approach is not the same as a last-minute program. Spontaneity is important in programming and must be recognized as a legitimate programming effort. The spontaneous program capitalizes on the creative uses of available resources. A spontaneous program may happen when you discover that in two days a well-known speaker will be on campus. You might try to arrange for that person to eat a meal in the residence hall with your residents or to have the person stop for an informal reception and discussion. Another spontaneous program might relate to a campus issue. You might respond by inviting somebody from the institution to come to discuss the issue.

The organized approach is the one that is most often successful and provides the greatest latitude for programming. It is simply not feasible to attempt to plan a canoe trip a hundred miles from your campus in 48 hours without some prior planning or much help.

Ten Steps to a Successful Program

The 10 steps given here are the organized way to do programming. This is the way most good programs are accomplished. This planned approach pulls in different resources and enables you to move clearly to a successful program.

Step 1. Assessed the Residents' Needs

All too often people attempt to arrange programs without assessing the needs of the group. Needs assessment can be handled in several ways. Many educational programming teams in residence halls begin the year by administering an *interest survey,* which lists a number of possible programs and asks people to evaluate how they feel about having such programs in the residence hall. You can generate your own list of ideas for an interest survey.

Interest surveys can be particularly helpful in gaining an understanding of the common interests of your residents. They can give you an idea of the scope of programming and also the way in which to direct your programming; that is, they give a general evaluation of the available options. They do not, however, permit people to create their own programming ideas. People respond on surveys according to the options you provide. If you use surveys, try assessing programming needs through the survey at the beginning of the year, and then, intermittently throughout the year, review the surveys with groups of your residents. This will help you discover new program ideas in the ensuing discussions.

Brainstorming at a floor meeting is another way to generate ideas for programs. *Brainstorming* is a very simple technique that requires a person to ask questions and facilitate the flow of conversation and ideas. The key to using this technique in a small group is to allow a free flow of ideas, no matter how bizarre, without any limitations on their feasibility. It is an idea-generating time. You may use the following brainstorming format:

1. A small group of people is called together and the general topic of programming is introduced.
2. The facilitator chooses a second person to assist by writing down ideas.
3. The group is instructed to imagine any possible program in which they or others might be interested.
4. Generally a time limit is placed on the length of this brainstorming activity. The facilitator may wish to extend the time limit or alter the time limit depending on the interests and ideas being generated by the group.
5. The facilitator asks the basic question, "What programs, activities, or interests would you like to see us undertake this year?"
6. The facilitator instructs the assistant to write down all the ideas that are generated. This is usually done best on a newsprint pad at the front of the room or on a large sheet of butcher paper.
7. The facilitator may offer a few ideas but should encourage the group to generate most of the ideas. It helps if the facilitator reinforces people who offer ideas with comments like "That's a good idea, let's get that one down," or "Great idea!"

8. When the group has run out of ideas, the facilitator brings the brainstorming session to a close.
9. The group is then asked to rank those programs in which they would like most to participate.
10. Feasibility of the programs may be discussed at this time, relative to the rank order.
11. The top three or four programs are discussed and selected consistent with the group's need.

Another version of this brainstorming approach is to take a number of items (such as a fountain pen, a ball, a book, and other objects) and place them in a box or paper bag. Ask the group to divide into smaller groups; then ask each small group to suggest programs they could arrange with each one of the objects in the box or bag. The small groups then share their programming ideas with the larger group. This can be conducted as a competitive contest among the small groups. These ideas can eventually be built into a series of programs.

Both brainstorming and interest surveys are formal techniques for determining programming needs within the hall. Informal contacts and discussions with students can also help determine needs. In your discussions with the residents of your living unit, certain needs may become apparent. For example, if a number of students mention some difficulties about meeting class assignment deadlines and are frustrated in their studies, perhaps they are expressing a need for a study-skills program. You may then wish to approach individuals in the living unit with such an idea to see if there is any interest. Or, you may be sitting in on a late night bull session during which the group begins to discuss their values related to sexuality. This might provide you with the opportunity to invite a speaker to discuss human sexuality and to answer some of the questions raised in the informal discussions.

Step 2: Set Objectives for the Program

An *objective* is a statement that describes the process by which a goal should be attained. It describes both the performance and the key conditions under which the performance is expected to occur (Mager, 1972). Objectives are useful in delineating exactly what you intend to do. They are particularly helpful in communicating to others what you are attempting to achieve and why. You can use the following five-step plan to state what is commonly referred to as a performance objective:

1. Identify who is to engage in a particular behavior (who will be affected).
2. Describe the behavior that is to be done in behavioral terms (what will be done).
3. Describe conditions under which behavior is expected to occur (how performance is to be manifested).

4. Specify standards of acceptable performance (how well behavior should be performed).
5. Specify criteria on which performance of behavior will be judged (how to judge behavior).

Examples of performance objectives are

- One hundred percent of the students in my unit will have participated in at least one floor and one hall program before the end of the winter term as measured by an informal poll of the residents on the floor during a floor meeting the week before finals week in the winter term.
- On June 4, there will be a program on human sexuality in the floor lounge at which at least 25 percent of the residents of my floor will participate and will rate it as "interesting or very interesting" on an evaluation form that I will distribute at the end of the program.

Objectives are important because they state for you and others exactly who is to be affected, what specifically will be done, how it will be done, and how you will know that it has been accomplished.

Step 3: Involve Others

One of the most important elements of learning takes place through direct involvement in programs. It is the most efficient way to arrange programs, as well as the most educational way to accomplish them. As an RA, you are in a position of responsibility requiring organizational and coordinating skills. However, you should not feel compeled to do all of the work in designing and implementing programs yourself because the programs then become your programs. Instead, most programs should be collective efforts. People are more likely to participate in programs to which they have contributed. If people design a program together, they become ego-involved in its success. On the other hand, if the program is your program, you must elicit the loyalty and faith of others for the program to succeed.

Two of the leadership styles which can be used to work with students are the autocratic style and the democratic style. The former is highly rigid and centralized. One person makes all the decisions and gives all the orders. This leadership style might be appropriate for combat or a police crisis, but is not useful for programming. The preferred leadership style is democratic. This style allows everyone to have input into the decision making, and there is shared responsibility for what is and is not accomplished. The democratic, or team-management approach, is the advisable way to work with students in programming. Although the autocratic approach may have limited success, it will not accomplish the goal of helping people involve themselves in their own education, nor will it be the best way to achieve the programs that you want.

Try these methods for involving others:

- Delegate. Delegation is essential to successful programming. Always select a specific person to assume responsibility. This is preferable to asking for volunteers because, when you do that, you are communicating that the responsibility is not very important and that anyone could do the job. What you communicate to a student with a statement like this is that he or she has a special talent of which the group has a need. This not only reinforces the student's self-esteem but also makes him or her feel special.
- Coordinate. The responsibility of a person organizing a program is to coordinate the program. This means attention to detail and continual follow-up with people to whom you have delegated responsibility. You may have asked others to assist with the program, but for the time being the success of the program is still your responsibility. Programming is a process, and students learn from that process. Coordinate the skills of others, keeping in mind that your ultimate goal is eventually to move to the next step.
- Abdicate. Abdicate your involvement when possible. Try to put someone else in charge of designing, organizing, and coordinating the program. Become a true advisor. Advise your residents on how they can accomplish what they need to do, but do not do it for them. The one exception to this rule will perhaps occur at the beginning of the year, when it is necessary to role model good organizational and programming skills to give your residents the opportunity to learn from you. One of your personal goals should be to turn over much of the programming responsibility to a group of students in your living unit. Ideally, these students should be the ones thinking of the ideas, arranging the programs, evaluating the programs, and gaining the reinforcement or glory from the success of those programs.
- Motivate. Encourage, support, and reward those in the group who are helping with a program. Mention in front of others the accomplishments of these students and tell them how much you appreciate their contribution.

Step 4: Preprogram Planning

By this stage, you have assessed the needs of the group, determined your specific objectives, and involved others in the formation of the ideas and the organization of the program. You and your residents are now ready to plan the program's general format. Essentially, you examine the feasibility of your proposed program. In this stage of the planning, you find answers to the following questions:

- Are facilities available?
- What resources will we need to accomplish this program?
- What tentative dates would be possible for this program? Are there any conflicts?
- What monetary support is necessary for the success of this program?
- What special equipment or facility (sound equipment and so on) is needed for the completion of this program?

- Who on the programming staff should be contacted to get approval for the program or to get additional information?
- Does this program comply with university policies regulating residence hall activities?
- Who will attend the program (coed group, people from other living units)?

Draw up a tentative plan. Does the plan meet the needs of the group? If it does not, revise the objective or revise the plan. You are now ready to plan the actual event.

Step 5: Plan Program

Every good program needs a good title, a title that will motivate, excite, and encourage people to attend. If the audience that you have defined in the preprogram plan is the residents of your living unit, your title may be different from one for a program intended for the entire residence hall or campus. If your audience will consist of the residents of your living unit, you may wish to choose a title like "The Art of Keeping the Group in the South Wing Quiet" or "Study Skills for the Stereo Buff." If the audience is to be the entire residence hall, you may wish to title the program something like "Academic Success Through the Art of Studying."

Good programmers keep accurate records. If you are writing to companies for promotional items or contacting speakers, it is necessary that you keep good records of these contacts. Try setting up a file for each program that you are planning. Although getting too meticulous about paperwork can inhibit programming and make it overly complicated, it is better to be slightly too organized than not organized enough to complete the program. You will find that good organization saves time.

Following is a general checklist of the sequence of steps to help you design a program.

1. Determine program title.
2. Set specific date.
3. Set specific location.
4. Delegate responsibilities.
5. Reserve facilities, equipment, and speaker(s).
6. Determine budget (if applicable).
7. Do publicity.
8. Set time for program.
9. Review policies related to program (if applicable).
10. Review program with hall director.
11. Set deadlines for each project and delegated assignment.
12. Confirm dates, time, place, topic, telephone numbers, money in writing.

Step 6: Publicity

If you have done everything correctly up to this point, you probably have the design of a reasonably good program, but the program will not achieve your objective unless people actually attend. No matter how much deemphasis is put on evaluating programs solely on the basis of attendance, attendance is important. If you spend $100 on a program that only one student attends, this is not a good allocation of money—even if the student really enjoys the program. Poor attendance can be attributed to (1) poor needs assessment, (2) poor planning and organization, or (3) poor publicity.

Publicity is a key element in the success of a program. Good publicity that motivates and encourages people to attend helps bring people in contact with what your program has to offer. Poor publicity turns people off (or doesn't reach them in the first place) and limits the success of your program. Preparing and distributing the publicity is not easy; it is hard work, and it takes a lot of time. This is why delegating responsibilities is a key. Publicity is one of the items that people most often do not like to do. If you find somebody who is interested, especially an artist, cherish that person dearly. He or she can help ensure the success of many of your programs.

Elaborate publicity is not generally necessary in a residence hall. It is more important to be creative in the way the program is advertised. Some publicity ideas that have been used successfully are

- a note about a program placed in a bottle hung in the shower.
- logos or buttons worn by residents carrying the time, date, and place of the program.
- a telethon within the residence hall.
- notes on the cafeteria line.
- flyers in the floor restrooms, on the back of urinals, and on the mirrors.

Do not forget the importance of a positive attitude and word-of-mouth. A group of people who communicate excitedly about having a program can often be the most effective publicity. People want to go to programs that other people are attending. If a group of your friends is attending a program, you are much more inclined to go whether or not you are interested in the specific topic. You can help communicate this idea when you talk positively and excitedly about the program. Ask specific people in your living unit to attend the program. When you go to a program, gather several other people to go with you. Ask several of the residents in the living unit to do the same. If you have five or six people who agree to bring four friends each, you now have a group of 25 to 30 people. That could be a reasonably good showing and will allow more people to be introduced to the program.

Step 7: Final Checklist

Simply check what you have done. Go through every step and make sure that you have accomplished what you need to accomplish. The checklist should be a review of your program plan. This is the time for you to check with everyone who has been delegated something to do to confirm that he has done it or will do it.

Step 8: The Day of the Program

On the day of the program, check your speaker or program material to see that everything is ready. Make sure that the facilities are clean, neat, and usable. If there are to be refreshments, call to confirm that they will be delivered or that somebody will pick them up. Have special publicity prepared for the day of the program and the day before the program. People usually notice new items on the bulletin board, so this is a good publicity technique to encourage attendance.

Be at the site of the program at least one-half hour before the program is to start. This will enable you to fix any unexpected problems or to answer any last-minute questions. Make sure that somebody meets the speaker or brings along the material necessary for the program.

Step 9: At the Program

If the program has a speaker, somebody needs to introduce him or her. This could be you, but preferably it should be someone else who has worked with the program. Make sure that the speaker is introduced to any administration representatives who may be at the program and make sure that the speaker has the opportunity to meet as many students as possible before the program begins.

Before the program, think of some questions that will help stimulate discussion. You may wish to provide a few members of the audience with questions ahead of time. People ask questions when they see others doing it. You can start the discussion by asking some general questions and having your friends do the same.

Remember, nothing succeeds like success. A successful program, well executed, will mean better attendance, more support, more involvement, and better attainment of your program goals. Poor programs produce opposite results. If a program is boring, too long, or does not meet the needs of the students, people will be unlikely to come to the next program.

Step 10: After the Program

Once a program has concluded, evaluate the degree to which it met your goals. You can do this in several ways. A survey is probably the most common although people often do not like to fill out surveys at the end of a program. Surveys are useful in that they give you a collective reaction. However, they are somewhat formal, and they may not be appropriate for all programs.

Another form of evaluation is an informal discussion that occurs later that evening or directly after the program. Make a point of asking people what they thought of the program—what they liked and what they did not like. Ask how they think the program could have been improved and whether they would recommend it to other people. Whether or not you hand out formal evaluations to a number of residents or talk informally with a group, you should make some summary comments on every program presented. After all, you cannot determine whether your objective has been accomplished until you evaluate it.

It is important to reinforce those students who helped with the program. This is best done publicly. Call them by name and say something like, "John found the speaker for this topic, and I think he has done a very good job. Let's give him a round of applause." Publicly congratulate and praise people who helped. This, after all, is the only payment that they will receive. Recognition and reinforcement are two key ways of communicating your thanks for their help. There is nothing worse than leaving a program that you have put much of your time into without some expression of thanks. If your program planners did not do well, reinforce what they did do well and make some suggestions on what could have been done better.

Thank-you notes to speakers are always appropriate. Never invite a speaker to your living unit without sending a formal thank-you letter. If it was a large program presented to the entire residence hall, it may be appropriate to send a formal thank-you letter to the speaker with a copy to his or her supervisor. You should check this idea with your hall director to determine which times it is appropriate.

Do not count on many rewards for yourself. Although you may feel a sense of accomplishment for what took place, people may not congratulate you. Your rewards will come later in knowing that you have presented a successful program and that people are interested and motivated to go to your programs. Other RAs in the building, as well as your hall director, will recognize your contribution to the success of this program.

How to Plan an Unsuccessful Program

If you really want to do a poor program, one that is almost guaranteed to fail, here is what you should do:

1. Guess at what you think others want to do.
2. Don't plan anything. Don't have any goals.
3. Wait until the last minute to prepare the program.
4. Don't involve anyone else—after all, you can do it better yourself.
5. Tell as few people as possible and make sure you wait until they have made other plans.
6. When you do tell people about the program, tell them how wonderful you were to have planned such a great program. Make sure to take all the credit and don't involve anyone else. People will especially like this.
7. Don't meet your guest speaker, but let him or her try to track you down in the best way he or she can. This will give him or her an opportunity to show resourcefulness. When you introduce a speaker, make sure you give a long introduction pointing out how important you are. Add unrelated details and give many unrelated facts about yourself.
8. Don't evaluate. Don't thank anyone. You won't want to see the evaluation, and you will get all the thanks you deserve.

Programming Tips

Following are some tips to make programming easier. Chances are that your hall director or other people on your residence life staff also have special tips that will help you:

1. Approval: Get approval from superiors for all programs.
2. Transportation: Do not use your automobile to transport people to a program unless your insurance covers such transportation or unless there is a special clause covering transportation related to your position as an RA.
3. Financial Transactions: Do not use your personal checking or savings account for any financial transactions.
4. Publicity: Publicity should be heaviest the day before a program and on the day of the program.
5. Speaker: A speaker should be informed beforehand of the conditions under which he or she will speak and whether there is a possibility that the group may be small.
6. Location of the Program: Central lounge locations where there is a heavy flow of traffic will attract a number of people. These locations are generally good for programs designed to accommodate the entire residence hall.
7. Room Setup: Do not trap students in the program by putting the speaker in front of the door. Keep a free flow of traffic for people to enter and exit easily if they choose.
8. Length of Program: Talk with the speaker or programming committee and determine an approximate length for the program. People's interest spans vary, but generally an hour to a maximum of two hours is considered a good length for programs. The topic and interest of the participants should ideally determine length. Make sure before the program starts that you know how long it is to last. This makes a difference to the person conducting the program. If a speaker knows he or she is responsible for a 30-minute lecture with 30 minutes of questions, that takes one type of preparation. If he or she is expected to present a longer program, this may mean that he or she can incorporate other activities into the program.
9. Time: The best programming time varies from campus to campus. Generally, Sunday to Thursday evenings prove to be the best time for programs. Most schools find that immediately after dinner—between the hours of 5 P.M. and 7 P.M.—is a good time for programs. Part of this depends on assessing the habits and interests of the people in your living unit. Groups that are already formed and have a particular interest, such as a club or hobby group, will set their own times.
10. Theme Programs: Theme programs or a series of programs on the same topic can be effective. These should be held, when possible, at the same time, place, and location each week. Movie series programs are often popular, although very expensive.

11. Refreshments: If refreshments are to be provided, this should be mentioned in the advertisements. Some people may come to have refreshments and listen to the speaker. Every program need not have refreshments. Work with the residence hall or campus food service to determine the quantity needed. Be aware of what packaged items can be returned to the food service for credit and which items cannot be returned. Compare the prices offered through the food service with the price of similar packaged goods at the grocery. Some items may be less expensive from the grocery.

Conclusion

The only limits to programming are those set by your institution or by your own creativity. Individual living units within residence halls have joined together to plan such programs as ski trips, field trips off campus, organization and promotion of a commercial carnival on campus, and speakers on almost any conceivable topic. Programming should be seen as an opportunity for your residents to share a common experience.

Although some educational programming may take funds, these usually can be obtained from the residence hall council or from your housing administration. Many programs can involve little or no expense. Some of the most creative programs take the least amount of money. Programs that permit people to interact and to learn organizational or leadership skills are always worthwhile.

Chapter 18
Community Development

Defining *Community* in the Residence Halls

Perhaps one of the greatest tragedies of the latter half of the twentieth century has been the breakdown of the community and the rise of individualism. *Community* is both a sense of attachment to a group and a set of values that are commonly shared within a group. As one writer has stated,

> The quest for a feeling of community has centered around three romantic or utopian hopes: that life be more caring, that people have more concern, affection, and love for each other, and that the immunition in social life be reduced; that life be more intimate, more like family that we idealize but rarely achieve, and that closeness replace the unconnectedness that so many people experience in their normal lives; that life have greater depth, that people mature to each other, and that this shared depth and meaning replace the superficiality and shallowness that are still characteristic of most social relations (Gibb 1978, p. 212).

Hillery (1955) in considering some 94 different definitions of community, discovered that there were many similarities among them. From these definitions he developed a single definition of community: "A group of individuals engaged in social interaction, possessing common interests and goals, who show concern for and are sensitive to the needs of other members, and are primarily interested in furthering the group's goals over all others" (p. 118).

For students in residence halls, community is the sense of belonging with the other members of the group and a set of shared experiences that bind them together and make them a mutually identifiable group. For the student, the attachment to the other people in the living unit forms an all-important sense of belonging. In many ways, it is like a substitute family.

Why is this important for you as an RA? Very simply, the behavioral setting and the influence of peers within that setting are connected. The behavior of students in the living unit is shaped by interaction with the other students who compose their group. Both the formal structure of the facilities and the informal structure of the peer subculture have an influence. If the peer subculture can be developed in such a way as to promote concepts consistent with a supportive community feeling, it follows that students will internalize these values, assist one another in the accomplishment of their goals, and in general learn to function as members of a mutually supportive and sharing group. The far-reaching effects of having grown in such an environment, both in terms of one's self-image and the residual effects through community involvement in later adult years, are evident.

Specifically, a community transmits common goals and values. It fosters the ability to achieve deeper, more intimate relationships with people, frees interpersonal relationships, and increases self-acceptance and acceptance of others. It aids in shaping and developing a sense of personal integrity and ethics, shapes attitudes and values, and modifies human behavior in a positive direction.

The community also acts as a reference point for the individual. It is an identifiable group to which the person may point and claim allegiance. It provides specific social ties for the individual, encourages the development of adult social skills, and helps identify social contacts. One of its most important functions is as a mirror to assist the individual in developing a more accurate picture of himself or herself. Peers are used as a way of gauging one's behavior relative to group standards. A supportive community not only reflects positive values, but can assist an individual in gaining a better perspective of his or her own behavior. Of more intrinsic value, the availability of a community in which the student trusts others aids the student in times of crisis, need, and emotional stress.

Elements of a Community

Two issues to ponder about a community are what is necessary to establish it and how you, as the RA, can help foster a supportive community that will aid students in the accomplishment of their goals. The establishment of a community includes the following elements:

- *Social contact:* There must be a degree of physical proximity to allow people to have appropriate social contact with one another.
- *Shared values and common primary group:* There must be an identifiable set of shared goals and values toward which the group commonly ascribes and that it is seeking to fulfill.
- *Primary group:* The individual members must view the community as constituting their primary group of friends and acquaintances.
- *Power and Authority:* The members must recognize that the group has the power or authority to act in some way.
- *Commitment to cooperative survival:* Members of the community must make a commitment to the community through a sense of energy output or self-sacrifice.
- *Personal transcendence:* Community members must recognize that the group is more important than any individual in it, and, by virtue of this belief, they must surrender some degree of individuality for the sake of the group.
- *Communion:* This is the sense of member identification, an acting out of a sense of self within the group.
- *Process:* The group must have a sense of informal or formal process by which it operates. This may be a parliamentary type of meeting style, or it may be some much more informal style of interaction. A process must exist in the minds of the members.
- *Survival need:* The community must be based on a sense of mutual dependence, and there must be some reason for this mutual dependence—that is, a sense that survival can be achieved only through cooperation.
- *Solidarity and solitude:* Community members must be able to distinguish the boundaries of the group. Solitude or some degree of isolation helps in defining the physical boundaries of the group.

- *Faith and abandonment:* In order for a community to survive at its most humanistic level, individuals must enter the community with faith in the ability of the community and with some degree of abandonment of their own personal desires in favor of those of the community.
- *Time:* Community is dependent on individuals having enough time to contribute to the community, to meet, to interact, and to share common experiences.
- *Standards:* A community is supported when it has the authority to define the laws, standards, or rules by which it will operate. In other words, the community defines a standard of behavior.

The literature about residence hall living speaks of different types of communities. One is a formal structured community, which often involves a special cooperative housing program, the support of the residence life staff, and a set of structured experiences that promote a "sense of community." These communities may take the form of living-and-learning center programs in which students may do many of the same things together by design of the program. Generally, these programs are characterized by a contract the student signs, faculty involvement, a set of goals to be accomplished during the committed experience, evaluation of the progress of the community, work as part of the students' contribution to the community, and similar activities designed to elicit a communal environment.

This is certainly one way of approaching the development of a community environment, and it proves very successful in many institutions. However, it is also possible to establish a "sense of community" in a unit within a residence hall and—depending upon the size of the building—perhaps in a residential building as well.

How to Establish a Community

At this point you know what a community is, what it tries to achieve, and some of the factors necessary for a community to exist. How can you, as an RA, stimulate a sense of community within the group?

The first thing you need is an appropriate physical setting that allows people to be in close proximity. Residence halls are ideal for this purpose, although large residence halls are less ideal than smaller living units. Groups of about 10 to 20 individuals offer the best hope of establishing community involvement in a living unit; however, larger groups can be structured to develop community by breaking down the groups into subgroups.

The physical structure of the living unit plays a major role in helping establish the community. If your living unit is somewhat isolated from other living units, through physical barriers such as walls and doors, or if the building that you occupy is small enough and isolated from other buildings, these physical divisions help define the boundaries or territory of the community.

The group needs to define its territory in some fashion. Many residence life programs permit students to "mark their territory," defining it as their own by decorating foyers, hallways, and lounges.

The second component in the establishment of a community is a set of mutually shared experiences. This is where programming and general group activities such as intramural sports play an important role. The more opportunities the students have to interact in the same experience and with the same goals, the greater the chance of community to exist. Intramural sports serve this function very well. If together students participate on a football team in competition with a group outside of the residence hall, they enjoy a mutually shared experience with a common goal—winning the game.

This experience helps build a sense of team accomplishment and requires that individuals commit to one another, share skills with one another, and depend on one another for the accomplishment of their mutual goal. Building something together is another way of helping to establish a mutually shared experience that will promote a sense of community. Whether this experience is sewing a quilt, building some cabinets in the lounge, or painting murals on the walls of the corridor, it contributes to students having a mutually shared experience with a common goal.

Communication and trust are intermingled to form the next element necessary for the development of a community. *Communication* means not just superficial talking, although this is obviously the first step, but more importantly, an exchange of values and a sharing of personal emotions of the kind that one shares only with trusted friends. Communication and trust are dependent on one another. These bonds can be enhanced by structured human relations experiences, such as may be found in the interpersonal training and self-awareness workshops that may be conducted by your campus counseling center, and by casual talks about values and beliefs that may occur in informal discussions in a person's room. You can act as a facilitator for the development of these discussions and can assist in further exploring the reasoning behind a person's values.

Through this communication and trust-building, a student should come to establish a sense that the group offers support for his or her individual accomplishments. This interpersonal support becomes self-perpetuating. It both enhances the community and maintains the importance of the community to the individual and collectively. People must be encouraged to share with one another at a level of personal intimacy and to feel that what they share on a personal level will not be used to their disadvantage at some later time.

Community seems to crystalize when the group is faced with a task to accomplish, is threatened in some way, or experiences a crisis. When these situations exist, the group can readily identify a goal, a reason to work together, a reason for mutual support. Through the crisis or conflict, the group comes to recognize a common purpose in sharing and mutual dependance. Whether this crisis is contrived or real, the result is the same. A sense of external threat helps to stimulate a sense of community.

It is unlikely that your residence hall will ever be threatened with attack from outside or that you will need to band together for mutual protection or support. There are other ways of developing a sense of community. One way is through the establishment of a common goal at a general meeting of all your residents. An identifiable common goal, something the group really wants to accomplish—winning a football trophy or remodeling the floor lounge—is a good way to inspire the commitment necessary for the development of a feeling of community. People must have some reason to band together. This reason must be recognized as important by the group as a whole and must be considered attainable.

Whatever the group identifies as its goal or common purpose, this purpose must be reaffirmed through a sense of communion within the group. The communion is a way of maintaining an inner group identity. It reaffirms the recognition of the community by the individual. Just seeing the entire living unit assembled is a visible sign of one's position within the community. But the members of the community need to be made to feel involved in the community's accomplishments and its failures as well as its rewards. Every person must be solicited for involvement. This contact serves to maintain the group. In a more tangible way, the involvement may take the form of social interactions, recognized group accomplishment, rewards given to individual members, mutual recognition of individual members by the group, and shared authority within the community group. Whether these group-maintenance activities are parties, football games, concerts, construction projects, decorations, a policy or program revisions, or new projects, they are important because they encourage the group to recognize and accept such activities as part of their identification with the group.

Conclusion

The French Revolution was predicated upon the basic premises of liberty, equality, and fraternity. The United States has done much in the past few years to help ensure liberty and has come a long way in trying to establish a policy of equality. Fraternity, or a sense of group community, has not been achieved, primarily because there are fewer opportunities for people to learn the skills of sharing with one another and to place allegiance to the group above commitment to self. Apathy on campuses across the nation is no less obvious than apathy in the voting booth. This situation needs to change. Community membership is not something that simply exists; it is a commitment that one must learn and experience.

Part 6

RA Survival Skills

Chapter 19
  Time Management

Chapter 20
  Study Skills

Chapter 21
  Stress Management

Chapter 19
Time Management

Learning to Manage Your Time

Time management is a system by which you determine your priorities and plan the allocation of units of time to accomplish what you believe is important. How well you learn to use the 24 hours that make up each day, the 168 hours of each week, and the 720 hours of each month is the degree to which you practice time management. People who organize and plan their time usually make better use of it.

Learning to manage your time is learning to manage yourself. Time management involves planning, self-discipline, maintaining a schedule, knowing your own habits, and learning to set priorities. The average college student taking a full academic course load and sleeping approximately 8 hours a night still has at least 80 hours of uncommitted or plannable time each week. How effectively the student uses this time for study, social activities, and recreation may have a major influence on the success of his or her college experience.

Making a schedule helps you get started. It is a way to prevent yourself from avoiding those subjects or duties you dislike. More important, it is a way to discover more time for the things you enjoy and to help control the time that is imposed on you by other people. By planning your schedule, you can eliminate last-minute cramming for exams and still have recreational time for yourself. Planning can make studying more enjoyable and will open new blocks of time that you can devote to other interests and better relationships with students in your living unit.

The most common mistake people make in planning their schedules is to overplan. Many people believe that they must schedule every minute of every day. Schedules need to be realistic. Every person needs time each day for some type of recreation and relaxation. Your psychological health is a key element in your ability to concentrate and in your motivation to study. The remedy for study problems is generally not more studying but more efficient and better use of the time used for studying—in other words, quality studying time as opposed to quantity studying time.

As you enter this time management system, remember that schedules are products of your own invention. They should be used to assist you in allocating your time and using it effectively. Do not be a martyr to your schedule. Let your life style determine your schedule, rather than allowing your schedule to determine your life style.

Time can be categorized as three general types. The first type of time is that over which you have little or no control. This can be thought of as *predictable time*. Such activities as classes, organizational meetings, a team practice, an RA staff meeting, eating in the cafeteria, and sleeping are predictable times. If you know that the cafeteria is open between 4:30 P.M. and 6:00 P.M., you probably plan to eat during some portion of that block of time. The same applies to sleeping. You can predict that you will spend between six and eight hours each day sleeping. Depending upon your life style, you can predict that this will occur sometime between 10 P.M. and 8 A.M. each day. Predictable time is time that is predictable for you, that your schedule dictates as committed time over which you have limited control. The only decision you exercise over this type of time is whether you choose to attend a particular class, to eat, to sleep, and so on.

Items such as studying, recreation, social activities, and most hobbies are plannable. These activities fall into the second time type, called *discretionary time*. This is time that is uncommitted. It is time that should be planned in a manner consistent with your life style toward the accomplishment of the priorities in your life.

The third type of time is *other-imposed time*. It is unpredictable time. Activities included in other-imposed time include emergencies, individual student crises, telephone calls, people coming to visit, and job- or school-related assignments.

Time management is a system of (1) learning to assign priorities to the tasks you wish to accomplish, (2) maximizing discretionary time by minimizing predictable time and other-imposed time, (3) planning the use of discretionary time, and (4) learning to be more efficient. The key to being an efficient time manager is learning to maximize discretionary time.

Predictable Time

As noted, predictable time is time set aside to accomplish a specific task. It is time over which you exercise the least amount of control. Although you may choose whether you wish to perform the particular task or attend a particular meeting, you have no real control over when you will do it. Students who are involved in many campus activities soon find that the number of meetings they must attend and the number of classes they must attend substantially increase their predictable time. When a manager in industry has a disproportionate amount of predictable time, the business experts usually say that he or she is letting the job run him or her, as opposed to him or her running the job. This can also apply to the RA position and to being a student.

Assume that an RA is enrolled for 15 semester hours requiring 15 hours per week of class attendance. The RA sleeps approximately 8 hours a night, spends at least 1½ hours a day eating, at least 1½ hours a day for personal hygiene, and a minimum of 1 hour a day for traveling to and from classes. This amounts to 93 hours per week of predictable time. In addition, say the RA has a daily exercise program of jogging that accounts for approximately 1 hour per day. This moves the RA's predictable time up to 100 hours a week. This leaves 68 hours of discretionary time each week.

When you think of scheduling your time, you are really considering about how to go about using these remaining 68 hours. Remember, this example considers a good amount of predictable time. RAs usually have much less. Most residence hall programs require that the RA take "duty" at least once a week, and many halls require that the RA work at the information desk a specified number of hours per week. These two responsibilities may account for another 10 hours of predictable, job-related time each week. Don't forget about the regular weekly

RA staff meeting. These vary, but they generally take at least 2 hours. Already the RA has at least another 12 hours of committed time per week. This does not include time that may be unique but predictable in any one week, such as an intramural event that the RA has helped to organize a program that the RA will hold that week, or a special committee or organization with which the RA is working.

On average, RAs devote at least another 2 to 3 hours per week to miscellaneous meetings and programs that are associated with their job. With this additional 3 hours, the predictable hours for the RA mounts to about 115, leaving only 53 hours of discretionary time.

On a piece of paper, list how much predictable time you have during a given week. Remember to include in that list the items that are predictable for you. If you spend an hour every night watching television, you can count that as predictable time. If you have a regular exercise routine, you can count that time as predictable time. If you belong to a fraternity or sorority and attend a regular chapter meeting once a week, you can count that as predictable time. Add up the number of hours you have as predictable time and subtract it from 168 (the total number of hours in a given week). The remaining time is discretionary time. You should find that you have between 50 and 60 hours of discretionary time per week. If you have more discretionary time than this, you are doing better than most. If you have less than 50 hours of discretionary time, chances are that you have a very tight schedule and may have possibly overcommitted yourself.

Discretionary Time

The 50 to 60 hours you have left per week is plannable time. You may start to plan this discretionary time by following four steps to time management: assessment, getting organized, a to-do-list, and scheduling time.

Step 1: Assess Your Own Situation

The first step in determining a schedule is to know yourself. People function differently. Some people are very active in the early morning and can accomplish much at that time. Others find that their peak intellectual time is later in the day. Make some assessments about yourself. To do this, try answering the following questions:

- At what time of day do you feel you can concentrate best (early morning, mid-morning, after lunch, late afternoon, early evening, late evening)?
- Do you like to go to bed early and get up early or go to bed late and get up late?
- When do you most feel like exercising (morning, evening, afternoon)?
- When are most of the people in your living unit available, during the day or evening (before dinner, after dinner, late evening)?
- When is your living unit most quiet (and thus more suitable for study) and when is your living unit noisiest (and thus most suitable for socializing)?

- When do you most often like to socialize?
- When are you most likely to engage in social activities such as dating (Friday night, Saturday night, or Friday and Saturday nights)?
- What is the most frequent reason you give for not accomplishing certain tasks such as studying?
- Are you the type of person who, when asked by a friend to go some place with him or her while you are studying, usually goes?
- When you have free time, in which ways do you most often spend it?
- What is the most frequent interruption you get that interferes with studying?

This information is used in planning your schedule, as described later. Set it aside for now.

Step 2: Get Organized

Purchase or make some type of scheduling notebook. This may seem like a rather simple task, but you would be surprised how many people do not use this necessary instrument. Many people who do have notebooks use the wrong type. A good scheduling notebook should have times listed for the times you do things. If you rise at 7 A.M. and work until 11 P.M., your scheduling notebook should include those hours as scheduled time. You can buy several good scheduling notebooks that come close to meeting this time-span. An appointment notebook, similar to the type found in many doctor's offices, is generally good. There is space allocated for the use of every 30 minutes during the day. When you open the scheduling notebook, you should be able to plan the entire week. This basic scheduling tool is an important part of time management.

Step 3: Prepare the To-Do List

Consider all the things that you wish to accomplish and make a list of them. Put the list on one sheet of paper, preferably in the notebook that you bought for that purpose. Use only one sheet of paper for this list. Do not put every item on a separate sheet of paper. You will find that this becomes very cumbersome and that shuffling papers will distract you.

This list is called a "to-do list." You should make a to-do list every day, listing on it every task that you wish to accomplish during that day. You should try and make this to-do list at the same time every day to ensure that the list will get done and will allow you some time each day (predictable time) to plan the day ahead. Though you will need to plan more than just from one day to the next, a day-to-day planning list is important to refresh your memory and set priorities for each day.

Once you have your list, assign priorities to the items on it, using the following three criteria:

1. First rate tasks that are directly related to the accomplishment of the most important task you have set for yourself with an A. Other items that rate an A are those directly related to the accomplishment of a goal about which there is some urgency.

2. Next rate items that are related to a less important goal or that do not have immediate urgency with a B.
3. Finally, give all other items a C.

Each day work on As first until they are completed. When you finish the As, begin working on B items. If you finish all the As and all the Bs, then do the Cs. Do C items only when everything else is finished. For example, suppose you have the following things to accomplish during the day:

- Read a chapter in history.
- Write a short essay for English class tomorrow.
- Buy some posters for your room.
- Do your laundry.
- Return a telephone call from a friend.
- Read the Wall Street Journal for your economics class.
- Find 10 new resources for your term paper in economics.
- Talk with your hall director about an upcoming program.

Having listed these eight tasks, you now must identify the ones you consider most important. Depending on your individual priorities, probably writing an essay for English class tomorrow would rate an immediate A. But equally important might be reading the chapter in history and looking up the 10 resource items for the term paper in economics. The rest of the items could be rated as B, except calling a friend, buying posters, and doing laundry, which would probably rank as Cs.

The most important thing that this system of ranking does is help you decide what you must accomplish and what can wait. You may find that some C items never get done. That is okay. Sometimes a C item becomes an A. When it does, do it. But until it does, do it only after you have finished all of your A and B priority tasks.

Step 4: Schedule Your Time

Use the appointment calendar and questions you answered in Step 1 to schedule your time as follows:

1. Using a pencil, write in all of your predictables with regularly scheduled hours for the week or as far in advance as you wish to plan (activities such as, classes, team practices, student organization meetings, church, and RA staff meetings).
2. Block out time for sleep. Be realistic. You may need eight hours a night to rest properly. If your class schedule or life style is such that you sleep until noon each day, that is fine. Start your schedule there.
3. Write in times when you usually eat. If you skip breakfast but have a late-night snack, then don't schedule breakfast but do schedule the snack.

4. Select some recreational time each day. For most college students, 4 P.M. to 7 P.M. tends to be a good time to plan some type of recreation. Include some type of physical exercise, if possible. This not only helps keep you healthy but occupies your mind and gives you an opportunity to escape some of the pressures of the day.

5. Using your to-do list, starting with the As, schedule the things you would like to accomplish for the day. If you just have a list of things to study, all of which are of relatively equal value, here are some study scheduling hints that may help you:

   • Plan roughly two hours of study time for each hour of class time. This varies with the difficulty of the course, the demands of the course, the demands of the individual professor, and your skill in the subject area.

   • Adapt the length of time you spend studying to the type of material being studied. For most subjects, studying in 20 to 30-minute blocks, with 5- to 10-minute breaks, for periods of approximately 1 hour per subject works well. This is only an approximation. Drill work involving rote memorization differs in length of time from reading a novel.

   • Eliminate dead hours from your schedule. If you have an hour between classes, do not waste it. Schedule that hour to review your lecture notes from the previous class or to prepare for the next class.

   • One hour of studying during the day can be worth as much as one and a half hours of studying time at night. Use daylight hours for studying whenever possible.

Other-Imposed Time

There are three types of other-imposed time: (1) necessary, (2) unnecessary, and (3) unavoidable.

Necessary Other-Imposed Time

Necessary other-imposed time involves legitimate crises or important issues that need your attention. Because you are an RA, you will have many of these contacts. A student who is undergoing some type of important emotional crisis has a right to interrupt you to discuss a problem. A fire drill, a fight in the residence hall, a student who is experiencing a major problem, or a program that you must attend is other-imposed time that is necessary for your job functions. Many times you are in a situation in which only you have the information or authority to make a needed decision. This also is necessary other-imposed time. The last form of necessary other-imposed time is employer-imposed time related to legitimate job functions. If the residence hall director must call a staff meeting on a particular day or needs your assistance, this is related to a legitimate job function and, therefore, falls into the category of necessary other-imposed time. These are situations for which you must learn to adjust your schedule. You can minimize them only to the extent that you can ask that some of them be handled at a later time.

Unnecessary Other-Imposed Time

Unnecessary other-imposed time is a serious problem for RAs. Items that fall into this category are telephone calls from people who wish only to chat, visitors for which you had not planned, regular meetings in which very little or nothing is accomplished, trash mail, poor communication that needs further clarification from your superiors, disorganized meetings, campus red tape, unavailability of people you need to contact, questionnaires, and writing reports that nobody ever reads. You can minimize unnecessary other-imposed time in creative ways. Try some of the techniques that others have found successful. They take some self-discipline, but they may help increase your discretionary time.

- Take the phone off the hook while you are studying.
- Avoid visitors by studying in places other than your room or by putting a sign on your door informing people that you are studying.
- Go to meetings on time and demand that they start at the time scheduled. If the meeting was to start at 1:30, demand that it start at 1:30 and not at 1:45 as is probably customary. If that does not work, just plan to be there at 1:45.
- When you receive trash mail, stack it in your room and read it when you get a chance or throw it out immediately without bothering to open it.
- For unclear communications, write on them that you do not understand their purpose, and ask the sender to explain.
- Bureaucratic red tape is a problem for everyone. You can find out who on your campus does what and send people to the appropriate person to begin with. Or, if it is an internal matter within the residence programs, the best course of action is to use the person under whom you work. Ask your supervisor to help work out the problem.

Unavoidable Other-Imposed Time

Unavoidable other-imposed time is time wasted over which you have no control. Everyone finds himself or herself wasting time for one reason or another. One such unavoidable other-imposed waste of time is traffic jams. There is no excuse for them, yet they occur and there is little that can be done about them. Waiting for an appointment in a doctor's office or a dentist's office is another kind of unavoidable other-imposed time. Being stopped in the hallway by a faculty member or stopped by a friend to talk is unavoidable other-imposed time. The important thing is to minimize these situations and not let them destroy your schedule.

Conclusion

Time is precious. You must learn to use it efficiently. Time wasted is time lost forever. You can use time well and gain maximum benefits from it by setting goals, organizing yourself, assigning priorities to your daily tasks, and scheduling your time. You will find that the better organized you become in working with your time, the more time you will discover that you have.

Chapter 20
Study Skills

Learning How to Study

The last chapter covered one of the critical elements of developing good study skills—time management. The solution to most study problems is not spending more *time* studying but learning how to study *better* in the time allotted. Some simple techniques about studying will help you in your academic pursuits.

Poor study skills produce anxiety and frustration. The need to achieve high grades is a reality. Students feel this pressure both in meeting their own personal goals and the expectations of parents. Often students' misbehavior in the living unit is a release of stress that has accumulated due to anxiety over not studying enough or not achieving academically for the amount of time invested in studying. It is a major stress producer for students.

Students seldom take the time to learn how to study. This chapter is devoted to this subject. It is divided into four areas: preparation, the basic skills, learning process, and test taking. The first of these deals with preparation for study. It addresses the study environment—how to get started in studying, procrastination, scheduling, and realistic attitudes about studying. The second section examines the skills necessary in acquiring the information. This includes text book reading, classroom behavior, notebooks and similar issues of how to acquire information. The third section covers the process of learning the information, and the final section is devoted to test-taking skills. Overall, we can look at studying as getting ready to study, hearing or reading information, learning the information, and giving the information back to the professor through a test, or term paper.

Preparing Yourself to Study

Preparing yourself to study is often overlooked by students. Most people need to get "psyched up" in order to concentrate on learning information. Preparing oneself to study follows an old adage "plan your work and work your plan." The first element of planning your work is learning to use a study schedule. The previous chapter on time management addresses how to create a workable schedule to allot maximum time for studying and other activities. If you have not already developed a study schedule, you should do so by reading the chapter on time management.

Creating Your Study Environment

Residence halls are reported as the location most often used by students to study. Libraries are generally ranked as the second location. Because residence halls are an important place to study, it is important that this environment be conducive to study. It is interesting to observe the myriad of distractions that many residence halls present. As you walk down the corridor of a residence hall, you can observe students attempting to study with their doors open and playing their stereos. Their desks are lined with pictures of girlfriends, boyfriends, their automobile, or other mementos, and different items may be dangling from strings overhead. In the corridor, a group of people may be talking, while in the room next door a group of people may be cheering over a Monday night football game.

This hardly presents a conducive study environment. It is true that students can learn to adapt to a noisy and distracting environment; however, studying in this environment requires greater concentration. If the noise is background noise, having little or no associative value, the distracting quality is diminished. A good example of this is a student who is studying and listening to the radio at the same time. If the background music is music with which the student has little association, chances are that it will present only a mild distraction. If, on the other hand, a song is played with which the student identifies, his or her thoughts will be inclined to drift toward the song.

Many students claim they can study better when their stereo is playing. This may be true for some students. There has been some research indicating that background music of a nonassociative value tends to help some males focus their concentration. For females this was not true. It could be that in some situations playing music of little associative value may help muffle or drown other distracting noises in the environment. Part of this preference and the degree to which it may influence one's ability to concentrate may have to do more with whether a person's primary way of perceiving the world is visual or audiological. People who perceive the world audiologically as their primary means of sensing may be more influenced by extraneous sound in the environment. Whatever your situation may be, the general principle for most people is that less noise is preferable when you are attempting to concentrate.

There are other kinds of distractions. Pictures, memorabilia, and items that students use to clutter their desks can also be distracting. A student looking up for a moment catches a glance of a picture pinned to the bulletin board in front of his or her desk and spends a few minutes recalling some past experiences. This break in concentration can be as distracting as an auditory disturbance.

In arranging your room for studying, you should attempt to place your study table or desk against a wall. Do not pin, paste, or post anything against this wall that may distract you. Do not place your desk in front of a window; the activity on the outside could be a distraction. Pay special attention to removing anything that will compete with your concentration. Proper lighting in this area is important. Glaring fluorescent or overly bright lights can be distracting, and they are more tiring to the eyes. If your desk has a plastic laminated top, light may reflect off the glossy surface into your eyes. This is easily solved by placing a cover or blotter over the top of the desk.

One key to using a study environment successfully is to develop positive study habits in that environment. If possible, try to use your study area only for study. Try not to play cards, sit and make telephone calls, or do anything else unrelated to studying in this area. This establishes a positive, reinforcing atmosphere for study in this location. Soon the area will become associated with concentration and study; eventually it will reduce the time necessary for you to prepare for concentration. The fewer distractions and the more prepared your environment is for study, the quicker you will be able to start studying. You will be able to spend less time studying because the time you spend will be of greater quality.

The principles for establishing a positive study environment are as follows:

- Use your study area only for studying.
- Have all materials available and within easy reach.
- Keep the area free from all distractions.
- Study at the same time and in the same location whenever possible.
- Spend your study time in this area wisely. If you cannot concentrate, do not spend time there.
- Keep the room moderately cool rather than moderately warm.
- Assume a posture conducive to work and not one suggestive of relaxation. Lying on the bed with your feet propped against the wall is not conducive to concentration.
- Study when you are most alert and best able to concentrate. For most people, this is during the day. It is generally held that one hour of study time during the day is worth at least an hour and one-half at night when you are less able to concentrate, have more distractions, and are more tired.

Staying Healthy

People who are healthy can study better. If you are tired, anxious, and irritable, it is difficult to concentrate and therefore difficult to study. Drugs, alcohol, caffeine, and foods high in sugar tend to detract from your ability to study. Sugary foods and alcohol make you drowsy. You should approach studying in college as you would approach a job. Unless your body is functioning well, it will be difficult to study.

Many students have a regular exercise routine. Exercise reduces stress, which is a major inhibitor to effective studying. Relaxation techniques such as meditation, biofeedback, and a host of other relaxation procedures may also be of assistance to individuals in reducing stress. If you are well in mind, body, and spirit, you have a better chance of performing at your optimum level.

Practical Realities of Studying

Before engaging in serious study, you must recognize some realities about the process. You will not automatically learn material by reading it. You may have to read some chapters in a textbook several times to understand it. In writing an essay or term paper, you will make more than one draft. The first draft is a general expression of ideas. Subsequent drafts are where you refine this information in a way that can be presented best to others.

Waiting until the last minute to undertake term papers or study for tests increases one's anxiety. Starting early allows you greater freedom to plan your time, review your work, and fine tune your knowledge. Try finishing an essay or paper two weeks before the deadline date—whenever possible. Let the paper sit for several days, and then reread it. You will find areas that you may want to improve.

The more you are pressured in study situations, the more stress you experience and the less you can produce. Some people claim they work best under pressure. This is usually not true. What is true is that some people are able to motivate themselves only when they are under great pressure. This does not mean they do their best work; only that when left with no alternative but to do the work, they finally do the work.

Remember that studying is a gradual process. It involves learning bits of information and stringing the facts together over time. Studying a little each day, doing your reading as required throughout the course, and reviewing the material as you go, is the process of studying. Putting everything off until the last minute and hoping to "cram" all the information the night before an examination is the last act of a desperate student. It seldom offers the reward that the student is seeking.

Getting Started

Plan the work you want to study within the time you have available. Set a goal for yourself for each study period. If your goal is to read one chapter in that scheduled period, then read the chapter and then do something else. Perhaps all you want to do is scan the chapter, or scan the chapter and take notes. Whatever you choose, make a conscious choice to do it. Plan it ahead of time.

If you just don't feel like studying, try easing yourself into the process by doing something mechanical such as surveying the chapter headings or rewriting or rearranging some of your notes. As you move through these tasks, spend time concentrating, examining, and questioning the material. This should begin to increase your concentration.

One deterrent to studying is the tendency to look at major projects as overwhelming. Thinking about the material that students must compile, analyze, and write in a term paper is so overwhelming for some students that they constantly put it off. If everyone approached their work in this way, very little would get accomplished. The best way to approach large projects, such as term papers or large books, is to break the project into small segments. If you think about writing a term paper 40 or 50 pages long as writing 10 segments of five pages, it won't seem nearly so difficult. If you need to read a book that has 50 chapters, you really only need to read 2 chapters a day for 25 days.

Procrastination

Procrastination is another word for avoidance or displacement. The energies that you should devote to studying are sometimes channeled into other areas. The more a person delays studying, the more anxious he or she becomes. Procrastination may serve another function. Some people procrastinate because they subconsciously prefer not to succeed. Others are not willing to surrender the freedoms or the time that is required for studying.

People procrastinate by replacing something that they don't want to do with an alternative. This way they avoid the task that they don't want to do. If a person procrastinates to the extent that he or she can no longer function in school or places himself or herself in situations that create great anxiety, then he or she probably needs to discuss this procrastination with a trained counselor.

It is probably true that everyone procrastinates to some extent and that a little procrastination is acceptable. However, when somebody avoids and delays a project that needs to get done to the extent that it causes great emotional stress, there is a reason for such behavior. As mentioned earlier, this is an issue worth exploring with a counselor. You may be able to help students who are experiencing this problem by having them talk about the reasons that they are procrastinating. You can offer them some encouragement and perhaps review some of their study techniques. It is possible that if their studying has been very unrewarding, this may be part of the reason for their procrastination. Students are more likely to undertake academic projects in areas in which they have succeeded than in areas where they have failed.

Types of Procrastinators

The Perfectionist: Perfectionists believe that everything they do must be perfect. One of their favorite expressions is "if it is worth doing, it is worth doing right." They often get bogged down in the minutia of a project, labor for hours over insignificant details, and construct all kinds of road blocks to the accomplishment of a project. Soon, each small assignment begins to look larger than life. All projects become major projects, and the weight of all this work causes the avoidance behavior.

The truth of the old adage about doing things right is that some things that are worth doing are worth doing even when they are not done right. The degree of care or precision should be in proportion to the task to be accomplished. So what if you cross out a word in a term paper? It hardly seems to justify retyping the whole term paper. If you are cutting the grass and you happen to miss a few blades of grass here or there, it really does not matter. This is not to say that students should approach all of their work in a less demanding way, only that there are varying degrees of precision required.

The self-downer: Self-downers have something invested in failing. They believe they are not any good at some things, so they don't bother to try. Mathematics, for some students, is a good illustration. If in high school students did not like math and barely got by, when they get to required math courses in college, they avoid doing the homework or studying for the exams. These students believe they will fail. To avoid confronting the failure, they fill their time with things they do well or prefer doing and use these as excuses to avoid the tasks that need to get done.

Of course, their deep belief that they will fail is realized. One of the interesting facets about this approach is that students can avoid owning the failure because they can explain the failure by not having studied, by not trying, or by filling the time with other things that support the rationalization of not having the time to do what was needed.

The Angry Pacifist: Angry pacifists spend all of their energy being angry at the person or events that created the need for the project to be completed. Instead of acknowledging the anger or confronting the cause, they avoid or delay doing the project as a way to get even.

The Excitement Junkie: Excitement junkies are hooked on being entertained. They believe their life should be filled with variety and excitement. When they get bogged down with anything less than exciting, they seek escape by finding more exciting things to do. In filling their time with all the exciting things, they procrastinate getting necessary schoolwork done. For an excitement junkie, reading a novel is not nearly as exciting as watching TV.

The Whiner: Whiners spend their time complaining about what they need to do but not doing it. They avoid the task by talking about how hard it is or how unfair it is. The result is that they keep complaining and not doing what needs to get done.

The Grasshopper: Grasshoppers like to jump around from project to project without making any progress on the project. They have low impulse control, meaning that they are quick to act on their impulses. They may start on a project but can only stay with it for a few minutes before they act on an impulse to do something else. Typical of a grasshopper is having a dozen different things going at the same time, hopping from one project to another without much progress on anything.

The Miner: Miners like to stockpile work. They are great organizers and great believers in that popular myth of procrastination, "The mood will strike someday." When the stockpile of work gets large enough, they get around to digging into it, but slowly so as not to disturb the elaborate structure of organization they have constructed in creating this mass of work. Often what happens is that after the miner spends all of his or her time stockpiling and organizing, he or she looks one day at the huge pile of tasks that need to be accomplished and becomes too overwhelmed to dig in.

The Myths of Procrastination

Manana Myth: "I'll do it tomorrow" is probably the most widely used excuse for not doing something that needs to get done. It is the favorite myth of dieters and last-minute Christmas shoppers. The myth is, of course, that tomorrow you will be more motivated, have more time, feel more like doing it, be in a better mood, and so on. The problem is that tomorrow you feel the same way as you did today.

Pressure Packer Myth: "I work better under pressure" is one of the favorite excuses of every student who has ever crammed for a test. Such students finally reach their threshold of tolerance for not doing something, and in an act of desperation they get something finished they should have been working on for some time. They believe that this shows that they work better under pressure. What is probably true is that when they are against a deadline with no room to procrastinate they finally focus their attention on the project that needs to get completed. One of the reasons they believe that they work better this way is that when they finally get the project finished they have such a sigh of relief they get a feeling of accomplishment and are reinforced for the behavior. It is difficult to believe people can do their best work under these circumstances. It is difficult to believe a person can do as good a job on a paper that he or she spent two hours on as a paper he or she spent two weeks on. Although greater effort spent is not always related to better work produced, expediency is surely not a cause of good quality.

The Inspiration Myth: People who subscribe to the inspiration myth believe that suddenly they will become inspired to achieve what needs to get done. They believe a bolt of inspiration will strike them, and they will be embodied with the creative inspiration to undertake the assignment they have been delaying. These people believe that their life is controlled by others and that somehow they are not responsible for their own actions. If they wait long enough, they will get inspired, and the project will get completed. Unfortunately, many times the bolt of inspiration misses them, and they either do not get it done or delay it until the last minute and do the project poorly. It is easy for such procrastinators to excuse their actions because it was not their fault that they never got inspired.

Life Is Always Fair Myth: Our need to be treated fair, to be rewarded when we do well, and to have others empathize with us are desires we all share. We sometimes translate these beliefs, or wants, into a faith that life is fair. Cognitively, most people understand that life is not always fair, but many people often find it difficult to accept situations when it is not. Unfair things take the form of a professor not recognizing all the work you may have done on a project, not asking the questions you thought should be asked on a test, or falling one point below the grade you would like to have gotten. It is easy to invest considerable energy into anger about the unfairness and let it get in the way of what needs to get done. People who buy into this system of believing life is always fair find people to blame when life is not fair. They get bogged down by procrastinating things that need to get done as a way to express their hostility.

Overcoming procrastination is not easy. You must honestly assess your ways of procrastinating and gain control of them. Once you have identified the problem(s), you can begin to address these behaviors directly. If procrastination is a serious problem for you and you have not been successful addressing it by yourself, do not be afraid to consult a counselor. This trained professional may help you uncover some of the hidden reasons for procrastinating.

Basic Skills in Acquiring Information

A person acquires information in one of four ways—reading, listening, experimentation/application, and discussion.

Textbook Reading

Textbooks are outlined to permit students to obtain an overview of the material. The outline for each chapter is determined by the headings and subheadings throughout the book. When you look at a chapter in a textbook, first become familiar with what that chapter covers. There are a number of methods for the initial reading in a textbook. One successful method employs a five-step process. First, survey the chapter to determine what the chapter will cover. Second, while you survey the chapter ask yourself some questions about the material to be covered. Third, read the chapter, looking for answers to the questions you have previously asked. Fourth, review the outline of the chapter again, and fifth, recite your answers to the questions and other pertinent information that you have discovered.

This is one method for reading a textbook. There are others that work just as well. Reading to answer questions and thinking about how certain material applies to specific situations will help you make the material meaningful. If you can associate the material in the textbook with an experience or in some way make it meaningful to you, your memory of the material is facilitated. Underlining or highlighting sections of the textbook aids in retention of the material. Highlight only the most important material. It does little good to highlight large segments of material. A similar technique is to write comments or questions in the margins of the book. This reinforces what you've read and helps you summarize. It will be particularly helpful to you in reviewing the material later.

Many students believe that they can read a textbook as quickly as they read a novel. Textbooks are not meant to be read with great speed. They are meant to be read, studied, and reviewed. It is often necessary to reread sections of a text in order to get the full meaning.

Classroom Behavior and the Lecture

The purpose of a lecture is to provide you with information that is not covered in the textbook or to explain textbook material in greater detail. In many courses the lecture is the focus of the course, and the textbook or other reading is used to augment the information covered in the lecture. Whatever the case, attending a lecture involves the process of active listening. Active listening does not just mean taking a voluminous series of notes. It does mean listening carefully to what is said, understanding the relationships provided by the lecturer, taking meaningful notes in an outline form that will aid in remembering the material covered in the lecture, and asking any relevant questions. Many students believe that they must take down every word that the lecturer says in order to take good notes. This is simply not true. Notes of this detail become awkward and cumbersome. Often a student is so absorbed in transcribing words that the important concepts are missed.

Good note taking should consist of formulating an outline in sufficient detail to stimulate your memory of the information covered in the lecture. It is helpful to include examples the lecturer gives. Lecturers provide examples and tell stories about experiences to aid students in drawing relationships between the information the lecturers are giving and its application. If students can associate the information with the example, it is easier to remember the information.

In taking notes, it is preferable to use single sheets of paper that may be placed in a loose leaf notebook. This enables you to add, rewrite, or modify your notes. Use only one side of the paper. Save the back side to add material later or to clarify examples that have been given.

Your notes should be an outline. You should use abbreviations where possible, include examples the professor gives, and make sure that you include statements that the lecturer has emphasized or stressed. Focus first on concepts and then on details. After the lecture it is helpful to recopy the notes. Although this takes additional time, it helps in review of the information and in the accuracy of the notes.

Students who record lectures usually will not get as much from the lecture as a person who is actively listening and taking notes. Having to relisten to lectures becomes cumbersome and time consuming. It's like having to do all the work again. It also is difficult to refer back to information unless one wishes to spend time spinning through tapes and relistening. Using a tape recorder is only helpful if the material is very complex, and you use it immediately following the lecture to supplement your notes. Remember, your notes do not need to be in such great detail that you catch every word. Your notes should be an outline of concepts, ideas, and important facts covered by the lecture.

Professors who lecture have the responsibility to teach. This means that as a student you paid for the right to ask questions and to talk with instructors during their office hours. They should be available to help explain material that you do not understand or have graduate assistants who can. Know the course instructor and do not be afraid to consult with him or her when you have questions. Generally, you will find that faculty members are available for these conversations and are more than willing to explain material that you do not understand.

Experimentation and Application

The third way students learn is through experimenting or applying information. Labs associated with chemistry, physics, and similar fields are examples of learning through experience. Art, music, and the area of rhetoric and public address are other areas in which we acquire information by experimentation and application.

One of the things you hear students say is that they find much of their academic work to be impractical because they are not able to see how this information will benefit them in later years. Information is easier to learn if you can see how it is to be applied. Doing research for an intercollegiate debate is a good example. Debaters usually do voluminous amounts of research on the given topic, becoming experts in that topic. They research both sides of the question so that they can argue on either side in a tournament. Debaters who seriously invest themselves in the activity are usually voracious researchers. They read to gather information, constantly thinking how that information might be put to use in a debate or in formulating their presentation of the issue. They have learned to read for specific information. This increases retention. By using the information in a debate, the debaters come to know the information better. They not only understand its application but have experimented with the information. Experimentation and application are important ways to acquire information.

Discussion

Because discussion involves the exchange of information through inquiry, debate, and rebuttal, students are forced to think about what is being said to formulate an intelligent response. Forced to defend a point of view, students employ their best reasoning skills. They will evaluate information presented and analyze the consistency of the other person's argument. Discussion is an effective learning style and one preferred by many students.

Unfortunately, large classroom lectures do not always lend themselves to open class discussion. Students who attempt to engage in protracted discussions with the instructor are sometimes pressured by peers to stop. People hear in different ways. Some people learn best through discussions, while others learn best by reading, seeing visual representations of ideas, or by hearing lectures. All are useful, and each has its place in college.

The Studying Process

Studying is a process of reading, organizing or outlining, reciting, and reviewing. Studying should be done on a regular basis and not just for exams.

In reading chapters of a textbook, you should focus on the outline presented, noting particularly the notes that you have made in the margin and facts that you have highlighted. The idea in reviewing the textbook is to digest concepts and the major facts presented. It is sometimes helpful to make an outline of the chapter with accompanying facts and details that you need to remember.

Reviewing your notes is done in a similar fashion. First, read through the notes and then condense this material into a shorter outline. Review the notes, and perhaps condense the outline again until you can remember it or understand it without having to look at it.

Review your text, outline, and the notes again and try to recite what is covered. Try to visualize the outline of the text and the outline of the notes that you have made. Think about how one supports or relates to the other. Focus particularly on examples that will help trigger the information you need.

Memorizing is required when you will be given objective examinations or need to access certain dates or formulas. Science courses tend to require more memory work than the humanities. Music requires more memory work for pianists and vocalists than for most other musicians. Memorize only the material you need to memorize.

Professors are usually interested in your understanding of the concepts and information presented. It may be necessary for you to demonstrate this by remembering certain facts about a particular battle or theoretical approaches that are attributed to a particular psychologist. However, it is generally more important to be able to discuss the psychologists' theories and what they mean, or describe and explain the causes and what happened during a battle than to present dates, facts, and figures.

Generalizations in this area are hard to make. Much depends on what individual faculty members are expecting. The best way to find out what faculty members think is important and what type of information they will require of you is to ask. Most instructors will answer candidly.

For memory work, first write the facts you wish to memorize on a sheet of paper, or on a series of 4 by 6-inch cards. Break down large sections of information that you need to memorize into smaller sections. Start by memorizing smaller sections and link these smaller sections together until you can memorize the larger piece of information. Visualizing the material can help. Either visualize what actually happened or visualize the actual words on the page. If you can associate facts that you need to remember with examples, your ability to remember those facts should be increased. One technique people use to remember other people's names, for example, is to associate the person's name with a physical feature of that individual. So if the person's name is Eileen, you may think of Eileen as a person who wears a certain type of eye glasses. You can adapt this same technique to studying.

Memorization is done by reviewing and reciting. Some techniques that help are to review and recite the information before you go to bed at night. At night you may dream about some of this information. First thing in the morning, try to recite the information. Review and recite again. Do this over a two- or three-day period, and the information will become yours. Some researchers say that the information must be recited verbatim at least seven times before you can retain it. The more times you use, review, and recite information, the more and the longer you will remember the information.

Anagrams can also help. If you need to know a seven-stage process or the bones of the leg, try making an anagram (a word) from the first letter for each component. The U.S. Government uses anagrams for many government programs. For example, HUD is the anagram for the Office of Housing and Urban Development. If you can remember the word, you will have the outline—the letters of the word—to help you recall the components.

Test Taking

Professors do not always ask the questions you would like to have them ask. You do not always have an opportunity to show them everything that you know about a given topic. Instead, they tend to test students to determine the varying degrees of information they have about a topic. In every test there should be some questions you cannot answer or find very difficult to answer. Testing does not test how much knowledge you have about a subject; it tests what information you have about the questions asked in a given format and your ability to take the type of test being administered.

To prepare to take a test, you first must know what type of test you will be asked to take. There are basically three types of tests: objective, multiple choice, and essay. Some tests are a combination of the three. A professor usually tells you beforehand what type of test is to be administered. If he or she does not, ask.

Objective Exams

An objective exam is one that requires total recall. It is the most difficult type of exam to take. Fill-in-the-blank type questions and short-answer questions are forms of objective tests. You either know the information being sought, or you do not. If you do not know the information, write what you think is the right answer unless the professor indicates that he or she will deduct points from your total score for incorrect answers. Go through the exam and answer those questions you know; then go back and answer the questions that you are less sure of, leaving the most difficult questions until last.

As with all examination questions, read thoroughly to make sure you understand exactly what the question is asking.

Multiple Choice Questions

Multiple-choice or multiple-guess questions come in many forms. The most obvious is where you are given a question and four or five alternative answers. Versions of this exam type include being given a question in which more than one of the alternatives may be correct and you are asked to pick the best answer. Sometimes such a test asks for all the correct answers. It is important to read multiple-choice questions carefully. The directions to them vary. Know particularly whether there is more than one right answer to each question.

First, look through the questions and answer those you know. Next, go back and examine each question you are unsure of. Eliminate the obviously incorrect alternatives. You should be able to narrow the options to two or three, thus giving you a better chance of determining the correct answer. Among these two or three, look for global statements such as *always, in every case, never,* and *absolutely.* You can usually eliminate one of these alternatives. It is rare that an authority would make such a global statement.

Finally, if you still cannot decide which is the correct answer, and the professor is not deducting from your total score for answering incorrectly, take your best guess. You have a chance of guessing right.

True and false questions are a form of multiple choice. If you don't know the correct answer in a true-false test, take your best guess (unless the professor deducts for wrong answers). Never leave a yes or no question unanswered. You always have a 50–50 chance of choosing the correct answer.

Essay Exams

Essay exams call for you to organize your thoughts and present them in a coherent way that speaks directly to the question asked. This is your opportunity to express in your own words your understanding of the question raised. Pace your time on essay exams. Do not spend all of your time writing an elaborate answer to one question, only to find that you do not have enough time to answer the remaining questions on the test. Start by outlining in the margin of your paper or in your head what you want to say. Each essay question is looking for certain facts the professor wants. Think what those key elements must be and organize your essay around them. If there are three parts to a theory that the professor has asked you to explain, start your essay by saying there are three parts to the theory and the first part is, the second part is, the third part is. The purpose of an essay is for you to explain what you know, not for you to create a great literary masterpiece. This does not mean that you should be careless with your grammar and spelling. Quite the opposite is true. If you express yourself clearly, using correct English, it will add to the credibility of your response.

Include only the information necessary in the essay. Don't waste your time and the instructor's time by adding extraneous material to pad the essays. If you feel you must pad the answers, do so in moderation. Remember that college professors are experienced students and experienced readers of essays. It is surprisingly simple to differentiate between students who have an understanding of the topic on a essay question and those students who are simply padding questions with extraneous information.

If you absolutely have no idea how to answer a particular essay question, and again the professor will not deduct for wrong answers, write something. Even if it is extraneous material, the professor may, out of pity, give you one or two points for your attempt.

Test Anxiety

Some students get so anxious about a test that they block (become unable to remember information they have studied). You might call this a type of stage fright. Students can feel nervous, have a headache, feel dizzy, and develop a fear reaction. In other words, they panic. There is more than one way to combat test anxiety. The one thing that always helps is to have confidence in your ability to do well on the examination. If you have studied and know the information, this will help provide you with the confidence to do well. Success on other tests also tends to help build the confidence in test taking. The more confident students feel about the information they have covered, the more confident they should be about taking the examination.

Even though some students are confident they have studied enough, they nevertheless panic when beginning the examination. Relaxing before the examination is one way to help reduce anxiety. Another way is to take several deep breaths before taking the examination and look through the examination to find the easiest questions first. Sometimes by answering a few easy questions in the examination the student builds enough confidence to answer some of the more difficult ones. Students should have a realistic perspective on any examination. Few examinations are a make-or-break situation for a student. If you experience some test anxiety, you need to think about positive test experiences that you have had. Admit to yourself that you are not going to be able to answer all the questions right. Remember that a test examines the depth of one's information, and it is normal for people to miss answers to some questions. If you cram just before a test, this may heighten your anxiety.

One of the techniques used by professional counselors to reduce test anxiety is biofeedback relaxation. They have the student explain each segment of taking an examination, starting with the student getting up in the morning and proceeding step-by-step through the student actually sitting down to take the examination. As a student relates each segment of his or her behavior, counselors have the student relax. This process takes place in a safe and secure environment. The student learns to associate the relaxation response with the experiences leading to the test. This process is usually coupled with some therapy that focuses on issues of self-esteem and fear of failure.

If you or some of your residents experience test anxiety to the extent where you cannot function during the exam, you should talk with a counselor about the problem. Some anxiety before a test is normal. It is not normal, however, to be so anxious and disturbed that you cannot remember or produce the information that you know you have learned.

One final word about taking examinations. Most exams are given in a specified amount of time, usually one class period. You need to be conscious of how much time you are allotting to questions and the value of those questions. In a 60-minute class period, it is not a good use of time to spend 30 minutes responding to a 10-point essay, leaving the remaining 30 minutes of the class period to answer questions for the remaining 90 points on the exam. A few professors will let students write as much as they wish with no time constraints. Find out beforehand how long you will be given to take the exam. If it will be one class period, use your time wisely, apportioning appropriate time to the value assigned to individual questions. If no specific value is assigned to each question, inquire as to whether all questions will receive equal weight.

Cramming

Cramming for a test is better than not studying at all, but it is not a substitute for studying the material over a period of time and learning it throughout the course of the semester. If you are in a position where you must cram, set aside a block of time and begin by condensing the material you have into an outline from which you can work. Try to get some help from another person in the class to determine what areas are particularly important in the course. Review the outline and the information the fellow student believes will be on the exam and disregard trying to read the entire textbook again or trying to copiously review someone else's notes.

If you must cram, do so systematically and from outlines that summarize the material covered. Use the outline to explore specific areas you believe are likely to be on the examination. Don't try to review everything in the course; it will overwhelm you and will squander your limited study time.

Academic Honesty and Dishonesty

A surprising number of students choose to cheat on examinations or plagiarize term papers. This reprehensible conduct seriously jeopardizes the academic integrity of the institution and raises the question as to whether that student should be permitted to continue at the institution. One of the reasons the institution exists is for the purpose of helping students master information. If a student chooses to represent to the faculty that he or she has mastered information that he or she has truly not mastered, it calls into question the purpose that, that person has in attending the institution. There is no excuse for academic dishonesty. Despite the pressures to get good grades or whatever personal problems may exist, it does not excuse the lack of integrity and breach of trust demonstrated by academic dishonesty.

Some students experience personal problems that prevent them from studying. The solution is not for them to press on with their course work but to explain the situation to the appropriate college authorities and seek their advice and help in resolving the problem. Most schools allow students to take incomplete grades when they have a legitimate reason. Students should be aware of when they can withdraw from courses and when that is no longer possible. In cases of serious mental, emotional, or physical health problems, the college counseling or health center will be able to assist the student in securing an extension for the course or perhaps a withdrawal. Whatever the institutional policies, there are usually alternatives. There are always alternatives if a student acts soon enough. Help students on your floor understand what their options are. The stigma of being expelled or suspended from a college for academic dishonesty is much greater than receiving a failing mark in a course.

Spend some time talking with the residents of your living unit about the issue of academic honesty. Help them understand that "everybody" does not cheat and that academic dishonesty will not get them through college. Make sure they understand the institution's position on academic dishonesty. They are issues of honor, integrity, and scholarship.

A college education trains not only the mind but also the character of the individual. It is the issue of the student's character that is questioned when he or she cheats in a course. If you know of academic dishonesty, you should confront the student(s) who is involved. It is appropriate for you to consult with your hall director on how your particular institution handles these situations and what is expected of you in this situation.

Chapter 21
Stress Management

Sources of Stress

Stress, is a reaction caused by intense exertion, strain, and effort. It is brought about by the continual adjustments and demands we place on ourselves as we react to given stimuli. The more we are called upon to adjust to changing situations, the more stress we acquire.

In the world in which we live each of us is exposed to some form of daily stress. It comes in a variety of forms: job stress, insecurities, perceptions of how other people feel about us, perceptions of our abilities, interpersonal relationship problems, and unfulfilled expectations. These issues and others create various levels of stress that influence our physical and emotional well-being.

As an RA, you are subject to the same stresses as other students. In addition you are exposed to the pressures of your job and the expectation that you will maintain a reasonable level of academic performance.

Stress is an interesting phenomenon. We use the term very loosely in our everyday language and we take it for granted. Yet stress is estimated to be associated with as much as 60 percent to 80 percent of all diseases. Even the most conservative medical journals have estimated no less than 50 percent of ailments are in this category! It is evident that stress is a significant factor in our lives and should not be taken lightly.

Not all stress is bad. A certain amount of stress is necessary to enable us to operate efficiently. For example, any form of exercise done as part of a physical fitness program generates stress on our bodies. Many students find that they may do their best work when they press themselves to achieve as their highest level—such as in competitions or examinations. The relationship between stress and an individual could be compared to the relationship between spices and cooking. The right amount of spices enhances the flavor of the product, whereas too much can destroy the taste.

Psychologically, any time a person feels threatened, is anxious, or is injured, the body reacts. First, the autonomic portion of the nervous system senses stress and automatically responds. It chemically transmits a signal to the pituitary gland, which releases two hormones known as adrenocorticotrophic hormone (ACTH) and thytrophic hormone (TTH). This stimulates the flow of adrenalin into the bloodstream. Between the pituitary gland and the endocrine system a series of hormones are released into the bloodstream, causing a series of reactions that prepare the body to respond more quickly to a threat. This physical reaction designed for survival has come to be known as the *flight or fight response.*

Fight or Flight

Fear, whether real or imagined, sets off a reaction of tension in the body that causes nervous impulses to increase and the adrenalin to be rushed throughout the body. Adrenaline is a powerful chemical that causes the body to enter a state of hyperactivation. As a result of this state the heart rate and blood pressure increase dramatically. The body temperature rises, and oxygen consumption and the production of carbon dioxide increase. The increase in blood flow to the muscles of the body can be as much as 300 to 400 percent.

Because we live in a civilized community, the need to fight or flee has been replaced with socially learned customs to deal with the same anxiety-producing situations. Modern society, however, has its own special set of stressful situations our ancestors never had to confront. Driving in traffic, the fear of failure of an exam, and living in close proximity to other people—such as in a residence hall—all produce stress.

Young people today have more stress than the people of past generations. Technology and less-structured moral options present more choices to them. Thirty years ago drugs were not as readily available as they are today, and there was little social pressure to experiment. Sexual activity among young people who were not married occurred, but there was strong social pressure against this experimentation, much more so than today. The technology of television, increased crime, the mobility of our society, the breakup of the nuclear family through divorce, and the perception that the economic future of the country is in doubt are some of the new issues confronted by young people today. The result of these issues is stress. Its effects can be seen in the disproportionately high suicide rates among adolescents, the use of drugs and other substances to escape, mental health problems, and violence among young people.

One of the major problems we all confront is stress produced by the pressure of time and time commitments, both at work and at home. We tend to place high expectations on ourselves, and these expectations tend to increase even though we now have many labor-saving and time-saving devices at our fingertips. More and more people find themselves carrying work home to do in the evenings and on weekends. It can be argued that the division between work and play has become blurred, or in some cases nonexistent. It is important to establish a reasonable division between work and play, and to engage in enjoyable activities during the hours when we are not working.

Most of us have difficulty saying no to additional obligations or demands. The ability to limit ourselves to an appropriate number of activities is a skill that must be practiced and learned as a student so that it can set a pattern for later adult roles. The sense of frustration that results from having too many things to do or not having sufficient time to relax results in stress. When this stress is extended over a long period of time, it negatively influences a person, mentally and physically.

Stress becomes intensified when it lasts for a long time or when a of stress producers accumulate over time. It is intensified when a person must confront a number of stressful situations or when the stress situations are coupled with other adjustment difficulties.

Coping with Stress

Considering the increasing complexity of all aspects of our lives, it is apparent that stress is a normal part of life and will continue to increase with increased responsibility and our increasing complex society. Each person learns some methods of coping with stress that are unique and appropriate to him or her. Fortunately, there are many techniques for reducing stress.

It is important to relieve stress as it accumulates. One method is to make stress work for you by doing something you find personally satisfying after a stressful situation. Find a way to relax or direct those energies to an enjoyable task.

For individuals who are having difficulty recognizing signs of stress, biofeedback training can be of help. Many institutions offer a minicourse in biofeedback training that can help a person become aware of physiological signs associated with stress and anxiety. A form of biofeedback is used in test-anxiety reduction programs offered by most college counseling centers. Through this program, students learn elements that produce stress, and they learn step-by-step methods of reducing this anxiety. The biofeedback training usually includes some type of relaxation training, as well as training in recognizing physical signs of increased stress.

Many people turned to some form of meditation technique to combat stress. Meditation first became popular in the Western world when the Maharishi Mahesh Yogi introduced transcendental meditation (TM) in the United States.The TM program was unique in that it involved a system of teaching meditation to large numbers of people and provided a system of follow-up that reinforced the individual's motivation to continue.

Since the introduction of this program, many books have been written that profess the ease with which individuals can teach themselves some form of meditation. Although TM has proved to be one effective method for reducing stress, it is not the only meditation method available that lowers stress levels. It is possible to teach oneself to meditate by learning some techniques in published materials and having the commitment to stay with the process.

Herbert Benson (1985), a notable author in this area, describes a response phenomenon that can be induced within the body that he refers to as the "relaxation response." Benson's research shows that by following a simple set of instructions for a 15- or 20-minute period a person can elicit a tranquil state of meditation within the body. The significance of the relaxation response is that it causes nearly an exact opposite set of reactions within the body as does the flight or fight response. For example, as the relaxation response goes into effect, the body experiences a decrease in metabolic rate, heart rate, blood pressure, oxygen intake, carbon dioxide production, and blood flow to the muscles. This response pattern continues for the 15- or 20-minute period and beyond.

Benson (1985) believes that the effect of the relaxation response may continue well beyond the daily meditative period and in fact may be cumulative. If this is true, then it would appear that practicing a relaxation technique in some fashion on a regular basis would not only allow an individual to combat stress regularly but would also place the individual in a situation where he or she could become more resistant to the impact of stress!

Another method of eliciting the relaxation response is to take advantage of a myriad of audio tapes designed to help people relax. Your counseling center or your health center should have tapes available. These tapes are designed to elicit a meditative state simply by listening. In most instances a speaker calmly and serenely provides instructions that you follow to achieve a meditative state that reduces the relaxation response. The use of these types of tapes along with headphones is particularly well suited for life in residence halls. This method enables an individual to engage in the meditative state without being disturbed by noises occurring in the hallway. These tapes also have an advantage in that no particular instruction is required.

Recently a number of medical research studies have begun to point at a possible relationship between stress and a number of major diseases, such as heart problems and cancer. Benson (1985), Pelletier (1977), and others have observed that some of the hormones released in the body as a part of the flight or fight response suppress the immune system.

It has been suggested (Benson, 1985; Pelletier, 1977) that it may be possible to boost the immune system through the regular practice of a relaxation technique combined with a process called "imaging." Imaging is similar to hypnosis. It allows an individual to influence the subconscious mind while he or she achieves a state of deep relaxation. Your campus health center or counseling center will be aware of these techniques and can help you explore them.

The problem in getting most people to practice a relaxation response is that it must become part of one's daily schedule. It is usually recommended that these techniques be practiced twice a day. However, once a day could be sufficient if an individual practices regularly. It is easiest to get 15 or 20 minutes in the morning before the school day begins. However, the primary benefits of practicing a relaxation technique can best be felt in the late afternoon, before dinner, or during the early evening before studying. At these times the sensations of relaxation seem to be felt most strongly.

Practitioners of these techniques often argue that the rest provided during these sessions is deeper and more effective than sleep. If this is true, these techniques could be very valuable tools for students.

Regular exercise is a good stress-prevention technique. It provides the opportunity to physically express aggressive feelings and frustrations through such exercise activities as walking, running, swimming, or biking. Being able to concentrate on a racquetball game, golf game, tennis match, or some other athletic endeavor for a short period of time provides the mind an opportunity to escape, if only temporarily. As mentioned in the chapter on time management, recreational time should be scheduled just like other activities. Time spent in regular exercise and recreation is time well spent—not wasted. Time spent in recreational and athletic endeavors contributes to your efficiency and your ability to deal with other tasks.

Sleeping has an interesting relationship to stress. When people become stressed to the point that they feel they can no longer cope, one way of retreating is to escape by sleeping. Psychologists look to sleeping patterns as indications of a person's personal problems. People who try to escape stress in this manner may regularly sleep from 12 to 15 hours a day.

Occasionally, a person may find a need to reduce sleep for the purpose of completing things that need to be done. Those who routinely try to exist on four hours of sleep a night for prolonged periods of time, believing that this increases their efficiency, are probably reducing their efficiency by not getting adequate rest.

People need varying degrees of rest at different stages in their life. Young children need more sleep than adults. The reason is that the complexity of learning new things and dealing with their new environment requires that they remove themselves from these situations and synthesize the complexity of their environment by sleeping. College students need more sleep than middle-aged adults, because of the complexity of their new environment and the academic demands placed upon them. Elderly people usually get more sleep, but in shorter periods. They tend to take four or five naps during the day. This is because their metabolism slows, and they get tired.

Emotionally, you can do much to prevent stress and relieve it by learning to talk about problems. One of the best skills for coping with stress is learning to talk about your problems with someone else. Sitting down and sharing the problem and gaining another perspective can alleviate some of the stress of a problem. The freedom to do this is important. Encourage others to talk about their stress producers with you and in turn share some of your stress producers with others. You will find that you not only gain insight into your problems, you will find that your problems are not unique.

Few of the stresses that we experience are about life-and-death issues. It is important to keep problems in perspective. View the situation realistically. The thought of failing a course, losing a girlfriend or boyfriend, not completing a term paper, or not finding a summer job may be very important and may be the source of much stress. However, you must keep these issues in perspective and consider other importance in your overall life goals.

Learning to accept things that we cannot change is part of being realistic. If you have no control over an event, it does little good to worry about it. If the decision-making authority is beyond your control, then the stress you experience by worrying about it is hardly worth the effort.

On occasion, psychological stress, occurring persistently, may be a sign of a physical problem. Consult a physician if you have this concern. If no medical problems are found to be the cause, discuss your stress with a physician or a counselor at the college. It is unwise to prescribe self-medication for stress producers. Self-prescribed medications seldom make the problem go away.

If stress reaches a point at which you cannot cope with it, you should discuss your stress with a counselor. Your counseling center is staffed by counselors trained to assist students with just these types of problems. You will find these people concerned and experienced in dealing with the stress that college students experience.

College is a very hectic time in a person's life. It is even more so because of your responsibilities as an RA. You must not only contend with the day-to-day pressures of academic work but also with stress associated with the intensity of personal relations strained by your job responsibilities and magnified by living with students that you are trained to assist.

Everyone needs quiet time each day—time in which you know that you will not be interrupted. This might be an hour set aside just for you to do whatever you want. If it is only for 15 minutes at the end of the day, it may help you to relieve some of the stress, deal with your job, and other people's problems more objectively.

Burnout

Psychologists have found that a person undergoing a series of major stresses in a short period of time can become overstressed or burned out. Some of the major stress producers include such events as a major job promotion, marriage, divorce, and a death in the family. An accumulation of too many of these major stress producers in a short period of time can overstress a person. Taking on a series of new leadership roles or committing to more than you can do will also lead to burnout.

Freshmen face a series of major stress producers. All change produces some stress. Freshmen confronted with moving away from home, adapting to a new living facility, a new roommate, and a new social system are under considerable stress. Some of the more colorful behavior in the first few weeks of school is no doubt a reaction to this overstress. Some of the homesickness that you may see on the part of some of your residents may be a result of overstress. Finally, some of the people that develop deep depression, suicidal tendencies, and similar problems may be exhibiting signs of overstress.

As an RA, you are a good candidate for burnout. People tend to place great demands on your time. School, parents, job expectations, the expectations of your residents, and your career objective can all be sources of stress; if you live in a hall that has frequent discipline problems with students or that is loud and congested, these factors will cause you stress, the accumulation of which may cause burnout.

You have two choices. You can stay in the RA position and find effective coping mechanisms (such as exercise, meditation, biofeedback, or counseling) or you can separate yourself from the stress. In other words, quit your job. Spend some time thinking about what steps you are willing to take to avoid burnout.

Conclusion

Stress affects everyone. The key to dealing with stress is to recognize when you are under stress and learn what situations produce stress for you. If you can learn to cope with and prevent stress in yourself, you can more efficiently accomplish the goals you have set for yourself. The regular practice of a relaxation technique or exercise will not only combat and relieve stress but may also provide additional benefits. Effectively dealing with stress enhances your health, general well-being, and productivity. Not confronting it can only lead to problems.

Bibliography: References and Selected Readings*

Chapter 1: The Roles of the RA

Greenleaf, E. (Eds.) (1967). *Understaduate students as members of residence hall staff*. Washington, D.C.: National Association of Women Deans Administrators and Counselors.

Chapter 2: History of Residence Halls

Abernethy, J., and Abernethy, B. (1949). *At home to students*. New Haven: Edward W. Hazen Foundation.

American Council on Education (1937). The student personnel point of view: A report of a conference on the philosophy and development of student personnel work in college and university (Series 1, Vol. 1, No. 3, June) Washington, D.C.: Author.

Association of College and University Housing Officers—International (1985). *The purpose and history of the association*. Columbus, Ohio.

Astin, A. W.; King, M.; and Richardson, G. (1981). *The American freshmen: National norms for the fall 1981*. Los Angeles: Laboratory for Research in Higher Education, University of California, Los Angeles.

Bess, J. L. (1973). More than room and board: linking residence and classroom. In J. Katz (Ed.), *Services for students* (New Directions for Higher Education, Series No. 3, Autumn). San Francisco: Jossey-Bass.

Birdseye, C. F. (1906). The college home life as a means for securing a right moral atmosphere for students. *Religious Education, 3* (6), 218–224.

Blimling, G. S. and Schuh, S. H. (1981). Influences, predictions, and recommendations. In Blimling, G. S. and Schuh, S. H. (Eds.) *Increasing the educational role of residence halls*. San Francisco: Jossey-Bass.

*The bibliography contains references cited in the text, those that were used as background information, and selected readings by chapter.

Brown, F. J. (1951). Higher education and the national emergency. Paper presented at the twenty-third anniversary conference of the National Association of Deans and Advisers of Men, St. Louis, March 30 (reported in the verbatim transcript of the conference proceedings, pp. 96–110).

Carnegie Foundation for the Advancement of Teaching, (1976). *The states and higher education: A proud past and a vital future*. San Francisco: Jossey-Bass.

Cooperative dormitories. (1938). *School and Society 48,* September 10, 1237, 343–344.

Cowley, W. H. (1934). The history of student residential housing. *School and society, 40* (1040), December 1, 705–712; (continued) 40 (1041), December 8, 758–764.

Cowley, W. H. (1937). The disappearing dean of men. Paper presented at the nineteenth annual conference of the National Association of Deans and Advisers of Men, Austin, April 2 (reported in the verbatim transcript of the conference proceedings, pp. 85–102).

Cowley, W. H. (1949). Some history and a venture in prophecy. In E. G. Williamson (Ed.). *Trends in student personnel work*. Minneapolis: The University of Minnesota Press.

Cowley, W. H. (1957). Student personnel services in retrospect and prospect. Reprinted in G. Saddlemire and A. Rentz (Eds.). (1983), *Student affairs— a profession's heritage: significant articles, authors, issues, and documents*. Carbondale, Ill.: American College Personnel Association.

Cowley, W. H. (1964). Reflections of a troublesome but hopeful Rip Van Winkle. Reprinted in G. Saddlemire and A. Rentz (Eds.). (1983), *Student affairs—a profession's heritage: significant articles, authors, issues and documents*. Carbondale, Ill.: American College Personnel Association.

Cowley, W. H., and Waller, W. (1935). A study of student life: the appraisal of student traditions as a field of research. Reprinted in *Journal of Higher Education, 50* (4), 377–388.

Dormitory system at the University of Minnesota, a. (1926, July, 2). *School and Society, 24* (604), 103.

Dixon versus *Alabama State Board of Education,* 294 F. 2d 150. U.S. Court of Appeals, Fifth circuit, 1961.

Eliot, C. W. (1909). The private dormitory. *Religious Education, 4* (1), 51–59.

Ferris, W. B. (1946). Comments made in response to S. Earl Thompson's paper entitled, The program of student housing, presented at the twenty-eighth anniversary conference of the National Association of Deans and Advisors of Men, Lafayette, IN, April 18–20, (reported in the verbatim transcript of the proceedings, pp. 102–103).

Findlay, J. F. (1936). The independent men's association—an effort to integrate the nonfraternity man. A paper presented at the eighteenth annual conference of the National Association of Deans and Advisers of Men, Philadelphia, April 30–May 2 (reported in the verbatim transcript of the conference proceedings, pp. 156–161).

Findlay, J. F, (1937). The origin and development of the work of the dean of men. Paper presented at the nineteenth annual conference of the National Association of Deans and Advisers of Men, Austin, April 3 (reported in the verbatim transcript of the conference proceedings, pp. 104–123).

Fitzgerald, L. E.; Johnson, W. F.; and Norris, W. (Eds.) (1970). *College student personnel*. Boston: Houghton Mifflin.

Funds for dormitories in Virginia institutions of higher learning. (1926, September 4). *School and Society, 24* (610), 294–295.

Gladieus, L. E. and Wolamin, T. R. (1976). *Congress and the colleges*. Lexington, Mass.: Lexington Books.

Greenleaf, E. A. (Ed.). (1967). *Undergraduate students as members of residence hall staff*. Washington, D.C.: National Association of Women Deans and Counselors.

Greenleaf, E. A. (1969). Residence halls 1970s. *NASPA Journal, 7* (2), 65–71.

Hughes, R. C. (1909). Factors in the dormitory problem. *Religious Education, 4* (1), 47–50.

James, E. (1917). College residence halls. *The Journal of Home Economics, 9* (3), 101–108.

Kolbe, P. R. (1936). Address of welcome. Speech presented to the eighteenth annual conference of the National Association of Dean and Advisers of Men, Philadelphia, April 30–May 2 (reported in the verbatim transcript of the conference proceedings, pp. 9–14).

Leonard, E. (1956). *Origins of personnel services in American higher education*. Minneapolis: University of Minnesota Press.

Levine, A. (1981). *When dreams and heroes die*. San Francisco: Jossey-Bass.

Levine, A. (1981). Going first class on the Titanic. *Change, 13* (2), 16–23.

Lloyd-Jones, E. (1949). The beginnings of our profession. In E. G. Williamson (ed)., *Trends in student personnel work*. Minneapolis: The University of Minnesota Press.

Low cost housing for students at the University of Wisconsin. (1938, November, 12). *School and Society, 48* (1246), 623.

Lind, M. (1946). The college dormitory as an emerging force in new education. *Association of American Colleges, Bulletin, 32* (December), 529–538.

Lowell, L. (1929). Residential houses at Harvard University. *School and Society, 24* (739), 262–264.

L.S.U. Student Handbook (1934–1935). Baton Rouge, La.: Student Y.M.C.A..

Mayhew, L. B. (1977). *Legacy of the seventies*. San Francisco: Jossey-Bass.

Moore, D. (1971). A letter from the president. *Journal of College and University Student Housing, 1* (1), 2.

Moynihan, D. P. (1975). The politics of higher education. *Daedalus,* Winter, 128–147.

Mueller, K. K. (1961). *Student personnel work in higher education*. Boston: Houghton Mifflin.

Murphy, R. O. (1969). Developing educational meaning for residence halls. *NASPA Journal, 7* (2), 61–64.

National Center for Education Statistics. (1981). *Digest of Education Statistics, 1981* (NCES No. 81–400). Washington, D.C.: U.S. Government Printing Office.

Newcomb, T. M. (1966). The general nature of peer influence. In T. M. Newcomb and E. K. Wilson (Eds.). *College peer groups: Problems and prospects for research*. Chicago: Aldine.

Orme, R. (1950). *Counseling in residence halls*. New York: Bureau of Publications, Teachers college, Columbia University.

Pierson, I. (1962). *Campus cues. 3rd ed*. Danville, Ill.: Interstate Printers and Publishers.

Pillinger, B. B. (1984). Early residential life: Vassar college in the nineteenth century. *Journal of College and University Student Housing, 14* (1), 7–9.

Proposed residential colleges at the University of Michigan. (1927, January, 1). *School and Society, 35* (627), 10–11.

Prostrollo versus University of South Dakota, 507 F.2d. 775, U.S. Court of Appeals, Eighth Circuit, 1974.

Residential colleges at Harvard and Yale. (1929, January, 26). *School and Society, 24* (735), 124–125.

Rudolph, F. (1962). *The American college and university: A history*. New York: Vintage Books.

Sanford, N. (1967). *Where colleges fail*. San Francisco: Jossey-Bass.

Schneider, L. D. (1977). Housing. In W. T. Packwood (Ed.), *College student personnel services*. Springfield, Ill.: Charles C. Thomas.

Shay, J. E., Jr. (1964a). The evolution of the campus residence hall. Part I: The decline. *Journal of the National Association of Women Deans Administrators and Counselors, 27* (4), 197–185.

Shay, J. E., Jr. (1964b). The evolution of the campus residence hall. Part II: The resurgence. *Journal of the National Association of Women Deans Administrators and Counselors, 28* (1), 25–33.

Shay, J. E., Jr. (1969). Freedom and privacy in student residences. *NASPA Journal, 7* (2), 76–80.

Sorenson, G. P. (1985). Indoctrination and the purpose of American education. : A 1930s debate. *Issues in Education, 3* (2) 79–98.

Stewart, R. B. (1941). Institutional housing policies. Paper presented at the twenty-third annual conference of the National Association of Deans and Advisers of Men, Cincinnati, April 17–19 (reported in the verbatim transcript of the conference proceedings, pp. 109–118).

Strang, R. (1949). *Counseling techniques in college and secondary school*. New York: Harper and Brothers.

Student housing facilities at land-grant colleges. (1931). *School and Society, 33* April 18, (851), 522–523.

Talbot, M. (1909). Moral and religious influences as related to environment of student life; dormitory life for college women. *Religious Education, 4* (1), 41–46.

Thompson, S. E. (1946). The program of student housing. Paper presented at the twenty-eighth anniversary conference on the National Association of Deans and Advisers of Men, Lafayette, In., April 18–20, (reported in the verbatim transcript of the conference proceedings, pp. 95–102).

Thwing, C. F. (1909). Dormitory life for college men. *Religious Education, 4* (1), 34–40.

Unseem, R. H. (1966). A sociologist views learning in college residence halls. *Journal of the National Association of Women Deans and Counselors, 29* (3), 116–121.

Van der Ryn, S., and Silverstein, M. (1967). *Dorms at Berkeley—An environmental analysis.* New York: Center for Planning and Development Research, Educational Facilities Laboratories.

Wilson, W. (1913). The spirit of learning. In N. Fobister (Ed.), *Essays for college men.* New York: Henry Folt.

Wrenn, C. G. (1951). *Student personnel work in college.* New York: Ronald Press.

Yoakum, C. S. (1919). Plan for a personnel bureau in educational institutions. Reprinted in G. Saddlemier and A. Rentz (Eds.). (1983). *Student affairs— a profession's heritage: significant articles, authors, issues, and documents.* Carbondale, Ill.: American College Personnel Association.

Young, D. P., and Gehring, D. D. (1977). *The college student and the courts.* Asheville, N.C.: College administration publications.

Chapter 3: A Philosophy of Residence Halls

Brown, R. D. (1972). *Student development in tommorrow's higher education: A return to the academy.* Washington, D.C.: American College Personnel Association.

Council for the Advancement of Standards for Student Services/Development Programs (1986). *CAS standards and guidelines for student services/ development programs.*

Chapter 4: The Influence of Residence Halls on the Development of Students

Albrow, M. C. (1966). The influence of accommodation upon 64 Reading University students—an *ex post facto* experimental study. *The British Journal of Sociology.*

Astin, A. (1973). The impact of dormitory living on students. *Educational Record,* Summer.

Astin, A. (1977). *Four critical years.* San Francisco: Jossey-Bass.

Astin, A. (1985). *Achieving educational excellence.* San Francisco: Jossey-Bass.

Beal, P., and Williams, D. (1968). An experiment with mixed-class housing assignments at the University of Oregon. *Student Housing Research, ACUHO Research and Information Committee,* February.

Blai, B. (1971). Roommate impact upon academic performance. Unpublished (manuscript), Harcum Junior College.

Blimling, G., and Hample, D. (1979). Structuring the peer environment in residence halls to increase academic programming in average ability students. *Journal of College Student Personnel, 20,* 310–316.

Blimling, G. (1989). A meta-analysis of the influence of college residence halls on academic performance. *Journal of College Student Development, 30.*

Blimling, G. (1988). The influence of college residence halls on students: A meta-analysis of the empirical research, 1966–1985 (doctoral dissertation, The Ohio State University, 1988).

Boyer, E. L. (1987). *College: The undergraduate experience in America.* New York: Harper & Row, Publishers.

Brandt, J. A., and Chapman, N. J. (1981). Student alteration of residence hall rooms: Social climate and satisfaction. *The Journal of College and University Student Housing, 11* (Summer), 37–43.

Chickering, A. (1974). *Commuting versus resident students.* San Francisco: Jossey-Bass.

DeCoster, D. (1966). Housing assignments for high ability students. *Journal of college student personnel, 7,* 19–22.

De Coster, D. (1968). Effects of homogeneous housing assignments for high ability students. *Journal of College Student Personnel, 9,* 75–78.

DeCoster, D. (1969). Some effects of coordinating classroom and residence hall assignments for college freshmen: A pilot project. Paper presented at a meeting of the American Personnel and Guidance Association, Las Vegas, March.

DeCoster, D. (1970). Some effects of different classroom conditions upon interpersonal relationships, personal adjustment, and achievement for college freshmen. *Dissertation Abstracts.*

Duncan, C., and Stoner, K. (1976/77). The academic achievement of residents living in a scholar residence hall. *The Journal of College and University Student Housing, (6),* Winter 6, 2.

Erikson, E. (1963). *Childhood and society.* 2nd ed. New York: Norton.

Erikson, E. (1968). *Identity, youth, and crises.* New York: Norton.

Eklund, C., et al. (1972). The effects of proximity, willingness to engage in social interaction, and sorority membership on the initial formation of friendship patterns among previously unacquainted college freshmen. Paper presented at Southeastern Psychological Association, Atlanta, GA.

Elton, C., and Bate, W. (1966). The effects of housing policy on grade-point average. *Journal of College Student Personnel,* 1966.

Feldman, K., and Newcomb, T. (1969) (Eds.). *The impact of college on students.* San Francisco: Jossey-Bass.

Hall, R., and Willerman, B. The educational influence of dormitory roommates. *Sociometry,* 1963.

Heath, D. (1968). *Growing up in college.* San Francisco: Jossey-Bass.

Heiweil, M. (1973). The influence of dormitory architecture on resident behavior. *Environment and Behavior, 5,* 377–412.

Huang, E. T. (1982). Impacts of environmental design on residential crowding. *Dissertation Abstracts International, 43,* (3), 984A. (University Micorfilms No. 82–18, 991).

Lehmann, I. Changes from freshman to senior years. In *The College Student and His Culture: An Analysis,* Yamamoto (Ed.). Boston: Houghton Mifflin, 1968.

Martin, R. (1974). Friendship choices and resident hall proximity among freshmen. *Psychological Reports, 34.*

Menne, J., and Sinnett, E. (1971). Proximity and social interaction in residence halls. *Journal of College Student Personnel.*

Morishima, J. (1966). Effects on student achievement of residence hall groupings based on academic majors. In Bagley (Ed.) *Research on Academic Input: Proceedings of the Sixth Annual Forum of the Association for Institutional Research.* Cortland, N.Y.: Office of Institutional Planning, State University of New York at Cortland.

Mortimer, K. (Chairman) (1984). *Involvement in learning: Realizing the potential of American higher education.* (National Institute of Education, U.S. Department of Education) (GPO Stock No. 065–000–00213–2). Washington, D.C.: U.S. Government Printing Office).

Murray, M. (1961). The effects of roommates on the scholastic achievement of college students. *Dissertation Abstracts.*

Newcomb, T. (1960). Exploiting student resources. In *Research on College Students,* Sprague (Ed.). Boulder, Colo.: The Western Interstate Commission for Higher Education.

Newcomb, T. (1962) Student peer-group influence. In *The American College,* Sanford (Ed.). New York: Wiley.

Ogden, G. (1969). The effect of modified class scheduling on student alienation. *NASPA Journal, 7,* 104–107.

Olson, L. (1964). Students' reactions to living-learning residence halls. *Journal of College Student Personnel.*

Pemberton, C. (1968). An evaluation of the 1967–68 living-learning experiment at the University of Delaware. *University Impact Study.* Newark, Del.: University of Delaware, November.

Priest, R., and Sawyer, J. (1967). Proximity and peership: bases of balance in interpersonal attraction. *American Journal of Sociology, 72,* 633–49.

Rockey, M. (1969). Living and learning at Central Washington State College. Paper presented at NDEA Institute for College Student Personnel Workers, Michigan State University.

Rohner, R. P. (1974). Proxemics and stress: An experimental study of the relationship between living space and roommate turnover. *Human Relations, 27,* 697–702.

Sanford, N. (1962). *The American college.* New York: Wiley.

Scott, S. (1975). Impact of residence hall living on college students. *Journal of College Student Personnel, 6,* 3.

Smallwood, F., and Klas, L. (1973). A comparison of the academic, personal, and social effects of four different types of university residential environments. *Journal of College and University Student Housing, 3* (2), 120–122.

Snead, R., and Caple, R. (1971). Some effects of the environmental press in university housing. *Journal of College Student Personnel, 12,* 189–192.

Sommer, R. (1969). Study conditions in student residences. *Journal of College Student Personnel, 9,* 232–237.

Taylor, R., and Hanson, G. (1971). Environmental impact on achievement and study habits. *The Journal of College Student Personnel, 12,* 445–54.

Upcraft, L., and Higginson, L., eds. (1975). Implementing a student development model in residence halls. (Paper presented at ACPA Convention, Atlanta, Georgia).

Upcraft, L. (1982). *Residence hall assistants in college.* San Francisco: Jossey-Bass.

Vreeland, R. (1970). The effects of houses on students' attitudes and values. In Whitley and Sprandel (Eds.), *The Growth and Development of College Students.*Washington, D.C.: American College Personnel Association.

Whittaker, D. (1969). Student subcultures reviewed and revisited. *NASPA Journal, 7,* 23–34.

Zirkle, K., and Hudson, G. (1975). The effects of residence hall staff members on maturity development for male students. *The Journal of College Student Personnel, 16* (1), 30–3.

Chapter 5: The Growth and Development of College Students

Blasi, A. (1980). Bridging moral cognition and moral action: A critical review of the literature. *Psychological Bulletin, 80* (1) 1–45.

Blyth, D. A.; Bulcroft, R.; and Simmons, R. G. (1981). The impact of puberty on adolescents: A longitudinal study. Paper presented at the annual meeting of the American Psychological Association, Los Angeles, August.

Case, F. D. (1981). Dormitory architecture influences: Patterns of student social relations over time. *Environment and Behavior, 13* (1), 23–41.

Chickering, A. (1969). *Education and identity.* San Francisco: Jossey-Bass.

Chronicle of Higher Education (1988). Fact file: Earned degrees conferred in 1985–86, 34 (18), January 13, p. A36.

Coelho, G.; Hamburg, D.; and Murphy, E. (1968). Coping strategies in a new environment. In Yamamoto (Ed.), *The college student and his culture: An analysis.* Boston: Houghton Mifflin.

Constantinople, A. (1969). An Eriksonian measure of personality development in college students. *Developmental Psychology, 1,* 357–372.

Duberman, L. (1975). *Gender and sex in society.* New York: Praeger.

Erikson, E. (1968). *Identity, youth, and crises.* New York: Norton.

Feldman, K., and Newcomb, T. (1969). (Eds.) *The impact of college on students.* San Francisco: Jossey-Bass.

Gilligan, C. (1981). Moral development. In A. Chickering and Associates (Ed.), *The modern American college.* San Francisco: Jossey-Bass.

Havighurst, R. *Human development and education.* New York: Longman's, 1953.

Heath, D. (1968). *Growing up in college.* San Francisco: Jossey-Bass.

Heath, D. (1978). A model of becoming a liberally educated and mature student. In C. Parker (Ed.), *Encouraging development in college students.* Minneapolis, Minn.: University of Minnesota Press.

Jones, M., and Bailey, N. (1950). Physical maturing among boys as related to behavior. *Journal of Educational Psychology, 41,* 129–148.

Knapp, M. L. (1978). *Nonverbal communication in human interaction* (2nd edition). New York: Holt, Rinehart and Winston.

Kohlberg, L. (1969). Stage and sequence: The cognitive-developmental view. In D. A. Goslin (Ed.)., *Handbook of socialization on theory and research.* New York: Rand McNally.

Kohlberg, L. (1973). Continuities in childhood and adult moral develoment revisited. In Bates and Schaie (Eds.), *Life-span development in psychology* (2nd edition). New York: Academic Press.

Kohlberg, L., and Kramer, R. (1969). Continuities and discontinuities in childhood and adult moral development. *Human Development, 12,* 93–120.

Kohlberg, L. (1981). *The philosophy of moral development, Vol. 1.* San Francisco: Harper & Row.

Kohlberg, L. (1984). *The psychology of moral development, Vol. 2.* San Francisco: Harper & Row.

LaVoie, J. (1976). Ego identity formation in middle adolescence. *Journal of Youth and Adolescence, 5,* 371–385.

Levinson, D. (1978). *The seasons of a man's life.* New York: Alfred A. Knopf.

Martin, R.D. (1974). Friendship choices and resident hall proximity among freshmen. *Psychological Reports, 34,* 118.

Moore, W. (1982). William Perry's cognitive-developmental theory: A review of the model and related research. Fernald and Fernald (Eds.), *Introductory psychology* (5th edition) (prepublication draft).

Mussen, P., and Jones, M. (1957). Self conceptions, motivations, and interpersonal attitudes of late and early maturing boys. *Child Development, 28,* 243–256.

Neal, J. (1981). Patterns of gender role conflict and strain. *Personnel and Guidance Journal.*

Newcomb, T. M. (1966). The general nature of peer influence. In T. M. Newcomb and E. K. Wilson (Eds.), *College peer groups: Problems and prospects for research.* Chicago: Aldine.

Parnell, R. W. (1958). *Behavior and physique: An introduction to practical and applied somatometry.* London: Edward Arnold.

Peskin, H. (1967). Pubertal onset and ego functioning. *Journal of Abnormal Psychology, 72,* 1–15.

Piaget, J. (1952). *The origins of intelligence in children.* New York: International Universities Press.

Priest, R. F., and Sawyer, J. (1967). Proximity and peership: Bases of balance in interpersonal attraction. *American Journal of Sociology, 72,* 633–649.

Rodgers, R. (1980). Theories underlying student development. In D. G. Creamer (Ed.). *Student development in higher education.* Cincinnati: American College Personnel Association.

Rubin, Z., and Shenker, S. (1978). Friendship, proximity, and self-disclosure. *Journal of Personality, 46,* 1–22.

Sanford, N. (1962). *The American college.* New York: Wiley.

Singer, J. E. (1964). The use of manipulative strategies: Machiavellianism and attractiveness. *Sociometry, 27,* 128–51.

Sorenson, R. C. (1973). *Adolescent sexuality in contemporary America.* New York: World.

Toder, N., and Marcia, J. (1973). Ego identity status and response to conformity pressure in college women. *Journal of Personality and Social Psychology, 26,* 287–294.

Turiel, E. (1974). Conflict and transition in adolescent moral development. *Child Development, 45,* 14–29.

Weidman, J. C. (1989). Undergraduate socilization: A conceptual approach. In J. C. Smart (Ed.), *Higher education: Handbook of theory and research,* Vol. 5. New York: Agathon Press.

Widgery, R. N., and Webester, B. (1969). The effects of physical attractiveness upon perceived initial credibility. *Michigan Speech Journal, 4,* 9–15.

Widick, C., Knefelkamp, L., and Parker, C. (1980). Student Development. In U. Delworth, and Hanson, G. (Eds.), *Student services: A handbook for the profession.* San Francisco: Jossey-Bass.

Widick, C. and Simpson, (1978), Developmental concepts in college instruction. In C. Parker (Ed.), *Encouraging development in college students.* Minneapolis, Minn.: University of Minnesota Press.

Zastrow, C., and Kirst-Ashman, K. (1987). *Understanding human behavior and the social environment.* Chicago: Nelson-Hall.

Chapter 6: Adjustment Problems in the College Years

Astin, A. (1977). *Four critical years*. San Francisco: Jossey-Bass.

Chickering, A. (1978). *Education and identity*. San Francisco: Jossey-Bass.

Coelho, G.; Hamburg, D.; and Murphy, E. (1968). Coping strategies in a new environment. In Yamamoto (Ed.), *The College student and his culture: An analysis*. Boston: Houghton Mifflin.

Coons, F. (1974). The developmental risks of the college student. In D. DeCoster and P. Mable (Eds.), *Student development and education in college residence halls*. Washington, D.C.: American College Personnel Association.

Feldman, K., and Newcomb, T. (1969). *The impact of college on students*. San Francisco: Jossey-Bass.

Havighurst, R. (1953). *Human development and education*. New York: Longman's.

Heath, D. (1968). *Growing up in college*. San Francisco: Jossey-Bass.

Kinsey, A.; Pomeroy, W.; Martin, C.; and Gebhard, P. (1953). *Sexual behavior in the human female*. Philadelphia, Penn.: Saunders.

Lehmann, I. (1968). Changes from freshman to senior years. In Yamamoto (Ed.), *The College Student and His Culture: An Analysis*. Boston: Houghton Mifflin.

Levinson, D. (1978). *The seasons of a man's life*. New York: Alfred A. Knopf.

Maslow, A. (1954). *Motivation and personality*. New York: Harper & Row.

Maslow, A. (1962). *Toward a psychology of being*. Princeton, N.J.: Van Nostrand.

Miller, T., and Prince, J. (1976) *The future of student affairs*. San Francisco: Jossey-Bass.

Mussen, P.; Conger, J.; and Kagan, J.: (1969) *Child development and personality* (3rd edition). New York: Harper & Row.

Newcomb, T. (1960). Exploiting student resources. In Sprague (Ed.), *Research on college students*. Boulder, Colo.: The Western Interstate Commission for Higher Education.

Perry, W., Jr. (1970). *Forms of intellectual and ethical development in the college years*. New York: Holt, Rinehart, and Winston.

Piaget, J. (1956). *The Origins of intelligence in children*. McCook (trans.). New York: International University Press.

Powell, J.; Plyler, S.; Dickson, B.; and McClellan, S. (1969). *The personnel assistant in college residence halls*. Boston: Houghton Mifflin.

Rossi, P. (1964) Effects of peers on socialization of college students, National Opinion Center, University of Chicago. A paper presented at the Research Conference on Social Science Methods and Student Residence, University of Michigan, Ann Arbor, Mich., November 28–29.

Sautter, J. (1974) *Understanding your residents: A residence hall paraprofessional counselor's handbook*. Lafayette, In.:

Super, D. E.; Starishevsky, R.; Matlin, R.; and Jordaan, J. P. (Eds.) (1963). *Career development: Self-concept theory.* New York: College Entrance Examination Board.

Super, D. E., Crites, J. O., Hummel, R. G., Moser, H. P., Overstreet, P. L., and Warnath, C. F. (1957). Vocational development: A framework for research. New York: Teachers College.

Whittaker, D.(1969). Student sub-cultures reviewed and revisited. *NASPA Journal.*

Chapter 7: Peer Counseling

Carkhuff, R. R. (1977). *The art of helping III.* Amherst, Mass.: Human Resources Development Press.

Corey, M. S., and Corey, G. (1989). *Becoming a helper.* Pacific Grove, Calif.: Brooks/Cole Publishers.

Danish, S. J., and Hauer, A. L. (1973). *Helping skills: A basic training program (leaders manual).* New York: Human Sciences Press.

Heaps, R.; Rickabaugh, K.; and Finley, R. Counseling evaluation inventory ratings of counselors and academic recovery through structured group counseling. *Research Report No. 23, University of Utah Counseling Center,* 1977.

Kennedy, E. (1977). *On becoming a counselor: A basic guide for non-professional counselors.* New York: Seabury Press.

Kiev, A. (1977). *A strategy for success.* New York: Macmillan.

May, R. (1975). *The courage to create.* New York: Norton.

Meier, S. T. (1989). *The elements of counseling.* Pacific Grove, Calif.: Brooks/Cole Publishing.

Chapter 8: Interpersonal Communication

Bernstein, B. (1971). *Class, codes, and control.* London: Routledge and Kegan Paul.

Bormann, E.; Howell, W.; Nichols, R.; and Shapiro, G. (1969). *Interpersonal communication in the modern organization.* Englewood Cliffs, N.J.: Prentice Hall.

Marsh, P. (Ed.) (1988). *Eye to eye: How people interact.* Topsfield, Mass.: Salem House.

Miller, G., and Steinbert, M. (1975). *Between people: a new analysis of interpersonal communication.* Chicago: Science Research Associates.

Stewart, J. (Ed.) (1972). *Bridges not walls: A book about interpersonal communication* (2nd edition). Reading, Mass.: Addison-Wesley.

Chapter 9: Behavioral Problems, Confrontation, and Counseling

Alberti, A. E., and Emmons, M. L. (1974). *Your perfect right* (2nd edition). San Luis Obispo, Calif.: Impact.

Fensterheim, H., and Baer, J. (1975). *Don't say yes when you want to say no.* New York: David McKay.

Gott verses *Berea College,* (1913) 161 S.W. 204, Court of Appeals of Kentucky.

Kurtz, R., and Jones, J. (1973). Confrontations: types, conditions, and outcomes. *The 1973 annual handbook for group facilitators.* LaJolla, Calif.: University Associates.

Lange, A., and Jakubowski, P. (1976). *Responsible assertive behavior: Cognitive behavioral procedures for trainers.* Champaign, Ill.: Research Press.

Shelton, J., and Mathis, H. (1976). Assertiveness as a predictor of resident assistant effectiveness. *Journal of Student Personnel, 17,* 368–370.

Smith, M. (1975). *When I say no, I feel guilty.* New York: Dial Press.

Wolpin, M. (1975). On assertion training. *The Counseling Psychologist, 5,* (4).

Chapter 10: Conflict Resolution

Cunningham, M., and Berryman, C. (1976). Conflict: How to deal with it effectively. Lecture presented at the First Annual Bowling Green All-Greek Leadership Conference, March 6.

Miller, G., and Zoradi, S. (1977). Roommate conflict resolution. *Journal of College Student Personnel. 18,* 228–231.

Chapter 11: Suicide Intervention

Balser, B., and Masterson, J. (1959). Suicide in adolescence. *American Journal of Psychiatry, 116,* 400–404.

Benensohn, H. (1976). Suicide attempts increase. *Guidepost.* July 22, 3.

Binstock, J. (1974). *The futurist.* April.

Cantor, P. (1972). The adolescent attempter. *Life Threatening Behavior. 2,* 252–259.

Coleman, J. (1972). *Abnormal psychology and modern life.* Glenview, Ill.: Scott, Foresman and Co.

Dublin, L. (1963). *Suicide: A sociological and statistical study.* New York, The Roland Press.

Engel, G. (1968). Bulletin of the Menninger Clinic, 32.

Kennedy, E. (1977). *On becoming a counselor: A basic guide for non-professional counselors.* New York: Seaburg Press.

Kiev, A. (1975). The nonconformist adolescent. *Excerpta Medica. 1,* 1–3.

Klagsbrun, F. (1976). *Too young to die.* Boston: Houghton Mifflin.

Kraft, S. (1983). Teen Suicide: Contagious social problem. *Baton Rouge Sunday Advocate,* August, p. 4H.

Lee, E. (1978). Suicide and youth. *The Personnel and Guidance Journal, 57,* 200–204.

National Center for Health Statistics (1983). *1983 Reports.* Washington, D.C.

Pretzel, P. (1972). *Understanding and counseling the suicidal person.* Nashville, Tenn.: Abingdon Press.

Santrock. J. W. (1987). *Adolescence: An introduction* (3rd edition). Dubuque, Iowa: Wm C. Brown.

Shneidman, F. (1969). *On the nature of suicide.* San Francisco: Jossey-Bass.

Shochet, B. (1970). Recognizing the suicidal patient. *Modern Medicine, 38.*

Stengel, E. (1964). *Suicide and attempted suicide.* Baltimore, Md.: Penguin.

Weiner, I. B. (1980). *Psychopathology in adolescence.* New York: Wiley.

Williams, D. (1978). Teen age suicide. *Newsweek,* August 28.

Chapter 12: Crime on Campus

Brothers, J. (1987). Date rape. *Parade Magazine.* Sept. 27, 4–6.

Federal Bureau of Investigation (1987). Crime in the United States: Uniform crime reports, 1987. Washington, D.C.: U.S. Government Printing Office.

Laird, B. (1988). Facts, figures behind the fears. *USA Today,* October 4, p. 6A.

Leo, C. (1987). When the date turns into rape. *Time,* March 23, 77.

McMillen, L. (1988). Colleges urged to step up efforts to prevent rape, a major menace to student on campus. *Chronicle of Higher Education, 34* (1), A1.

National Crime Prevention Council (N.D.a). Sexual assault: Reducing the risk and coping with an attack. The Woodward Building, 733 15th Street, N.W.; Washington, D.C. 20005.

National Crime Prevention Council (N.D.b). Being forced into having sex— even if it's by someone you know—is rape and it's a crime. The Woodward Building, 733 15th Street, N.W., Washington, D.C. 20005.

National Crime Prevention Council (N.D.c). Be smart. Be alert. A safe campus starts with you. The Woodward Building, 733 15th Street, N.W., Washington, D.C. 20005.

Smith, C. (1988). *Coping with crime on campus.* New York: Macmillian.

USA Today, (1988). Crime on campus. October 4, p. 1A.

Zastrow, C., and Kirst-Ashman, K. (1987). *Understanding human behavior and the social environment.* Chicago: Nelson-Hall.

Chapter 13: Substance Abuse

Alcohol resource information manual (1976). East Lansing, MI: Residence Hall Program Office, Michigan State University.

Archer, J., and Lopata, A. (1979). Marijuana revisited. *Personnel and Guidance Journal. 57,* 244–252.

Archer, J., and Lopata, A. (1978). Marijuana—a summary of current research on psychological efforts. A report prepared for the Delaware Advisory Commission on Marijuana.

Brecker, E., and Editors of Consumer Reports (1972). *Licit and illicit drugs.* Boston, Mass.: Little, Brown and Company.

C.H.U.C.K. (1979) Committee halting useless college killings. P.O. Box 188, Sayville, NY, 11782 (Newsletter).

DeHaes, N., and Schuerman, J. (1975). Results of an evaluation study of three drug education methods. *International Journal of Health Education, 18,* 1–16.

Department of Health, Education, and Welfare (1974). Second special report to the U.S. Congress on alcohol and health. June (DHEW Publication No. HSM–72–9099).

Engs, R. (1977). Drinking patterns and drinking problems of college students. *Journal of Student Alcohol, 38,* 2144–2156.

Engs, R. (1977). Let's look before we leap: The cognitive and behavioral evaluation of a university alcohol education program. *Journal of Alcohol and Drug Education, 22,* 39–48.

Fielder, J., Neil, M., & Olson, B. (1976). Alcohol manual for resident assistants at Michigan State University. East Lansing, MI: Residence Hall Program Office.

Gonzalez, G.M., and Wendy, W. (1981). The incidents of alcohol usage as a factor in student disciplinary cases. *NASPA Journal, 19,* (2), 33–38.

Harris, L. and Associates, Inc. (1974). Public awareness of the National Institute on Alcohol Abuse and Alcoholism advertising campaign on public attitudes toward drinking and alcohol abuse. Study No. 2355. National Institute of Alcohol Abuse and Alcoholism. In *Alcohol and Health.* Second Special Report to the U.S. Congress, U.S. Department of Health, Education, and Welfare, Public Health Service. Washington, D.C.: U.S. Government Printing Office.

Hecklinger, F. (1971). How to deal with the drug problem on campus. *NASPA Journal. 9,* (1), 37–42.

Jessor, R., and Jessor, S. (1975). Adolescent development and the onset of drinking: A longitudinal study of youth. *Journal of Studies on Alcohol. 36,* 27–51.

Keller, J. E. (1971). *Drinking problem?* Philadelphia: Fortress Press.

Kendler, H. (1963). *Basic Psychology* (2nd edition). New York: Appleton-Century-Crofts.

Kraft, D. (1979). Alcohol related problems seen at the student health services. *Journal of the American College Health Association. 27,* February.

Kubistant, T. (1982). Bulimarexia. *Journal of College Student Personnel, 23,* 333–339.

Lingman, R. (1974). *Drugs from A to Z: A dictionary.* New York: McGraw Hill.

National Institute of Alcohol Abuse and Alcoholism (NIAAA). (1972). *Alcohol & alcoholism: problems, programs and progress.* Department of Heath Education and Welfare. Washington, D.C.: U.S. Government Printing Office.

National Institute of Alcohol Abuse and Alcoholism (NIAAA). (1974). *Facts about alcohol and alcoholism.* Department of Heath Education and Welfare. Washington, D.C.: U.S. Government Printing Office.

National Institute of Alcohol Abuse and Alcoholism (NIAAA). (1976). *The whole college catalog about drinking.* Department of Health, Education, and Welfare. Washington, D.C.: U.S. Government Printing Office.

National Institute of Health, (1978). *1977 National high school senior drug abuse survey.* Rockville, Md.: National Institute on Drug Abuse.

National Institute on Drug Abuse (1990). *1989 National high school senior drug abuse survey.* Rockville, MD: U.S. Government Printing Office.

Nuwer, H. (1978). Dead souls of hell week. *Human Behavior.* October.

The Prudential Insurance Company of America (1971). *Questions and answers about drug abuse.*

Park, F. (1975). Sex-role adjustment and drinking disposition of women college students. *Journal of Studies on Alcohol.*

Pawlak, V. (1975). *A conscientious guide to drug abuse.* San Francisco: Do It Now Foundation.

Rachal, J., Williams, J., Brehm, M., Cavanaugh, B., Moore, R., and Eckerman, W. *A National study of adolescent drinking behavior, attitudes & correlates.* Research Triangle Park, N.C.: Research Triangle Institute, 1975.

Schifferes, J., and Synovitz, R. *Healthier living.* New York: Wiley, 4th edition, 1979.

Snodgrass, G., and Wright, L. (1983). Alcohol and polydrug use among college undergraduates. *NASPA Journal, 21,* (2), 26–35.

Tebrock, H. (N.D.). *Drug abuse and misuse.* General Telephone and Electronics Corporation.

U.S. Department of Justice, Drug Enforcement Administration, (N.D.). Controlled substances: uses and effects. Washington, D.C.

Wilsnack, S., and Wilsnack, R. (1982). Sex roles and adolescent drinking. In Chafetz and Blane (Eds.), *Youth, Alcohol, and Social Policy.* New York: Plenum Press.

Zucker, R. A. (1968). Sex-role identity patterns and drinking behavior of adolescents. *Quarterly Journal of Studies on Alcohol, 29,* 868–84.

Chapter 14: Sexuality

"AIDS in America—a 1986 Update" *Medical essay—Mayo Clinic health newletter,* Mayo Clinic, January, 1986.

American College of Gynecology (1987). Methods of contraception. Planned Parenthood pamphlet.

Avery, Caryl S. "Flirting with aids." *Human sexuality annual editions 89/90.* 14th Edition. Guilford, CT: Dushkin Publishing Group, 1989.

Bendet, Peggy. (1989). Hostile eyes. *Human sexuality annual editions 89/90.* 14th Edition. Guilford, Conn.: Dushkin Publishing Group, pp. 193–196.

Boston Women's Health Collective, *The new our bodies ourselves,* New York: Simon and Schuster, 1984.

Bruess, Clint and Glen Richardson. *Decisions for health.* 2nd Edition. Dubuque, Iowa: Wm. C. Brown, 1989.

Can we rely on condoms? *Consumer Reports, 54* (3), pp. 135–141.

Caron, Sandra L., and Bertran, Rosemarie M. "What college students want to know about sex." *Human Sexuality Annual Editions 89/90.* 14th Edition. Guilford, Conn.: Dushkin Publishing Group, 1989.

Caron, Sandra L., Bertran, Rosemarie M.; and McMullen, Tom. AIDS and the college student: the need for sex education. *Human Sexuality Annual Editions 89/90.* 14th Edition. Guilford, Conn.: Dushkin Publishing Group, 1989.

Chlamydia: The Silent Epidemic. *Time.* February 4, 1985.

Doshi, Mary L. Accuracy of consumer performed in-home tests for early pregnancy detection. *American Journal of Public Health 76,* May 1986.

Facts about aids. Pamphlet printed by U.S. Department of Health and Human Services, August, 1985.

Fraser, Laura. (1989) "Pill politics." *Human Sexuality Annual Editions, 89/90.* 14th Edition. Guilford, CT: Dushkin Publishing Group, pp. 109–112.

Future of abortion in America. (1989) *Newsweek, 114,* July 17, pp. 14–27.

Hatcher, Robert A., Guest, Felicia; Stewart, Felicia; Stewart, Gary; Trussell, James; Bowen, Sylvia; and Cates, Willard. *Contraceptive Technology 1988–89.* 14th Edition. Atlanta, Ga.: Printed Matter, Inc., 1988.

Keeling, Richard P. *AIDS on the college campus—ACHA Special Report.* 1986.

Maio, Jacqueline. Pregnancy test kits: no sure thing but sometimes helpful. FDA Consumer—HEW Publication No. 79–4017.

Smith, Sandra, and Smith, Christopher. *The college student's health guide.* Los Altos, Calif.: Westchester Publishing Co., 1988.

Surgeon General's Report on AIDS. U.S. Department of Health and Human Services. 1987.

Viscott, David. *How to live with another person.* New York: PA Kangaroo Book. 1977.

What is safe sex? (1985). Pamphlet printed by Justice, Inc., Indianapolis, Ind. October.

Whitfield, Charles L. *Healing the child within.* Deerfield Beach, Fla.: Health Communications, Inc., 1987.

Wilbur, Amy E. (1986) The contraceptive crises. *Science Digest.* September.

Yarber, William L. Aids: what young adults should know. Pamphlet written for the Indiana State Board of Health, 1987.

Chapter 15: Cults on Campus

Blimling, G. S. (1981). Cults, college students, and campus policies. *NASPA Journal, 19,* (2), 2–11.

Citizen Freedom Foundation (1983). Destructive Cults: Mind Control and Psychological Coercion. (Author).

Clark, J. (1979). Cults. *Journal of the American Medical Association, 1979a, 242,* (3), 179–281.

Conway, F., and Siegelman, J. (1978). Snapping: America's epidemic of sudden personality change. Philadelphia: J. B. Lippincott.

Conway, F. (1979). Testimony before a special U.S. Senate Committee entitled. Information meeting on the cult phenomenon in the United States. (Transcript of proceedings.) February 5.

Cox, H. (1977). Eastern cults and western culture: Why young Americans are buying oriental religions. *Psychology Today, 11,* (2), 36–41.

Delgado, R. (1977). Religious totalism: gentle and ungentle persuasion under the first amendment. *Southern California Law Review, 51,* (1), 1–98.

Delgado, R. (1979). Testimony before a Special U.S. Senate Committee entitled Information meeting on the cult phenomenon in the United States. (Transcripts of proceedings.) February 5.

Galanter, M., Rabkin, R., Rabkin, J., and Deutsch, A. (1979). The 'moonies': A psychological study of conversion and membership in a contemporary religious sect. *American Journal of Psychiatry, 136,* (2) 165–170.

Lifton, J. (1961). *Thought reform and the psychology of totalism.* New York: Norton.

Perry, W., Jr. (1970). *Forms of intellectual and ethical development in the college years.* New York: Holt, Rinehart, and Winston.

Chapter 16: Cultural Diversity

Bernstein, B. (1971). *Class, codes, and control,* London: Routledge and Kegan Paul.

Betts, N., and Newman, G.(1982). Defining the issue: sexual harassment in college and university life. *Contemporary Education. 54,* 48–52.

Carnegie Council on Policy Studies in Higher Education (1980). *Three thousand futures: The next twenty years for higher education.* San Francisco: Jossey-Bass.

Chronicle of Higher Education (1988). 1986 minority enrollment at 3200 institutions of higher education. July 6, A20.

Deane, N. H., and Tillar, D. L. (1981). *Sexual harassment: An employment issue.* Washington, D.C.: College and University Personnel Association.

Kallman, F. J. (1952). Comparative twin study on the genetic aspects of male homosexuality. *Journal of Nervous and Mental Disease, 115,* 283–298.

Kinsey, A. C., Pomeroy, W. B., and Martin, C. R. (1948). *Sexual behavior in human males.* Philadelphia: W. B. Sanders Publishing.

Marsh, P. (Ed.) (1988). *Eye to eye: How people interact.* Topsfield, Mass.: Salem House Publishers.

Martin, S. E. (1984). Sexual harassment: The link between gender stratification, sexuality, and women's economic status. In S. Freedman (Ed.), *Women: A feminist perspective.* Palo Alto, Calif.: Mayfield Publishing, pp. 54–69.

Project on the Status and Education of Women (1978). Sexual harassment. (June). Project on the Status and Education of Women, Association of American Colleges, 1818 R. Street, N.W., Washington, D.C. 20009.

U.S. Bureau of the Census (1986). Statistical abstract of the United States, 1986. Washington, D.C.: U.S. Government Printing Office.

U.S. Merit System Protection Board (MSPB) (1981). Sexual harassment in the federal workplace. Is it a problem? Washington, D.C.: U.S. Government Printing Office.

Zastrow, C., and Kirst-Ashman, K. (1987). *Understanding human behavior and the social environment.* Chicago: Nelson-Hall.

Zuger, B. (1976). Monozygotic twins discordant for homosexuality: A report of a pair and significance of the phenomenon. *Comprehensive Psychiatry, 17,* 661–669.

Chapter 17: Educational Programming

Leafgren, F. (1981). Educational Programming. In G. Blimling and J. Schuh (Eds.), *Increasing the educational role of residence halls.* San Francisco: Jossey-Bass.

Mager, R. F. (1972). Goal Analysis. Belmont, Calif.: Fearon Publishers.

Repp, S. E. (1981). *Perspectives on RA Training: A sourcebook.* Mt. Pleasant, Mich.: Association of College and University Housing Officers—International.

Schuh, J., ed. (1977). *Programming and activities in college and university residence halls.* Columbus, Ohio: Association of College and University Housing Officers.

Wilson, W. (1913). The spirit of learning. In N. Fobister (Ed.), *Essays for college men.* New York: Henry Folt.

Chapter 18: Community Development

Crookston, B. B. (1974). The intentional democratic community in college residence halls. *Personnel and Guidance Journal, 52,* (6), 382–389.

Ender, K.; Kane, N.; Mable, P.; and Strohm, M. (1980). *Creating community in residence halls: A workbook for definition, design, and delivery.* Cincinnati, Ohio: ACPA Media (Publication No. 29).

Gibb, J. (1978). *Trust: a new view of personal and organizational development.* Los Angeles: The Guild of Tutors Press.

Hillery, G. (1955). Definition of community: areas of agreement. *Rural Sociology, 20,* (2), 118.

Keyes, R. (1975). *We, the lonely people, searching for community.* New York: Harper & Row.

Chapter 19: Time Management

Lakein, A. (1974). *How to get control of your time and your life.* New York: Signet Book, The New American Library.

Mackenzie, R. (1982). *The time trap.* New York: McGraw Hill.

Oncken, W., Jr. (1977). Managing management time. A video course presented for the Saga Food Corporation.

Chapter 20: Study Skills

Bednor, R., and Weinberg, S. (1970). Ingredients of successful treatment programs for underachievers. *Journal of Counseling Psychology 17,* 17.

Briggs, R.; Tosi, D.; and Morley, R. (1971). Study habit modification and its effect on academic performance: a behavioral approach. *The Journal of Educational Research, 64,* 341–350.

Burka, J., and Yuen, L. M. (1982). Mind games procrastinators play. *Psychology Today, 16,* 32–37, 44.

Creaser, J. (1963). Evaluation of a college study habits course using scores on a Q-sort test as the criterion. *Journal of Educational Research, 56,* 272–274.

Danskin, D., and Bennett, C. (1972). Study techniques for those superior students. *Personnel and Guidance Journal, 31,* 181–86.

Ellis, A., and Knaus, W. J. (1977). *Overcoming procrastination.* New York: Signet.

Pauk, W. (1974). *How to study in college.* 2nd edition. Boston: Houghton, Mifflin.

Sherman, J. (1971). The student's study skill needs. *Improving College and University Teaching, 19,* 214–216.

Silver, M., and Sabini, J. (1982). When it's not really procrastination. *Psychology Today, 16,* 39–42.

Chapter 21: Stress Management

Altmaier, E. M. (Ed.)(1983). *Helping students manage stress.* San Francisco: Jossey-Bass.

Benson, H. (1985). *Beyond the relaxation response.* New York: Berkley.

Erikson, E. *Childhood and society.* 2nd edition. New York: Norton, 1963.

Pelletier, K. (1977). *Mind as healer, mind as slayer.* New York: Dell Publishing.

Index